REINVENTING THE STATE

Social Liberalism for the 21st Century

REINVENTING THE STATE
Social Liberalism
for the 21st Century

Edited by

DUNCAN BRACK

RICHARD S. GRAYSON

DAVID HOWARTH

POLITICO'S

First published in Great Britain in 2007 by
Politico's Publishing, an imprint of
Methuen Publishing Limited
11–12 Buckingham Gate
London SW1E 6LB
www.politicospublishing.co.uk

10 9 8 7 6 5 4 3 2 1

A CIP catalogue record for this book is available from the British Library.

ISBN: 978 1 84275 218 0

Printed and bound in Great Britain by Biddles Ltd, King's Lynn, Norfolk
Cover design by Jonathan Wadman.
Designed and typeset in Minion by Duncan Brack.

Contents

Foreword *by Menzies Campbell*   vii

Acknowledgements   viii

Introduction *by Duncan Brack, Richard S. Grayson and David Howarth*   ix

Contributors   xvii

Principles

1   What is Social Liberalism?   1
David Howarth

2   Equality Matters   17
Duncan Brack

3   Liberal Environmentalism: A Liberalism that Matches the Age We're In   37
Ed Randall

4   Global Giants   55
Matthew Taylor

5   Me, Myself and I   75
Simon Titley

6   Liberalism and the Search for Meaning   93
David Boyle

7   Rights and Responsibilities   111
Elspeth Attwooll

Individuals, communities and the state

8   Using Community Politics to Build a Liberal Society   131
Mark Pack

9   Status versus Friendship and the Common Good   145
by Lynne Featherstone

10   The Politics of Parenting: Confronting the F Word   159
Matthew Taylor

Economics

11 Globalisation and the Role of the British State   175
    David Hall-Matthews

12 The Economy and Climate Change   195
    Chris Huhne

13 The Limits of the Market   211
    Paul Holmes

14 Repoliticising Politics: The Case for Intervention   231
    Tim Farron

Decentralising the state

15 The Case for Localism: The Liberal Narrative   241
    Chris Huhne

16 The State and Education   255
    John Howson

17 Reforming the NHS: A Local and Democratic Voice   269
    Richard S. Grayson

Constraining the state

18 Rebuilding Trust in the Criminal Justice System   287
    Tim Starkey

19 Tackling Terrorism: A Liberal Democrat Approach   301
    by Nick Clegg

Britain in the world

20 To be a Briton: The Citizen and the State   325
    William Wallace

21 A Rational Defence Policy   345
    Tim Garden

Conclusions

22 Communicating Social Liberalism   363
    Steve Webb and Jo Holland

Foreword

Menzies Campbell

British people are tolerant, energetic, enterprising and compassionate. But they are badly served by a centralised and failing political system that excludes the views of most of them. Britain is also an increasingly unequal society in which too many are prevented from making the best of their lives. And it has been burdened by governments which have failed to face up to long-term challenges such as climate change.

I believe that a different Britain is possible – one in which people and communities are able to wield real political power on their own behalf, where people are not shut out by a lack of income or wealth or respect, and where the environment is valued and protected. The Liberal Democrat commitment to making Britain free, fair and green – the slogan adopted by our policy review last year – can meet these goals.

But liberalism is constantly evolving, in response to new challenges and new thinking. That is why I particularly welcome this book's contribution to liberal political thought, as relevant outside the Liberal Democrats as it is inside, because liberalism's combination of political freedom, social justice and internationalism are needed now more than ever. I hope liberals everywhere will read and respond to its arguments.

Menzies Campbell MP, Leader of the Liberal Democrats

Acknowledgements

This book has been in gestation for quite some time, and we acknowledge our debt to authors of other books on the future direction of Liberalism that helped to convince us that there was a need for such a volume – including Paul Marshall, David Laws and their colleagues in *The Orange Book: Reclaiming Liberalism* (Profile Books, 2004) and Julia Margo and hers in *Beyond Liberty: Is the Future of Liberalism Progressive?* (IPPR, 2007). A number of individuals, including Alistair Carmichael, Gareth Epps and Ali Goldsworthy, contributed thoughts and encouragement particularly in the earlier stages.

The Joseph Rowntree Reform Trust Ltd made the publication of the book possible, through a generous grant to cover publication costs. Our thanks also go to all those involved in the production of the book, including Jonathan Wadman and Alan Gordon-Walker, at Politico's Publishing, Siobhan Vitelli, for meticulous proofreading, and Deirdre Razzall and Jayne Martin-Kaye, at *Liberal Democrat News*, for providing the cover illustration.

Most of all, though, our sincere thanks go to all the chapter authors, without whom the book would not have been possible.

Duncan Brack, Richard S. Grayson and David Howarth
August 2007

Introduction

Duncan Brack, Richard S. Grayson and David Howarth

This book is about a different way of governing Britain. It is about reinventing the British state so that it delivers social justice and environmental sustainability through a decentralised and participatory democracy.

Throughout much of the last two decades, much of the political debate, both in the country in general and in the Liberal Democrats in particular, has focused on the values of the market in economic, social and environmental policy. The limitations of the market, however, are becoming increasingly obvious. Conservative and Labour governments obsessed with market-based solutions have built a more unequal and unfair society than Britain has experienced at any time since before the Second World War. The ever-more serious threat of uncontrolled climate change cannot be met by market mechanisms alone. And the introduction of markets into the public services has had – at best – mixed results.

This is nothing new to British Liberals, who have argued for well over a century that the market suffers from a number of limitations, and that there is, therefore, an important role for the state. This was the social liberal approach of the New Liberalism of the early twentieth century that laid the foundations of the British welfare state. At the same time, however, Liberals have always recognised the danger of government-based solutions that rely on, or lead to the establishment of, remote and insensitive bureaucracies.

Yet over the last decade New Labour has presided over an expansion of precisely this kind of remote bureaucracy. Furthermore, it has governed in an increasingly authoritarian and controlling manner. The positive argument for the role of the state has become accordingly more difficult to make because the idea of government action has become tainted by New Labour's approach.

Yet the need for collective responses to the problems we face remains overwhelming. Despite growing prosperity, individuals are increasingly unhappy. Britain is seen as a divided and unfair society, where individuals and communities are powerless in the face of bureaucracies and companies which treat them only as passive consumers. People feel that they cannot control their own destinies – or even their own local services, from schools and hospitals to post offices and community facilities. The Labour and Conservative approach to the breakdown of traditional social structures is to descend to mere consumerism, promising the voters more of everything – or at least more services and possessions, but never values, or community spirit, or social solidarity.

This book therefore puts the case for reinventing the state so that it is creative and enabling, rather than centralising and stifling. We believe that government is not helpless in the face of the market, however globalised it may be. We believe that individuals will re-engage in politics if they are given a real opportunity to exercise control over their own futures. We believe that a reinvented state can deliver social, economic and environmental advances in a responsive, democratic and decentralised manner.

A Liberal Democrat agenda based on this approach will differentiate the party clearly from both Tories and Labour, with their common obsession with the private sector and with their equally centralising record in government. It is the right approach for the country and for the party.

Beliefs: what is social liberalism?

We start with an examination of social liberal beliefs. David Howarth explains in Chapter 1, 'What is social liberalism?', the emergence of a distinctive social liberal ideology out of the older classical liberalism. Like their forebears, social liberals believed in the core value of freedom. They held that the state should as far as possible leave people alone to make their own decisions on how to live their lives, but they believed in addition that freedom was not attainable without a fair distribution of wealth and power. This in turn led to support for redistributive taxation as a way of fairly distributing wealth, and for democracy as a way of fairly distributing power.

David Howarth also explains the confusion about 'economic liberalism', which is sometimes portrayed (usually by journalists trying to blow up minor differences into major 'splits' in the interest of a good story) as a distinctive, and opposed, strand of liberalism. In reality, as the chapter makes clear, economic liberalism is simply 'a preference for market mechanisms not in opposition to redistribution but as a method to be used in the detailed design of mechanisms for it', and those party members who journalists like to identify as economic rather than social liberals are in reality both. There are far more urgent (and interesting) discussions to be had in British politics today than whether a particular public service can best be delivered by the market or the state – which, in any case, is a question which has no general answer.

Clearly, there are, and will always be, differences between Liberals over the details of philosophy and policy – we would hardly be Liberals if there were not. (Even our contributors display this, as well as some differences over terminology.) But this is better described as a difference – or, to more accurate, a continuous spectrum – between maximalist and minimalist social liberals, who differ primarily over the extent of the redistribution they believe necessary to achieve the conditions for political freedom. No social liberal, however, disagrees with the contention that there must be some redistribution.

The following three chapters set out the case for state action in areas we believe are the most urgent. Duncan Brack, in Chapter 2, 'Equality matters', argues that Britain's highly unequal society, in terms of income and wealth distribution and low rates of social mobility, is failing. Standards of health and well-being, rates of crime and anti-social behaviour and levels of community and political participation are all worse than they would be in a more equal society. He therefore argues that Liberals need to recognise the essential role that equality plays in achieving freedom, and to make social justice a more explicit part of the Liberal Democrat programme.

In Chapter 3, 'Liberal environmentalism', Ed Randall presents the other great priority of today's politics, the need to tackle accelerating climate change. He argues for a new liberal environmentalism based on the concept of responsible stewardship – the Earth held in trust for future generations – implemented through democratic means and in ways that respect social justice. No other form of environmentalism has a chance of mobilising the necessary popular support.

Matthew Taylor, in Chapter 4, 'Global giants', incorporates these approaches into a broader look at human society, first in the UK and then outside its borders. He finds that while the post-war welfare state built upon the blueprint of the Liberal William Beveridge has addressed the five giants Beveridge identified – want, disease, ignorance, squalor and idleness – they still remain pervasive in the UK, though in mutated forms, posing new, more subtle and more complex threats to material and subjective security. Throughout the developing world, however, Beveridge's five giants remain unconquered, and are now joined by a sixth, environmental degradation, which threatens us all.

The next three chapters look at the social liberal agenda in relation to individual motivations and political structures. Simon Titley, in Chapter 5, 'Me, myself and I', examines how the transformation in the sense of self, in the way people perceive themselves, has changed society in far-reaching ways. But while the disappearance of the old deferential hierarchies in many ways has been positive, in others it has degraded society, breaking down people's sense of social solidarity and trust in institutions. Politicians have responded by adopting an essentially consumerist approach, promising people instant gratification; no wonder trust in politics has declined and voters view parties as indistinguishable. The chapter calls on Liberals to find a way to rebuild the social fabric, to help individuals develop the meaning they want in their lives – and for the Liberal Democrats to differentiate ourselves by challenging this consumerist approach, by 'being true to themselves and not trying to please everyone'.

David Boyle, in Chapter 6, addresses the same question, 'The search for meaning', in a different way. He looks at the religious aspects of Liberalism's heritage, including the sense that there is something more than the bottom line, that people have something unique to offer in their ordinary lives, and that people and communities make things possible. He argues for a series of social liberal measures to decentralise the state and create structures in which people matter and can make a difference – and also, that Liberals should cease to portray themselves as mere secular technocrats and recognise the element of spirituality that lies within their history.

In Chapter 7, Elspeth Attwooll takes a systematic look at the extent to which political decision-making involves choices about fulfilling claims and allocating responsibilities. From the perspective of social liberalism, she argues, it is a mistake to prioritise claims – which risks treating society as no more than a set of atomised, competing, individuals – or responsibilities – which risks treating individuals as undifferentiated, subservient, components. Rather, a social liberal approach starts with a concept of social goods of which human beings are the main beneficiaries.

The policy agenda

The remainder of the book fleshes out these beliefs and principles into more detailed policy proposals. Chapters 8, 9 and 10 all continue the debate about the relationship between individuals, communities and the state. Mark Pack, in Chapter 8, 'Using community politics', looks at how the Liberal adherence to the principle of community politics can be applied in highly practical ways – not merely to win elections (which is what it has all too often come to mean) but to allow people to take power into their own hands. A series of proposals are put forward, for central and local government, and for party campaigners, to change the state from being an organisation that does things for people to one through which people do things for themselves.

Lynne Featherstone, in Chapter 9, 'Status versus friendship and the common good', picks up Simon Titley's and David Boyle's theme, and examines the extent to which the balance between status, as defined primarily by possessions, and friendship (and neighbourliness, and social solidarity), has become seriously out of kilter. She identifies what is needed to address the malaise and ensure that society comes to place more value on individual responsibility and the common good.

In Chapter 10, 'The politics of parenting', Matthew Taylor argues for a new approach to family policy – and an urgent one, given the current levels of unhappiness, ill-health and insecurity amongst British children. He analyses how the obsession with work amongst policy-makers has undermined the value of parental interaction with children and is placing mothers and fathers in an impossible balancing act between work and family. Liberals must reassert the value of parental involvement (by both parents) and create structures that make it possible.

The next four chapters consider economic policy. David Hall-Matthews, in Chapter 11, 'Globalisation and the role of the British state', examines the extent to which – contrary to much recent government rhetoric – nation-states can in reality exercise control over the impacts of globalisation. Indeed, not to do so risks strengthening the hand of those who oppose globalisation and its benefits – sometimes xenophobic nationalists, but often ordinary citizens despairing of their government's ability to control their future. The government has a clear responsibility – and ability – to assist those who are least well-equipped to benefit from globalisation, and to check its negative impacts.

In Chapter 12, 'The economy and climate change', Chris Huhne develops Ed Randall's theme into a detailed set of policy proposals. Decarbonising the economy will require a coordinated response across the private and public sectors unlike any other policy challenge that we have faced in peacetime. Yet we already largely possess the technology and the policy framework – what is needed is leadership, with an understanding and commitment that can deliver serious change. Importantly, the chapter shows how a policy programme can be constructed without hurting the poor or compromising on redistribution.

Chapters 13 and 14 both look at the limits of the market. Paul Holmes analyses the failures of market-based solutions to deliver what has often been claimed for them, by governments of both other parties, for the last three decades. The chapter gives examples, in health, education and housing, and a counter-example, of the success of local-council-led regeneration in Chesterfield. PFI schemes are revealed to have delivered little of value. Tim Farron addresses the same theme from the viewpoint of rural communities. A lack of affordable housing and employment opportunities, and agricultural markets in which farmers are at the mercy of major purchasers, such as the supermarkets, have devastated many rural villages. Both chapters reach the same conclusion: that there is much that the market cannot deliver that nevertheless is valued, and that social liberals do not have to accept market outcomes as immutable.

The next section discusses a crucial element of the social liberal state: its decentralised nature. Chris Huhne, in Chapter 15, puts the case for localism as a core part of the Liberal narrative. He argues that the current failure of the British state to deliver much of what its people want is undermining the entire political process. The answer is localism: 'the decentralisation not just of management decisions but of political responsibility to a human scale where voters can once again identify – and complain to, or praise, or boot out – decision-makers in their community'.

John Howson and Richard Grayson then apply this principle to education and to health. John Howson argues that to provide for an education system that is responsive to the needs of both individuals and the local community, a top-down system between central government working with the private or not-for-profit sectors cannot work. The community element must be preserved. Similarly, Richard Grayson puts the case for reforming the NHS so that it is run by democratically accountable local people with wide-ranging powers. Without this local power, local people will be continually asking for health care that is not on the menu, and for which they have not been given a price. Radical devolution has happened elsewhere in Europe, and it works. The challenge now is to apply it to the UK.

The social liberal state is not just decentralised; it is constrained. It respects human rights and civil liberties, even – perhaps especially – in the face of serious challenges from crime and terrorism. In Chapter 18, 'Rebuilding trust in the criminal justice system', Tim Starkey criticises Labour's centralising approach, fondness for knee-jerk legislation, obsession with targets and undermining of judicial independence. He proposes instead a series of ways in which the workings of the state can be made more efficient, more decentralised and more democratic.

In Chapter 19, 'Tackling terrorism', Nick Clegg argues that there can be no accommodation between liberalism and Islamist terrorism, which represent value systems which are diametrically opposed to one another. In other words, liberalism must be forthright in its own defence. The chapter proposes greater engagement with the mainstream Muslim community, together with reforms to the intelligence services, police and the judicial system to strengthen anti-terror prosecutions. 'Our aim should remain steadfast and simple: to protect both our lives and our liberties, and to refuse to accept that one requires the sacrifice of the other.'

The final policy section looks at Britain's place in the world. Liberals are instinctively internationalists and individualists, opposed to the closed communalism that nationalism encourages. Yet, as William Wallace, in Chapter 20, 'To be a Briton', argues, national identity is still important; democratic government can be supported and redistributive welfare can be maintained only by a commitment to shared institutions and values, rooted in shared understandings of their origins and rationale. At present confused and contested, it is a Liberal task to clarify and redefine them. In Chapter 21, Tim Garden puts forward the case for a rational defence policy, ensuring national security while also meeting international challenges. Given the escalating costs of defence technology, and the current over-stretch in the British armed forces, he argues for sharing capabilities through NATO and the EU. 'In defence, perhaps more than any other policy area, we need to reinvent the role of the state by accepting that the sovereignty of the state can be most effectively exercised through international collaboration.'

Conclusions

The last chapter in the book, 'Communicating social liberalism', by Steve Webb and Jo Holland, brings us back to our starting point. The social liberal argument has three steps. First, relying exclusively on unfettered market mechanisms to deliver a liberal and democratic society is doomed to failure. Second, positive state intervention to tackle market failures is not only perfectly compatible with Liberalism, it may be actively necessary for a full understanding of individual freedom. Third, Liberal interventions in markets are different in kind from socialist interventions, being always as local as possible and as accountable as possible.

The chapter goes on to develop the basic framework for a social liberal message, and points to the trends in public opinion which will make it a popular approach – the widespread resentment at gross inequalities in income and wealth which appear to bear little relation to effort or talent; the public demand for coordinated international action on climate change; the growing awareness of the problems caused when market players become too powerful; a clear desire for exercising control over decisions affecting local public services; and continued concern over the 'nanny state', particularly in reaction to rafts of centralised targets that seek to micro-manage the public sphere.

Our goal in all these things – the goal of all this book's contributors – is to enable the individual to make the most of his or her life. This will not happen if the state stands idly by. Nor will it happen if the state steps in to control. But it will happen if the state enables, if the state hands power back and if the state tames the power of the market.

To achieve these aims requires the reinvention of the British state. The country's current structures of government and society do not work, and the ideologies – if one can call them that – of Labour and Conservatives do not provide a solution. Given the challenges that the UK now faces – the external threats of climate change, terrorism and unchecked globalisation, the internal ones of an unequal and unparticipative society – but also given the basic values and tremendous capabilities of Britain's people, when treated as the responsible and intelligent human beings they mostly are, social liberalism's combination of political freedom, social justice and democracy are needed now more than ever.

Contributors

Elspeth Attwooll has been the Liberal Democrat MEP for Scotland since 1999. She is a member of the Regional Development, Fisheries and Employment & Social Affairs Committees. She is also the Scottish Liberal Democrats' Europe spokesperson and President of the Scottish Women Liberal Democrats and the Scottish Section of Liberal International. Born in 1943, she was educated at St Andrews University: Queen's College, Dundee, and taught jurisprudence at the University of Glasgow. Her political career spans more than three decades, beginning in 1974 when she stood as a Parliamentary candidate in Glasgow Maryhill.

David Boyle is the author of *Blondel's Song* (Penguin), a fellow of the New Economics Foundation, and a member of the Liberal Democrat Federal Policy Committee. He has also written a number of books about money, social trends and the future, including *The Little Money Book*, *The Tyranny of Numbers* and *Authenticity: Brands, Fakes, Spin and the Lust for Real Life*. See www.david-boyle.co.uk.

Duncan Brack is a freelance researcher, mainly on international environmental issues. A former Director of Policy for the Liberal Democrats (1988–94), he currently chairs the party's Federal Conference Committee and was vice-chair of the 'Meeting the Challenge' policy review group in 2005–06. He is also the Editor of the *Journal of Liberal History* and has co-edited a series of books, including the *Dictionary of Liberal Biography* (1998), *Dictionary of Liberal Thought* (2007), and *Why I Am A Liberal Democrat* (1995).

Nick Clegg is MP for Sheffield Hallam and Liberal Democrat Shadow Home Secretary. He studied at Cambridge, Minnesota and College d'Europe before training as a journalist. He then worked as a development and trade expert in the EU, sat as an MEP (1999–2004), lectured at Sheffield and Cambridge universities, and was elected as an MP in 2005. He served first as Europe spokesperson and then Shadow Home Secretary, a role in which he has spearheaded the Liberal

Democrats' defence of civil liberties, promoted a liberal approach to immigration and campaigned for prison reform.

Tim Farron was elected as MP for Westmorland & Lonsdale in 2005. He is Parliamentary Private Secretary to Menzies Campbell, Chair of the All-Party Parliamentary Group on Hill Farming, and a member of the House of Commons Environment, Food and Rural Affairs Select Committee. He is currently also the district councillor for the Milnthorpe ward on South Lakeland District Council. He chaired the recent South Cumbria NHS Inquiry and is active in campaigns to protect and enhance the Westmorland General Hospital in Kendal.

Lynne Featherstone was elected as MP for Hornsey & Wood Green in 2005. She was a Haringey councillor 1998–2006, and a member of the Greater London Assembly 2000–05. Before being promoted to the Liberal Democrat Shadow Cabinet as the Shadow Secretary of State for International Development in 2007, Lynne was part of the home affairs team, as well as being the spokesperson for London. Lynne was short-listed for the 2006 Channel 4 Political Awards, while her blog has twice been nominated for the *New Statesman* New Media Awards.

Tim Garden was the Liberal Democrat spokesperson on Defence in the Lords. He was a pilot in the RAF for thirty-two years, and eventually became responsible for forward planning for all three services. After retirement as an air marshal, he was Director of Chatham House, and a visiting professor at the Centre for Defence Studies at King's College London, where he worked on defence diplomacy, NATO Reaction Forces, and European defence capabilities. His chapter here was one of the last pieces he wrote before dying, just as this book went to print.

Dr Richard S. Grayson was Director of Policy of the Liberal Democrats in 1999–2004, during which time he was one of the principal authors of the party's manifestos for the 2001 general election and the 2004 European election. He stood for Parliament in 2005 in his home town of Hemel Hempstead, and has been reselected in the same seat for the next election. He was Director of the Centre for Reform in 1998–99. Since 2004 he has lectured in British politics at Goldsmiths, University of London, and has been Head of Politics there since 2006.

Dr David Hall-Matthews is a lecturer in the School of Politics and International Studies at Leeds University. He has conducted research on nineteenth-century India and contemporary Malawi, publishing a number of articles and a book, *Peasants, Famine and the State in Colonial Western India* (Palgrave Macmillan, 2005). He is currently working on a contemporary history of South Asia for

Blackwell. He has advised several Liberal Democrat international development spokespersons and served on policy working groups on development, international trade and investment and, currently, the UK response to globalisation.

Jo Holland is Senior Researcher to Steve Webb MP, and runs his Parliamentary office in Westminster. She has worked with him on the health and social security portfolios, and now in his role as manifesto chair. She sat on the Liberal Democrat Children and Families policy working group in 2006 and co-authored the chapter 'Children, the family and the state: a liberal agenda' in *The Orange Book* in 2004. She was elected as the party's Parliamentary Staff Chair in 2002–03 and is currently an executive member of the Liberal Democrat Christian Forum. She has an MA in History from Cambridge University.

Paul Holmes is Liberal Democrat MP for Chesterfield. He joined the SDP-Liberal Alliance in 1983 and the Liberal Democrats in 1988. He was elected as MP for Chesterfield in 2001 and co-founded the Beveridge Group. In the 2001–05 Parliament he was a member of the Education and Skills Select Committee, the Lib Dem spokesperson for people with disabilities, and a Friend of UNICEF in the Commons. In 2005 he was elected as Chairman of the Parliamentary Party and in 2007 joined the Shadow Cabinet as Shadow Minister for Housing.

David Howarth is the MP for Cambridge. He is currently a member of the Liberal Democrats' shadow cabinet with responsibility for legal affairs. Before his election to Parliament he taught law and economics at the University of Cambridge, served on the Liberal Democrats' Federal Policy Committee and led Cambridge City Council.

Professor John Howson has been an adviser to four Liberal Democrat shadow secretaries of state for education over the past ten years. He is a director of Education Data Surveys, a leading research company in the field of education. He started his teaching career in Tottenham in the 1970s and his political career in Devizes during the 1966 general election, while still at university. In the 2005 general election he fought Reading East for the Lib Dems.

Chris Huhne is MP for Eastleigh and the Liberal Democrat Shadow Secretary of State for Environment, Food and Rural Affairs. He was runner-up in the 2006 leadership contest, and was previously Shadow Chief Secretary to the Treasury, and economic spokesman for the pan-European Liberal group in the European Parliament from 1999 to 2005. He is a former City economist and journalist for the *Independent, Independent on Sunday, Guardian* and *Economist*.

Mark Pack is Head of Innovations for the Liberal Democrats, having previously worked in the Campaigns & Elections Department for seven years. He was the campaign manager for Lynne Featherstone's 2005 victory in Hornsey & Wood Green. Before working for the party, Mark had a series of jobs in IT and academia, and he completed a doctorate in nineteenth-century English elections. He writes here in a personal capacity.

Ed Randall is a lecturer in politics and social policy at Goldsmiths University of London. He was a councillor in Greenwich for sixteen years and a Liberal Democrat parliamentary candidate in the borough. He is the author of *The European Union and Health Policy* and *A Union for Health*, and he edited the *Dictionary of Liberal Thought* with Duncan Brack. Ed has recently written for the *Political Quarterly* on Liberal policy and politics and for the *Journal of European Public Policy* on European regulatory governance. His current research is concerned with politics, risk and food.

Tim Starkey has practised as a criminal barrister for six years, appearing in courts at all levels from the Magistrates' Court to the Court of Appeal. Over this time he has both prosecuted and defended in a wide range of cases, gaining valuable insights into the problems of the criminal justice system. He was on the Federal Party working group which produced the policy paper *Together We Can Cut Crime.*

Matthew Taylor was first elected MP for Truro & St Austell in 1987, aged 24, and remained the youngest MP for ten years. He has held several key positions in the Liberal Democrat Shadow Cabinet, including environment, education and Shadow Chancellor. He has also been the Chair of the Parliamentary Party and Head of Communications and Campaigns. After two decades as an MP, and following his marriage to partner Vicky and the birth of their son Arthur, he will be standing down at the next election to dedicate more time to his family.

Simon Titley is a writer and public affairs consultant based in Brussels. He writes regularly on political and public affairs, and recently contributed a chapter to the global standard reference work, *The Handbook of Public Affairs*; he is also on the Editorial Board of the *Journal of Political Marketing*. His political activities focus on writing and producing *Liberator* magazine. He was a Liberal parliamentary candidate in the 1983 election, and a member of the party's election HQ team in 1987 and 1992. He was born in Lincoln in 1957 and educated at the University of Keele, where he read International Relations.

William Wallace (Lord Wallace of Saltaire) is Deputy Leader of the Liberal Democrats in the House of Lords, and spokesman on foreign affairs. He is also emeritus professor of international relations at the London School of Economics, where he taught full time from 1995 to 2005, and chair of the LSE's Cold War Studies Centre. He has written on European international politics and transatlantic relations, as well as on British foreign policy and on the links between foreign policy, history and national identity.

Steve Webb has been MP for Northavon since 1997, and now chairs the Liberal Democrat manifesto group. From 1999 to 2005 he was the party's spokesman on social security and from 2005 to 2007 on health. Prior to being elected to Parliament he worked for nine years as an economist at the Institute for Fiscal Studies, before being appointed Professor of Social Policy at Bath University in 1995.

Chapter 1

What is Social Liberalism?

David Howarth

Sometime in the late nineteenth century, liberalism began to divide into two different streams. One stream, which came to be called 'classical liberalism', confined liberalism's ambitions to establishing a robust framework to protect individuals from a rapacious and power-hungry state. It aimed to control the size of the state, especially its military expenditure, and to promote international free trade, both for its own sake and as a way to encourage peace. Its ideal was a state that left us alone to get on with our lives. It valued political freedoms – especially of speech and of belief – but also tended to see property rights in themselves as an important bulwark against oppression.

Some classical liberals shaded into what ought to be called libertarianism rather than liberalism. They came to view property rights as natural rights existing outside the framework of the state, so that the state may not even redefine property rights without committing a wrong.

The other stream, which has come to be called 'social liberalism' (but which might better be called 'social justice liberalism'), also valued political freedom, also thought that the state should as far as possible leave us alone to make our own decisions on how to live our lives, also opposed militarism and also believed that international free trade was a way to preserve peace, but it believed in addition that liberalism required a commitment to a fair distribution of wealth and power, which in turn led to support for redistributive taxation and public services as ways of fairly distributing wealth and for democracy as a way of fairly distributing power .

Fairness can be seen both as a condition for the legitimacy of the state itself (the characteristic 'social contract' view as revived by John Rawls) and as a condition for meaningful freedom. In contrast to the views of libertarians and some classical liberals, rights of property came to be seen by social liberals as instruments of state policy that had to contribute to broader political goals rather than as goals in themselves.

In some countries, the division of liberalism eventually led to the creation of two separate liberal parties. An early example was the separation of the Danish Venstre and Radikale Venstre. Later examples include the Dutch VVD and D66 and the division of the French Radical Party into the Radicaux de Gauche and the Valoisien Parti Radical. But in Britain, and in a different way in the United States, 'liberalism' has come simply to mean social liberalism. British and American liberals believe not just in political freedom but also in social justice and in democratisation.

As a consequence classical liberalism does not have its own political home in Britain. Some classical liberals have ended up in the Conservative Party, but that has never been a particularly comfortable home for them because of the ever-present authoritarian and socially illiberal strands in Conservative thinking.

The confusion about 'economic liberalism'

Occasionally the idea comes up that some British liberals are 'social liberals' whereas others – for example some of the authors of *The Orange Book*[2] – are 'economic liberals', and that there is a fundamental difference between them. This is a confused view, which comes about through not understanding the difference between means and ends. All British liberals are social liberals, even the ones who claim to be more 'economically' liberal than others. To take an example often cited by commentators, David Laws, regarded by many as an 'economic liberal', is nevertheless an advocate of a very social-liberal view of redistribution. 'Freedom is curbed by poverty and inherited disadvantage', he has written, 'which is why liberals have been concerned about these issues for more than a century'.[3] Economic liberalism, for Laws, is about the way in which we pursue social liberalism, not about the aims of social liberalism. He has further explained that his often-expressed view that British liberals should 'reclaim our economic liberal heritage'[4] has been 'misunderstood and misrepresented, as implying a downgraded commitment to the party's social liberal roots … The argument is that social liberal goals should be pursued with economically liberal means.'[5]

The confusion comes about because 'economic liberalism' is an ambiguous term. One possible meaning is that it is identical with 'classical liberalism', with the view that liberals need not be concerned about redistribution or with democracy but only with limiting the scope and activity of government. If that were what 'economic liberalism' meant, it would indeed sometimes come into conflict with social liberalism. That is not, however, the meaning used by 'economic liberals' within British liberalism. Their version of 'economic liberalism' is a preference for market mechanisms not in opposition to redistribution but as a method to be used in the detailed design of mechanisms for it. For all social liberals, whenever the use of the market might undermine the central aim of social liberalism – namely a society that protects effective freedom for all and which thus can generate and recognise a legitimate form of government – the market has to give way. The political goals of liberalism are always more important than any particular method of achieving them.

Reasonable social liberals can disagree about the desirability and practicality of specific proposals for delivering social liberal goals. Market mechanisms will always have attractions for liberals, because they decentralise decision-making and encourage innovation – both important liberal enthusiasms – but market mechanisms will never be more than means rather than ends in themselves. The inherent limitations of market mechanisms, even in the absence of barriers that all liberals, including classical liberals, have always recognised, such as monopoly, are now very well-known. Asymmetries of information, transactions costs, and our limited capacity as human beings to calculate and imagine ('bounded rationality') all inevitably contribute to market failure. That does not mean, of course, that other mechanisms – state regulation or voluntary action – will do any better, but the possibility that they might should not be excluded. Above all, liberalism, as opposed to libertarianism, sees markets, and the property rights on which they rest, as intimately connected with the state, since markets, other than the most elementary and short term, fail without state guarantees of rights. Thus, for liberals, whether a market exists is a matter of policy choice, not a matter of brute fact.

It is an oddity of British political debate that so much emotional energy is expended on a question that almost certainly has no general or stable answer, namely whether public services should be organised using market or administrative mechanisms – except that no one now disputes that the state should compete for labour in the labour market and not be able to direct people into its jobs (though perhaps even that is not fully accepted by some in the National Health Service, who have recently attempted – with disastrous results – to introduce a directed labour element to the employment of junior doctors in training to become consultants). As a practical matter, some kinds of service at some times are better suited to be delivered through commercial contracts with separate organisations, whereas other kinds of service at other times are better delivered by directly employing the providers of the service. For example, where the aims of a service are in dispute or in transition, and so the criteria for its success or failure are unclear, governments would be well-advised not to attempt to contract the service out but instead to retain the flexibility of direct employment and management. On the other hand, simple services with uncontroversial aims might be better managed through a contract with another organisation. The fact is that British politics – largely because of a party structure that originally organised itself around the 'sides' of industry – elevated issues of personnel and resource management into matters of fundamental principle, while paying very little attention to issues that really are fundamental, such as political freedom, the development of democracy and the effects of gross inequalities of wealth and power.

The common core of liberalism

One should not, however, exaggerate the differences between classical and social liberalism. Both begin, and end, with the view that a state that fails to secure political freedom is not legitimate. Both reject the conservative view, for which the main advocate in Britain is the Labour Party of Tony Blair and Gordon Brown, that security is always more important than liberty. That view attributes to the state a wildly exaggerated capacity to provide security – not only because of the all-too-apparent limitations of the competence of state officials to keep us safe but also because, as the arbitrary power of the state increases, the more the state itself becomes a source of insecurity. The citizens of the Soviet Union were not more secure because of the immense arbitrary power of the Soviet state – they were less secure. The politics of fear, as practised in Britain by Labour, is ultimately self-defeating. It will destroy both the very freedoms it is the state's task to preserve and security itself.

That is not to say that liberalism denies any significance to security. It is just that it values security only in so far as it contributes to freedom. Tony Blair's view, in contrast, seemed to be that the only right that matters is the right to life. He would have sacrificed any political freedom if he thought that by doing so he would save a single life. One wonders what our forebears who sacrificed their lives for political freedom, from the seventeenth century to the twentieth, would make of the view that political freedom is not worth a single life. One wonders what the Blair doctrine would have implied in 1940, when we could have avoided a great many deaths in exchange for sacrificing the political freedom of the whole of Europe. For Labour, however, political freedoms are only 'traditional', as if they were a form of folk dance, and as such are merely romantic indulgences be sacrificed on the altar of the 'modern'. In contrast, for liberals of all kinds, unless the state guarantees political freedom, it has no moral claim on us at all.

Admittedly, to the extent that liberalism is built upon a social-contract view of politics, it cannot ignore existential threats. The social contract is not a suicide pact. But, as Lord Hoffmann has said, aptly but to the fury of large numbers of conservatives in the Labour Party and beyond, the current threat from terrorism is not existential. We are not faced with 1940. The greater threat is from laws that remove political freedom.[6]

Indeed, if there is an existential threat that creates a need to readjust the basic liberal social contract about what powers we ought to cede to the state, it is not terrorism, but climate change. But even a real existential threat such as climate change does not justify the erosion of fundamental liberties such as freedom from arbitrary arrest.

Nevertheless climate change does pose a challenge for classical liberals who are tempted by libertarianism. If one believes, as libertarians do, that property rights are fundamental and pre-political, one will find climate change a very thorny issue. Libertarians typically deal with environmental problems by saying that they depend on deciding which person, the polluter or the pollutee, has the better property right. But the global and existential nature of climate change makes this analysis very difficult for libertarians to apply. The consequence of saying that the polluter has the better right will be to undermine all property by destroying the physical conditions in which property has any meaning. But, because carbon emissions are so pervasive in our way of life, the consequence of saying that pollutees have the better right is to undermine such a broad range of property rights that one would be close to having to abandon any pretence of giving absolute priority to property rights. The exception would have swallowed the rule. Perhaps this dilemma explains why some libertarians tend towards climate change denial.

Classical liberals who are not libertarians, however, should have no difficulty with the idea that property rights should be designed by the state so that catastrophic effects such as climate change are avoided.

Two forms of social liberalism

Social liberalism moves beyond classical liberalism in two ways – a commitment to redistribution and a belief in democracy. But both are affirmations of liberalism's attachment to political freedom, not contradictions of it. The fundamental idea is that the over-concentration of power is itself a threat to political freedom. Excesses of wealth and poverty are themselves threats to freedom because they tend to produce self-perpetuating oligarchies who buy up the political system, either directly or through politically influential actors such as the media. On the other side, democracy, with its basic rule of political equality (one person, one vote) tends towards the dispersal of power, which safeguards liberty, especially if it takes the form not just of the passive democracy of occasional voting for representatives but also the active democracy of taking part in public decision-making. Social liberalism thus opposes gross inequalities of wealth and supports the extension and deepening of democratic decision-making.

Stating the basic principle does not, of course, settle how far to take it in particular circumstances. Indeed there is a disagreement within social liberalism about whether the principle that freedom should be safeguarded from the consequences of economic inequality is sufficient in itself or whether it should be supplemented by some further principle of fairness (for example John Rawls proposed two such principles: 'la carrière ouverte aux talents' – the principle that state jobs should be held only on the basis of ability; and his 'difference principle' – that material inequality should only be tolerated to the extent that it benefits the least advantaged). No social liberal would allow a supplementary fairness principle to undermine their commitment to political freedom, so that for all social liberals there is a clear hierarchy of value between freedom and equality (and one that is the opposite of that held by socialists), but there is disagreement about whether state policy should promote economic equality beyond the point strictly required by the goal of safeguarding political freedom.

What is sometimes interpreted as a difference of approach between 'social' and 'economic' liberals in Britain is often merely a difference within social liberalism between those who recognise supplementary fairness principles ('maximalist' social liberals) and those who recognise only the principle that there should be redistribution to the extent that maintains the conditions for political freedom ('minimalist' social liberals).

One point, however, tends greatly to reduce the practical distance between minimalist and maximalist social liberalism. Nearly all social liberals accept that the existence of formal political rights cannot be enough by itself to create a liberal society. Citizens need to be in a position to exercise their rights. That principle, which sounds modest, in reality implies a far-reaching programme of public services that goes beyond the classical liberal list of 'public goods' (such as defence). It implies in particular a commitment to the broadest possible provision of education, not for the sake of economic development, as in the socialist and utilitarian traditions, but to ensure that citizens can exercise their democratic rights in practical ways and not fall victim to political fraud and demagoguery. It also implies government guarantees in health care, since citizens who are ill or constantly in fear of illness are hardly in a position to give their time to public affairs.

Democracy – dialogue, community and localism
The commitment of social liberalism to democracy, especially to democratic participation, introduces another potential point of tension between social liberalism and markets. Markets are essentially a way in which people can communicate their desires and their abilities to other people without saying very much. Information flows through markets by the device of the price mechanism alone. The process of bidding prices up and down communicates all that needs to be communicated about preferences and costs. Democracy, however, especially in its participative form – but even in its representative form, when the representatives engage in debate – implies a much richer form of communication. Both

markets and democracy use forms of rationality, but the rationality of the market is closed. It is limited to working out the consequences of what we happen to want. Democracy, especially in its deliberative forms, goes further, into open discussion of what we ought to want.

Social liberals are drawn to markets because of their ability to disperse power and to promote innovation, but they are often also repelled by their impersonality. Moreover, markets seem potentially to undermine political freedom by undermining political activity. They do this by providing a means for obtaining what one wants without having to engage in anything but the thinnest of dialogues with one's fellow human beings. The extensive availability of the option of 'exit', to use Hirschman's venerable but still useful vocabulary,[7] tends to dissolve the option of 'voice'.

The dangers of replacing political participation with markets are apparent in British society today. It is connected with the rise of consumer politics, in which one's vote is seen not as a responsibility to choose what is best for all but as an instrument of self-interest. It is one of the factors behind growing disillusion with politics, which in turn is a major threat to political freedom, as disillusion turns inevitably to cynicism. If politics is seen simply as 'buying' products in a political marketplace, it will soon lose all coherence, and hence, in the longer term, it will lose all credibility. Pure manoeuvre replaces attempts to reflect values. That in turn leads to endless disappointment, since, unlike in a real market transaction, if voters choose incoherently, as they are likely to do if they follow only their immediate desires (more services *and* lower taxes) they can and will blame 'politicians' for their own incoherence.

In contrast, political participation in decision-making (and not only in campaigning – single-issue politics can only be entry-level politics, not the full deal) is an education in political responsibility. It gives an insight into understanding the problem of political value and choice. To govern is to choose, but if only a few people understand that fact, and the rest are infantilised into believing that they can have everything they want, democratic government will not endure.

The classical liberal view that all the state should do is guarantee rights and then move out of the way leads to a situation in which politics appears not to be necessary. Social liberals fear that this classical liberal dream is a dangerous delusion, for there never can be a society in which rights are so firmly guaranteed that no political action is necessary to secure them. That is because securing rights can only take place through human institutions, such as the legal system, and human institutions are populated by human beings, who are not necessarily to be trusted. Any attempt to create such a perfectly non-political society (what might be called 'legal liberalism') will have the unintended but serious effect of making rights ultimately less secure. Liberalism, to be sure, values the rule of law, but social liberalism also recognises that law should not attempt to replace or abolish politics. Instead, law should be seen as a form of vitrified or frozen politics, a form that is valuable because it deliberately slows down some kinds of decision and because it is more firmly committed than the rest of the political system to ideas of procedural justice; but we also need the means by which other decisions can be taken more quickly, whether in the marketplace or in politics.

The value social liberals give to dialogue and democratic participation also emerges in another theme of British liberalism, that of community. If one were to read only recent liberal political theory, and ignore the practice of liberal politics in Britain over the past forty years, one might conclude that the idea of 'community' was the exclusive possession of an anti-liberal group of politicians called 'communitarians'. It is true that anti-liberal, and indeed illiberal, communitarians exist. But they are not the only politicians interested in community. The liberal idea of community arises from the democratic ideal of people taking and using political power[8] rather than from any metaphysical notion that people only exist in their relations with other people – a view liberals would reject, even though they value opportunities for rich human interaction. Liberal community politics can be criticised as tending to confuse society and the state, but its deeper meaning is as a form of active democracy, in which people come together, decide what they want to change and then work to bring that change about. The idea is not that politics should reflect the views of existing 'communities' – the amorphous groups within which communitarian (and specifically Labour) politicians want to trap people – but that it should create communities. More than that (and this is where the practice of community politics can go wrong), liberal politics should aim to create liberal communities.

All this explains why localism is a long-standing social liberal commitment. Local government combines all the liberal desiderata, not just some of them. It helps to disperse power and to promote experimentation and diversity, but, in addition, unlike markets, it can facilitate political participation. It has a human dimension that markets tend to suppress. Classical liberals sometimes criticise social liberals for claiming to believe in decentralising power but failing to promote further decentralisation from local government to individuals through markets. The social liberal response is that political freedom depends on active participation in politics and that can best happen, both from a practical point of view and from the point of view of avoiding the dangers of excessive concentrations of power, in local government.

Localism lies at the heart of what social liberals mean when they talk of reinventing the state. If the units of decision-making are small enough, more people will believe that their participation can make a difference and hence they will be more likely to participate. But, even more importantly, they have to believe that the unit of government in which they are invited to participate can make decisions that make a difference. The first condition of wider participation in local government is that local government needs to have effective power. Undermining that power, by, for example, purporting to 'devolve' power further to individuals in markets, will defeat the whole exercise. This is why both Labour and Conservative versions of localism will ultimately fail.

Classical liberals might object that the implication of localism is that, as long as the state is decentralised, it should be permitted to displace the market entirely. But this is not the implication of localism, at least for social liberals. Social liberalism's devotion to localism arises principally from its commitment to preserving political freedom through encouraging political participation. The degree to which localised state institutions should displace market mechanisms, or quasi-market mechanisms such as voucher and insurance schemes, depends on the degree to which such mechanisms might undermine political participation, and the degree to which local political control might encourage political participation.

Because social liberalism supports localism for its political effects, for its contribution to liberty rather than to fairness, it ought to be supported by all types of social liberal, both minimalist and maximalist. The difference between them will be that minimalist social liberals will be satisfied if localism succeeds in safeguarding political freedom. Maximalists,

however, will want to use local power to further their extended fairness goals. Maximalists will also argue that the dangers of state action
for freedom itself will be less acute if that state action is taken at local
level, since power will inherently be less concentrated and individuals
will retain an option to exit (that is, to move house) that will usually be
fairly easy to exercise. But maximalist social liberalism is not socialism.
Ultimately it values political freedom above fairness, and it should not
ignore the real dangers of the abuse of power at local level.

Getting the economy out of the state – beyond public choice
Classical liberalism enjoyed an intellectual and academic renaissance
between thirty and forty years ago largely because of the rise of public
choice theory.[9] The basic premise of public choice theory is that since
politicians and public administrators are humans too, their behaviour
can be explained in the normal economic way of assuming that they are
maximising their own welfare. Political behaviour in a democracy, for
example, is explicable through the fact that politicians need to win re-
election. Bureaucratic behaviour is explicable in terms of bureaucrats'
desire to maximise their number of subordinates. Both incentive structures lead to obvious inefficiencies. Public choice thus became the study
of state or bureaucratic failure, a study that parallels, supplements and,
crucially, changes the policy conclusions of economic thinking about
market failure. Its central policy message was that market failure does
not necessarily imply state intervention because state or bureaucratic
failure might be worse.

Public choice theory has important weaknesses. Its view of what
politicians want is very thin, because it ignores the role of political values
and ideals. It promotes a view of democracy that is entirely passive –
as a marketplace for desires in which votes are expressions of existing
preferences, not as a forum in which desires are formed and changed. It
assumes that political actors have no concept of virtue or public service
whatsoever, an assumption that has the potential to feed back into a sub-
stantive belief that politicians in reality have no such concepts. It turns
the older liberal-republican idea that, although political virtue exists, it is
limited in supply and thus needs to be husbanded carefully[10] into a conception of politics that dissolves all virtue and seems to require politics to
be suppressed altogether.

Nevertheless public choice theory has a kernel of truth. The theme that political discretion is often dangerous and should be minimised forms part of the intellectual background to policies of all the main British political parties. It crops up not only in the Conservative privatisations of the 1980s but also in the quintessentially Liberal Democrat policy of independence for the Bank of England, a policy subsequently stolen by Labour.

There is, however, a problem. Public choice theorists tended towards libertarianism, and therefore tended to downplay the part played by the state in creating and structuring markets. They thought that if state activity were to be replaced by market activity, politics would be less important and we could all sleep more safely in our beds. This turned out to spectacularly wrong. The privatisations of the 1980s and '90s were accompanied by the biggest-ever rise in lobbying, especially by business. The consultancy sector in the UK rose by a factor of thirty-one (or elevenfold in real terms) between 1979 and 1998.[11] What happened was that for privatisation to work, the state had to create, through regulation, a series of new organisations and markets, but it also created, in the form of the newly privatised companies themselves and others who might have an interest in them or their activities, a vast number of people who might benefit or lose according to precisely how the government chose to regulate. Furthermore, these organisations, unlike the previous state organisations, had budgets to spend on influencing those decisions.

British politics is now dominated by corporate lobbying. Lobbying lies at the heart of the crisis in party funding, for example, and the cash-for-honours scandal. It also contributes to alienation from politics, and ultimately from democracy itself, because the power of big economic interests to get their way demonstrates to everyone else their powerlessness and encourages a belief that political activity is pointless. Corporatism was not killed off by Thatcherism, as the public-choice theorists hoped. It has merely been reborn in a new form, with, for the most part, only one 'side' of industry being represented, but still otherwise intact.

Although we should be wary of the dangers of public choice theory's libertarian anti-politics, its anti-corporatism remains entirely admirable. Public choice theory's error lay not in hoping for the end of corporatism but in promoting methods of pursuing that goal that only made things worse. But the anti-corporatist theme itself, and especially the aim of rolling back the corporatist-lobby state, is entirely in line with social liberal instincts.

The role of a social liberal party

The question remains: how broad a church should a social liberal party be? Clearly there is no difficulty in holding within itself social liberals with different ideas about how to pursue social liberal goals, such as 'economic liberals'. Almost as clearly, the gap between 'minimal' and 'maximal' social liberals does not lead to insuperable difficulties. The question in practice is about the degree of desirable redistribution or equality of opportunity, not the desirability of those things in the first place. And all social liberals can agree about democratisation and the redistribution of power.

The case of classical liberals, however, is more difficult. Classical liberal adherence to the common core of liberalism, namely the ultimate importance of political freedom, provides a very substantial shared base. But where classical liberalism starts to look like libertarianism, with pre-political theories of property rights and suspicion of all politics including democratic politics, there is more difficulty. Perhaps the issue is ultimately a practical one for classical liberals – do they feel more uncomfortable with fellow liberals who happen to believe in redistribution and democracy or with people who are not liberals in the first place?

There is also, and finally, the question of the relationship between the party and personal liberalism. Liberals in politics are often liberals in their own lives as well. Many liberals hold liberalism as a 'comprehensive' doctrine – one that offers guidance for all aspects of life – and not just guidance for politics. 'Comprehensive' liberalism means, for example, not just that the state should refuse to condemn other people's choices when it does no one harm but themselves, but also that we should refuse to do so personally as well. Ultimately, personal liberalism comes down to the idea, derivable from the philosophy of Immanuel Kant, that there is no 'core' self that we cannot escape. We should be prepared to abstract away from any allegiance or prejudice and be prepared to start again.[12]

There are difficult questions here. Comprehensive liberalism has political implications, for example about the extent to which we should tolerate illiberal behaviour within other people's communities. Should

13

we tolerate communities that do not allow people to leave them, for example? Irrevocable membership violates the most basic comprehensive liberal view, that people always have the capacity to change, and that denying that capacity denies their humanity. But should the state intervene to preserve that capacity for people who seem not to believe in it or to want it to be preserved?

If we accept the reality that a social liberal party will always have as its bedrock people who are comprehensive and personal liberals, the question becomes whether such a party should discourage from membership liberals whose liberalism is not personal but only political? That is, what about people who are not liberal in their own moral views but who are only liberal to the extent that they believe that, in public life, we should refrain from invoking arguments that appeal only to those from very specific cultural backgrounds or with very specific religious views (roughly 'political' liberals in Rawls' sense)? Or what about those who would not even go that far along the route of restraining their own commitment to their own moral view but who believe that the only way to create a tolerable state of affairs in a society dominated by competing and incompatible comprehensive views is by a non-aggression pact, or more accurately a no-attempts-at-domination pact ('modus vivendi liberals')?[13] These questions are particularly pressing in a party that has always welcomed religious minorities and dissenters (for example the Nonconformist tradition) but whose political line tends towards secularism.

The best tradition of the party is that it should welcome liberals of all sorts, although it should recognise the tensions that will arise as a result. Liberalism, although as strong a political force in Britain as anywhere in Europe, is not so strong that it can afford to divide its forces. And it is also no longer possible to imagine, as Ralf Dahrendorf once did, that there is no need for a separate liberal party because the other parties could be sufficiently suffused with liberalism to make them safe. The rise of illiberalism, both in the media and in the New Labour government, has been too strong in the past decade to make that a plausible stance.

Social liberalism's combination of political freedom, social justice and democracy are needed now more than ever.

Notes

1   See G. Gaus, 'On Justifying the Moral Rights of the Moderns' in E. Paul, F. Miller and J. Paul, *Liberalism: Old and New* (Cambridge University Press, 2007).

2   P. Marshall and D. Laws, *The Orange Book: Reclaiming Liberalism* (Profile Books, London, 2004).

3   J. Astle, D. Laws, P. Marshall and A. Murray, *Britain After Blair: A Liberal Agenda* (Profile Books, London, 2006) p. 144.

4   D. Laws, 'Size isn't everything' in J. Margo, *Beyond Liberty: Is the future of liberalism progressive?* (IPPR, London, 2007) p. 145.

5   Ibid., pp. 145–46.

6   See Lord Hoffmann in *A v Secretary of State for the Home Department* [2004] UKHL 56 at 95–97.

7   A. O. Hirschman, *Exit, Voice and Loyalty: Responses to Decline in Firms, Organisations, and States* (Harvard University Press, 1970).

8   See B. Greaves and G. Lishman, *The Theory and Practice of Community Politics* (Association of Liberal Councillors Campaign Booklet 12, Hebden Bridge, 1980).

9   For a quick summary see the reissue of G. Tullock, *The Vote Motive* (Institute of Economic Affairs, London, 2006).

10   See B. Ackerman, *We, The People: Foundations* (Belknap Harvard University Press, 1991), ch. 7, 'The Economy of Virtue'.

11   D. Miller 'The Rise of the PR Industry in Britain, 1979–98', *European Journal of Communication* 15 (1), 2000.

12   See A. Ryan, 'Newer than What? Older than What?' in Paul, Miller and Paul, *Liberalism: Old and New.*

13   Ibid.

Chapter 2

Equality Matters

Duncan Brack

The Liberal Democrats exist to build and safeguard a fair, free and open society, in which we seek to balance the fundamental values of liberty, equality and community, and in which no one shall be enslaved by poverty, ignorance or conformity ... We reject all prejudice and discrimination based upon race, colour, religion, age, disability, sex or sexual orientation and oppose all forms of entrenched privilege and inequality ... We recognise ... that the market alone does not distribute wealth or income fairly. We support the widest possible distribution of wealth ...

Extracts from the Preamble to the constitution of the Liberal Democrats

Of the three 'fundamental values' which the party's constitution claims we 'seek to balance' – liberty, equality and community – equality has traditionally held least appeal for Liberal Democrats. The very title of the 2002 policy paper on Lib Dem philosophy, *It's About Freedom*, relegates it explicitly to, at best, second place. As the paper made clear:

We place the principle of freedom above the principle of equality. Equality can be of importance to us in so far as it promotes free-dom. We do not believe that it can be pursued as an end in itself, and believe that when equality is pursued as a political goal, it is invariably a failure, and the result is to limit liberty and reduce the potential for diversity.[1]

I served on the working group that produced that paper, so I share the responsibility for the statement. I now believe, however, that it drastically understates the importance of the pursuit of equality as the essential underpinning of our ultimate aim of individual freedom, Similarly, equality underpins the type of communities in which individuals thrive best. The pursuit of both these other values will be compromised by a lack of attention to equality. Furthermore, I don't mean just equality of *opportunity*, the Liberal get-out for most of the past century. I mean equality of *outcome* – or to be more accurate, a significant reduction in *inequality* of outcome.

This chapter will argue the case for promoting (or restoring) equality to the place where the party put it in its founding constitution, as a 'fundamental value' balanced against – rather than subordinate to – the other two. My case is based on three main arguments. First, that the extent of income and wealth inequality in modern-day Britain is seriously undermining the fabric of society, and needs urgently to be tackled by government – not just for the sake of those at the bottom of the income and wealth pile, but for all of us.[2] Second, that a commitment to reduce levels of income and wealth inequality fits naturally into our Liberal philosophy. Third, that it's smart politics.

Is Britain unequal? Income and wealth inequality

First, we need to examine the extent of income and wealth inequality in modern-day Britain. Is Britain in reality an unequal society?

The answer is emphatically yes. After falling in the 1970s, income inequality grew significantly under Thatcher, and has declined only slightly since. By 1979 the percentage of the population living in relative poverty[3] had fallen to about 14 per cent, a post-war record. By 1996–97 this had almost doubled, to 25.3 per cent, and by 2006–07 it still stood at 21.6 per cent, representing 12.7 million people.[4] As the Institute for Fiscal Studies found:

> Inequality rose dramatically over the 1980s … The scale of this rise in inequality has been shown elsewhere to be unparalleled both historically and compared with the changes taking place at the same time in most other developed countries … Over the first two terms of the Labour government, the net effect of these changes was to leave income inequality effectively unchanged and at historically high levels.[5]

Wealth distribution remains even more unequal than that of income, partly because of the substantial rise in house prices. Between 1990 and 2001 the proportion of wealth held by the wealthiest 10 per cent of the population increased from 47 per cent to 56 per cent.[6] A Joseph Rowntree Foundation study published in July 2007 concluded that Britain was becoming an increasingly segregated society in terms of wealth distribution. The last fifteen years have seen an increase in the total number of households living in poverty. At the same time, households in already wealthy localities have tended to become even wealthier, with many rich people now living in areas segregated from the rest of society. This widening gap between rich and poor has led to a fall in the number of 'average' households (neither rich nor poor), with those families gradually disappearing from London and the South East. The report concluded that 'Britain is moving back towards levels of inequality in wealth and poverty last seen more than forty years ago'.[7]

The filthy rich

That income and wealth inequality grew dramatically under the Thatcher governments is no surprise. It was a predictable side-effect of the reductions in the higher levels of income tax, the shift from direct to indirect taxes, cutbacks in government spending on public services, and government-engineered recessions which saw unemployment soar. It was not countered significantly, however, by the recovery in employment and output experienced from the mid 1990s onwards.

Why is this? One might have expected a Labour government to be more concerned about inequality than their Conservative predecessors. In fact Labour's tax and benefit reforms have helped the poorest groups, though only since 2000–01, after they dropped their rigid adherence to Tory spending plans. Since then, significant increases in means-tested benefits and the use of tax credits have helped to raise the income of most of the poorest 40 per cent by more than the average, although the poorest 10 per cent have not done nearly so well. The complexity of the tax credit system has led to significant administrative problems, and redistribution has also has been counteracted by substantial increases in Council Tax, which affects those on lower incomes more heavily.

The other main reason why inequality has remained stubbornly high is because the highest rate of growth of incomes, in both absolute and proportional terms, has been experienced by those in the top 10 per cent: the rich have got even richer. This is not really surprising; when Peter Mandelson said, in 1998, that New Labour was 'intensely relaxed about people getting filthy rich', he really meant it.

Partly this is the outcome of government policy – the way in which the tax system operates, or can be manipulated, to benefit the super-rich. Overall, the poorest fifth of the population pays a higher percentage of their gross income in tax than the richest fifth. The House of Commons Treasury Select Committee's recent investigation into private equity firms revealed how the tax relief structure on capital gains tax has helped many in that industry pay less than 10 per cent on their investments,[8] even if they paid tax legitimately. More broadly, chief executives' pay levels have increased enormously. In 1979, FTSE100 chief execs earned on average about ten times as much as the average worker on the shop floor. By 2002, the ratio had increased from 10 to 54, and by 2006 to 76.[9] Last year FTSE100 chief execs' pay rose by 30 per cent on average; the average pay of their staff increased by 2.8 per cent.

Can't this be justified by improved performance and competitiveness? After all, the British private sector in 2006 has a rather better image than its predecessor in 1979. A University of Manchester study comparing corporate performance from 1983 to 2002, however, showed that the sales of the top 100 quoted companies on the stock exchange rose by an annual 2.7 per cent, as did pre-tax profits, while the pay of their chief executives rose almost ten times faster, by 26.2 per cent.[10] The study concluded that 'giant-firm CEOs might be just another averagely ineffectual officer class', who have in effect been 'value-skimming', quietly enriching themselves for mediocre performance. This picture was reinforced by a Work Foundation study in 2006 showing that higher pay rates could be justified neither by higher levels of personal risk (the turnover rate for their jobs was lower than the national average; only one was made redundant, and he left with £5m compensation) nor by competition in the global market (most CEOs of British companies are British, and promoted from within their companies).[11]

Does this growth in the super-rich really matter? I return to this question below, in terms of its indirect impact on social cohesion, but there are direct impacts too. As the Rowntree Foundation study highlighted, the concentration of super-rich households in some urban and suburban areas is pushing house prices way out of the reach of even the better-off. Shops and restaurants follow the trend, helping to create super-rich ghettos – the real impact of 'trickle-down'. The super-rich increasingly buy their own media and then use it to promote the political parties that come to them for funds, as ordinary party membership dwindles.

No way out: social mobility

None of this need matter so much if people have a reasonable chance of escaping from poverty, of climbing into the ranks of the rich – or even into those of the average. But on top of the UK's current pattern of income and wealth inequality, the country suffers from low and declining social mobility.

A 2005 study showed that the chances of children born into low-income groups of moving into high-income groups as adults were lower in the UK than in the Nordic countries or Germany, and the chances of upward movement were significantly lower for people born in 1970 than for those born in 1958. There is a far stronger relationship between educational attainment and family income in Britain than in other European or North American countries. Young people with parents with higher professional jobs, for example, are four times more likely to go to university than those with parents in routine manual employment.[12]

The UK performs very poorly in international comparisons of social mobility. A league table of eight developed states found that only the US had lower social mobility than the UK. In contrast, the four Scandinavian countries, along with Canada, are all nearly twice as socially mobile as Britain. Social mobility appears to be related to, or at least strongly correlated with, the degree of income inequality.

And despite the small fall in levels of inequality, social mobility is not improving. A 2006 Rowntree study on persistent poverty suggested that the chance of a poor child growing up to become a poor adult were still growing.[13] An Institute of Education report in June 2007 showed that by the age of three, children from disadvantaged families were already lagging a full year behind their middle-class contemporaries in social and educational development.[14]

The impacts of inequality: health and well-being[15]

Clearly, then, Britain is a deeply unequal society in terms of income and wealth distribution. It is also relatively socially immobile: your life chances are determined heavily by your parents' social class and status. Self-evidently, this is bad news for those at the bottom of the pile.

Its has been recognised for almost thirty years that standards of health and well-being are closely related to income levels. As far back as 1980, the Black Report, *Inequalities in Health*, concluded that from birth to old age, those at the bottom of the social scale had much poorer health and quality of life than those at the top. Recent studies show that the gap is still widening – the areas with the highest life expectancy a decade ago are the places that have seen the biggest increase in life expectancy since.[16] These disparities in health standards are nothing much to do with the NHS: social and economic factors such as income, wealth, employment, environment, education, housing and transport all affect standards of health more fundamentally, and all favour the better-off.

So inequalities in health are an outcome of inequalities in society. Life expectancy in rich nations correlates precisely with levels of equality – so Greece, with half the GDP per head, has a longer average life expectancy than the US, the richest country in the developed world, but also the most unequal. The people of Harlem live shorter lives than the people of Bangladesh. Average male life expectancy in the Calton area of Glasgow is eight years less than in Iraq, even after more than ten years of sanctions, war and insurgency.[17] A study of 528 cities in the US, UK, Sweden, Canada and Australia showed a strong relationship between death rates and inequality levels within each city. The two most egalitarian countries in the developed world, Japan and Sweden, also have the longest life expectancies.

This is not just about differences between extremes of wealth and poverty; there is a continuous gradient in death rates all the way through society. The higher people's status, the longer they live. A study of government office-workers in London in the 1970s and '80s found that death rates from heart disease were four times as high among the most junior office workers as among the most senior administrators working in the same offices; intermediate levels had intermediate death rates. Only a third of these differences could be explained by risk factors such as smoking, exercise and diet. Considering all causes of death, not just heart disease, the most junior workers were three times as likely to die prematurely as the most senior. As Polly Toynbee put it, if one office was found to be killing three times more than another next door, it would be evacuated instantly – but the social environment doesn't matter as much as environmental pollutants like asbestos.[18]

The impacts of inequality: violence, trust and social cohesion

This link between inequality and health standards is relatively familiar. What is much less appreciated is just how strongly levels of inequality are correlated with other social outcomes – which in turn mean that inequality is bad not just for those at the bottom of the pile but for everyone. Unequal societies function badly.

Violence is more common in societies where income differences are larger. About half the variation in homicide rates between different states or provinces in the US and Canada is accounted for by differences in levels of equality. Most criminologists regard this relationship as the most firmly established link between homicide and *any* environmental factor. Levels of imprisonment in a country can be shown to be related to income inequality and levels of literacy and mathematical ability – which are themselves closely linked to inequality.

This link between violence and inequality is not just exhibited in murder rates; it reaches all the way along the 'spectrum of hostility'. Both racial hostility and discrimination against women in US states is greater where inequality is higher. One British survey in the 1990s showed that families living on less than £10,000 a year were more than twice as likely to have daily arguments as those living on more than £20,000.

Perhaps most striking of all for Liberal Democrats, the extent to which communities work as communities is also highly correlated with levels of equality. In the US, levels of trust between individuals – the essential underpinning of any functioning community – can be shown to be higher in the more equal states. In the most equal states, only 10 or 15 per cent of the population feel they cannot trust others, while in the most unequal ones the proportion rises to 35 or 40 per cent.

The US Professor Robert Putnam has worked on people's involvement in community life, using a range of indicators, including the proportion of people belonging to voluntary groups and associations, propensity to vote in local elections, and readership of local newspapers. In Italy, he showed that involvement was highest where inequality was lowest. Although there was a tendency for local government performance to be better where the region in question was richer, a stronger correlation could be demonstrated with his index of 'civic community', which was in turn linked to equality.

Underlying causes: why inequality is harmful

Why is there such a pervasive relationship between inequality and social outcomes? The underlying reason, it is believed, is the stress caused by living at the bottom of the pecking order, on the lowest rung – the continuous stress of low social status, disrespect and exclusion.

Humans are a social species, and the quality of the social relations we experience matters enormously. Feelings of shame and embarrassment are powerful ones, and in extreme cases can lead to violence. Similarly, in Britain today, small premature babies are not, with a few exceptions, caused by bad diet – even poor nutrition, by British standards, will rarely harm a foetus. It is stress in pregnancy that does the real damage, and the poorer the mother, the more likely she is to be stressed. This is hugely important – maternal stress in pregnancy affects the son or daughter throughout their life, from behavioural patterns to standards of health to life expectancy. And these are further affected, of course, by stress levels in the children themselves. An orphanage in post-war Germany found that children on the same diet were found to have grown most under the kindest matron and least under the unkindest matron.

The stress hormone cortisol appears to be responsible. Cortisol is the most important hormone involved in preparing the body for sustained physical activity in meeting a threat. It shifts the body's functions away from housekeeping activities like digestion, energy storage, fighting infection and growth – a sensible move when fleeing from a predator or an enemy, but of less use in dealing with pervasive shame and disrespect. Long-term elevation of cortisol levels impairs immune system efficiency, raises blood pressure, causes diabetes and arteriosclerosis – and reduces birth weight amongst the children of stressed mothers.

How can stress levels be reduced? Primarily through improving the quality of social relations. We need to build a society which relies less on social status and more on friendship, which tend to vary inversely. Status and friendship have their roots in fundamentally different ways of resolving the problem of competition for scarce resources. Status is based on pecking order, coercion and privileged access to resources, while friendship is based on a more egalitarian basis of social obligations and reciprocity. Lynne Featherstone's chapter in this book explores this theme in more detail. It is a complicated and difficult area for government to be involved in, but an important one. Here I concentrate on the extent to which the reduction of income and wealth inequality can contribute to this strategy.

Why equality matters to Liberals

So tackling inequality is hugely important for those at the bottom of the income and wealth distribution, those lacking disposable income and assets and, furthermore, trapped by social immobility, where too much of an individual's future is determined before she is born. It is also important for the rest of us, for those lucky enough to live on a reasonably decent income and to enjoy possession of some level of assets, but who nevertheless exist in the middle of a broken society, riven by distrust, unhappiness and failing communities.

That's fine in practice; how does it work in theory? Aren't Liberals more concerned with freedom than with equality? Don't we fear that too much attention to equality risks creating a society of dull uniformity, where initiative, choice and innovation are frowned upon?

No. The Liberal commitment to equality derives *from* the Liberal commitment to freedom; it is neither separate from it nor subordinate to it. This belief can be traced right back through the long history of British Liberalism, and can perhaps best be expressed as a commitment to *equality of justice*.[19]

The fundamental belief in freedom leads logically to a corresponding belief in a diverse and tolerant society, where individuals are able to exercise freedom of choice, conscience and thought. Since such a society cannot exist where individuals are treated differently by the law or by government institutions because of their nature, 'equality before the law' has been one of the great rallying cries of Liberalism, from the earliest days of the Whigs in the seventeenth century.

The French Revolutionary slogan of 'liberty, equality, fraternity' (transposed in the Liberal Democrat constitution into 'liberty, equality, community') was not simply a list of three separate words; the three concepts interlinked and reinforced each other. 'Liberty' did not mean merely the freedom of choice that consumers experience in modern market democracies – it meant not being subordinate to arbitrary power, whether exercised by monarchy, aristocracy or clergy. The concept of freedom was very closely bound up with the extent of differences in social status and social exclusion, and the belief in equality (and in fraternity) in the levelling of those differences.

This Liberal belief in equality was expressed in the nineteenth century primarily through the removal of barriers – to the right to vote, to the right to practise one's beliefs free of discrimination, to the right to trade freely across national borders. From the end of the century onwards, however, it became obvious that this was no longer enough. Industrialisation, urbanisation and the drastic changes in the structures of society that resulted had led to the spread of poverty, slums, ignorance and disease. Not only were these all serious impediments to freedom, to the ability of people genuinely to exercise control over their own lives and destinies, but they were also impediments that it was difficult, if not impossible, for the affected individual to remove by themselves. Negative liberty, the removal of constraints on the individual, would not necessarily lead to freedom of choice for all, as not everyone enjoyed access to the same opportunities; freedom of choice was therefore heavily constrained.

Equality and social liberalism for the twentieth century

Thus was born the New Liberalism, which came to be the dominant ideology of the early part of the twentieth century. As Michael Freeden put it, this was 'the crowning achievement of British liberalism … its subtle and intelligent integration of the requirements of social welfare into a continuing respect for individual liberty, a formula that encapsulates its commitment to both individual and social progress'.[20]

The great reforming Liberal government elected by a landslide in 1906 took up this agenda of social justice. Asquith, Lloyd George and Churchill laid the foundations of the modern welfare state. Labour exchanges were introduced, old-age pensions were paid by the state for the first time, the national insurance system was created, taxation was raised in aggregate and made more redistributive. This was the realisation of the New Liberal programme – removing the shackles of poverty, unemployment and ill-health so as to allow people to be free to exercise choice and realise opportunity. Thus freedom and equality remained interlinked. As the New Liberal thinker L. T. Hobhouse put it:

The struggle for liberty is also, when pushed through, a struggle for equality. Freedom to choose and follow an occupation, if it is to become fully effective, means equality with others in the opportunities for following such occupation. This is, in fact, one among the various considerations which leads Liberalism to support a national system of free education, and will lead it further yet on the same lines.[21]

Or, as it is more commonly attributed, 'liberty without equality is a name of noble sound and squalid result'. This belief underpinned the system of redistributive taxation and social services which Labour built on after 1945 and which brought Britain to its lowest level of inequality – until Thatcherite Conservativism came to reverse the achievements of the previous seventy years.

Equality and social liberalism for the twenty-first century

Thatcherism did not, of course, appear out of thin air. The growth in the size of the state throughout the twentieth century, partly consequent on its new welfare role, led to new problems, including the increased power of bureaucracies, and the infringement on civil liberties that may entail, the tendency for elites to capture elements of state power (leading to market distortions such as subsidies), the growth of corporatism, a rising burden of taxation, and so on. The centralised and directive state that Labour built – very different from that which the Liberal Party would have created – helped to create the Thatcherite backlash, and its consequent legacy of inequality.

So, in taking action to reduce inequality, it is important that we do not simply recreate the centralised state. Many chapters in this book stress the need for a more decentralised, responsive and participatory structure and style of government. It is not just the structure and size of the state, however, that is the problem. More fundamentally, the redistribution of resources needed to reduce inequality must, to the greatest extent possible, equalise conditions (or endowments, or birthrights), while respecting choices.

There are two main reasons why inequality may exist. First, because individuals choose different lifestyles. I have worked all my life in the voluntary sector; I have had fulfilling jobs, for the party, for a trade union and for a think-tank, but I have been consistently paid less than my university friends who went into the civil service, or law, or public relations. That was my choice, and I don't regret it (usually). Given the ability to choose freely, people can and should choose different types of jobs, or different mixes of work and leisure. No system of redistribution should counteract that, or reduce the incentives for effort and enterprise.

What we are concerned with, of course, is the inequality which stems from the unequal distribution of endowments. We have seen already how parents' income, social class and levels of education affect the life-chances of their children, so markedly that this can be measured even by the age of three. Similarly, people experience different levels of health and ability and access to knowledge, generally through no choice of their own. Liberals have always opposed vigorously discrimination based on gender or race or sexuality or disability; should we not also oppose just as vigorously discrimination based on inherited poverty and ignorance?

The trick, of course, is to create a system that redistributes resources while preserving choice and incentives. This is not easy, either in practice or in theory, though it has occupied the time of many of the liberal thinkers of the later twentieth century.[22] John Rawls developed his 'difference principle', which stated that inequality could only be justifiable if it proved to be to the greatest benefit of the least advantaged members of society. Perhaps more importantly, Ronald Dworkin's theory of distributive justice, or equality of resources, claims that how people fare in life should, as far as possible, depend on their ambition, or personality, but not on their endowment, or circumstances. Dworkin defended the post-war structure of progressive taxation, unemployment insurance and universal health provision, while at the same time arguing for the option to buy private health insurance, in order to maximise choice.

A series of further writers, including Bruce Ackerman, Philippe van Parijs and John Roemer, have suggested various means of putting Dworkin's approach into practice. This includes, most commonly, the idea of allocating some form of basic income or ownership of wealth to every citizen, regardless of their status. Roemer has argued for a programme of 'compensatory education', investing more in the education of children from poorer families and communities. What these approaches have in common is their aim of giving everyone a more equal share of society's resources, and thus a fair start in life. As R. H. Tawney observed, opportunities depend 'not only upon an open road, but upon an equal start'.[23] This is more than just the traditional Liberal approach of aiming to guarantee equality of opportunity (the 'open road'); we recognise that whatever people choose to do later in their life, it is socially just to start them from a position where they have as equal as possible a prospect for a good life (the 'equal start').

Equality and liberty

It should be obvious, then, why Liberals should support a substantial reduction in inequality. First, because it is an important extension of freedom for those suffering from low levels of income, wealth, education, etc., though no fault of their own – the equality of justice argument. In that sense, *It's About Freedom* was right to point out that equality is important *because* it promotes liberty.

Clearly, though, if income and wealth are to be redistributed, some people will have their freedom restricted, for example by being subject to higher levels of taxation. The classical utilitarian argument in favour of this is that the marginal utility of income decreases as income increases – i.e. an extra £1,000 a year is worth a lot more to someone living on £10,000 a year than it is to someone on £100,000. In addition, however, as I have tried to show above, there are direct benefits to everyone, no matter what their levels of income and wealth, from living in a more equal society. Lower levels of crime and anti-social behaviour, stronger political institutions, and more thriving communities provide a benefit to set against the cost of redistribution. Thus, once again, equality promotes liberty, in that a well-functioning society provides an easier and better environment in which to live.

And a more equal society is probably a more economically efficient one too. Higher levels of inequality tend to lead to lower educational attainments, on average, wasting the talents of those at the bottom of the pile. A focus on the equality agenda will be essential to deal successfully with the pressures of competition from the developing world (particularly China and India) and economic migration – both clearly of benefit to world development and to the migrants themselves, but both also leading to downward pressures on wages for the low-skilled in developed economies, including the UK. Once again, equality promotes liberty by spreading prosperity.

At this point opponents of reducing inequality will generally come up with the argument that the danger of pursuing equality is that in practice it limits liberty, stifling initiative, destroying the incentive to work, and generating uniformity. This may be true, at least in theory, if equality is pursued as an end in itself, regardless of the consequences. But why should we do that? One could just as well criticise the pursuit of freedom as a dangerous slippery slope. No one (no Liberal, at least) quarrels with the need to force people to drive on the left, be educated to a minimum age or pay taxes – yet we can still regard liberty, or freedom, as one of the party's fundamental principles. We do not pursue it to its extreme conclusion any more than we need pursue equality – or, indeed, community.

The question then becomes, how much equality is enough? It is hardly necessary for Liberals to give a precise answer, any more than they need answer how much freedom is enough, or how much community. I would settle for the levels of equality seen in most of the Scandinavian states, but in the mean time Britain is so far away from that level that it would take a government dedicated to reducing inequality many, many years to reach it – so let us at least make a start. The reality is that the degrees and forms of freedom, equality and community that best suit a country at any particular point in time will vary, and will themselves depend on circumstances and political compromises.

If you want a theoretical answer, though, I would argue that it is not the difference in outcomes that derives from individual preferences that should worry us; rather, it is the inequality in outcomes that arises from the structures of society which should, as far as possible, be eliminated. Different outcomes should be the result of choice, not inheritance.

Liberty and equality are not a zero-sum game; on the contrary, the ability to enjoy the opportunities provided by a democratic society is *increased* by the redistribution of wealth and power. Equality is *not* just another desirable objective in the party's list of three, but the essential precondition for liberty and community. Too much inequality limits freedom and destroys community.

An equality agenda for Liberal Democrats

What does all this mean in practice? In the same way as the party has tried, with some success, to ensure that a commitment to environmental sustainability underpins all our policy proposals, not just those relating directly to DEFRA, a commitment to reducing inequality should similarly underpin our programme. This is a logical outcome of the 'Meeting the Challenge' policy review exercise of 2005–06, which concluded that 'tackling inequality is one of our top two political priorities'.[24] I do not have the space to do more than outline a few headings, but here are some thoughts.

To redress the great injustice of inequalities of income and wealth in Britain today requires a commitment to a thoroughly redistributive taxation system. To a significant extent the party now has this; its two recent policy papers on taxation[25] aim to make the system more progressive by removing many of the exemptions and tax reliefs enjoyed by the upper income groups, reducing the basic rate of income tax, and replacing Council Tax with local income tax. Nevertheless, this is a complex and not easily communicated package, and there is a strong case, in due course, for increasing the top rate, both to increase the extent of redistribution and as a clearly visible commitment to a fairer society. It's worth remembering that Britain has lower top tax rates than almost all other comparable countries – in 2004 it was twenty-third (just ahead of Turkey) in the list of thirty OECD countries ranked by top marginal tax rates. Push it up to 50 per cent and it would rise only to eleventh.[26]

As has been seen, part of the problem of inequality is caused by excessive pay rates and tax loopholes for the super-rich. The party's approach of closing tax loopholes should help with the latter, but can we do anything about high rates of pay? Legislation in this area is notoriously difficult, but there may be scope for exposure – along the lines of the Treasury Select Committee's investigation into the private equity industry. I would suggest converting the Low Pay Commission into a Pay Commission, analysing and commenting on the disparities in pay rates within major companies, and their relation (or lack of one) to performance indicators – if not company by company, at least on a sectoral basis. Shareholders could be encouraged to require companies to justify, at their AGMs, increases in top executives' salaries greater than the rise in the average company wage.

The tax papers did not address the issue of a wealth tax, or even the related one of a property tax. Yet this is a hugely important area; as has been seen above, inequalities in the distribution of wealth are more pervasive than inequalities in the distribution of income, and thanks to the housing market are changing the social fabric of many communities.

The introduction of land value taxation for domestic properties, sensibly adjusted for the income of the owners, needs exploring.

Along with the taxation papers, the party's 2007 policy paper *Freedom from Poverty, Opportunity for All: Policies for a Fairer Britain* goes a long way towards creating a programme based on social justice in the areas of pensions and benefit, education, employment and housing. The idea of the 'pupil premium', increasing the funding available to schools for pupils from the most disadvantaged backgrounds, fulfils John Roemer's aim of 'compensatory education', touched on above. Similar principles need to underpin the party's approach to health and social services.

Studies of health standards in the workplace show that people are healthier, with lower death rates, where they have more control over their work. Industrial democracy – employee participation and share ownership, and support for cooperative enterprises, creating a more equal society at work – used to occupy a prominent place in Liberal manifestos. They have, however, steadily disappeared from Lib Dem programmes: the 1992 commitment to a right to participate in decision-making had become, by 2001, simply a right to consultation, while by 2005 the topic was entirely absent.[27]

It's about equality

Undoubtedly there is much more that needs to be added to this programme – but much of this is already party policy, or has been at various points in the recent past. Perhaps my main conclusion is that the party needs to talk about it all more. As I observed above, Liberal Democrats tend to talk about 'freedom' and 'community' much more than 'equality'. The party's new tax package, although it is more redistributive than the old one, does not look like it very obviously. The party runs the risk of failing to engage with the electorate about why redistribution is so necessary, leaving the field open for our opponents to focus only on perceived negatives around such policies. As Steve Webb has written, 'a comprehensive expression of liberalism must not simply accommodate fairness as some reluctant and unwelcome travelling companion, but must embrace it as an indispensable partner'.[28]

Furthermore – and this is the final reason for advocating a greater emphasis on reducing inequality – it should be popular with the kind of people who are likely to vote for us, generally highly educated, socially liberal and progressive, concerned about the quality of life, not just personal consumption. Private polling for the party before the 2005 election suggested that the 'fairness' component of the 'freedom, fairness, trust' slogan used in the run-up to the election resonated well with the electorate. It made a welcome return in the 2006 policy review document *Trust in People: Make Britain Free, Fair and Green*, and we should keep it.

Because the equality agenda is all about fairness. An unequal society is not a fair one. Too many of its members start off hobbled by inherited disadvantages which are enormously difficult, by themselves, to remove. Almost all of its members are affected by the breakdown in neighbourliness and social cohesion which they did nothing to choose themselves. A stress on fairness would resonate with these people – and, possibly, already does. The coverage given to the Treasury Select Committee investigation into the private equity industry is one symptom; Harriet Harman's condemnation of a £10,000 handbag is another. No minister today would dare repeat Peter Mandelson's affection for people 'getting filthy rich'. Opinion polling regularly shows that a substantial percentage – 73 per cent of people in 2004 – considers the gap between those with high and those with low incomes to be too large.[29]

Can the other parties adopt this agenda? David Cameron has argued that society is 'broken'. As we have seen, in many ways it is, but it is almost impossible to see even Cameron arguing for the fundamental redistribution of income and wealth than is needed to help heal it. Labour under Gordon Brown could go further – though it was the government in which he was Chancellor that failed to do more than reduce inequality marginally, and has seen social mobility levels decline. Furthermore, part of the fairness agenda is about democratic and civic equality, building on and supporting the redistribution of income and wealth by a redistribution and decentralisation of political power – not a subject Labour is particularly familiar with.

A hundred years ago the New Liberals faced many of the same challenges of deeply ingrained inequality as we see today. They rose to this challenge, recognising that however much one removed constraints upon individual liberty, there were some things that individuals could not accomplish by themselves – and therefore could not be truly free.

Now we face the same challenge, to accept that there is a limit to what we can do to promote health and well-being, reduce violence and disorder and build functioning communities without tackling the underlying problem of a deeply unequal society, where social relations are dysfunctional and the stress of low social status, disrespect and exclusion is widespread. We need to accept the central role that the assault on inequality plays in all our attempts to promote both liberty and community. They can't be won without it.

Notes

1   Liberal Democrat Policy Paper 50, *It's About Freedom* (Liberal Democrats, 2002), p. 8, para 1.10. The paper itself did not have a separate section on equality.
2   This chapter is primarily about income and wealth inequality. I recognise, of course, that other forms of inequality – e.g. those deriving from race or gender – are also serious issues, but I do not deal with them here because I think the party's position on them is right.
3   Sixty per cent of median income.
4   Mike Brewer, Alissa Goodman, Alistair Muriel and Luke Sibieta, *Poverty and Inequality in the UK: 2007* (Institute of Fiscal Studies Briefing Note 73), p. 29. Figures are after taking housing costs into account.
5   Ibid., pp. 19–20.
6   Will Paxton and Mike Dixon, *The State of the Nation: An audit of injustice in the UK* (IPPR, London, 2004), p. 60.
7   *Poverty and Wealth Across Britain 1968 to 2005* (Joseph Rowntree Foundation, July 2007).
8   By the admission of the British Private Equity and Venture Capital Association's chief executive – he resigned two days later. 'Private equity boss quits after Commons mauling', *Daily Telegraph* 15 June 2007.
9   Larry Elliott, 'Nice work if you can get it: chief executives quietly enrich themselves for mediocrity', *Guardian* 23 January 2006; Polly Toynbee, 'I was only the hapless decoy duck for David Cameron', *Guardian* 28 November 2006.
10 Julie Froud, Sukhdev Johal, Adam Leaver and Karel Williams, *Financialisation and Strategy: Narrative and Numbers* (Routledge, London, 2006).
11 Nick Isles, *The Risk Myth: CEOs and Labour Market Risk* (The Work Foundation, London, December 2006).
12 Liberal Democrat Policy Paper 76, *Trust in People: Make Britain Free, Fair and Green* (Liberal Democrats, 2006), para. 3.1.2.
13 Jo Blanden and Steve Gibbons, *The Persistence of Poverty Across Two Generations* (Policy Press / Joseph Rowntree Foundation, 2006).
14 Kirstine Hansen and Heather Joshi (eds.), *Millennium Cohort Study: Second Survey* (Centre for Longitudinal Studies, Institute of Education, University of London, June 2007).
15 Except where noted, all references in this and the next two sections are from Richard Wilkinson, *The Impact of Inequality* (Routledge, 2005).
16 'What's the prognosis?', *Guardian*, 7 September 2005.
17 Audrey Gillan, 'In Iraq, life expectancy is 67. Minutes from Glasgow city centre, it's 54', *The Guardian*, 21 January 2006.
18 Polly Toynbee, 'Inequality kills', *Guardian* 30 July 2005.

19   See Duncan Brack and Richard Grayson, 'Equality', in Duncan Brack and Ed Randall (eds.), *Dictionary of Liberal Thought* (Politico's, 2007).

20   Michael Freeden, 'More than freedom: the ideology of liberalism', in Julia Margo (ed.), *Beyond Liberty: Is the future of liberalism progressive?* (IPPR, London, 2007), p. 28.

21   L. T. Hobhouse, *Liberalism* (Williams & Norgate, London, 1911).

22   For summaries of their thinking, see the relevant entries in Brack and Randall (eds.), *Dictionary of Liberal Thought*; and Will Kymlicka, *Contemporary Political Philosophy* (OUP, 2nd ed., 2002), particularly Chapter 2, 'Liberal Equality'.

23   R. H. Tawney, *The Acquisitive Society* (G. Bell & Sons, London, 1921).

24   Liberal Democrats, *Trust in People: Make Britain Free, Fair and Green*, para. 3.2.4.

25   Liberal Democrat Policy Papers 75, *Fairer, Simpler, Greener* (Liberal Democrats, 2006) and 81, *Reducing the Burden: Policies for tax reform* (Liberal Democrats, 2007).

26   OECD Tax Database, 'Taxation of wage income', table I.4; available at http://www.oecd.org/document/60/0,3343,en_2649_37427_1942460_1_1_1_37427,00.html. Figures include central and local taxation, employee social security contributions and tax credits.

27   See Stuart White, 'Liberalism's progressive past: post-war Liberalism and the property question', in Margo (ed.), *Beyond Liberty*.

28   Steve Webb, 'Free to be fair or fair to be free?', in Margo (ed.), *Beyond Liberty*, p. 135.

29   Michael Orton and Karen Rowlingson, *Public Attitudes to Economic Inequality* (Joseph Rowntree Foundation, 2007).

Chapter 3

Liberal Environmentalism: A Liberalism that Matches the Age We're In

Ed Randall

Refashioning liberalism

Liberalism needs to be refashioned, not simply reclaimed.[1] We should value and cherish liberal verities but the greatest challenge of our times requires us to make the most of human – especially, though not exclusively, liberal – creativity. In an age of unprecedented global dangers, political argument and economic theory have struggled to keep up and we now face challenges that most of the great liberal thinkers could hardly have imagined.

Few people doubt that the Liberal Democrats have been getting steadily greener or that liberal environmentalism has become an increasingly important plank of Liberal Democrat politics and policy.[2] However, pinning down liberal attitudes to environmental politics is far from straightforward. This is partly because scientific understanding of the interaction between humankind and the planetary environment keeps shifting and also because environmentalism represents a profound challenge to a liberal politics based on optimism about the social and political, as well as the economic, benefits of growth in a free society.

A number of core principles have come to define liberal environmentalism, and the enthusiasm with which these principles are applied will show how ecologically responsible Liberal Democrat environmentalism can be.[3]

The great liberal thinker John Stuart Mill anticipated an age when economic advance, defined primarily in terms of increased personal consumption, would come to an end. His view of an advanced liberal polity anticipated a society in which material consumption would no longer be regarded as the key to individual fulfilment. In his *Principles of Political Economy* Mill wrote:

> It must always have been seen ... by political economists, that
> the increase in wealth is not boundless: that at the end of what
> they term the progressive state lies the stationary state, that all
> progress in wealth is but a postponement of this, and that each
> step in advance is an approach to it ... I cannot ... regard the sta-
> tionary state ... with the unaffected aversion so generally mani-
> fested towards it by political economists ... It may be a necessary
> stage in the progress of civilisation ... not a mark of decline, for it
> is not necessarily destructive of the higher aspirations and heroic
> virtues ... It is scarcely necessary to remark that a stationary
> condition of capital and population implies no stationary state of
> human improvement.[4]

Mill's sanguine attitude to the end of growth – not development – may
come as a great surprise to many of those who criticise liberalism for
holding a purely instrumental attitude to the riches of the Earth. Indeed,
liberal environmentalism entails a commitment to a series of ideas and
propositions that seek to divorce human fulfilment and the pursuit of
international justice from an endless expansion of consumption. That is
the first principle of liberal environmentalism: human development and
economic growth should not be treated as the same thing; they can and
should be distinguished from one another.

This notion has recently been boosted by the work of Richard Layard,
who promotes what he calls a 'new science' of happiness.[5] Layard's challenge to some versions of liberal political economy is not really that new;
in fact it rests upon another proposition that is at the core of liberal environmentalism. Conventional measures of wealth and welfare, which rely
heavily on prices established in market exchange, can gravely mislead us
about what is truly valuable and what makes us happiest.

It is a core belief of liberal environmentalists that environmental
treasures, such as clean air, have a value that conventional measures of
human wealth do not capture. Liberal environmentalists feature promi-
nently amongst those who seek ways of attaching prices to environmental goods and services that will help to harness market logic to their
preservation.[6] Making markets the servants rather than the masters of
our valuation of ecological systems is a vital part of liberal environmentalism. The valuation of ecological systems, whether for their own sake

(a dark green rather than a liberal environmentalist goal), or for the services they provide and the pleasure they afford us, is closely allied to yet another liberal environmentalist principle: polluters should pay.

Some may object to what they regard as environmentalist soundbites. Isn't the assertion that 'we should make markets the servants rather than masters of our environmental goals' an example of simple-minded sloganising? Liberal environmentalists once again turn to J. S. Mill to help them explain what may easily appear to be a contradictory approach (for liberals at least) to the role of markets in valuing environmental goods. Surely, the prices established in free markets for natural resources simply reflect individual utilities expressed by personal purchasing decisions. Where else can human valuations come from but from individuals?

Mill sought, in his essay *On Liberty*, to define a domain of personal freedom that he hoped would be inviolate in a liberal democracy. He invoked the *harm principle* to do so. Offending others is not the same as harming them; therefore, what individuals do, so long as it does not harm others, should go unregulated. Surely personal consumption decisions, expressed in the form of purchases in a free market, should be free from government interference?

Liberal environmentalists are not the only liberals who doubt that such a simple rule can stand unchallenged. Acid rain, traceable to coal-fired power stations, illustrates the problems encountered by third parties who are harmed by the consensual acts and purchases of others in a free market. Acid rain harms people who are not directly involved in an economic transaction hundreds and possibly thousands of miles away. Many market transactions in free societies have externalities which are harmful to others. Liberals are not alone in finding it difficult to balance rival interests in circumstances where significant externalities have been identified. We cannot avoid the question: 'In dealing with the harms we do to each other how wide should the net be cast, who should cast it and at what cost?'

The thought that one person's carbon footprint could adversely affect the lives of others thousands of miles away did not occur to Mill, but it has come to preoccupy thoughtful liberals around the globe. The proposition that the harm principle needs to be continually refashioned, in order to take account of our greatly enhanced understanding of the interconnectedness and interdependency of the modern world, is one that has profound implications for liberals.

For those liberals who believe that the concepts of individual liberty and well-being are quite discrete, liberal environmentalism may threaten a new road to serfdom. In other words, it is feared that empowering elected representatives to tax and regulate, so that they can protect the environment and pursue the cause of international environmental justice, risks handing dictatorial powers to politicians who will then be able to justify more or less any assault on liberty in the name of environmental responsibility. Liberal environmentalists reject such sweeping opposition to government intervention to protect the environment. The idea that freedom and opportunity are yoked together and bound up with the ways in which seemingly unconnected individuals alter the common environment means that liberal environmentalists accept there are likely to be many instances when public intervention is not only desirable but essential.

If one person's opportunity to pursue or make their own plan of life is critically dependent upon environmental goods that another person thoughtlessly or selfishly destroys, then the freedom of the former may be imperilled unless the environmental impact of the latter is controlled. Shared resources need to be safeguarded by appropriate government regulation and intervention if markets cannot be left alone to do the job. In circumstances where practical means do not exist for those who are adversely affected to hold those who endanger them to account, liberal environmentalism will be defined by its willingness to intervene and regulate: to exercise responsible stewardship.

Responsible stewardship is another vital component of liberal environmentalism. It recognises the interests of the poor, the vulnerable and those who have not yet been born – those who are worst placed to defend their own interests. John Rawls formulated a *just savings principle*, which was designed to guide stewards in balancing the interests of one generation against another.[7] Liberal environmentalists acknowledge principles of justice that require each generation to weigh the interests of their own against those of generations to come.

When the Brundtland report, *Our Common Future*, was published in 1987 it established the notion of *sustainable development*.[8] It is a concept that is found at the heart of liberal environmentalism and encompasses the just savings principle. Indeed, sustainable development encapsulates and unites the notions of responsible stewardship, justice between generations, and the proposition that environmental obligations should be indifferent to national boundaries. Sustainable development was defined by Brundtland as development that 'meets the needs of the present without compromising the ability of future generations to meet their own needs'. However, one of the attractions of the concept was also a source of its greatest difficulty for environmentalists: it could be interpreted in ways which made it easy to muddy the committed environmentalist's distinction between economic growth and development. Sustainable growth might be reconciled with a trio: responsible resource management, reductions in social and economic inequality *and* rising living standards. The proposition that it is possible to square economic growth, as conventionally defined, with economic justice is particularly attractive to political leaders of the world's most developed societies. The slippery notion of sustainability is, of all the different ideas that have been woven together in liberal environmentalism, the one that environmentalists are most likely to disagree about. Beliefs about sustainability vary not only with the relative importance accorded to particular ecological systems but also according to how data about natural systems are interpreted.

Not unreasonably, therefore, liberal environmentalism rests very heavily on scientific argument and evidence. Reason and the findings of climate and other ecological sciences are expected to play a central role in shaping public debate and policy-making. As scientific research into climate change has become more certain in presenting its findings about anthropogenic climate change, the extent to which it remains possible to reconcile economic growth, as conventionally defined, with sustainability has become the subject of desperate manoeuvres at international meetings and a potentially highly divisive matter, even amongst environmentalists.[9] Liberals who follow the scientific debate closely cannot help but be struck by the growing body of scientific opinion now supporting the proposition that the speed of climate change has been underestimated and that the scale of reductions in greenhouse gas emissions needed in the near term is much greater than has generally been recognised.[10] The strength of responses to the sounding of such scientific alarm bells will undoubtedly play a very important part in the evolution of liberal environmentalism.

Liberal environmentalism can be defined not only by the principles and positions it espouses but also by those that it rejects. In 1995 Robert

Eves and his colleagues, in an article written for *Parliamentary Affairs*,[11] distinguished between three lines of environmental political thought and action: liberal, green and survivalist environmentalism. Liberal environmentalism was characterised by its support for democratic and relatively gradual change in response to environmental imperatives. The liberal path was one in which the economy was coaxed by judicious market interventions and regulation along a more responsible environmental road. International trade continued and the prospects for economic growth were only a little dimmed.

What Eves and his co-authors labelled green environmentalism insisted on sharp reductions in consumption in the first world. Self-reliance and local provisioning would be encouraged. This was consonant with a world in which global economic integration was halted and then reversed. Local economic independence would be complemented by political decentralisation and democratisation. Small autonomous production units were represented as the key to sustainability as well as part of a politically and culturally desirable self-sufficiency. Political and economic independence was presented as the vital ingredient in a better, not just a more sustainable, way of life.

Eves and his colleagues went on to describe survivalist environmentalism. It was the most radical and authoritarian. Survivalists were, it was suggested, committed to limiting population growth and ready, even determined, to adopt authoritarian policies to ensure that demand for scarce resources was speedily reduced. Control population and patterns of consumption would be radically changed, even if hearts and minds failed to follow. The goal for greens, by contrast, was a cultural change that depended on a dramatic shift in popular beliefs. For the greens, public understanding was critical to halting climate change and their goal of realising a wholesale abandonment of consumerism.

The survivalists, intent on population control, had little faith in environmental salvation without the adoption of draconian measures. Liberal environmentalism is, in this company, marked out by its optimism and its insistence that change without consent is not only undesirable but unworkable.

While liberal environmentalism positively welcomes localism and self-sufficiency it does not accept that it will be sufficient to manage the transition that is undoubtedly needed to a more sustainable way of life for thousands of millions of people. Small is beautiful, as the liberal E. M. Schumacher observed, but most liberal environmentalists believe that it is far from sufficient. Energy self-sufficiency or substantial independence is also highly attractive to Liberal Democrats, and liberal environmentalists, generally because it is a necessary requirement for any political community that wants to pursue an ethical foreign policy in a world where a small number of unreliable fossil-fuel supplying states have disproportionate leverage.

There is also – and this is particularly important – common ground between green and liberal environmentalists in their insistence on the importance of public understanding. However, liberal environmentalists have generally been more willing to recognise how extraordinarily difficult it is to persuade others of both the necessity and the practicability of adapting to environmental imperatives. For liberals – and it is important that they acknowledge this – it is also vital to explain why they have come to regard environmental issues as paramount. This is especially important because liberals have a long history of being amongst the keenest advocates and ideological proponents of economic growth. Liberal environmentalists have responded and are now in the front rank of those who have come to accept that it is no longer possible or reasonable to treat the Earth's bounty as unlimited or unconditional.[12]

What is to be done?

Jonathan Porritt has argued that intelligent and essentially liberal capitalism can be reconciled with environmentalism.[13] He draws on five key authors: David Korten, Jeff Gates, Gretchen Daily and Katherine Ellison, and Margaret Legum.

Korten complains of predatory financial systems driven by one overriding objective: boosting exclusively financial returns on capital. This is, he insists, a narrow objective and serves to intensify the depletion of 'real capital', which consists of those resources (most especially but by no means exclusively natural resources) upon which humanity's long-term prospects depend. He observes:

> The truly troubling part is that so many of us have become willing accomplices to what is best described as a war of money against life. It starts from our failure to recognise that money is

not wealth. In our confusion, we concentrate on money to the neglect of those things that actually sustain a good life.[14]

Jeff Gates points to a 'curious and dangerous inconsistency' in modern capitalism:

> It extols ... private ownership. Yet while the capital is there and so is the capitalism, what is missing are people who can rightly be called capitalists. The reason for this is poorly understood: contemporary capitalism is not designed to create capitalists, but to finance capital ... A more participatory capitalism could gradually displace today's exclusive, detached and socially corrosive ownership patterns.[15]

A capitalism that finds it increasingly difficult to accommodate capitalists and a price system that falters badly in valuing the natural environment should surely motivate liberals to refashion their liberalism.

Daily and Ellison recognise that philanthropy and government regulation are necessary but insufficient to protect the value we know exists in natural systems. Something more is needed to husband and harvest natural systems responsibly. They refer, as many others have, to the 'tragedy of the commons', a negative-sum game in which 'each individual [appears to have] more to gain by ... launching another fishing boat than to lose as the fishery is depleted'. The fishers eventually find that their livelihoods have been destroyed along with the fishery upon which they all depended.

In the absence of prices, Daily and Ellison believe that 'nature becomes like an all-you-can-eat buffet'. It is time to 'launch bold initiatives to find financial incentives for environmental conservation' that reward innovators and 'change the rules of the game ... to produce new incentives for environmental protection geared to both society's well-being and individual's self-interest'.[16]

The view that sustainability calls for environmentally aware enterprise, able to respond to the carefully crafted rules of a new game, and an international trading system that strengthens rather than undermines the world's most disadvantaged people, is especially well presented in Margaret Legum's *It Doesn't Have To Be Like This*. Legum, an admirer of the great liberal economist John Maynard Keynes, begins by deploring the rejection of proposals Keynes made at the end of the Second World War for the establishment of an International Clearing Union. Her insistence that capitalism can and must serve the interests of ordinary people echoes Jeff Gates's manifesto for an 'ownership solution'. Legum quotes, with particular approval, Keynes' oft-misunderstood expression of sympathy for those who:

> would minimise rather than maximise economic entanglements between nations. Ideas, knowledge, art, hospitality, travel – these are the things that should of their nature be international. But let goods be homespun whenever it is reasonable and conveniently possible, and above all let finance be primarily national.[17]

Policy and politics

Korten directs our attention to the thralldom of distorted measures of wealth. First among those measures are national accounting systems that hide, or at best obscure, much of what is critical to our well-being. Conventional national accounting skews and frustrates public debate. It is a proposition now widely accepted,[18] and it leads directly to a very important policy conclusion. Liberal environmentalists must, as one of their first orders of business, insist on the wholesale reform of national accounts. It is, in the words of *The Economist*, vital, if we want to correct a warped official view of how well off we are, that national accounting should account for 'leisure, inequality and the environment'. And, for liberal environmentalists – as well as *The Economist* – national accounts must 'take account of pollution and the using-up of non-renewable resources'.

Jeff Gates's advocacy of what he calls the ownership solution should appeal to Liberal Democrats. Gates believes that the best, most socially and environmentally responsible enterprises aim to make all those who work in and for them partners. He is full of admiration for the John Lewis partnership in Britain and Herman Miller in the United States. Liberal environmentalism should embrace Gates's ownership solution as one of the most attractive ways to engage the working population in enterprises that are equipped to care about more than the return on one kind of capital. Gates believes that co-operators are much more likely to take the long-term view. A Britain able to maintain a fiscal environment that is attractive to private equity firms should also be capable of developing tax policies that favour co-operators who work in businesses that make sustainability an integral part of their corporate culture and mission.

Daily and Ellison give the example of water, what they call 'urban blood'. Safe drinking water justifies substantial public investment, which is likely to require us to make important ecological choices with significant political and economic consequences. In the case of New York's water supply, a subject they have studied closely, they report a determination to maintain the natural watershed from which the city's water is drawn. The alternative entailed the construction of a water filtration system reliant on hugely expensive technologies. It is one of a number of examples of conservation schemes which hinge on the valuation of ecological services all too often taken entirely for granted. Their conclusion, that it is possible to make a business case for protecting the environment and, with a little ingenuity, develop ways to value environmental goods and services, should be regarded as an open invitation to liberal environmentalists to combine the process of planning (to realise ecological goals) with markets and profits. In short Daily and Ellison describe forms of environmental entrepreneurship that should inspire environmentalists. There can be little doubt that the attractions of such environmental entrepreneurship can be readily communicated to the general public. Indeed Daily and Ellison offer telling examples of responsible environmentalism that utilises an economic logic that is widely understood in market societies.

Margaret Legum is a champion of intelligent self-sufficiency. Her advocacy of fair trade and debt cancellation should be welcomed by liberal environmentalists. She argues that dependency, which entrenches poverty, not only frustrates development but exacerbates problems of environmental degradation. Liberal environmentalists, and others who are committed to sustainable development, cannot help but observe the closeness of the relationship between the adverse terms upon which the world's poorest producers trade (and borrow) and their poor prospects of escaping poverty and limiting damage to the environment.

It is hard to disagree with James Martin, author of *The Meaning of the 21st Century*, that empowering the poor, particularly women, in the world's least developed societies, is the most effective antidote to poverty and environmental destruction.[19] Poor societies facing serious environmental degradation should be able to trade on terms that enable them to build local capital and social enterprises that equip them to play a leading role in provisioning themselves and in minimising ecological damage.

Sustainability and fairness

Amongst the great challenges human societies face is deepening social inequality – a problem intimately connected with environmental degradation. At the 1972 UN World Environmental Conference in Stockholm, Indira Gandhi is reported to have said that 'poverty is the biggest polluter',[20] a phrase that has struck home with liberal environmentalists who believe that sustainable development binds ecological responsibility to social justice.

An assault on social and economic inequality is a critical part of any truly liberal and democratic project for environmental sustainability. Jonathan Porritt has pointed to the kinds of enterprises that are needed if we are to move closer to sustainability: they link the pursuit of sustainability to fairness. What kind of capitalism is consistent with sustainability?

> It must be as much about new opportunities for responsible wealth creation as about outlawing irresponsible wealth creation; it must draw upon a core of ideas and values that speaks directly to people's desire for a higher quality of life, emphasising enlightened self-interest and personal well-being … [because] … environmental degradation and social injustice are increasingly feeding off each other.[21]

We must not divorce the objective of sustainability from liberalism's abiding concern with social justice. Not only does it appear to be the case that, in the world's richest society, the distribution of wealth, income and opportunity has grown more unequal, but it has also been suggested that this is occurring at a time when the environmental burden of acquisitive behaviour, in the world's wealthiest society, is having an increasingly detrimental impact on the global environment.[22]

Liberals must not avert their eyes from the numerous places where environmental degradation and social injustice feed off one another.

Neither must they overlook the opportunity costs of what are extraordinarily wasteful and environmentally profligate patterns of consumption in the world's wealthiest societies. Greatly to his credit, Nicholas Stern did not attempt to disguise the extent to which poverty and environmental degradation are yoked together. Climate change, if it is not contained, will profoundly damage the world's poor and add many millions to the numbers of people living on less than $2 a day. It will also greatly increase child mortality as the 21st century progresses. As Stern also shows, the prospects for sustainable agriculture, amongst the poorest inhabitants of the globe, can be dramatically improved if carbon emissions can be reduced.[23]

Wanted: genius to protect freedom, promote opportunity and respect for the natural environment

Liberal Democrats who want to draw on the ever-expanding treasury of policy proposals and ideas aimed at facilitating sustainable development could do worse than begin by consulting David Pearce's *Blueprint for a Green Economy*.[24] Written jointly with Anil Markandya and Ed Barbier, it was first published in 1989 and remains a seminal text for liberal environmentalists. Its authors described a basic choice between anticipatory policy responses to climate change and adaptive policy responses. Pearce, had he remained alive (he died in 2005), would have continued to advocate the use of market incentives to achieve environmental ends and gone on urging political leaders and policy-makers to present the strongest case possible for anticipatory rather than adaptive policy-making. That is something that Liberal Democrats have taken a lead in doing.

For those who are convinced that science, technology and business can be allies of liberal environmentalism the library of sustainability now includes the works of Janine Beynus, and of Paul Hawken and Amory, as well as Hunter, Lovins. What Benyus calls *biomimicry* looks to scientific research and insight as a source of ideas and new technologies capable of employing and adapting the highly evolved solutions found in the natural world to the challenges of human survival and environmental adaptation.[25] There is little doubt that nature has answers to many of humanity's most pressing problems, but only if we have the good sense and humility to recognise them.

The Lovins, along with their good friend Paul Hawken, have described a smarter and much more environmentally aware capitalism.

Their core argument is that it is technically feasible to triple and even quadruple outputs from manufacturing processes, without increasing either the energy or material inputs.[26] Their argument is sustained by dozens of case studies in which they have been able to show that productivity (and profitability) can be dramatically increased if changes in public policy, innovations in technology and alterations in business practice can be combined intelligently. The ecological dividend from altered business practice, change in public policy and application of technological innovation is, they argue, dependent on a hard-won integration of commercial practice, public policy and science. However, they come to the conclusion that this is a greater challenge than boosting productivity and resource efficiency alone. Indeed this is the political and cultural challenge that researchers working at the Stockholm Environment Institute have been trying to address for many years. What Måns Nilsson and Katrina Eckerberg[27] refer to as Environmental Policy Integration (EPI) has become the greatest challenge for liberal environmentalists.

Those who want to make the most of the very best environmental practice need to understand that it depends on how deeply and securely it can be embedded in the way we live our lives and in the way that we govern ourselves. The very same message is contained in Paul Raskin's presentation of what he calls the great transition to a *new paradigm*.[28] His transition looks to a free, responsible and harmonious world, a world that liberal environmentalists dream of.

The specific instruments and policies which liberal environmentalists are able to commend now form part of an impressive – some might say, intimidating – portfolio. Many of those instruments have been widely debated and have been generally available to governments since economists, most notably David Pearce, started to describe in detail the types of taxes and incentives that could be introduced to assist Britain and other advanced economies move on to a more sustainable economic path.

The failure to apply many of those instruments with the rigour that is necessary, if we are to achieve sustainable development, has been deeply disappointing to committed environmentalists. It continues to frustrate Liberal Democrats who, at their September 2006 conference in Brighton, demonstrated their willingness to deepen the party's commitment to sustainability. Their endorsement of the *Green Tax Switch* also confirmed the party's well-developed environmental conscience and appreciation of what is required to make Britain's economy more environmentally sustainable.

It is essential for Liberal Democrats to match the willingness they demonstrated in Brighton, to take the lead in environmental policy-making, with a determination to proselytise for sustainable development (not growth), international justice and environmental responsibility. The party is exceptionally well placed to do this. It is freer of special interests and less likely to be captured by producer interests than its principal rivals. It is committed to the European Union having a leading role in environmental policy-making. The strength of the EU is critical to the prospects for effective regulatory action and eco-taxation capable of protecting the environment. The income from intelligent and enforceable eco-taxes is vital for funding such things as conservation of the natural environment, improvements in energy efficiency and ecologically responsible and sustainable transport. Indeed the international adoption of environmentally responsible policies and energy efficient technologies may well depend on how successful the EU is in getting its member states to adopt them.

Conclusion – necessity and opportunity

In the thirty-year update to *Limits to Growth*, Donella Meadows and her colleagues opened by explaining that their original report had not predicted abrupt limits to economic growth.[29] The original publication had acknowledged great uncertainties while confidently predicting that 'global ecological constraints would have significant influence on global development in the twenty-first century'. Lack of certainty about the precise timing and fine detail of ecological constraints on economic growth should not have delayed 'early action … to reduce the damage caused by approaching (or exceeding) global ecological limits'. Although 'The end of growth … seemed … to be a very distant prospect in 1972', their dismay at how little action has been taken is undisguised. 'There seemed to be time enough for deliberation, choice, and corrective action – even at the global level.' Opportunity after opportunity to begin a process of adjustment has been missed. The difficulties that humanity is likely to encounter in moving from what is unsustainable to sustainability have sharply increased. And, in recognising that, Meadows and her colleagues wrote that they were well aware that: 'No modern political party has [yet] garnered broad support for a programme' capable of: 'increas[ing] the consumption levels of the world's poor, while at the same time reducing humanity's ecological footprint'.[30]

Meadows and her colleagues were surely justified in drawing attention to the absence of a single successful political party able to 'garner broad support' for a radical environmental programme. But that should encourage rather than deter Liberal Democrats. Those who speak from knowledge and conviction and anticipate what is coming stand to win an invaluable asset in a liberal democracy: a reputation for prescience and, if they have the courage of their convictions – when the telling is far from easy – a reputation for facing up to inconvenient truths. Indeed, those who see ahead and share their insights can expect to be well placed to define the common purpose and to put their imprimatur upon the public response to the events and circumstances that they have anticipated.

Liberal Democrats, at the beginning of the twenty-first century, need to be prepared to ask hard questions of authorities that have shown great timidity in the face of convincing scientific evidence. Confronted with incontrovertible evidence of profligacy and irresponsibility and of its consequences for our planet we must change course. Now that we have been made aware of the price that has been paid, is being paid and is likely to be paid, it is time to take the lead in advocating change.

Change in a free society requires the consent and active support of the electorate. Political authority in a liberal society depends upon persuasion. Refashioning the economic system so that it supports and encourages sustainability will not be possible unless the political system is also refashioned. Framing the means requires liberals to change and adapt markets so that they signal much more accurately than they do now the central role that the natural environment plays in all our lives. This will mean curtailing the influence and reducing the power of very well-organised commercial interests, and encouraging and rewarding those who have the best ideas and schemes for marrying human ambitions and environmental imperatives.

There are very real risks – as there always have been – in advocating more, and more determined, government action. There are enormous risks, to human well-being and individual liberty, if we fail to find better ways of caring for the commons upon which we all depend. Just as the creation of legal systems and the development of rule-governed trading systems helped to realise the ambitions of millions of individuals in times past, it has now become necessary to refashion governments, legal systems and markets so that they are our servants rather than our masters in the period of ecological consequences that we have now entered.

George Monbiot, an improbable clarion of liberal thought, has ventured a definition of a free market that should stimulate and challenge liberals who want to paint from a palette that includes many shades of green, including the most verdant greens:

> A genuine free market is surely one which is [open to] everyone, rather than one in which the powerful are free to squeeze economic life out of everyone else. The prerequisite of freedom ... is effective regulation. This means that in some respects the state will have to become not weaker – as both the anarchists and the neo-liberals insist – but stronger. It must be empowered to force both producers and consumers to carry their own costs, rather than dumping them on to other people or the environment. It must be allowed to distinguish between the protection of workers, consumers and the ecosystem and trade protectionism.[31]

A liberal society that ensures that producers and consumers carry their own costs and pay a fair price for nature's services is not something that we can expect to appear of its own accord. It is a work that will demand extraordinary ingenuity, generosity and honesty and immense political courage. It is the greatest challenge that liberals have ever faced, but face it they must if they want human societies to survive so that they can prosper while protecting and enhancing human liberty *and* caring for the shared environment.

Notes

1   See Ed Randall, 'Yellow versus Orange – Never a Fair Fight: An Assessment of Two Contributions to Liberal Politics Separated by Three-quarters of a Century', *Political Quarterly* 78(1), 2007, pp. 40–49.

2   See, for example: Robert Eves, Geoffrey Woodcock and Barry Munslow, 'Liberal-Environmentalism and its Impact on UK Political Parties', *Parliamentary Affairs* 48(3), 1995, pp. 473–83; Tony Beamish, 'The Greening of the Liberals?', *Journal of Liberal History* 21, 1999, pp. 15–19; and Paul Burrall, 'The Environment: A Winner for the Liberal Democrats?', *Political Quarterly* 78(1), 2007, pp. 50–58.

3   Readers may find it helpful to look at Steven Bernstein, 'Liberal Environmentalism and Global Environmental Governance', *Global Environmental Politics* 2(3), 2002, pp.

1–16 and Duncan Brack, 'Environmentalism' in Duncan Brack and Ed Randall (eds.), *Dictionary of Liberal Thought* (Politico's, London, 2007).

4   John Stuart Mill, *Principles of Political Economy*, Book IV, Chapter VI (Charles C. Little & James Brown, Boston, 1848), pp. 313–17.

5   Richard Layard, *Happiness: Lessons from a New Science* (Penguin Press, New York, 2005).

6   See, for example, Al Gore, *Earth in the Balance: Forging A New Common Purpose* (Earthscan, London, 1992), pp. 337–45.

7   Erin Kelly (ed.), John Rawls, *Justice as Fairness: A Restatement* (Belknap Press, Cambridge, Mass., 2001), pp. 159–61.

8   Gro Harlem Brundtland, *Our Common Future* (Oxford University Press, 1987).

9   See, for example, Mark Lynas, *Six Degrees: Our Future on a Hotter Planet* (Fourth Estate, London, 2007), pp. 263–300.

10   See James Hansen et al., 'Climate change and trace gases' in *Philosophical Transactions Royal Society* Series A 365(1856), 2007, pp. 1925–54 for recent information on the speed of change; and Stephen Pacala and Robert Sacolow, 'Stabilisation Wedges: Solving the Climate Problem for the Next Fifty Years with Current Technologies', *Science* Vol. 305, August 2004, for an authoritative account of how reductions might be achieved.

11   Eves, Woodcock and Munslow, 'Liberal-Environmentalism and its Impact on UK Political Parties'.

12   See in particular Al Gore, *An Inconvenient Truth: The Planetary Emergency of Global Warming and What We Can Do About It* (Rodale, Emmaus, 2006).

13   Jonathan Porritt, *Capitalism as if the World Matters* (Earthscan, London, 2006).

14   David C. Korten, 'Money versus wealth' in *Yes! A Journal of Positive Futures*, Spring 1997.

15   Jeff Gates, *The Ownership Solution: Towards a Shared Capitalism for the Twenty-First Century* (Penguin Books, London, 1998), pp. xvii and xxiv.

16   C. Gretchen Daily and Katherine Ellison, *The New Economy of Nature: The Quest to Make Conservation Profitable* (Island Press, Washington, 2002), pp. 12–13.

17   John Maynard Keynes, 'National Self-Sufficiency', *Yale Review* Vol. 22, June 1933, pp. 755–69.

18   See, for example, 'Grossly Distorted Picture' *Economist* 9 February 2006; Adair Turner, *Just Capital: The Liberal Economy* (Pan Books, London, 2001), pp. 107–31; Greg Ogle, 'Green National Accounting', *Environmental Politics* 9(3), 2000, pp. 109–28.

19   James Martin, *The Meaning of the 21st Century: A Vital Blueprint for Ensuring Our Future* (Transworld Publishers/Eden Project Books, London, 2006), pp. 53–64.

20   Gro Harlem Brundtland, '*Our Common Future* – Seventeen Years Update' (lecture series on Human Health and Global Environmental Change, Center for Health and the Global Environment, 2004, available at http://tinyurl.com/2uhfse.

21   Porritt, *Capitalism as if the World Matters*, pp. 20, 210.

22   Clive Ponting, *A New Green History of the World: The Environment and the Collapse of Great Civilisation* (Vintage Books, London, 2007), pp. 402–03.

23   Sir Nicholas Stern, *The Economics of Climate Change: The Stern Review* (Cambridge University Press, 2007), pp. 126–27, 613.

24   David Pearce, Anil Markandya and Edward Barbier, *Blueprint for a Green Economy* (Earthscan, London, 1989).

25   Janine M. Benyus, *Biomimicry: Innovation Inspired by Nature* (Harper Collins, New York, 1997).

26 Paul Hawken, Amory B. Lovins and L. Hunter Lovins, *Natural Capitalism: The Next Industrial Revolution* (Earthscan, London, 1999).

27 Måns Nilsson and Katrina Eckerberg, *Environmental Policy Integration in Practice: Shaping Institutions for Learning* (Earthscan, London, 2007).

28 Paul Raskin et al., *Great Transition: The Promise and Lure of Times Ahead: Report of the Global Scenario Group* (Tellus Boston, and Stockholm Environment Institute, 2002), and Paul Raskin, 'Global Scenarios for a Sustainable Future', Harvard Center for Health and the Global Environment lecture video, 2007, available at http://tinyurl.com/3ylysk).

29 Donella H. Meadows, Jorgen Randers and Dennis Meadows, *Limits to Growth: The 30-year Update* (Earthscan, London, 2004).

30 Ibid., pp. x, xi, xv.

31 George Monbiot, 'Turn the Screw', *Guardian*, Tuesday 24 April 2001.

Chapter 4

Global Giants

Matthew Taylor[1]

> Want is only one of five giants on the road of reconstruction
> and in some ways the easiest to attack. The others are Disease,
> Ignorance, Squalor and Idleness.
>
> *Social Insurance and Allied Services, Report by Sir William*
> *Beveridge, November 1942*

The Beveridge Report of 1942 set the agenda for the establishment of the modern welfare state after the Second World War. Beveridge's prism sharpened the Liberal focus and laid down the central principles with which to make sense of society's ills. Setting the ideological framework for post-war British Liberalism, Beveridge provided the vocabulary and concepts with which *social* liberalism could express itself, and the Liberal agenda progressed into the latter half of the twentieth century with clear enemies.

The present challenge, however, is for British Liberalism to reinvigorate the battle. The widespread absolute poverty and severe disadvantage with which Beveridge contended have become relatively obsolete for large parts of society (although of course not all), making it too easy to assume that his giants have been defeated. In reality, however, while they no longer obstruct domestic well-being as they once did, the giants now pose new, more subtle and more complex threats to the material and subjective security of individuals and groups. The truth is that want, squalor, disease, ignorance and idleness remain pervasive, though in new and different ways, and innovative and creative solutions will be needed to overcome them. The first step in attacking their modern incarnations lies in recognising them, and to do so Beveridge's classification, reconceived in the modern UK context, is as relevant as it ever was.

While liberals face changed giants at home, however, we are now confronted with more familiar giants abroad. Beveridge's metaphor applies almost unchanged to the developing world, and comprises the central threats to international stability and peace. If British Liberals are to remain true to the rights agenda underpinning our own country's welfare state, we must embrace an extended ethics, devoted to slaying these global giants. Growing interdependence and a commitment to *universal, human* rights bring the evils plaguing far-off states much closer to home. It is both in the national interest and is a moral – liberal – duty that these giants be brought down.

Beveridge's conception of need therefore continues to provide a liberal agenda for action, both at home and abroad. One addition that should be argued for, however, is the sixth giant, an unprecedented threat to human prosperity, with unknown, indiscriminate and far-reaching consequences: the environment. While environmental degradation is doing more damage to the developing world than elsewhere, the UK cannot escape the dangers caused by climate change and the risks of global pandemics.

In moving forward with the welfare agenda, liberalism can never underestimate the importance of cultural relevance. Practices and institutions for distributing welfare must always derive from the needs and norms of the society in question. This is not only morally right, but is also vital for the success of these designs as, unless they reflect the society for which they are created, they simply will not last. Liberals should not be seeking to install what has essentially been a British model of welfare, specific to a particular set of geographical and historical circumstances, in a multitude of societies which diverge hugely in their politics, economics and value systems. The imperative for liberals is nevertheless to identify the universal elements of our belief, meaning the fundamentals that should be the entitlement of all people in all places, the breach of which is to us indefensible regardless of historic, nationalist or cultural 'justifications'. This is not cultural imperialism, but a belief in universal principles which progressive liberals have a moral duty to work for globally, whilst recognising the many different ways in which they may be delivered. It is here that twenty-first century liberals must take a stand at home and abroad.

Giants in the UK: want

The 'want' that Beveridge identified in 1940s' Britain related to a sheer poverty that for many has now been overcome. It is not completely obsolete, of course – for example 1.3m British children in are estimated to be living in severe poverty[2] – but it is no longer the norm. Historically high levels of affluence in the UK have frequently led the fortunate to declare victory in the war against poverty. Such celebration is dangerous, however, as want continues to inhibit individuals and groups, though in less obvious ways.

The evolution of want can be explained in terms of the evolution of need. According to current British standards, the basic list of a person's essential needs has grown, meaning that there are now more goods in which it is possible to be lacking. The satisfaction of basic human needs is no longer enough, as other barriers dictate a person's ability to engage fully with society and realise their potential. Absolute needs, such as hunger, or the need for shelter, have been replaced with relative needs.

It is doubtful that Beveridge would have thought much about the concept of relative needs. But while the absolute poverty he fought has largely been slashed, relative poverty is a scourge that is growing in force. As the gap between Britain's rich and poor continues to widen, certain goods that most of society takes for granted are increasingly inaccessible for the worst-off, and without them they are unable to engage fully in modern life and so are denied the opportunities available to others. Technology provides a striking example of the way in which new needs determine well-being. For example, for those people who cannot afford a car, access to quality products and services is hugely restricted, leaving them isolated and with only the worse and most expensive options. Shopping on the internet is increasingly becoming the best way to obtain goods and services at affordable rates for low-income groups, but it is precisely those groups who lack access to computers with internet connections.

Further up the ladder social pressures generated by affluence are at the heart of *perceived* relative needs. Base, essential, needs have for many been replaced with materialism on a sliding scale. Endlessly updating mobile telephones, cars, clothes and other goods have led to short-lived contentedness and an unprecedented consumerism. Good enough is, simply, rarely enough. Britons are working longer hours than anywhere else in the developed world,[3] often leading highly stressed lives in which there is little time for family – or, indeed, anything else – in order to keep up with the ever-shifting goalposts of what is felt to be a 'good' standard of living.

What is more, in tandem with the new consumerism, want has evolved as subjective values, such as happiness and emotional security, have taken on a new importance in the collective imagination. Never before have there been so many studies into people's conceptions of their own emotional well-being. For the middle classes at least, 'lifestyle fulfilment' is the new benchmark of quality of life, as the top tiers of their hierarchy of needs – food, shelter and so on – are satisfied. And many people are dissatisfied. The pursuit of essentially material goals often fails to bring long-term gratification.

Giants in the UK: squalor

The typical expression of severe want has always been squalor. All of the giants walk hand in hand, but their mutually reinforcing relationship is rarely ever as pronounced as between these two.

Generally speaking, the UK has banished squalor as it was once known. The majority of British households are now connected to an adequate basic infrastructure, with access to effective sanitation, fuel and energy. The entrenchment of a 'health and safety culture' has ensured that acceptable standards of buildings and facilities are generally upheld, and even in cases where this is not so, the overwhelming consensus is that it should be.

Despite these improvements, however, it is possible to identify a new kind of squalor, best conceived of through the concept of 'squalid communities'. In disadvantaged areas it is common to find cycles of unemployment, racial tension, drug abuse, teenage parenthood and prostitution spiralling out of control and eroding the social fabric. These conditions are the result of webs of multiple deprivation, where disadvantage breeds disadvantage, condemning entire communities to hardship. Out of poverty and squalor comes frustration, which in turn finds expression in apathy, addiction and violence. State neglect leads to poor public services, and these communities are left to struggle on substandard education, health care and social services.

As a result they become instilled with a sense of hopelessness. As I discuss elsewhere in this volume (see Chapter 10), deprivation and social exclusion pass down from one generation to the next, locking young people into self-destructive patterns, often manifest in disorder and anti-social behaviour. The rage that can be found within this growing underclass is easily manipulated, hence the correlation between high socio-economic deprivation and racial tensions. Britain now trails well behind other industrialised nations in terms of child well-being, and, according to UNICEF research, scores exceptionally badly on young people's behaviour, risk-taking and sense of security.[4] Given the persistence of squalid communities, this is less surprising than it first seems. Large groups of alienated young people have been left feeling that they have no stake in society, and therefore do not carry responsibilities or obligations within it. Their societal withdrawal makes their communities more squalid, and so the cycle continues.

Giants in the UK: disease

Of all the giants at home, disease has been dealt the greatest blow by the welfare state. Indeed, for many the most revered element of Beveridge's legacy has been a national health system funded by all through taxation and free at the point of delivery. The fact is that disease is no longer the mortal threat it once was.

However, a glance at contemporary debates makes it immediately apparent that the provision of health care remains paramount in British politics today. It is one of the most emotive issues in current popular discourse, and has retained the power to mobilise what is generally an increasingly disengaged electorate. Deficits, waiting lists, staff shortages and a range of other issues frequently dominate the news, both at local and national levels.

Given that disease is no longer the imminent and pervasive threat that it was in Beveridge's era, this is, perhaps, surprising. People are living longer than ever, infant mortality rates are at an all-time low, and diseases that used to claim many lives are now extinct, yet the obsession with this giant continues. This can be understood as a result of the rise in expectations caused by advances in medical science. Medical technology has made possible treatments that the founders of the NHS could never have imagined, and consequently, as a society, we are encouraged to aim for a very high standard of health care. Ironically, however, it is these advances that actually prevent the realisation of this standard.

Developments in medicine have brought vastly escalating costs – leading directly to the rationing of many treatments throughout the country, confounding the rising expectations that were unimaginable in 1948. Contrary to Beveridge's prediction, universal health care has not, in the long run, reduced the financial burden of disease on the state.

The lesson has been that there is always more that can be usefully spent. High costs have meant that British health care in the twenty-first century does not match the idealisation of what it could be, as what is possible is not what is affordable. The discrepancy between what the public believe is possible for health care and what public money can provide makes it very easy to attack governments on inadequacies in health care provision. It thus remains a key political weapon and high on the political agenda.

Giants in the UK: ignorance

Compulsory secondary schooling in Britain has transformed the battle against ignorance. While there are, of course, continuing debates over the quality of education and the number of young people going on to further training, it cannot be denied that compared to Beveridge's era the situation today may be deemed a success. Whereas half a century ago large numbers of people could not read and write, now the vast majority of people are educated to GCSE standard at least in maths, English, science, arts and the humanities.

Despite these improvements, however, modern ignorance has a new face. Rather than describing a lack of knowledge, primarily concerned with facts, it relates to a lack of tolerance. The ignorant are the unenlightened, who do not accept the existence of alternative views and whose narrow mindsets lead them to treat those who are different with suspicion and contempt.

The growth of these groups has become a matter of increasing concern over recent decades. As in other parts of Western Europe, the UK is experiencing a renewed interest in right-wing ideologies amongst certain sections of society. In particular, there has been a rise in support for the BNP and an increase in faith-based fundamentalism. Counterintuitively, the tolerance that presumably should have followed widespread education has not embedded as a social value across the board, and pockets of extremism are a growing problem.

Much of the cause of this has already been discussed. In particular it is the alienation felt in squalid communities that leads to frustration and rage, which is easily manipulated by right-wing individuals and groups looking to recruit support. Further, the growth of new communications can also be seen to have contributed to modern British ignorance. In twenty-first-century Britain, in contrast to the 1940s, far from there being a shortage of knowledge, there is a bewildering array of it, especially through satellite TV and the internet. Just twenty years ago, there were only four national TV stations. Now there are dozens. In 1998, less than 10 per cent of households had access to the internet. By 2006, that figure was over 57 per cent.[5]

The growth of a 'knowledge society', however, has not led to overall enlightenment. The great many 'truths' available for understanding have, for some, been overwhelming, encouraging what may prove to be a renaissance of extremist thought. As the UK has become saturated with information and individuals are confronted with a multiplicity of information sources, many people tend to rely on only one or two, contributing to a very narrow view of the world, reinforced by unlimited contact (often via the internet) with only fellow-believers. In an age when people can share their lives with others from very specific interest groups, the attractions of geographic communities are greatly reduced, thereby minimising people's contact with those who disagree with them.

This is creating a society in which people are disconnected from the community around them, and increasingly, from the national community which expresses itself in politics. Thus, if Beveridge were around to fight the battle against ignorance today, here he would find a very different dilemma, based more on the abundance of information rather than barriers to its dissemination.

Giants in the UK: idleness

The idleness that plagued mid-twentieth-century Britain derived from the absence of gainful work for many. People were either exploited, working gruelling, dangerous jobs for a meagre existence, or else opted out, often turning to crime. The current situation is, of course, very different. Legislation on the age of workers, working hours and the minimum wage has replaced the forced child labour and extreme working conditions that Beveridge saw. Significant minorities are, however, still mistreated, but they are at least exceptions rather than the rule.

Instead, modern British idleness refers to widespread disengagement from the working world, or at least the side of it that contributes to fulfilment or prosperity. As explained above, cycles of cross-generational deprivation have fostered a growing British underclass. Many of the policies pursued in the 1980s and early 1990s aimed to give people more responsibility for their lives, to take away government support and to leave people to rely upon themselves and their families. However, although relevant to the growing middle class and the elite, this approach left behind a section of society that was unskilled and simply did not have the resources to take advantage of opportunities. Failures in the education system have made this situation worse, blocking the only real ladder out of poverty and deprivation for a significant minority. In particular, the shift to a national, undifferentiated secondary curriculum has failed these young people.

For these individuals, there are two 'choices' (although there may not be much choice involved): to work or not to work, neither particularly appealing. Unemployment results in reliance on state support, and the dependency culture inherent to the current tax and benefits system encourages those who sign up to benefits to do so for life. Indeed, the loss of earnings in tax for even those in very low-paid jobs is a huge deterrent to re-engaging with the working world once someone has spent time out of it. The other possibility is crime, as those who feel disempowered perceive few opportunities to improve their prospects. For those who take this route and get caught, prison sentences often do more damage rather than rehabilitate. Reoffending rates are embarrassingly high, and too many people who enter prison as petty offenders come out as hardened criminals ready to commit more serious offences. Sixty-seven per cent of inmates are reoffenders, up from half in the early 1990s.[6]

The other option, then, is to work. As I discuss elsewhere in this book (see Chapter 10), the current government's drive to work is forcing many adults into poorly paid, thankless and unfulfilling jobs, in which they have few opportunities to advance and develop their skills so as to progress themselves, and nor can they earn enough to lift themselves out of poverty. Parents and their children are suffering particularly, as mothers and fathers are coerced into working punishing hours for very little return.

Global giants: want

While the giants have changed greatly in the UK, the global picture would be a great deal more recognisable to Beveridge. Across the planet pure, unadulterated, abject poverty exists in abundance. A staggering 40 per cent of the world's population live on less than $2 a day,[7] and in sub-Saharan Africa around two out of every five people live on just $1 a day.[8] The world's 500 richest people have a combined income of over $100 billion (not including asset wealth), exceeding the combined income of the poorest 416 million.[9] And despite constant reassurances by G8 leaders that things are getting better, the United Nations predicts that some 380 million people will miss the Millennium Development Goal to halve extreme income poverty by 2015.[10]

The most severe manifestation of global want is hunger. Eight hundred and twenty million people in developing countries are undernourished, having dropped a mere three million since the early 1990s.[11] Bluntly, much of the world is starving. Malnutrition contributes to over half of under-fives' deaths in developing countries, and in some states, such as India and Bangladesh, almost a third of all babies are born underweight.[12]

The leading principle in the international response has been aid, and an entire industry has built up around its delivery. This is, however, proving both unsustainable and insufficient. Aid packages, although vital, particularly in humanitarian emergencies, do little to provide long-term solutions. Aid alone cannot enable developing nations; it cannot provide them with the tools for self-sufficiency. Indeed, in some ways the charitable element of the aid agenda has been to the detriment of the developing world, reinforcing its role as the dependent party in international relations.

To tackle global poverty a fundamental change to the economic order will be required, in which the global South engages in commerce on a more level footing. If the universal right to equality of opportunity is to be realised, a fundamental overhaul of internationally regulated trade practices will be needed. A commitment to the role and authority of multilateral governance – and so the United Nations and the World Bank – from all nations is key in countering the vested interests of those states and elites already benefiting from the inequality that characterises the global economic order. As one of those beneficiaries, the UK has a particular responsibility to act in ways that promote global fairness, and ensure that people across the world are not going hungry and are lifted out of extreme poverty, as should be their intrinsic human right.

Global giants: squalor

Squalor also plagues the developing world in the traditional sense. Rather than a subjective sense of despair, it exists more as an objective constraint on realising a basic level of existence. Millions of people in the developing world live in conditions which would be unthinkable in the UK. Two billion six hundred million people do not have adequate access to sanitation,[13] with an indisputable impact on health. Poor sanitation leads to a degrading environment, often with open sewers and refuse spilling into streets, and yet the UN estimates that the water lost by dripping taps in wealthy countries each day is more than is available to over one billion people.[14] The lack of clean water results in huge economic expense, based on health costs, productivity losses and labour diversions. In sub-Saharan Africa it amounts to an estimated 5 per cent of GDP each year, some $28.4 billion, exceeding the amount given to the region through aid and debt relief for the whole of 2003.[15]

Beyond water, other elements of failing infrastructure perpetuate global squalor, and many states suffer from an extreme lack of investment in roads and transport, energy, and buildings. In Brazil some one million people live in Rio's six hundred shanty towns – 'favelas' – where families huddle in tiny tin huts, perhaps five or six meters squared, in villages so riddled with crime that even the police will not visit them.[16]

Efforts to raise basic living standards abroad have frequently been undermined by the widespread misappropriation of aid by corrupt and autocratic elites. Politically, a tradition of non-interference by the international community has allowed various undemocratic governments to sustain their campaigns of neglect towards their own people, as has been seen in Zimbabwe, to name but one. National sovereignty, so fiercely guarded, continues to paralyse the development of an effective set of sanctions against those governments who thus destroy their own people. Defeating squalor, bound up in the war against want, therefore requires political action. In tackling this global giant British Liberalism must ground its foreign policy in the primacy of international institutions, and must advocate the pooling of sovereignty into a United Nations with the teeth to enforce the requirement for basic standards. Progressive liberals cannot duck our essential belief in universal values that – by definition – we believe should apply abroad as well as at home.

Squalor can only be eliminated when its victims are themselves empowered to prevent it. Democratisation is the means of emancipation whereby populations may, with the initial support of the developed world, relieve themselves of the squalor that immobilises them. The appropriate models and processes in different countries and regions are dependent on the social practices, values and traditions already in place, and the export of a one-size-fits-all Western liberal democracy is not the answer. However, while it is vital to reject cultural imperialism and simplistic policies that seek to recreate Western political structures in places where they are not best suited, liberalism at its core must remain true to the fundamental right to freedom. Political institutions, therefore, may vary in their blueprints, but ultimately must all be designed so as to facilitate and reflect the self-government of peoples. It is through this empowerment that squalor, and indeed all of the giants, can be permanently defeated.

Global giants: disease

While health has greatly improved in the UK, health expectations in much of the developing world have not progressed in the same way. Worse, the extremity of the risks facing populations and the lack of basic resources (let alone advanced technology) capable of dealing with them have increased for many communities since 1945. Squalor provides fertile breeding ground for its bed-partner, disease. Diseases that now sound anachronistic in the UK rage through other parts of the world. While the UK did not experience a single case of cholera in 2006, in Senegal there were over 31,000.[17] The infant mortality rate here is 0.5 per cent, whereas in Angola it is 15 per cent,[18] and while UK life expectancy is 77 for a man and 81 for a woman, in Zambia the majority of people will not live beyond 40.[19]

A widespread lack of water and sanitation, overcrowding, poor education and limited basic health resources mean vast numbers of people have very little protection from illness and premature death. Scant education in particular is playing a huge part in the global HIV/AIDS epidemic: 39.5 million people were living with HIV in 2006.[20] In that year alone 530,000 children were infected, and 2.9 million people died. Almost two-thirds of all of the people living with HIV live in sub-Saharan Africa, and in Swaziland a devastating one in three adults has the disease.[21]

To counter the conditions within which disease can fester, want and squalor must be purged. British Liberals must therefore pursue policies abroad that deliver this, as they once did at home. Indeed, the UK's present sanitation system was born out of the Liberal-led social and industrial revolution of the Victorian era, and hygienic, modern systems for sanitation must once again register high on the liberal agenda. It is the responsibility of British Liberals to condemn those regimes that fail to invest in basic standards. Besides the ethical arguments supporting this, the duty to tackle disease internationally is further grounded in the national interest. Disease has no respect for borders. This has been underlined by the pandemic scares witnessed in recent years, notably SARS in 2003 and avian flu more recently. Neither have (yet) claimed the death tolls that were feared, but they have exposed the weak defences that many states would have against a modern-day plague, and 'bird flu' in Europe has been a stark reminder of the UK's vulnerability.

The fact is that the modern global society, criss-crossed by rapid movements of both goods and people worldwide, with people living in the most overcrowded mass populations in history, and with the delivery of goods and services depending on increasingly interdependent transnational industries, means that we are more vulnerable to plague and its consequences than ever before. Unsurprisingly, it is the poorer nations who are less equipped to take the preventive measures necessary to avoid disaster, but it is foolish to believe that Beveridge's NHS is a defence against all possibilities. Mankind has created the perfect laboratory conditions for plague and its attached social and economic breakdown worldwide; the UK is not immune.

Global giants: ignorance

While the abundance of information is a challenge in the UK, the global issue is still one of restriction. Although new communications are by nature transnational, their reach is not without bounds. In Ghana more than half of all adult women cannot read and write; in Burkina Faso, the figure is 83 per cent.[22] What is more, the world's poorest have little or no access to computers and the internet. Plus, in countries where there is no democracy, authoritarian regimes exert considerable control over incoming information. For example, all communication on the internet in China must pass through government-controlled routers, and sites thought to be subversive are blocked. This censorship has been used against various human rights websites, including Amnesty International.[23]

Orthodox access to information is also denied in many parts of the world, as many young children are driven into work by extreme poverty at the expense of their education. In Laos, for example, in 2005 84 per cent of children were in primary school, but this had dropped by over half to 38 per cent in secondary school, and just 8 per cent in tertiary education.[24] Where children are in school, facilities in developing countries are often hugely stretched, with large classes and few books and writing materials, let alone computers or qualified teachers.

The lack of education abroad must strike a chord at home, as ignorance, for liberals, has always been the enemy of liberty. The doctrine's Enlightenment fathers based their reverence of knowledge on its power to free man from the shackles of totalitarianism. Men are equal in their capacity for free will, but it is education that converts choice to reason. Without education the giants roam uninhibited, as the arguments that underpin them go unchallenged, and creative solutions cannot be found to punishing problems. Ignorance, combined with poverty, need and frustration, breeds violence and aggression. Tolerance, conversely, requires exposure to variety, and empathy – a vital component of sustained peace – must be learnt alongside understandings of differing and conflicting world views.

When British Liberals talk about ignorance abroad they must of course be wary of culturally imperialist prescriptions based on spreading 'western' values and remaking the developing world in the image of richer nations. However, such sensitivity cannot be a deterrent to the belief that a universal human right to freedom exists, and that true freedom is only realisable on the basis of autonomy, self-determination and the tolerance of others. Without access to education this becomes impossible. Further, liberals must stand by the demand that education is accessible to *all*, irrespective of wealth, race and gender, and must not bow to elites who justify discriminatory systems on the basis of faith or doctrine. In other words, the need for education provision to reflect a society's values and practices cannot be an excuse for racist, sexist or elitist institutions.

Global giants: idleness

The out-and-out employment abuse that pervaded the world half a century ago lives on in the international context. Exploitation has been characteristic of recent centuries, as various empires have pillaged the natural resources of their colonies, and have broken up traditional patterns of life and work. In many ways, since decolonisation imperial practices have been replaced by the near-identical practices of big business. People are forced by poverty and ignorance into work which does not meet their needs, and which does not build up their communities. Multinational companies, and their local sub-contractors, make huge profits as they sell goods for Western prices, but frequently they (or more often their local suppliers) pay their workers at subsistence level or below, only exposed from time to time by sweatshop scandals and the work of human rights organisations.[25]

The problems of exploitation in the developing world do not stop with the private sector. In some cases, the leaders of those countries create new problems or at the least exacerbate those that already exist. Robert Mugabe in Zimbabwe is a prime example. He has closed down many of the farms in his country because they were owned and run by white Zimbabweans. This has not resulted in greater employment for black farm-workers, but has instead generally left the farms standing idle or in the hands of his cronies, with former employees left to search for other work. There are no reliable statistics, but some observers have estimated that most are still unemployed. Further more, many are also facing government attacks on the shanty towns they have been forced to live in. In a country which is in a state of economic crisis there is no welfare provision, and the unemployed can find themselves starving. This situation is worsened because so many of the farms are out of action, and so the rate of food production is reduced. Mugabe further deepens the plight of his people by hoarding what food there is, and refusing to allow aid agencies to help the worst-affected areas.

Sadly, Mugabe is not unique. In many developing countries democracy is not fully established, and where it is in place in many cases it is open to abuse from corrupt officials and politicians. Corruption and the greed of elites fuel much of the intra-state conflict characterising the current world order. Growth and innovation become blocked by instability, which acts as a major deterrent to foreign investment, and work – stable, fulfilling, empowering work – is impossible. Without the opportunity for such meaningful work the individual has no control, no independence, and without the power to affect his or her life chances, there is no real freedom.

The sixth giant – the environment

It is clear, then, that while the giants at home have changed – no longer the pure incarnations that Beveridge challenged but rather the more resilient, more subtle and often better-hidden ills infiltrating British welfare, those abroad are easily recognised. There is, however, a new threat to social well-being at home and abroad, a sixth giant: the environment.

In the 1940s, environmental politics did not exist in any significant way, and it is unsurprising that Beveridge had nothing to say on the subject. Yet today the sixth giant resonates in the collective imagination as never before. The current era is characterised by unprecedented environmental degradation. It is said that the world's population as a whole ceased to live sustainably in about 1986, when for the first time people began using more resources than the Earth produces. Today, the human impact on the environment – or ecological footprint – is 2.5 times greater than in the early 1960s, and is estimated to be at least 20 per cent beyond what the planet can actually sustain. As explained by the Worldwide Fund for Nature, 'effectively, the Earth's regenerative capacity can no longer keep up with demand – people are turning resources into waste faster than nature can turn waste back into resources'.[26] Furthermore, since 1970, around 30 per cent of the planet's species have been wiped out through hunting or as their habitats have been destroyed.[27] Decreasing biodiversity weakens the web of life itself and makes human existence more precarious, rippling out in entirely unpredictable ways.

The global North has until now been cushioned from the impact of this reality, while in the developing world it is already being cruelly felt, be it the fisheries of West Africa that have been plundered and laid waste by EU trawlers,[28] or the villages in Indonesia that have been crushed by the landslides caused by deforestation.[29] This is despite the fact that developed countries have a much bigger impact on the global environment than others. For example, the per-person use of resources is a world average of 2.2 hectares per year, but in the US it is 9.5 hectares, and in UK, 5.4.

Colonialists of the past thought little about the effects of degrading foreign environments to enrich themselves, and the habit has continued, again with multinational corporations playing a large part. In addition, lacking the funding to invest in sustainable technologies and under economic pressure, many people in developing countries are continuing to act in ways which damage their own environment.[30] Deforestation creates landslips and desertification, kills rivers and threatens the existence of millions of species, from unknown insects to the orang-utan, one of man's closest relatives. Failures to remove waste safely from industrial plants ruins rivers and coastal areas, poisoning people and plants alike. Big businesses export parts and products cheaply to the West from a supply chain relying on lax regulations and corner-cutting over environmental regulation and human protection. The present ten-year boom in most developed countries has been underpinned by the increasing plunder of the resources of the poorest countries in the world.

The growing threat of pan-Earth climate change, however, is, levelling the risk. Here, the giant looms indiscriminately over East, West, North and South alike. Global energy use has increased by 700 per cent between 1961 and 2001, and is having the biggest impact of any human activity.[31] Although it is natural for the Earth's climate to change from century to century, the vast majority of scientific opinion agrees that human activity is causing changes that go well beyond what is natural, and at rates that will not allow species to adapt, with potentially devastating consequences. Scientists estimate that average temperatures are likely to rise by between 1.4 and 5.8 degrees by 2100,[32] with a catastrophic impact on the way people live their lives. Here in the UK a particular fear is that as polar ice caps melt, there will be flooding on a huge scale, with large parts of southern England permanently under water.[33] In addition, the beech and oak woodlands of southern England will be severely affected by more extreme heat in the summer. Some land in Western Europe may turn to desert due to temperature increases,[34] and food production patterns across the world will change. There will also be challenges to human health, such as an increase in the number of people at risk from tropical diseases such as malaria.[35] Half the world's coral reefs may disappear within a century,[36] and some experts predict extinction for the polar bear in the same timeframe.[37] Unless we act now to tackle these problems, both through politics and lifestyle, those alive today will bear an enormous responsibility for the difficulties faced by future generations.

Conclusion

So the five giants which stalked Beveridge's land still face us today, altered in the UK but clearly recognisable in the developing world. They have also been joined by a sixth. The bare bones of the solutions to these problems, indeed even the beginnings of solutions, would take at least an entire manifesto to set out. The point here, then, has been to revisit the ideological framework that gave British Liberalism its focus over sixty years ago and to see what it can do for British Liberals today.

At home, the giants as Beveridge faced them are a touchstone. They allow us to see what has been achieved and what is yet to be done. For the lower strata of society, they exist as they always did – abject poverty, dank and dark living, no work and no route out; but, for the majority, this is no longer the case. However, it is naive to celebrate their eradication. The giants still exist, but they hold society back in different ways. Primarily they combine in cycles of exclusion and relative deprivation that enhance alienation and community breakdown.

Abroad, the giants recall Beveridge's original conception – starvation, death, disease, exploitation – and it is the duty of British Liberals to revive Beveridge in these foreign battles. This duty is grounded in both ethics and pragmatism. With regard to the former, if progressive liberals are to stay true to achieving the fundamental human rights underpinning Beveridge's welfare system – the right to a basic level of existence, to not going hungry, to freedom from disease, the right to work, the right to liberty and thus autonomy, education and self-government – then we must extend the moral sphere across the globe. In other words, the universality that is claimed to be at the core of the welfare state must be truly universal.

In terms of pragmatism, British Liberals must recognise the alleviation of global want, squalor, disease, ignorance and idleness as central to international, and thus domestic, stability. Recent decades have witnessed an unprecedented rise in intra-state violence. Frustration and desperation enable elites to mobilise large populations and so become manifest in conflict. War, as it is today in many parts of the world, is about welfare. It is, however, very easy to blame these protracted social conflicts on ethnic tensions, perpetuating the myth that the developing world is simply less civilised than its Western counterpart. These explanations are not only misleading, but they absolve developed nations from their duties in improving global welfare, not least to bring an end to violence and instability.

Finally, then, while this chapter made no claims that it could offer complete solutions, it has laid out the necessary framework for a new, reinvigorated, inclusive, global path for British Liberalism. Opting out of politics, today's 'fashionable' option on the doorstep, cannot be the answer domestically, and ducking out of pressing the liberal cause internationally is both morally wrong and ultimately likely to rebound on us at home. Collective action will be crucial in rising to contemporary challenges. Vitality, commitment and political expression will be necessary to tackle the alienation and disengagement sweeping Britain, and to guide our government to pursue the right policies abroad. In these policies we must avoid the trap of benign imperialism and the imposition of ideals specific to our culture. However, at the same time we must be clear about who we are and what we believe, and aim for nothing short of the global spread of the fundamental, essential conditions to which progressive Liberals believe all people should have the right.

Notes

1   I am grateful to Zena Elmahrouki for her assistance in preparing this chapter. I would also like to thank Claire Bentham and Richard Grayson for their work as long ago as 2004 in helping to produce an early draft of it for a different purpose.
2   Save The Children, *Severe Child Poverty in the UK*, 19 June 2007.
3   International Labour Organisation, *Working Time Around the World: Trends in Working Hours, Laws and Policies in a Global Comparative Perspective*, June 2007.
4   UNICEF, *Child Poverty in Perspective: An Overview of Child Well-being in Rich Countries*, 2007.
5   Office of National Statistics, *Society: Internet Access*, 23 August 2006; available at http://www.statistics.gov.uk/CCI/nugget.asp?ID=8&Pos=&ColRank=1&Rank=374.
6   BBC News, 'Why more inmates are reoffenders', 30 January 2007, available at http://news.bbc.co.uk/1/hi/uk/6312863.stm.
7   United Nations Development Programme, *Human Development Report 2006, Beyond Scarcity: Power, Poverty and the Global Water Crisis* (UNDP, 2006), p. 269.
8   Department for International Development, *Poverty Factsheet*, November 2006, available at http://www.dfid.gov.uk/mdg/poverty.asp.
9   UNDP, *Human Development Report 2006*, p. 269.
10 Ibid.

11 Food & Agriculture Organisation, *The State of Food Insecurity in the World 2006 – Eradicating world hunger – taking stock 10 years after the World Food Summit* (FAO, 2006).
12 Department for International Development, *Hunger Factsheet,* February 2006, available at http://www.dfid.gov.uk/mdg/poverty.asp.
13 UNDP, *Human Development Report 2006,* p. 2.
14 Ibid, p. 5.
15 Ibid, p. 6.
16 'Favela fight', *The Guardian,* 1 June 2007, p. 25.
17 World Health Organisation, *Weekly Epidemiological Record,* 4 August 2006, available at http://www.who.int/wer/2006/wer8131.pdf.
18 World Health Organisation, *Core Indicators,* 19 June 2007, available at http://www.who.int/whosis/database/core/core_select_process.cfm.
19 Ibid.
20 World Health Organisation, *Global Summary of the Aids Epidemic,* December 2006, available at http://www.who.int/hiv/mediacentre/02-Global_Summary_2006_EpiUpdate_eng.pdf.
21 UNAIDS/World Health Organisation, *HIV Factsheet: Sub-Saharan Africa,* November 2006, available at http://www.who.int/hiv/mediacentre/20061121_EPI_FS_SSA_en.pdf.
22 Ibid.
23 Amnesty International, *People's Republic of China Controls Tighten as Internet Activism Grows,* 28 January 2004, available at http://web.amnesty.org/library/Index/ENGASA170012004.
24 UNESCO Institute for Statistics, 14 June 2007, at http://stats.uis.unesco.org/unesco/TableViewer/document.aspx?ReportId=198&IF_Language=eng.
25 Human Rights Watch, *Corporations and Human Rights,* available at http://www.hrw.org/about/initiatives/corp.html.
26 Worldwide Fund for Nature, *Living Planet Report 2006,* p. 2, available at http://assets.panda.org/downloads/living_planet_report.pdf.
27 Ibid.
28 BBC News, 'Fishing for a future', 19 March 2003, available at http://news.bbc.co.uk/1/hi/business/2846219.stm.
29 BBC News, 'Indonesia mudslide buries bus', 24 April 2004, available at http://news.bbc.co.uk/1/hi/world/asia-pacific/3655069.stm.
30 See, for example, Fairtrade Foundation, *Unpeeling the Banana Trade* (FTF, 2000), p. 11; available at: http://www.fairtrade.org.uk/downloads/doc/unpeeling_the_banana_trade.doc.
31 WWF, *Living Planet Report 2004,* p. 14.
32 BBC News, 'Guide to climate change', available at http://news.bbc.co.uk/1/shared/spl/hi/sci_nat/04/climate_change/html/climate.stm.
33 Department for Environment, Food and Rural Affairs, *Flood and Coastal Defence Project, Foresight: Future Flooding,* 22 April 2004, available at http://www.foresight.gov.uk/Previous_Projects/Flood_and_Coastal_Defence/.
34 BBC News, 'Southern Spain "dust bowl" threat', 28 June 2004, available at http://newsvote.bbc.co.uk/1/hi/world/europe/3929507.stm.

35 Meteorological Office, *The Impacts of Climate Change on Human Health* (Met Office, 1999); available at: http://www.metoffice.com/research/hadleycentre/pubs/brochures/B1999/imp_human_health.html.
36 BBC news, 'Action needed to save coral reefs', 13 February 2004, available at http://news.bbc.co.uk/1/hi/sci/tech/3487869.stm.
37 http://news.bbc.co.uk/1/hi/sci/tech/2642773.stm.

Chapter 5

Me, Myself and I

Simon Titley

W hat is the most significant and fundamental change to have occurred in our society in the past fifty years?

Television, perhaps? Widespread car ownership? Women's liberation? Computers? The internet? Multiculturalism? Higher education? Credit cards? Cheap air travel? Sex? Drugs? Rock 'n' roll? It is none of these (though each has had profound effects).

The answer is obvious, but most people fail to see it, because the change has altered the prism through which we perceive the world. The answer is you. Or rather, it is me. It is our sense of self.

This transformation has been the greatest revolution of the post-war era. Amongst other things, it has completely changed the context in which politicians must operate. It is a revolutionary social change yet it is taken for granted. An effective political strategy cannot be developed without a grasp of this change.

The revolution in the head[1]

The most profound social change to occur in the past half century in Western societies has been a transformation in the way people perceive themselves. Our self-perceptions are radically different. People now think of their lives primarily in terms of self-actualisation rather than adherence to the group.

Until the 1960s, most people had their identities given to them by the traditional groups to which they belonged: family, geographical community, social class or church. Today, most people create their own identities and select their own peer groups. We make ourselves. This individualism has been brought about by a combination of affluence, education, secularisation, technological advance and sexual liberation, which has released the majority of people from lives that are circumscribed by day-to-day subsistence and group dogma, and has popularised the concept of 'lifestyle choice'.

Throughout human history until recently, the majority of people in our society were focused on the daily battle for survival and a reflective outlook on life was a luxury in which few could indulge. Mass affluence has brought lifestyle choice within reach of most of us. A change as profound as this has not gone unnoticed but it tends to be misinterpreted. The most popular analysis sees the social revolution in terms of 'the sixties'; not the real 1960s of perpetual sterling crises and the Black & White Minstrel Show, but the mythical decade of peace and love, when centuries of tradition were apparently thrown out of the window.

The irony is that conservative politicians who continually rail against the sixties and the 'permissive society' are arguably its greatest beneficiaries. Margaret Thatcher's victory in 1979 would not have been possible without the individualism the sixties spawned. The much-derided 1960s hippies, meanwhile, far from being harbingers of a new individualism, may well have represented the last gasp of the old communitarian values.

Few politicians really understood this social revolution but, if they had cared to look, a cogent analysis of what was happening was readily available. The psychologist Abraham Maslow predicted the revolution in people's heads as early as 1943. The now familiar pyramid diagram of 'Maslow's hierarchy' describes this process in terms of self-actualisation as the summit of human fulfilment.[2]

However, the process of individual liberation has proved something of a double-edged sword because, although it has enabled most people in Western societies to lead easier and more pleasant lives, it has also led people to forsake social cohesion for material individualism, and to abandon deferred pleasure for instant gratification.

Haven't we been here before?

This may not be the first time human beings have been radically transformed. In a recent study of the history of collective joy, Barbara Ehrenreich notes the beginning of an epidemic of depression in the early 1600s, brought on by a mutation in human nature:

> This change has been called the rise of subjectivity or the discovery of the inner self, and since it can be assumed that all people,

in all historical periods, have some sense of selfhood and capacity for subjective reflection, we are really talking about an intensification, and a fairly drastic one, of the universal human capacity to face the world as an autonomous 'I', separate from, and largely distrustful of, 'them' ... The new emphasis on disengagement and self-consciousness ... makes the individual potentially more autonomous and critical of existing social arrangements, which is all to the good. But it can also transform the individual into a kind of walled fortress, carefully defended from everyone else.[3]

If this analysis is correct, the recent surge in individualism is not an isolated event but a lurch forward in a process that began 400 years ago.

And might it be the case that the 'culture clash' we are experiencing with Islam is basically because Islamic societies have not experienced our mutations, neither the changes of the 1600s nor those of the 1960s? Our world must seem incomprehensible to someone who cannot conceive of a subjective and autonomous identity distinct from one's family ties.

Is everybody happy?

Despite the growth in material wealth and the sense of liberation brought about by the recent social revolution, it seems that we are no happier than we were fifty years ago.[4]

This phenomenon has attracted much academic interest. In America, Robert Putnam's book *Bowling Alone*[5] has been hugely influential in developing the concept of 'social capital'. In Britain, Professor Richard Layard's work on 'happiness economics'[6] and Oliver James's book *Britain On The Couch*[7] are two leading examples of attempts to analyse and tackle the current malaise.

There may be no agreement on the cure but there is widespread agreement on the fundamental cause of people's unhappiness: a loss of social solidarity. The traditional close-knit community could often be stifling and is now widely regarded as outmoded, but it did at least provide a sense of security. The pillars of society on which most people once relied – the extended family, the friendly neighbours, the local priest, the trades union and the social club – have largely gone. People's lives are dislocated and material consumption cannot fill the ensuing social and spiritual void.

The symptoms are not hard to find. We witness them in day-to-day phenomena such as the rise in uncivil behaviour, a coarsening of relationships between strangers in which common courtesies have been forgotten. Or there is the way in which adults have lost confidence in their ability to tackle misbehaviour by other people's children, instead relying on the local council to issue ASBOs. A more profound effect, however, is people's loss of confidence in humanity and an abandonment of faith in the possibility of human progress, which is most evident in the popular brand of environmentalism that sees human beings as an excrescence on the planet.

We are also witnessing a massive breakdown in trust, which is not confined to politics. Everywhere one looks, once-respected individuals and institutions are losing popular trust. Doctors, the police, big business, the royal family – groups that once enjoyed a 'blue chip' reputation have seen their respect and trust eroded.[8] Traditional elites are being rejected and, because they do not understand why, their responses are inept.

People now live in a more impersonal world with an uncertain future. John Kampfner, examining the popular mood during the 2005 general election, pointed to the spiritual emptiness in our modern, atomised society:

> A reliable flow of disposable income does not automatically translate into security or well-being. Look around your average British small town. By day, you see high streets denuded of character as the big retailers dominate and, at night, people out on benders staggering from pub to pub. This is not part of an audition for Grumpy Old Men. This is what people, who resent being valued only as consuming objects, told me ... It is this emptiness, I would argue, that is being manifested now.[9]

We have more wealth and choice than ever before, but never have people felt more alone. They inhabit a world of alienation from the cradle to the grave. They are born in industrial-scale maternity units (remember the machine that goes 'ping' in Monty Python's *Meaning of Life*?). They are educated in factory schools designed for a bygone industrial age. They hate their insecure jobs (45 per cent of employees in large private sector companies in the UK will leave their jobs in the next three years[10]). They retire to an uncertain pension and die in large hospitals, wired up to more machines that go 'ping'.

People are better educated and more assertive. At the same time, most of their social relationships have been replaced by economic ones, and their isolation makes them feel that shared problems are actually their own fault. They have 'choice' but mainly of a trivial, consumerist variety, and feel they have little control over their lives. Their growing sense of powerlessness is leading to a higher incidence of psychological distress.[11] Their anger and frustration may be incoherent but are no less real for that.

Who surfed the wave?

Did the social revolution have to work out this way? Individualisation was perhaps an inevitable consequence of mass affluence. The first people to identify this revolution were advertisers and marketers, and they have done more than anyone else to mould the change. They could deploy the one force both ready and able to satisfy the new demand for independent identity, consumerism.

Before the 1960s, people tended to sublimate their aspirations into the needs of the traditional group to which they belonged. It was not just that people didn't have any money; they instinctively understood the need for deferred pleasure, an understanding that distinguishes adults from children.

As people began to cast off their traditional social identities and search for something new, consumerism filled the void. We can have a good laugh now about the sort of faux-sophisticated goods with which middle-class Britons in the 1960s sought to establish their new identities – Babycham, After Eight mints and hostess trolleys – but these first faltering steps into the bright new world of consumerism are evidence of who was identifying and exploiting social trends.

Since the 1960s, people have enjoyed not just unprecedented wealth but also access to easy credit. Material prosperity is infinitely preferable to poverty so we must be clear: the problem is not one of prosperity but of maturity. People now demand individual gratification and, childlike, they want it all and they want it now. Consequently, as most adults have lost the capacity for deferred pleasure, society has undergone a process of infantilisation. 'I wish it could be Christmas every day' sang the pop group Wizzard in 1973. It seems this wish has come true.

It was not until the 1990s that most politicians began to realise what was happening. They responded by adopting a consumerist strategy, moving from leadership to followership, from ideological positioning towards consumer appeal, with an emphasis on opinion polls and focus groups.

However, unlike the marketer of a consumer product, able to target a niche market, politicians are simply unable to satisfy millions of individualised wants simultaneously. Voters perceive this inability as impotence or dishonesty, and a vicious cycle of disillusionment and alienation sets in. This situation has been exacerbated by the mass media, which has reduced the level of political debate to a series of soundbites, and globalisation, which has created the widespread impression that there is little or nothing the individual can do to affect decisions.

Politicians should therefore consider why it is that pressure groups, such as the Royal Society for the Protection of Birds, with its million-plus members, are able to attract and mobilise support in a way that political parties no longer can. The answer is that pressure groups pursue a narrow agenda and provide a tailored offer that meets individual consumer wants. Political parties, on the other hand, necessarily demand compromises of their supporters. They offer a comprehensive package of policies that cannot satisfy every individual want and that voters perceive politicians cannot deliver.

The losers in this revolution have been politicians but the winners have been marketers and pressure groups. This trend has profound implications for the whole democratic process. We face a number of serious policy challenges, foremost among them climate change and pensions, that demand a degree of deferred gratification from the electorate if they are to be tackled successfully. Such a demand flies in the face of our consumer culture.

Interlude: politicians in the 'me' decade
Politicians have been slow to understand the change going on around them. Despite politicians having little intellectual grasp of the social revolution, by the 1980s the effects on them were plain to see. This was the decade when they became less the agents of change and more its dupes.

The right felt liberated from social obligations and adopted the ideology of economism, reducing all social facts to economic dimensions and insisting that the forces of supply and demand trumped any other considerations. This was accompanied by 'public choice theory', which took the cynical view that people were motivated only by self-interest and that the market was a better substitute for democratic politics or social relationships.[12]

It is one thing to recognise a damaging trend, quite another to exalt it. The economist Amartya Sen illustrated the absurdity of public choice theory in the following scenario: 'Can you direct me to the railway station?' asks the stranger. 'Certainly,' says the local, pointing in the opposite direction, towards the post office, 'and would you post this letter for me on your way?' 'Certainly,' says the stranger, resolving to open it to see if it contains anything worth stealing.[13]

The left, meanwhile, should not be allowed off the hook. The right may have believed that 'there is no such thing as society' but there is a tendency to forget that, during the 1980s, the left became just as self-indulgent. It was the decade of being 'right on', when the left abandoned its traditional social concerns and instead emphasised the solipsistic obsessions of identity politics, a movement that rapidly descended into our present-day culture of victimhood.[14]

(One might ask what British Liberals were doing at that time. The answer is that they had developed their own brand of self-obsession, and all their talk was of pacts, deals and coalitions).

The 1980s were an appalling decade. The politics of this era were not the fundamental cause of social atomisation but they did celebrate and accelerate it. For this, the left is as much to blame as the right.

The role of the media
A major influence on the social revolution has been television. While consumerism has shifted people's expectations from deferred pleasure to instant gratification, television has moved people's perceptions from the rational to the emotional. Al Gore explains this change well in his recent book, *The Assault on Reason*:

> To understand the reason why the news marketplace of ideas
> dominated by television is so different from the one that emerged

in the world dominated by the printing press, it is important to distinguish the quality of vividness experienced by television viewers from the 'vividness' experienced by readers. I believe that the vividness experienced in the reading of words is automatically modulated by the constant activation of the reasoning centres of the brain that are used in the process of co-creating the representation of reality the author has intended. By contrast, the visceral vividness portrayed on television has the capacity to trigger instinctual responses similar to those triggered by reality itself – and without being modulated by logic, reason, and reflective thought.[15]

Gore adds:

Any new dominant communications medium leads to a new information ecology in society that inevitably changes the way ideas, feelings, wealth, power, and influence are distributed – and the way collective decisions are made.[16]

Our politicians remain obsessed with the influence of Britain's national daily newspapers, which, despite falling circulations, are perceived as influential because of the biased role they tend to play, in contrast to the legally enforced neutrality of broadcast news.

This blinds politicians to the true influence that television has. The problem with TV is not party or ideological bias, but that it has moved political discourse from the lengthy exposition to the short 'soundbite', and from rational deliberation to emotional reaction.

This development has had a potent effect on the transformation of people's identities and the conduct of politics. It has led to the phenomenon of the 'permanent campaign', when the line between campaigning and governing has blurred, pollsters are consulted on nearly every matter of policy, and politicians organise their lives around a never-ending succession of initiatives intended primarily for media consumption.[17] Such a public-relations-led strategy was the main failing of the Blair government.[18]

The primacy of emotion is meanwhile having a disastrous effect on policy-making. This is particularly evident in popular attitudes to risk.

The public has become obsessed with safety and a 'blame culture' is evolving, even though fears are often irrational. The recent panic over the MMR vaccine, for example, shows the extent to which political decisions are not always based on sound science, because of the power of irrational fears amplified by the media.

The consequences for politicians

Although most politicians will not admit to it openly, they must feel increasingly frustrated by what appears to be such unreasonable behaviour on the part of the public. Some might privately echo Bertolt Brecht's satire on the events in East Germany in 1953:

> After the uprising of the 17th June
> The Secretary of the Writers Union
> Had leaflets distributed in the Stalinallee
> Stating that the people
> Had forfeited the confidence of the government
> And could win it back only
> By redoubled efforts. Would it not be easier
> In that case for the government
> To dissolve the people
> And elect another?[19]

One Liberal Democrat politician showed no reticence in her desire to dissolve the people. Shortly after her defeat in the 2001 general election, the former MP Jackie Ballard wrote an article in the *Independent* headlined 'What a politician really thinks about her ungrateful voters':

> The voters expect us [the politicians] to solve all their problems for them. They expect the council to do something about noisy neighbours, to mend all the potholes, to provide them with a house if they need one, to detect child abuse from five miles away (when the people next door haven't noticed anything amiss) and to dispose of their rubbish regularly without polluting the air with incinerators or using valuable land space. But they don't want to pay Council Tax. They want the government to lock up criminals but not to put a bail hostel or prison anywhere near

them. They don't want to get asthma or to have their house flood-
ed but they must drive their car 200 metres down the road. They
don't want to have to wait a long time for a hospital operation
and they want their children to have a good education. They don't
mind other people paying higher taxes, but they don't want to
themselves. They want their politicians to be 'normal' people who
they can relate to, but they also want them to work 100 hours a
week and be available any time of the day or night to sort out
their problems.[20]

Mrs Ballard, having left parliament for good, could afford to express such
sentiments. Most other politicians are struggling to understand what is
going on and are desperate to arrive at some accommodation with the
electorate, if only they could find out what people really want.

On the whole, politicians have been slow to recognise and exploit the
underlying social transformation. But the broad trend has been a switch
from leading public opinion to following it. This is a consequence of a
number of factors.

The first is what has been described superficially as 'the end of ideology'. The end of communism led not just to the fall of the Soviet empire
in Eastern Europe but also to the discrediting of traditional state socialism in Western Europe. At the same time, globalisation limited politicians' freedom of manoeuvre and capacity to deliver. Ideology has not
ended, but the range of ideas has narrowed considerably, politics has
been replaced by managerialism, and the argument within the political
mainstream is confined to a debate about nuances or replaced by personality issues.

The disappearance of profound ideological differences in the 1990s
was accompanied by the importation from the US of election campaign
techniques modelled on the psychoanalytical methods developed in
advertising and marketing, in particular the use of focus groups. These
electoral techniques replaced an ideological approach with a consumerist one, characterised by emotional appeals to the self. Focus groups were
highly influential upon New Labour. Former spin-doctor Derek Draper
once joked, 'A bunch of eight people sipping wine in Kettering determined pretty much everything Labour did'.[21]

This is why the public thinks that all politicians sound the same. Just as most modern cars look the same because every car manufacturer's wind tunnel tests produce the same results, so politicians sound the same when they derive their policies from opinion polls and focus groups.

There has meanwhile been an extraordinary rise in the power of NGOs (non-governmental organisations). Single-issue pressure groups have succeeded because they are more in tune with the new political and social climate. They understand the social revolution and how to exploit it. Traditionally, politicians acted to reconcile competing interests, but the change in popular attitudes from group allegiance to self-gratification has made it more difficult for politicians to achieve this. Pressure groups, by contrast, with no formal responsibilities, can focus on a single issue and are better able to satisfy public opinion. Pressure groups also understand the importance of emotional appeals and do not rely solely on rational argument.

The consequence of these changes is that politicians, instead of engaging in ideological argument with one another, now compete to agree with public opinion. They no longer have any incentive to support a cause unless it can already demonstrate public support. Thus public opinion is increasingly driving political issues – even though, ironically, the public (in the form of socially atomised individuals) feels powerless to do anything. This paradox is explained by what economist Fred Hirsch called 'the tyranny of small choices'[22] – in other words, consumer power is real but incoherent.

Despite their attempts to pander to what they perceive as popular desires, politicians continue to lose popular respect. They are confronted by a shift in the voters' behaviour from deferential/group attitudes to more assertive individualistic postures, with a growth in an infantile expectation of immediate gratification. The inability of politicians to satisfy these self-centred wants is at the root of popular dissatisfaction with the whole democratic process.

Having lost power over so many things that matter, politicians have attempted to claw back power in other ways. One is to try and regulate matters previously considered part of the private sphere, such as diets or parenting skills. The other is to exploit the fear of terrorism to award themselves draconian powers. Government lectures about obesity or assaults on civil liberties can therefore be seen not as a sign of strength but as a symptom of impotence.

The consequences for business

It is not just politicians who have experienced difficulty in accommodating to the revolution in the head. Business has also had its problems.

We have seen that it was the marketers and manufacturers of consumer goods who surfed the wave of individualism better than politicians. You might expect business to be riding high, but now it is suffering from an erosion of trust similar to that suffered by politicians.

As the social revolution took hold and people became more individualistic, business demanded a different relationship with its consumers. It shifted its equity from tangibles (bricks and mortar, plant and equipment) into intangibles (brand values and corporate reputation). In other words, a company's greatest asset nowadays is what people think about it. Through the growth in importance of the brand, business demanded a more emotional attachment from consumers, rather than a rational assessment of the functional benefits of its products. But, in its reliance on emotion, business got more than it bargained for. It became more vulnerable to criticism with a popular emotional resonance.

In this world of brand values, it is crucial for a corporation to maintain public trust to stay in business. As the stock of politicians and government sinks, people perceive business, especially multinational corporations, as alternative loci of political power. Business therefore finds that it needs the public's 'permission to operate'. The less business is perceived to be trustworthy, the more it faces popular pressure to modify its behaviour. It is important to understand that it is this force, leveraged by pressure groups, and not the proverbial 'nanny state', that is driving the demand for regulation of business. This consumer power has also shifted the political debate about industry from production to the impact of production.

The need of business to cope with this force, given the vulnerability of its brand images, is why there has been such a huge growth in the public relations and lobbying industries. In 1999, a UK government report noted that there were three times as many people in Britain employed as public relations consultants as there were coal miners.[23]

In the popular imagination, it is now big multinational corporations rather than national governments that are perceived to wield power. Looked at from inside a corporation, however, the world appears very different. Business finds itself in a much more volatile world, where consumer loyalties are more fickle, and where a corporate reputation can be wrecked in a single afternoon by an unexpected attack from a pressure group making emotional appeals through the mass media.

Business has been hoist with its own petard. For the past thirty to forty years, business leaders have lobbied enthusiastically for the replacement of democratic politics by market mechanisms. In the process, they have unwittingly exchanged coherent opposition for incoherent, predictability for unpredictability, and rationality for emotion.

The traditional analysis is that consumerism has shifted power from governments to corporations. A more plausible explanation for what is going on may be that power has evaporated altogether.

The consequences for the party

The greatest crisis for the Liberal Democrats – and all other political parties – brought about by the social revolution is the catastrophic collapse in party membership. Those who counsel recruitment drives as the solution are missing the point entirely.

To understand what has happened, I need to tell you about my first drink. It was the late 1960s, I would have been about eleven or twelve, and one evening my Granddad took me through the back streets of Lincoln to his local Labour Club, where I was allowed to drink half-pints of shandy while watching the snooker. I was experiencing a now lost world in which the Labour Party was not a discrete political organisation but was woven into the social fabric, with a network of social clubs and union branches providing solidarity, not as a left-wing slogan but as a practical reality. My Granddad was a Labour voter all his life, not from an abstract ideological conviction but because it was the natural thing to do.

Ten miles down the road, my Great Aunt, my Granddad's sister, was a lifelong Conservative member and voter. So far as I know, she never canvassed, delivered leaflets or staffed a committee room. It was simply that in rural Lincolnshire, joining the Conservatives was just something you did, because it was part and parcel of the social fabric of the village.

It was as natural as arranging flowers in the local church or stopping for a chat in the village store.

It is hard to recall this world now. Political parties were once social movements, a genuine expression of people's identities, which in turn were a product of traditional affiliations to social class and settled geographical communities. Parties nowadays have been reduced to a small knot of political hobbyists, declining in number and rising in age, and in the process they have lost much of their democratic legitimacy.

The era of mass-membership political parties is over, because the traditional culture of social solidarity that underpinned it has gone. Most people have disengaged from politics and, to the extent that they engage with the political system at all, their interaction is more analogous to shopping at the supermarket than it is to attending the moot hall.

The social revolution is also calling into question the campaign style of the Liberal Democrats. If people adhere less and less to their geographical communities, either because they move house often or because they have reoriented their lives around non-geographical social networks, then the traditional diet of parochial grievances aired in the party's local *Focus* leaflets will have less traction.

The party needs members and votes. Is it looking in the right place?

Conclusions

Politicians cannot reverse the profound social revolution of the past fifty years. The toothpaste of self-actualisation cannot be put back into the tube.

And anyway, isn't this individualisation what liberals want? Up to a point. Recent experience has shown that people are not really 'free' if society has atomised and they are left isolated and insecure. Genuine liberation is about being ourselves, not being alone. Most of us can flourish as individuals only with the support of others. This is what the 'social' in 'social liberal' should mean.

We need a truly liberal definition of individual freedom. Real liberation is about meeting the innate human need for 'agency', the ability to influence and change the world in which one lives. Power must be devolved so that people may make real and meaningful choices about their lives, not merely consumer choices.

The 'revolution in the head' calls for a radical rethink by Liberal Democrats of their policy and strategy. How can liberal values best be promoted in this new world of the self?

In terms of policy, it is clear that a priority for Liberal Democrats must be to help rebuild the social fabric, the 'glue' that holds us together as human beings. This idea must be promoted in ways that are liberating, not stifling or autocratic.

More astute readers will have noticed the minimal use of the word 'community' in this essay. The omission is deliberate. The word has become so debased as to be stripped of all meaning – 'care in the community', the 'business community', the 'banjo-playing community' and even, dare one say it, 'community politics'. We must stop leaning on this verbal crutch and say what we actually mean.

People tend to lead more fulfilling lives in the company of others, but politicians cannot dictate to people what their social relationships should be. The last thing we need is for government to behave like a Butlin's Redcoat, enforcing state-sanctioned communality. The need for social solidarity must never be interpreted as a licence for bossy people to force others into uncongenial arrangements.

People, left to their own devices, will build social networks and band together for mutual support. Politicians cannot build this social fabric but they can help to foster it. More importantly, they can prevent harm being done to it.

The necessary preventive steps take many forms, but they include an end to our 'cloned' High Streets, the protection of social hubs such as village pubs, and planning decisions that preserve or create spaces where people can naturally gather. A multitude of such small, local initiatives is likely to be more productive than a vain search for a silver bullet.

In terms of ideology, Liberal Democrats must reject economism, the economic reductionism that insists the individual citizen may exercise power only through buying or selling. This ideology corrodes social solidarity by promoting selfish behaviour and subordinating social relationships to the market. Liberals must reassert the view that the things in life that really matter are family, friends, neighbourhoods, the arts, the natural world and the pursuit of intellectual curiosity. The economy is no more than a means to these ends. Material prosperity remains vital but that is not the same thing as instant gratification.

Likewise, in their appetite for public office, Liberal Democrats must resist the temptation to assume that government can replace the complex social network that in practice provides most of our social solidarity. Statist solutions may be well-intentioned but they often do more harm than good by destroying close-knit geographical communities or undermining voluntary work.

In terms of electoral strategy, the Liberal Democrats must make a conscious choice whether to pander to consumerist voters or challenge them. We have seen how politicians have resorted to opinion polls and focus groups in an attempt to satiate popular demands. Unlike the Tories or Labour, the Liberal Democrats cannot afford opinion polls and focus groups but they have adopted a position that is morally equivalent. They practice a form of 'pavement politics' that treats the voters as supplicants and promises to sort out all their problems for them. By default, they have chosen to pander.

This strategy may deliver short-term electoral dividends but ultimately it fails. Trying to 'give them what they want' paradoxically turns off the voters. It causes political parties to converge on some mythical 'middle ground' and makes them seem indistinguishable. Being 'all things to all men' disaffects parties' core support and benefits only the fringe.

Politics is ultimately about making moral choices, so politicians have a duty to offer a moral direction rather than a moral vacuum. It would be healthier for all political parties, not just the Liberal Democrats, to be clear what they stand for and to fight for coherent positions with integrity. It is a myth that people don't like political arguments. Argument is what differentiates parties and provides people with a real choice. What people actually don't like is when all the mainstream parties look and sound the same.

Two recent examples demonstrate this point. Ken Livingstone, the Mayor of London, is one of Britain's least consensual politicians. His signature policy has been the introduction of the congestion charge to central London, a road-pricing policy that attracted much unpopularity and vilification in the press. Despite – or more likely, because of – this, Livingstone has built substantial respect, even from his opponents, to the extent that both the Conservatives and the Liberal Democrats have experienced great difficulty finding a credible candidate prepared to stand against him in 2008.

Or consider the 2007 presidential elections in France. Faced with a real choice, the turnout soared to over 80 per cent. Moreover, the French voters, in choosing Nicolas Sarkozy, elected the less consensual and more robust of the two leading candidates. The cause of low turnouts is obviously not 'apathy'.

The Liberal Democrats' biggest handicap is their fear of causing offence. They would be much better off being true to themselves and not trying to please everyone. Their policies on, for example, Europe or civil liberties are deeply unpopular in some quarters. The party should learn to accept this and recognise that, as the brave stand taken against the Iraq War in 2003 demonstrated, there is more to gain by building support among those who share its values than by trying to appease those who don't.[24]

One cannot attract without also repelling. The social revolution has led most politicians to pander to an imagined 'middle ground' but the party should avoid the temptation to pull its punches. On issues such as pensions or global warming, it must not pander to demands for instant gratification but should insist that deferred pleasure is necessary.

A combination of 'agency' and social solidarity is the best way of combating the demand for instant gratification because, apart from the intrinsic benefits, it confronts people with responsibility for the consequences of their own actions.

What should mark out social liberals from economic liberals is their support for social solidarity. It is only through such solidarity that we can reconcile our demand for individual liberty with a recognition of the value of unselfish behaviour. The problem with the right, on the other hand, was well expressed by the comedian Emo Philips: 'Libertarians believe consenting adults have the right to do whatever they choose except band together.'[25]

But we must not make the mistake of assuming that the answer is for the state to organise our social arrangements for us. Social liberalism should be about fostering social solidarity, not social democracy.

Notes

1   See Ian MacDonald, *Revolution in the Head* (Fourth Estate, London, 2nd edition, 1997), Introduction, pp.1-33. The introductory essay in this book about the Beatles is the best available (if somewhat pessimistic) analysis of how and why the social revolution took place in the 1960s.

2   See Abraham Maslow, *Motivation and Personality* (HarperCollins, New York, 3rd edition, 1987).

3   Barbara Ehrenreich, *Dancing in the Streets* (Granta Books, London, 2007), pp.137-8.

4   See the GfK NOP opinion poll on happiness conducted for the BBC in October 2005 and published online, 2 May 2006 (http://news.bbc.co.uk/1/hi/programmes/happiness_formula/4771908.stm).

5   Robert Putnam, *Bowling Alone* (Simon & Schuster, New York, 2000).

6   For example, see Richard Layard, *Happiness: Lessons From A New Science* (Penguin, London, 2005).

7   Oliver James, *Britain On The Couch* (Century, London, 1997).

8   See PR agency Edelman's annual 'Trust Barometer' (www.edelman.com/trust/2007).

9   John Kampfner, 'Platitudes won't win the election', *Observer* (27 March 2005).

10   Adecco and the Institute of Employment Studies, *Corporate Warming* (Adecco UK, April 2007).

11   See David Smail, *The Nature of Unhappiness* (Constable & Robinson, London, 2001).

12   For a more thorough critique of public choice theory, see David Howarth's chapter elsewhere in this book.

13   Quoted in Linda McQuaig, *All You Can Eat* (Penguin, Toronto, 2001).

14   Robert Hughes skewered this trend brilliantly in *Culture of Complaint* (Oxford University Press, New York, 1993).

15   Al Gore, *The Assault on Reason* (Penguin, New York, 2007), Introduction, p.19.

16   Ibid., p.20.

17   See Norman Ornstein and Thomas Mann (eds.), *The Permanent Campaign and Its Future* (AEI Press, Washington DC, 2000).

18   This tendency was lampooned in the television sitcom, *The Thick Of It* (BBC, 2005-7).

19   John Willett & Ralph Manheim (eds.), *Bertolt Brecht: Poems 1913-1956* (Methuen, London, 1976), 'The Solution', p.440.

20   Jackie Ballard, 'What a politician really thinks about her ungrateful voters', *Independent* (11 June 2001).

21   Interviewed in the television documentary series by Adam Curtis, *The Century of the Self* (BBC, 2002).

22   Fred Hirsch, *Social Limits to Growth* (Routledge & Kegan Paul, London, 1976).

23   Richard Scase, *Britain Towards 2010* (UK Foresight Programme, 1999, at www.foresight.gov.uk), Ch. 3 'Work, employment and occupations', p. 23.

24   For a fuller exposition of this argument, see my chapter 'Roots and wings' in Graham Watson & Simon Titley (eds.), *Liberalism – something to shout about* (Bagehot Publishing, Langport, 2006), pp. 51-62.

25   www.emophilips.com.

Chapter 6

Liberalism and the Search for Meaning

David Boyle

In 1955, the former Liberal MP for Barnstaple, Sir Richard Acland, resigned from his party – he had by then migrated to Labour – over their support for the hydrogen bomb. He lost his seat in the election that year, helped set up CND and became instead a teacher of religious education.[1]

Those were particularly depressing years for RE teachers. It was widely believed by educationalists that children could not, and should not, be taught abstract ideas. In the days before comparative religion and multiculturalism, that reduced the scope of religious education to narrow debates about right and wrong – without reference to religious or moral principles – and a steady diet of unquestioned Bible stories.

The result, for Acland, was his explosive book *We Teach them Wrong.*[2] The problem with this simplistic version of religious truth was that it spread atheism, he said, but not just atheism. The trouble was that it took no account of people's innate religious sense and the religious questions that young people, especially, struggle with. If they were led to believe that religious truth was a simple matter of whether or not Jonah was actually swallowed by a whale, the result – when they came to seek out religious answers for themselves – was just as likely to be some kind of unthinking fundamentalism. If they were led to believe that religion was about whether every mythic story actually happened or not, rather than deeper questions about what lay behind life and the world, then they might reasonably think that fundamentalism and atheism were the only choices.

In the half-century since his resignation, I believe that Acland has been proved to be right. Educational theory accepts that children can learn abstract ideas, but formal education rarely dares tackle them. I know primary school children who asked difficult but fascinating questions about who made the universe – and whether there was any point in anything if the sun was simply going to explode one day – who were told they should consult Askjeeves on the internet to find the answer.

Worse, the prevailing culture encourages this same simplistic understanding of religious truth. If you got all your religious education from the media – and many do – you might be forgiven for thinking that the core issues of Christianity were something to do with a tussle over homosexuality and the literal truth of the Virgin Birth.

Our culture seems increasingly uncomfortable with any kind of truth that isn't unambiguously material. This is Richard Dawkins, for example, complaining about a lecture he attended on the literature of figs, in which the lecturer made the mistake of referring to the Genesis story of Adam and Eve: 'The speaker obviously knew that there never was a Garden of Eden, never a tree of knowledge of good and evil. So what was he actually trying to say?' writes Dawkins:

> I suppose he had a vague feeling that 'somehow', 'if you will', 'at some level', 'in some sense', 'if I may put it this way' it is somehow 'right' that the fruit in the story 'should' have been a fig …'[3]

This knockabout stuff is actually rather puritanical, and therefore dangerous. When people are encouraged to believe that the only things worth saying are scientific – deriding any truth but the literal – they don't just deride symbolic, philosophical, moral or historical discussions. They don't just limit how we can talk about life. Nor do they just bang the drum for atheism, as they believe they intend. They encourage a creeping fundamentalism in all areas. They are lining up behind those who peddle a similar kind of narrow, intolerant religious truth.

Politicians are caught in the same trap. How do they discuss anything about principle, morality, tradition in this climate? The media do not understand it. The language they once used is corroded. Rightly or wrongly, they believe people think it's rather dull stuff, like telephone engineers talking about diodes or doctors talking about intestines. So the BBC obsesses about strategy in its political reporting, or personalities, with barely a nod towards the real stuff of politics that lies beneath it. It's just too 'religious'.

Of course not all discussion of values has to be religious, but the danger is that – such is the emerging animus towards religion, and such is the underlying utilitarianism of our political culture – that any statements about belief that are not utilitarian, including what we believe about right and wrong, are being similarly sidelined. This has brought with it something of a crisis of values inside the forces of liberalism. Liberals are often at the forefront of those who are turning away from religious language and tradition in reaction against the rise of intolerant fundamentalism, and against the terrorism, the violent placards outside theatres, and the religious automatons with their texts – Christian and Muslim – we encounter in the street or in the newspapers.

It has become increasingly de rigueur on the political left to lump religious attitudes and traditions together on the other side. To talk about the 'problem' of religion in Us and Them language, taking the side of tolerant secularism versus intolerant religious bigotry. On both sides of the Atlantic, there is the rumbling sound of the secular left girding themselves to hold back the tide of resurgent religion, forgetting just how deep religious attitudes go in most people – 77 per cent in the UK describe themselves as 'religious' – and blinding themselves to the inhumanity of secular corporatism. As if the only choice, as Benjamin Barber puts in, was between Jihad and McWorld.[4]

You can see why, of course. George Bush's version of religion is hypocritical at best and abhorrent at worst. But this narrow version of the politics of religion fails to understand the roots of religion in our civilisation and our political traditions. Nor does it recognise the way that both Jihad and McWorld – both Bush and bin Laden – are each fuelled by the other. In the rest of this chapter I am going to argue that social liberalism has deep and important ideological roots in religious faith, that faith is an integral part of many people's liberalism, and that taking a more sophisticated stance on the problem of religious faith is vital for political success.

Liberalism's religious roots

The social liberal tradition in Britain borrows from a range of philosophical positions, but it draws on three political traditions in particular. It draws on eighteenth-century romanticism, which may not be conventionally religious but carries within it the seeds of belief, certainly of awe, in creation and creator. It also draws on radical utilitarianism, the technocratic flowering of radical politics in the early nineteenth century. Out of that mix, between the liberalism of Jefferson and the liberalism of Bentham, emerged a political force which has dominated two centuries, forged together with the third tradition in Britain: religious nonconformity, the heirs of the revolutionary idealists of the seventeenth century. Those three elements went together to underpin the philosophical underpinnings of modern social liberalism. All three elements are obvious even on the Liberal Democrat benches in the modern House of Commons.

The agnostic radicals and the religious nonconformists have worked side by side ever since, but the Nonconformist tradition runs deep in the Liberal tradition in the UK, and is inseparable from the rest. Modern secularism suggests that religious teaching is bound to be intolerant, and there is no doubt that the worst of it is precisely that. Yet far from being a source of political intolerance, which had to be balanced by radicalism, it was Nonconformity which underpinned liberal tolerance, and in some ways, still does. The former nun Karen Armstrong points out that, two generations ago, religious nonconformity was on the side of the left.[5] In the Liberal Democrats, it still is.

It is a tolerance that believes people's conscience, and therefore their freedom to act, is sacrosanct – limited as always by the philosophy of John Stuart Mill. But it is also based on a very distinctive theology, not exclusively Christian but drawing primarily on the New Testament: that creation underpins human freedom, that God designed human freedom, and that Christ's teaching implies that human freedom is vital in God's creation. As a Liberal myself, I derive a great deal of my inspiration from the deliberate tolerance advocated in the Gospels: towards unbelievers, sinners, racial minorities – but also towards humanity itself. There is no implication that people should be forced by the state, or anyone else, to lead a properly religious life: quite the reverse. Those who imply anything of the kind are roundly condemned.

Nobody who has read the Bible closely could fail to stumble over the bloodthirsty cruelties that are described, especially in parts of the Old Testament. But there is a clear thrust towards tolerance in the Gospels which has inspired people politically, and continues to do so. It might not be the only inspiration that drives people towards political liberalism, but it undoubtedly has done so in the past and it almost certainly still does.

If we assume, as the left is beginning to do, that Liberals are now emphatically on the side of secularism – buying the story that cruelties are primarily religious affairs in human history – we risk losing half our tradition and many of our allies. We also risk losing some of the insights in the Liberal tradition that derive partly from faith. I am not, of course, arguing that Liberalism is a predominantly religious creed. It clearly isn't. I am saying that it needs to accept the religious aspects of its own intellectual heritage, and in three areas in particular.

The sense that there is something beyond the bottom line

It is widely recognised that economic growth, as expressed by GDP, is not a very good measure of national progress. GDP is not actually a measure of standard of living; it is a measure of the amount of work going through the economy, and those are very different things. Maybe all the money is being exchanged cleaning up pollution or oil spillages, or solving murders, or chopping down trees to make into paper cartons for fast-food purveyors. GDP is then higher, but life is certainly no 'richer' – yet governments for half a century have mortgaged themselves to this misleading measure, just as they are now forcing local services to conform to a whole range of other misleading targets.

The present Labour government, which must be the most utilitarian since the embalming of Jeremy Bentham, has been gripped by a perversion of this reductionist bottom-line mentality, which you might call the 'McKinsey fallacy'. The government's management consultants of choice, McKinsey, have a slogan which claims that 'everything can be counted, and what can be counted can be managed'.

This is wholly inaccurate. The truth is that everything that is most important – health, education, love, humanity – can't be measured, so what is less important (disease, exam results, late trains, etc.) gets managed. Because it is so hard to measure what is really important, governments and institutions have to pin down something else, which means that all their resources get focused on achieving something they never quite intended.

What distinguishes social liberals from either Fabian socialists or conservatives is this scepticism about the bottom line, whether it is money or some other metric. But it is a scepticism that also derives partly from the religious aspect of the Liberal tradition, which insists on a more holistic understanding of human beings. It is an understanding of humanity that recognises that individuals break out of any kind of numerical definition, just as this understanding of the uniqueness of individuals underpins the Liberal approach to human rights.

Liberals depart from Fabians and conservatives because they do not believe individuals are disposable: they see beyond the demands of the market and the state. But the principle that we protect each individual for their own sake, not just because it happens to be better for the greatest number, is a principle derived primarily from a religious understanding of the world. Not just from a religious understanding, but that is one of the strands in Liberalism that gave us this belief – and it is a belief that can be debated between religious and non-religious alike.

The sense that people have something unique to offer in their ordinary lives

Liberals believe that people are not just important for moral reasons, but for practical ones, because every individual is also a resource which society needs.

Since socialism has departed from the scene as a coherent political philosophy, we are left with the competing understandings of conservatism and liberalism when we look at society around us. Do we see something basically fearsome, the corroding result of a feckless working class, as gut conservatives do? Or an undiscriminating market for consumer products, like the market conservatives? Or do we see people, not as the tentacles of a vast engine, but as people who – often in difficult circumstances – are bringing up families, or living in relationship or neighbourhoods, with love and generosity and resourcefulness?

People are resources because of the potential that education can help them reach. But they are also important – and here Liberalism diverges from New Labour in practice – for what they do in their ordinary lives. Where Whitehall under the Blair government regards people's ordinary lives with suspicion and some disdain, Liberalism sees the millions of small efforts that happen below the political radar every day; not just formal volunteering or mentoring, helping out in schools, making tea for patients in casualty, but in vital ways like bringing up children. They regard the endeavour of ordinary living as unique, vital, wonderful and creative. Yet that insight is missing in public policy, leading to arrogant, inhuman institutions, often cloaking their fundamental inflexibility with the rhetoric of choice.

The sense that the people and communities make things possible

The option of collective action is a vital check on an over-mighty, an over-interfering or an incompetent state. Voluntary collective action has been a lynchpin of Liberalism since its beginnings. Again, this has theological roots, though it clearly comes from other ideological positions as well: there is an assumption at the heart of most faiths that a spiritual life should include active involvement in the world.

The idea of 'active citizenship' has now gripped the ideologues of all parties, though there was a time when Conservatives doubted whether anything done outside the market was worth doing, and socialists felt the same way about the state. Back in 1972, the Labour chair of Lewisham's housing committee – who had forced through London's first self-build scheme against the fervent opposition of his colleagues – complained that they seemed to believe that, if something was worth doing, it was worth the council doing it *for* people.[6] Liberals have warned against this Fabian view throughout the twentieth century. Liberalism rejects the technocratic approach to housing, which assumes tenants ought to be grateful, passive recipients of services, is sceptical about giving tenants a say, and downright dismissive about their needs for community, self-help, green space, privacy or any of those other aspects of modern life that modernism rejected.

When Lord Beveridge had finished his famous report, he wrote two more which had not been commissioned by the government. The third emphasised his argument that the new NHS should not unravel the existing voluntary structures that had been created to provide health care.[7] Unfortunately, his pleas were not heard by the Attlee government. Nor, despite their rhetoric, are they well understood by contemporary Labour governments, which – like other recent incumbents – are suspicious in practice of people's ability to act independently.

None of these are exclusively spiritual insights, but they have at their heart something which is also a spiritual truth, even if it is not a specific religious truth: that the value of individual human beings goes beyond money, statistics, institutions, existing mores and bias, and beyond their utilitarian value to the state or the collective. It is a spiritual truth and a human truth as well: that people break out of systems, and that is a hopeful and not a frustrating reality.

'What lies hidden behind all the figures by way of genuine, personal, human experience?' asked the great liberal dissident Vaclav Havel in 1975, challenging the penchant of Czechoslovakia's communist regime for similarly utilitarian statistics:

> Supposing we ask, for example, what has been done for the moral and spiritual revival of society, for the enhancement of the truly human dimensions of life, for the elevation of man to a higher degree of dignity, for his truly free and authentic assertion in this world?[8]

That is a recognisably Liberal question, but it is based on a belief that a moral and spiritual revival – whatever is meant by that – is possible and worth struggling for. It is not a meaningful ambition for Fabians or market conservatives, or for anyone who subsumes human beings to the demands of the market or state. It is not uniquely derived from a spiritual understanding – you could imagine a modern humanist expressing that kind of ambition in related terms – but there is no doubt that its roots also lie in a Liberal view of religious faith.

Liberalism is a complex animal. It gave birth to utilitarianism, which tends to be corrosive of many of these values once it is divorced from its Liberal roots. It gave birth also to modernism, just as it gave rise to economism, and both of these philosophies played a role in overthrowing the status quo of previous generations. The growth of liberal economics over the centuries has devastated ecclesiastical and aristocratic privilege alike – money has that effect. But that does not mean that the mercantile traditions that make up modern Liberalism can be reduced to an interest in money alone.

Both modernism and economism turned out to be dead ends. Modernism tried to reduce people to machines; economism tried to reduce them to money values. Both attempt to invent a new streamlined kind of human that is easy to measure and easy to control. Both are themselves a kind of faith, but in the end both reject the central pillars of the humanistic tradition: that human beings are individuals, awkwardly difficult to categorise or cajole. This is humanism of a particular kind:

the humanism of Erasmus and More, rather than that of Dawkins. It is a humanism that does not deny that humans have spiritual needs, and it is humanism which carries a critique of the status quo.

Modern liberalism rejects both modernism and economism and it does so on the basis of its own faith: that there is no measuring system that can sum up human beings; that there is no political system that can control them. That only when you allow people the imagination and skill to solve the problems that confront them does humanity move forward. That need not be a religious faith, but it is a belief nonetheless, and it derives from a religious dogma that was originally theological, recognising – as it does – that there is an element of the divine in all people, whatever their class, race or creed. One of the characteristics of good religion – and by good religion, I mean any religion that derives from more than simply authoritative texts – is that it shares this insight.

None of those three insights listed above derive exclusively from the faith traditions that went to make up modern Liberalism: both British Nonconformity (and its scepticism about power) and Catholic social doctrine (and its scepticism about centralisation). But they all imply a sceptical approach to the world as it is, a refusal to accept measures of power or wealth as they claim to be. They all demand a different bottom line to measure institutions, beyond value for money. These are ways of seeing the world that are as much Platonic as Christian, but they are a theological understanding that the real value in human beings goes beyond the conventional worldly measures of class, income or normality. Out of this mix comes the Liberal Democrat belief that 'no one shall be enslaved by poverty, ignorance and conformity.'[9]

Liberalism's religious challenge

I have argued that religious belief has traditionally brought people to Liberalism, and that faith remains a vital part of many people's Liberalism. The danger, if social liberalism forgets these aspects of its past and turns its back on all religion, is that we lose the sources of this inspiration. We also risk losing that scepticism in Liberalism, leaving it as a technocratic and utilitarian philosophy of measurement, without secure intellectual links to the original reasons for tolerance.

But anyone who argues against the secularisation of Liberalism clearly has to face up to the threat that aspects of religion now pose to

Liberalism around the world – the intolerant creeds, derived from fundamentalist adherence to absolute scriptures, narrow interpretations of religious truth, condemnatory and violent. We can see the results of the rise of this kind of religion, not just in Islamic terrorism but in Christian fundamentalism in America. We can see it in the threats to freedom of expression and emerging intolerance to sexual freedom, feminism and religious tolerance, as religious questions – whether people can wear crosses or cover their faces at work or in school. We can see it, also, in the challenge to liberal values based on interpretations of authoritative texts rather than on liberal principle or scientific reality.

In those circumstances, should Liberalism retreat into secularism to defend itself? I don't believe so, and for the following reasons:

Not all religion is intolerant: No sane person can deny the influence of religion behind some of the fiercest conflicts in the world, but nor can they deny the pivotal role played by liberal Anglicans in the defeat of apartheid or liberal Catholics in the liberation theology of Latin America, just as they could not deny the impact of liberal Protestants campaigning against slavery two centuries ago. Yet blanket secularism disempowers the tolerant creeds – and tolerant religious people – by treating them as if they were bigoted fundamentalist sects. It assumes that religious people will be intolerant by definition and plays, therefore, into the hands of the fundamentalists.

Not all religion is fundamentalist: It would be a terrible error to treat everyone adhering to any religious faith as if they were simplistic believers in literal and authoritative religious texts, when many – if not most – ordinary religious people are not: 77 per cent of Britons describe themselves as religious. To lump them together with the fundamentalists would be to abandon the kind of questioning, sceptical and spiritual religion that many people in this country believe in.

Religious questioning is a basic human need: The latest research suggests that religious needs, questions and experience are universal human phenomena, and concern people with no formal religious belief.[10] But if that is the case, to collude with fundamentalists – accepting their point of view that all religion is intolerant, slavish and unquestioning – can only encourage fundamentalism. Richard Acland was right. On the contrary, Liberalism should accept that people have spiritual needs and questions – whatever they actually believe about them – and that this is reasonable, human and tolerant in itself, and not something that should be excised from our institutions in the name of secular purity.

What that means for policy

This chapter is partly an argument that the heart of Liberalism – a refusal to accept the measurement of the world on its own terms – is an insight that derives as much from the theological roots of Liberalism as it does from its secular roots. But it is also an argument that social liberalism needs to build on those theological roots if it is ever going to meet the demand for a non-technocratic politics that accepts this insight.

The past century in Britain has been dominated by technocratic political parties with very different beliefs about human beings at their core. It is hardly surprising that the political mainstream has migrated to other issues – the role of the state, public spending, class issues and similar – which Liberalism was not designed primarily to address. Yet in an increasing minority of the population, there are new issues that appear initially to be on the fringes of mainstream politics, but which are very central to the Liberal traditions I describe above. The importance of local institutions, the right to health, not just health care, the threat of giantism and inhuman technocratic systems, public and private: all these are core issues for social liberalism, and their re-emergence in mainstream debate implies that we need to start developing policies that address them directly. These are likely to include:

- *New bottom lines*: GDP is not an accurate way of measuring national success, any more than the target regime is an effective way of moulding public services. Both have to go, to be replaced with broader and more human measures of well-being, health and mental health, and these must be embedded in our institutions.
- *New kinds of radical decentralisation*: not just to local democratic bodies, but to professionals – recognising the central importance of the 'People Principle' to making things happen: *if you employ imaginative and effective people at local level and give them the freedom to innovate, they will succeed – no matter what the programme. If you don't, they will fail, no matter what the programme.*
- *Investment in co-production*: public services need systems that can measure and reward the efforts that people are making to help broaden and deepen the services provided locally. That means

a shift in training for frontline staff so that they become enablers rather than gatekeepers, who can see the abilities of those before them rather than just their needs. It means transforming public service institutions into local engines of regeneration and community renewal.

- *Investment in human scale*: breaking down the monster hospitals, schools and training systems, so that relationships between client and professional are possible again, because this is the only force that is capable of making change happen.
- *Commitment to anti-trust*: a return to the ferocious approach to business monopoly that used to be at the heart of every Liberal programme, recognising that modern business monopolies undermine choice, wreck legitimate businesses and suppliers, impoverish local economies and reduce us to supplicants.
- *Reviving the voluntary sector*: the biggest 1.6 per cent of charities now hoover up two-thirds of all the charitable income in the UK. Increasingly delivering public services on behalf of the public sector, they are constrained and co-opted in similar ways by Whitehall targets. We need new financial instruments that are capable of delivering sustained and independent funding for the voluntary sector.

But it also means developing policies to deal with the threat from fundamentalism, and to do so in such a way that we support peaceful and liberal religious questioning, rather than pretending such a thing is impossible. Liberalism needs to reclaim its core commitment to freedom of expression, and all the other freedoms. But it also needs restating more precisely, to distinguish the political creed of social liberalism from the prevailing mainstream, which is liberal by default. We believe in the central and creative importance of human freedom, but this is freedom, not for its own sake, but for a purpose. Social liberals have found themselves tempted to allow the props of a healthy society to erode as well, forgetting how social networks, social institutions and family life underpin human happiness. Liberal freedom is freedom to achieve human well-being, but more than that: in the words of Vaclav Havel, it is for 'the moral and spiritual revival of society'.

We also need policies that recognise people's spiritual needs and take them seriously. For that reason, I am not one of those Liberals who believe that faith schools are somehow incompatible with Liberalism. Of course, children should not be educated in isolation from people different from them, but federated groups of schools – so that Muslim, Anglican and secular schools would be encouraged to share resources or specialist staff – would solve that problem without abolishing the whole idea of a spiritual basis to education.

As their opponents point out, the educational results of faith schools are no better than those of their secular counterparts. It is patronising, therefore, to condemn all those who want their children to go to one as social climbers, just as it fails to understand what the demand for faith schooling means. It is widely acknowledged that faith schools are also popular, rightly or wrongly, with parents of no religious faith. A sizeable minority in the UK, many of them avowedly liberal – and often *because* they are – look to faith schools because they want their children to have some belief in values beyond those of the world as it is, some spiritual dimension to their education, some civilised rooting which has depth and history.

They may be wrong that secular schools are incapable of providing this. But they are right to look at some of the soulless technocratic teaching that pupils are sometimes offered with great suspicion (comprehension tests but never the whole story, bans on music or art in the year before SATS, narrow religious education without theological or moral roots). The point is that the undeniable demand for religious education from people who might have little conventional faith themselves is as much a critique of secular schooling as it is any kind of enthusiasm for organised religion.

They look at state, and increasingly at independent education as well, despite the obvious commitment of so many teachers, and see a system which needs an injection of meaning. They see an infrastructure that provides no anchoring culture, no means for navigating and understanding the moral universe, no core values and a consequent vacuum that is easily filled by consumerism and the products of mass marketing. The fear of that emptiness at the heart of culture is not just a reasonable one, it is also a Liberal one, and progressive politicians ignore it at their peril.

None of this should imply that faith schools need no reform. They require the kind of federation with other local schools that the Liberal Democrat administration in Somerset is currently organising, so that pupils automatically find themselves mixing with a wider group of pupils of other faiths and of none. The whole basis of education must be the encouragement of self-exploration and questioning about the world, and the least society can expect from faith schools is that they provide this – and admit enough pupils from other faiths to make it possible. The problem is not that faith schools are uniquely incapable of encouraging this kind of questioning but that technocratic teaching systems, factory schools and an obsession with examinations all collude to make this difficult. In many ways, a religious faith can and should mean more questioning, not just about spiritual issues but about the way the world is. A blanket condemnation of all faith schools obscures this central issue, and simply closing them without addressing this basic need is illiberal and counter-productive.

What this means for religion

There is another reason why Liberals should avoid positioning themselves as a wholly secular philosophy. Because although many people who are attracted to Liberal politics are not religious, many are also searching for some kind of spiritual understanding. In the United States, it is widely argued that the Democrats have been making a mistake by aligning themselves wholly with secular modernity, and driving those who are sceptical about it into the arms of the so-called 'theo-cons'.[11]

The figures for those who still struggle with spirituality in the UK, rather than just those who go regularly to church, suggest that these 'theo-cons' are exploiting a real human need which progressives dismiss at their peril. It is a need that many, both rich and poor, face at some point in their lives, and described in the United States by Rabbi Michael Lerner as a 'crisis of meaning'.[12]

They want their lives to be about more than just money and material security. They search for a language in which to express this politically, finding it often in green campaigns or similar. Yet the more they search for that language in politics, the more the progressive forces concentrate on material security and suppress anything remotely spiritual, for fear that it is represents a kind of conservatism in disguise. 'It is imperative that liberal and progressive forces develop an understanding of this spiritual crisis, and a progressive politics of Meaning to counter the right-wing politics of Meaning,' wrote Lerner. That is a North American interpretation, but it is relevant here too.

Part of the problem is the mistaken assumption by the secular left that religious belief is different from any other kind of belief – that religious people believe what they do wholly because of the authority of scriptures which are closed to outsiders. In fact, most people derive their religious beliefs in much the same way as they do everything else they believe: a tension between experience, conscience and tradition. 'I am suspicious of any religion that doesn't involve the mind,' said Michael Ramsey, then Archbishop of Canterbury, and he was right: we should be. But to claim that nobody with religious beliefs can discuss them with outsiders, or check them against their own conscience – that they have no freedom of thought beyond the self-referential claims of scripture – means agreeing with the fundamentalists about the nature of religion. And – as Liberals – we must not do that.

We may face a threat from religious bigotry, but we will not win the struggle against it by withdrawing from the field and defending everything about modern technocracy, which is quite as corrosive of life and liberty as Bush's religious conservatism. We must not yield any part of the argument to the fundamentalists, and especially not their claims about the nature of religion. In political terms, Liberals need to claim their right to be religious, just as much as the conservatives and the fundamentalists, and to interpret what that means according to their Liberal conscience. Religious conservatives do not have a monopoly of spirituality, and we should not let them appear to.

Of course, there is a danger for Liberals here. We live in a period when Liberalism is wary of making judgements about other people's beliefs, despite the fact that we judge other people's political beliefs every day. To win this struggle, we are going to have to start judging religious belief in the same way as politics, because – as Cardinal Manning once said – every political issue has a theological disagreement behind it. The alternative is to abandon the battlefield to those who have real political ambitions which are the opposite of our own. We are going to have to rediscover a sense, which our predecessor Liberals were born with, of what is good religion and what is bad, and to stake out that definition for the future.

It is not the job of politicians to *define* Bad Religion. But we can still recognise it from some tell-tale signs:

- Intolerance against minorities, condemned in all mainstream religious traditions;

- Intolerance towards non-believers and those of other faiths;
- A tendency to embrace violence and a worrying enthusiasm for the end of the world;
- Over-reliance on a literal interpretation of scripture that obscures its deeper meaning, allowing peculiar, exclusive and intolerant interpretations that are alien to all mainstream religious traditions;
- A superstitious and selfish belief that human suffering can be bypassed, and all kinds of minor whims granted, only to true believers – again alien to all mainstream religious traditions.

Good Religion is not definable either but it clearly involves love, caring for others, gratitude, generosity and – far from being wish-fulfilling of minor material wants – it tends to involve some kind of self-denial. It also balances divine revelation from religious texts with the insights of tradition, conscience and also something beyond either. It is also open to the insights of other religious traditions, and there is a long tradition of the influence the holy men of one religion have had on those of others.

The language of Us and Them, which is used so often by progressive politicians about the religious world, is tantamount to backing ourselves into a corner of secular unbelief. It threatens to hand the fundamentalists a monopoly of spiritual values. Liberals should reserve the right to be a spiritual force themselves and to start recognising and addressing the need for meaning among their potential supporters in the electorate, and to distinguish, not so much between religious and secular values, but between good and bad religion.

I am a Liberal Democrat, but I do not regard myself as being on the side of secular technocracy, the force that regards human beings as endlessly expendable machines. I do not regard myself as being on the same side as corporate identikit culture, of Murdoch-style cultural mush or rootless modernity. Nor do I see this as any contradiction. Liberalism has its roots in spiritual insights and Liberals should never abandon the debate about spirituality, the idea that there is a reality beyond the world – whether that is formally religious or not – to political creeds that are inimical to everything Liberalism stands for.

Notes

1 I met Sir Richard Acland shortly before he died, while I was still at school, and he had an enormous influence on me.

2 R. Acland, *We Teach Them Wrong: Religion and the Young* (Gollancz, London, 1963).

3   R. Dawkins, *Climbing Mount Improbable* (Penguin, London, 2005), p. 1.
4   B. R. Barber, *Jihad Versus McWorld: How the Planet Is Both Falling Apart and Coming Together and What This Means for Democracy* (Random House, New York, 1995).
5   K. Armstrong, *The Battle for God: Fundamentalism in Judaism, Christianity and Islam* (HarperCollins, London, 2000).
6   N. Taylor, *The Village in the City* (New Society, London, 1973).
7   W. H. Beveridge, *Voluntary Action: A Report on Social Advance* (George Allen & Unwin, London, 1948).
8   Jan Vladislav (ed.), *Living in Truth: Twenty-two Essays Published on the Occasion of the Award of the Erasmus Prize to Vaclav Havel* (Faber, London, 1989).
9   From the Preamble of the federal constitution of the Liberal Democrats.
10 See for example D. Hay, *Something There: The Biology of the Human Spirit* (Darton, Longman & Todd, London, 2006).
11 J. Wallis, *God's Politics: Why the American Right Gets It Wrong and the Left Doesn't Get It* (HarperOne, New York, 2004).
12 M. Lerner, *The Left Hand of God: Taking Back our Country from the Religious Right* (HarperSan Francisco, New York, 2006).

Chapter 7

Rights and Responsibilities

Elspeth Attwooll

The 'rights and responsibilities' debate has been a consistent one for decades in political disputes over the role of the state in the UK. However, it has become particularly central in a number of policy areas over the last ten years because of its importance to the rebranding of Labour as 'New Labour'.

Aware that Labour had come to be seen as on the side of the criminal rather the victim, or the 'scrounger' rather than 'hardworking families', Tony Blair used the rights and responsibilities theme in successive speeches before becoming Prime Minister.[1] It has since been deployed by successive ministers who have argued that rights are contingent on the appropriate exercise of responsibilities. For example, as Home Secretary, David Blunkett applied it to the issue of citizenship.[2] The same line regarding citizenship has been taken recently by Jack Straw.[3] It has also been applied to welfare reform, for example in the area of unemployment benefits,[4] and on many other issues.

From an early stage, liberals have seen this approach as problematic. Commenting on a speech by Blair made in Amsterdam early in 1997, Conrad Russell argued that the premise that rights come with responsibilities was 'unexceptionable' and fell into the 'motherhood and apple pie' category. However, he pointed out that there were some highly problematic questions which were 'being smuggled through underneath the baby's mattress', arguing that there was a continued responsibility on society to be responsible for those who acted irresponsibly.[5]

Such rejections of New Labour's rights and responsibilities have been the trend within the Liberal Democrats – yet there have been efforts to move into similar ground, through *The Orange Book: Reclaiming Liberalism*[6] and its successor *Britain after Blair: A Liberal Agenda.*[7] For example, in his introduction to *The Orange Book,* Paul Marshall writes:

The notion of responsibility has arguably been neglected in a Liberal tradition so closely associated with the struggle for individual rights. But the two go together. A society of responsibilities without rights is reminiscent of the post-feudal order against which the early Liberals were reacting. A society of rights without responsibilities leads eventually to ... civic disaggregation ....[8]

Though I am far from disagreeing with his next point – that there is a balance that needs 'to be found in a mutual reciprocity between individual and society' – this chapter maintains that the balance should not be explained in terms of rights and responsibilities. More widely, it argues that, whilst there are many thought-provoking ideas in both books, some of the ideas contained in them on rights and responsibilities are based on mistaken understandings and do not provide a suitably liberal agenda for the twenty-first century.

Such a liberal agenda involves setting the conditions under which all individuals are enabled to maximise their own potential, in a manner compatible with that of others to do the same. To this end, principles of political, economic and social liberalism have to be combined so as to achieve this purpose with what the American jurist, Roscoe Pound, called 'the minimum of friction and waste'.[9]

Why talking about rights and responsibilities misses the mark

First of all, rights and responsibilities are not really on a par with one another. Rights are properly the creatures of rules. In most contexts these rules are legal ones, although we do sometimes think of rights as flowing from other well-developed social norms. For rights are found where it has been accepted that certain claims people have are strongly justified and that they should be made secure through the operation of political and legal structures.

Indeed, there is an argument to be had as to whether anyone can be said to have a right if it is not actually secured to him or her. In consequence, some would take the view (although I do not) that human rights, in certain parts of the world, are not really rights at all, since there is no way in which the duty to respect them can be enforced. The same applies, in many places, to certain social rights – such as the right to a decent house – because, even where there are organisations charged with their provision, there is no guarantee of actual supply as far as any particular individual is concerned.

Looked at in this way, what rights correspond with are duties – and possibly only with clearly located and/or enforceable duties. The real debate, then, should be about the competition between claims and responsibilities: which of these should achieve the status of rights and duties and for whom.

The nature of claims and responsibilities

Claims and responsibilities are alike in many ways. First, they are social concepts. Having a claim is different from simply experiencing a desire, because it must be regarded by other people as something they ought to accommodate. For example, I may have a desire to regale a peacefully reading stranger on a train with the highlights of my summer holiday or photos of my latest grandchild but I do not have a claim to do so. Similarly, others may regard me as having responsibilities without my experiencing any feeling for them.

Second, as social concepts, claims and responsibilities are – or at least can be – vague as to their content, their 'ownership' and the means of fulfilling them. This means that they may not always be matched with one another. It is possible to have a claim without anyone having a clear responsibility to meet it. For example, it is widely accepted that everyone has a claim to reproduce but, short of the reaching of certain specific agreements, there is no one with whom the responsibility for providing the egg or sperm needed for them to do so actually rests.

Equally, it is possible to have a responsibility without any clearly identified person or group to whom it is actually owed. So, while it is generally accepted that we have a responsibility to protect the environment, this is usually couched in terms of the world population in general, both present and future.

Third, both claims and responsibilities can take various forms. Claims may simply be to be left unhindered, whether by the actions of other people or by rules. An example is that to walk from one place to another, whether in the course of window-shopping, rambling or as part of a protest march. Claims of this kind we think of as liberties.

Or they may be to do or achieve something, such as to cast a vote at elections or to find a job. These can be described as opportunities, and may require the active support of other people. Finally, claims may be to receive something – for example, treatment when ill or the return of a debt – and in such cases there is always an onus on someone else to act. Claims like these may be thought of as benefits.

Responsibilities fall into similar groups. There are those to refrain from interfering with others, so respecting their liberties. One such responsibility is to afford them privacy by not reading their correspondence unless invited to do so. Then there are those to provide people with opportunities, such as that to have input into shared activities, if only on the level of 'what should we have to eat tonight?' Finally, there are – at least in the case of those nearest to us – responsibilities to provide necessities and, where we can, tokens of affection over and above these.

It is obvious that there can be conflicts between the claims individuals have, on the one hand, and their responsibilities, on the other. For example, the claim I have to benefit from the fruits of my own labour competes with the responsibility I have toward supporting others, whether fulfilled through voluntary giving or the payment of taxes.

But we can also find many examples of conflicts that occur within the various sets of claims or responsibilities that belong to us. The set of responsibilities attaching to companies provides a useful illustration. It can be said that these are owed to their shareholders, to their suppliers, to the consumers of their goods or services, to their workforce and to the wider social world. In so far as their responsibility to their shareholders is conceived exclusively (or even primarily) in terms of making a profit, then this could be fulfilled – in the short term at least – in a manner detrimental to all the other concerns. So there is a need for some kind of balance to be struck.

What is significant about claims and responsibilities is that such conflicts are resolved through a weighing up of their strength and importance. The strength has to do with the closeness of the relationship between those holding the responsibility and those to whom some liberty, opportunity or benefit might attach. Rightly or wrongly, we consider the responsibility to feed our own families to be far stronger than that to prevent starvation elsewhere, although we may be moved to cut down on certain luxuries to contribute to a famine appeal.

The importance has more to do with the moral or political value attached to the achieving of a particular social good. We no longer dispute the need for safe working conditions and, within certain parameters, they have become accepted as a greater social good than profitability. To this extent, companies' responsibility to their workforce is currently regarded as overriding that to their shareholders.

This brings us to the fourth and final point about claims and responsibilities – that they are relatively free flowing. The strength and importance accorded to them may vary over time and from one part of a society to another. Conflicts between them are usually resolved on an ad hoc basis. Consequently, if any of them are extinguished, it is normally only as a result of a long process of erosion. Even now, for example, we have not fully resolved the conflict between the claims of parents to discipline their children and the claims of children not to have physical harm inflicted upon them.

How rights differ from claims and duties differ from responsibilities

Rights and duties are, like claims and responsibilities, social concepts. But they differ in a number of respects. Rights and duties, in the strict sense at least, always correspond with one another. The players are clearly identified and the expectation is that relationships between them will be conducted according to certain rules. The content is more or less clearly defined.

Further, whilst conflicts of claims and responsibilities are ongoing and, as already indicated, resolved, if at all, largely on an ad hoc basis, and according to an immediate assessment of their weight and importance, conflicts of rights and duties are seen as a 'design fault'. Any resolution is intended to be permanent and is usually effected by reducing the scope of one or the other.

Similarly, whilst the contents of claims and responsibilities are relatively free flowing, those of rights and duties are crystallised at a given time. Many political campaigns are directed toward raising awareness of a mismatch between them. A clear contemporary example of this relates to the environment, where there is increasing acceptance – particularly in the light of climate change – that our duties fall short of our responsibilities.

Where such campaigns are successful, debate will then centre on the means of ensuring that the claims or responsibilities concerned are fulfilled. It may be regarded as appropriate to leave matters to social pressure (perhaps through market mechanisms) or by developing soft laws, such as codes of practice. Alternatively, it may be felt necessary to bring about changes to the current set of formal rights and duties.

One recent discussion illustrative of this concerns corporate social responsibility (CSR). Is it enough to promote the business case for CSR or should observance of the OECD guidelines for multinational enterprises become compulsory, and/or 'triple bottom line' accounting be introduced, with a requirement for social and environmental reports to produced in addition to financial ones? Currently, however, the extent to which companies involve themselves in CSR remains largely a matter of commercial judgement, whereas conformity with minimum health and safety standards offers no such option.

The conversion of claims and responsibilities into rights and duties is usually the result of a desire of those in political power to bring some of them into greater prominence. This may be as part of a mandate to implement a particular programme, in reaction to a perceived emergency or in order to cultivate popular opinion. Of course, these pressures can equally lead to the downgrading of certain claims or responsibilities, with a consequent loss of rights or decrease in duties.

Recent measures taken to counter the threat of terrorism provide a stark reminder of the former. As an aside, it may be remarked that, traditionally, the doctrine of the sovereignty of the Westminster Parliament means that our liberties always remain at the level of claims – being simply the area where the law has not yet intervened to restrict our behaviour. Since the incorporation of the European Convention on Human Rights into our domestic law, this perception should have changed. The present government, however, seems to have some difficulty in making the necessary adjustment.

The upshot
Talk about rights and responsibilities, then, deals with concepts of a different kind and ones that cannot properly be matched with one another. A further reason for abandoning this approach is that it puts a kind of straitjacket on discussion. This is because the means of fulfilling claims and responsibilities is not always through the creation of rights and duties in the strict sense.

For example, the means of addressing certain opportunity and benefit claims may simply be by way of empowering or assisting some body or
organisation to fulfil them, rather than placing them under an obligation
to do so. One need think only of the importance of the role played by the
voluntary sector and of the problems that arise where this is inadequately
funded.

Similarly, some claims may be addressed indirectly, by establishing
the conditions under which it is believed that the claim can be fulfilled
without further intervention. Thus, offering different types and levels of
education and training is seen as a key factor in the claim an individual
has to maximise his or her own potential in the world of work. Yet, at
the same time, this claim may need further protection, as evidenced by
recent legislation – largely generated by action at EU level – preventing
discrimination on grounds such as gender, sexual orientation, ethnicity,
age and disability.

In short, establishing rights and duties is one route, but by no means
the only route, toward the fulfilment of claims and responsibilities.

Would a debate about claims and responsibilities, then, be more helpful to Liberal Democrats?

The answer to this question must be a firm no, unless it is set in a wider
context. For a debate that is directly about claims and responsibilities is
likely to prioritise either the one or the other.

I argued earlier that claims are social concepts, in the sense that they
must be widely regarded as something that ought to be accommodated.
Even so, they focus on the freedoms, opportunities and benefits that
individuals or groups may desire or demand for themselves.

This gives rise to a competitive social model which, at its worst, is
a kind of free-for-all. However justified the claims of others may be in
principle, I need accommodate them only to the extent that they do not
encroach on my own. These are there for me to fulfil, if I can, irrespective
of the results for others. Effectively, the only kind of desire or demand
that is not acceptable as a claim in this context is that of an individual to
use force to achieve his or her ends, as this would lead to chaos. To provide
sufficient security, then, a mechanism is needed to limit freedom to this
extent. This takes the form of a protection agency – a minimal or 'night-
watchman' state – for the funding of which all have a responsibility.[10]

Paradoxically, although this gives very limited functions to the state, it could be still be a highly authoritarian one. This is because it has a monopoly over the use of force and there are no clear constraints on the manner in which it uses such force to maintain security.

The only way in which, under this approach, one can envisage a requirement for the kinds of protection against arbitrary arrest and detention found, for instance, in the American Bill of Rights or the European Convention on Human Rights is by subscribing to some kind of natural law theory. It is, though, difficult to imagine the existence of a natural law restricted to establishing these kinds of rights (and duties) alone. Yet, to accord it any wider remit would clearly undermine the idea that the only kind of desire or demand that cannot be justified as a claim is that of an individual to use force to achieve his or her own ends.

That said, if we could find some means of ensuring that it did not lapse into authoritarianism, a state that functioned simply to provide security for individuals to pursue their own ends might seem to offer a number of attractions. This is the kind of approach taken by Adam Smith in the *Wealth of Nations*.[11]

The argument here is that human beings operate according to certain principles of motion, in the form of selfishness or self-interest. Leaving them to bring their industry and capital into competition with others will produce an equilibrium that is conducive to the greatest production of wealth.

However, Smith admits that economic realities mean that his state will have to do more than simply maintain the conditions for peace. Taxes will also be needed to support the administration of justice, to create roads, bridges, canals and harbours, where doing so would not be profitable for individuals, and to provide basic education. He argues, though, that people benefiting from these should contribute to them. The state also has a role in reform – outdated property laws are an example – and in breaking up monopolies.

Even in the *Wealth of Nations*, then, it is difficult to see Adam Smith adopting the competitive social model for any other reason than the belief that it will lead to the creation of social goods. Further, it is a model that must be supplemented or corrected when it proves inadequate in this respect.

Smith's approach, accordingly, is considerably removed from the kind that focuses purely on the individual and the liberties, opportunities and benefits to which he or she aspires. Such an 'atomisation' of the individual is a mistake which opponents regard as intrinsic to liberal philosophy. They may be right where some of its exponents are concerned – particularly some contemporary 'neo-liberals' – but not about Adam Smith, or many others.

This becomes even clearer from Smith's other major work, *The Theory of Moral Sentiments*.[12] In this the principle of motion is that of sympathy, which leads us, through a process of interaction and adjustment to the perspectives of others, to the formation of general rules of morality that are 'universally acknowledged and established, by the concurring sentiments of mankind'.[13]

So, if claims, as social concepts, are – unlike desires and demands – conditioned by this morality, then it must also provide us with some idea of their limits, their relative weight and importance and the extent to which, and the manner in which, their fulfilment should be secured. None of this can be adequately achieved without a parallel consideration of responsibilities.

Even more to the point is the fact that, under the 'atomised individual' approach, we can make no real distinction between liberties, opportunities and benefits. For they all collapse into raw freedoms – those things we can do, achieve or acquire without assistance. Even liberties, which we do not always distinguish from freedoms, require some input from others, even if this is just a responsibility to hold back from interfering.

Actually prioritising responsibilities would, however, give rise to just as many difficulties as prioritising claims. The main danger is that of society being conceived as an organic whole, separate from and superior to its members, who are valued only for the contribution they make to it. In this context true freedom is seen as self-mastery, where one's own desires and demands are subordinated to the requirements of the higher good, and those who cannot achieve this for themselves have to be 'forced to be free'.[14]

On this kind of account, all people have are responsibilities – and to society, not to others – with claims not coming into the equation at all. Adam Ferguson, a philosopher of the Scottish Enlightenment, recognised the problem long before this kind of ideology was put into political practice, as it was in various fascist and communist regimes:

> Man is, by nature, the member of a community; and when considered in this capacity, the individual appears no longer made for himself. He must forego his happiness and his freedom, where these interfere with the good of society. He is only part of the whole; and the praise we think due to his virtue, is but a branch of the more general commendation we bestow on the member of a body, on the part of a fabric or engine, for being well fitted to occupy its place or produce its effect.
>
> If this follows from the relation of a part to its whole, and if the public good be the principal object with individuals, it is likewise true, that the happiness of individuals is the great end of civil society: for in what sense can a public enjoy any good, if its members, considered apart, be unhappy.[15]

Whether or not we agree with Ferguson that 'man is, *by nature*, the member of a community', it is clear that the vast majority of human beings do actually belong to one and that our ways of seeing the world are conditioned by the form it takes. In fact, at times, we are misled into believing that certain social constructs are natural features of it. Thus, the seeming normality of a tradition of awarding higher damages to women for facial injuries and higher ones to men for those affecting their limbs.

A Liberal Democrat approach, then, needs to find a way of acknowledging that we are component parts of a whole, without treating that whole as something separate from and superior to us. Here the philosopher Emile Durkheim gives us a clue when he writes of the system that is formed by the association of individuals representing a specific reality that has its own characteristics. We develop ways of acting, thinking and feeling which are external to us and according to which we interact with other individuals in ways that cannot be explained by reference to the parties alone. Amongst such facts of social life are our customs, law and morals.[16]

Despite their different starting points, there are, then, considerable similarities between the views of Durkheim and of Adam Smith, at least as expressed in *The Theory of Moral Sentiments*. These offer us the kind of social understanding into which both claims and responsibilities can be fitted, without either being accommodated to the necessary exclusion of the other.

A practical application

In a settled society, much of the disagreement about claims and responsibilities is around the margins. Returning to the issue of health and safety at work, legislation on working time provides a prime example. The issues are complex ones. First, employees may be regarded as having a claim to work as many hours as they desire. This can only be a liberty-type claim, requiring lack of legislative hindrance, as there is clearly no corresponding responsibility on the employer to provide opportunities for overtime.

For John Stuart Mill (and so for many Liberal Democrats), it could be regarded as a legitimate claim, even if the long hours result in damage to the employee's health, since – on that view – our liberties should only be restricted where they do direct harm to others. Indeed, to limit working hours could be regarded as harmful if this reduces the employee's capacity to provide benefits for self or family, so affecting his or her fulfilment of the responsibilities involved. Equally, though, long working hours can be detrimental to personal or family life and so counterproductive where parallel responsibilities are concerned.

Even those who have been most concerned to ensure the continuation of the UK opt-out from the 48-hour average working week under the Working Time Directive appear to baulk at the idea that anyone might be expected (or even allowed) to work twenty-three hours a day, seven days a week. This suggests that their real argument is not so much about principle as about where the line should be drawn as a matter of convenience.

The stronger argument for restricting hours in terms of safety considerations, however, relates to the potential for harm to others. This is particularly so in certain cases, for example those in the medical profession or transport, where being tired may lead to serious misjudgements. In these instances, at least, there seem to be good grounds for maintaining that someone, somewhere, has a responsibility for ensuring that such situations do not arise, and it is difficult to see where, other than the employer, this should rest.

At the same time, the employers have a claim, also of a liberty type, to organise their workforce in the manner best suited to meet their production needs. In certain cases, particularly seasonal work or urgent orders, long hours may be needed for the purpose. Failure to permit this may affect not just the firm's profitability but its very viability. This would have an adverse effect on the fulfilment of its responsibilities to shareholders, suppliers and consumers and, on some understandings at least, to the workforce itself. The last is most likely to be recognised in small enterprises, where a personal relationship between employer and employees has developed.

Yet, at the same time, the employers' claim to organise the workforce as suits them cannot be an unrestricted one. Were it so, we would be living in a system of forced labour. Rather, we regard working people as having a claim to dispose of their own time which can only be limited with their agreement. In some occupations, at least, there is an understanding that work beyond a specified number of hours should be both voluntary and paid at a higher rate. Again, the employees may feel a responsibility to the employer to do overtime, even where this would not be their first choice, in an emergency situation – although this, too, is more likely to be so in the case of small enterprises.

Also running counter to the employers' claim to organise their workforce to suit is the more general responsibility not to exploit their employees' weaker economic situation. This means, for example, avoiding making demands on them that negate their claims, such as those not to have their health affected by adverse working conditions, and to a personal and family life.

One argument is that the only certain way of ensuring this is by imposing duties on employers – to issue protective clothing, for example (with a benefit right on the part of employee to receive it and a parallel responsibility to wear it). Some would take a similar approach to long working hours, whereas others would insist that the only need is to find a way of making sure that, where these are undertaken, it is genuinely on a voluntary basis. The problem lies solely in finding a mechanism that will be properly effective in this regard.

It is not the intention of the present chapter to suggest how Liberal Democrats should resolve this particular issue (although the writer does have her own ideas). It is, rather, to point to the fact that it cannot properly be done without some overall vision of society and a view as to how claims and responsibilities can best be adjusted to give effect to that vision.

This vision we can find expressed in the Preamble to our party constitution, expressed most generally in the first paragraph:

> The Liberal Democrats exist to build and safeguard a fair, free and open society, in which we seek to balance the fundamental values of liberty, equality and community, and in which no one shall be enslaved by poverty, ignorance or conformity. We champion the freedom, dignity and well-being of individuals, we acknowledge and respect their right to freedom of conscience and their right to develop their talents to the full. We aim to disperse power, to foster diversity and to nurture creativity. We believe that the role of the state is to enable all citizens to attain these ideals, to contribute to their communities and to take part in the decisions that affect their lives.[17]

And, most directly relevant to the issue of working time:

> We will foster a strong and sustainable economy which encourages the necessary wealth-creating processes, develops and uses the skills of people and works to the benefit of all, with a just distribution of the rewards of success. We want to see democracy, participation and the co-operative principle in industry, within a competitive environment in which the state allows the market to operate freely where possible but intervenes where necessary.[18]

How helpful, then, is distinguishing between personal, political, economic and social liberalism in this respect?

David Laws draws such a distinction in Chapter 1 of *The Orange Book*. Personal liberalism is regarded as being concerned with the protection of the individual from oppression – whether by the state, a tyrannous majority or prejudice. Political liberalism is to do with democracy, particularly an insistence on freedom of information, accountability and transparency in political structures and on the decentralising of power. Economic liberalism he sees as 'the belief in the value of free trade, open competition, market mechanisms, consumer power, and the effectiveness of the private sector. These beliefs are combined with opposition to monopolies and instinctive suspicion of state control and interference, particularly in relation to the owner-ship and control of business.'[19]

Finally, social liberalism is seen as the New Liberalism of the early twentieth century, which is about achieving the kind of positive free-dom that comes when people are relieved from poverty, ignorance and ill-health. Paul Marshall notes, in the introductory chapter, its genera-tion by thinkers such as Hobhouse and Green, and sees it as being about striving 'to equip and encourage each individual to realise his full poten-tial and play his full part in society'. Marshall looks to 'the principle of citizenship' as embodying the balance between negative liberty (freedom from) and 'the positive connotation of responsibility (to family, children, the community, environment …) and participation (in the workplace, schools, housing associations, neighbourhood watches and in local and national government)'. [20]

David Laws, however, argues against 'nanny-state liberalism' where 'personal rights and freedoms [are] compromised by the pursuit of other, no doubt well-intentioned, objectives', such as animal welfare.[21] He goes on to advocate (as do several later writers) the marrying of economic lib-eralism to social liberalism. A programme for the latter should include, for example, 'Introducing more choice, competition and consumer power into public services such as health, while preserving the principle of access to all on the basis of need, not ability to pay'.[22]

Aside from the fact that these analyses take no account of much more recent contributions to the philosophy of liberalism – the approaches of John Rawls and Ronald Dworkin notably amongst them – they seem to me to be seriously muddled.

Although I am in broad agreement with Marshall about the prin-ciple of citizenship, his way of putting things seems to be setting what has been identified in the analysis as personal liberalism on one side and political liberalism on the other. Yet one aspect of personal liberalism involves promoting a positive freedom – to participate in the decisions that affect one's life. For this claim (classified earlier in the chapter as an opportunity one) provides a measure of security against the kind of oppression by the state, a tyrannous majority or prejudice to which Laws refers. Economic forces could well be added to this list.

Paralleling the claim to participate, there is, arguably, a responsi-bility to do so, although not a duty except in a system where voting is compulsory. And actual participation clearly produces a further responsibility to have regard to the needs of 'family, children, the community, environment' etc. So, the principle of citizenship may well involve addressing a number of competing claims and making choices as to which of them it is most important to pursue.

In this context, I believe that David Laws, though correct in wishing to marry economic and social liberalism, is mistaken in the manner in which he does so. This is because the four different types of liberalism cannot be treated as operating at the same level.

Economic liberalism involves a commitment to the idea that a free market (or at least one that is subject to a minimum of restrictions, aimed mainly at the maintenance of competition) is the one most conducive to the production of wealth. Political liberalism is concerned with the creation of a thriving democracy. The tenets of economic and political liberalism are, accordingly, about the conditions for the achievement of their respective goals. By contrast, personal and social liberalism are expressed as goals in their own right. It can, moreover, be argued that social liberalism collapses into a rich form of personal liberalism – in that it looks to an individual who is not simply not oppressed by the circumstances in which he or she lives but is actively empowered to shape them.

Of course, arguing for personal liberalism to be seen as a goal, and for the collapse of social liberalism into it, risks the accusation that, in centring on the individual, it ignores the claims of 'family, children, the community, environment etc.'. Yet this need not be so if it is acknowledged that the empowered individual cannot be an atomised one, since such empowerment is impossible without a notion of citizenship involving reciprocal claims and responsibilities.

For this reason, it seems to me that it is better to return to a social vision and look to the setting of conditions under which all individuals are enabled to maximise their own potential in a manner compatible with that of others to do the same. We can move from a four-fold classification to a three-fold one. Each type of liberalism is directed toward establishing a set of conditions. In the case of political liberalism it is of those for a truly participatory democracy. With economic liberalism it is those most conducive to the production of wealth. And, for social liberalism, it is those that provide for a good quality of life, including the relationship these have with the production and use of wealth.

Of course, the classification is still a somewhat arbitrary one, since, as liberal principles, there is much that is shared between them. For example, one cannot have a free market unless it is informed by the political principles of transparency and accountability. Nor can one have functioning democratic structures without the existence of some wealth to support them and (at least on a Western model) the incorporation of an element of competition into them. Equally, wealth has to be created before it can be put to use.

Yet, arguably, wealth is unlike other social goods. All these are worth having both in themselves and because they contribute to one another. Many, for example, know to their cost that finding work without a home address, and an acceptable one at that, is far from easy. Similarly, there is currently more and more emphasis on the importance of education for wealth creation. But, as Jo Swinson puts it in *Britain after Blair*, GDP growth is not the only indicator of quality of life.[23] In other words, the value of wealth lies in what else it makes achievable.

Conclusion

Where, then, I find myself in disagreement with many of the arguments put forward by some proponents of economic liberalism is in their one-sidedness. A reluctance to accept the principles of social liberalism, as setting constraints on the production and use of wealth, is combined with a propensity to 'let rip' with those of economic liberalism when it comes to the creation and maintenance of other social goods. There seems, too, to be a tendency to employ (or not) the principles of political liberalism to suit, with too great a faith – particularly where the workplace is concerned – in the current capacity of the individual, acting alone, to ensure that her or his own welfare is adequately safeguarded.

To me, accordingly, the balance – set out in the Preamble to the Liberal Democrat constitution – between the values of liberty, equality and community has become distorted. The writers concerned are, of course, correct to warn against over-regulation. As indicated earlier, there are many interesting ways of allowing the fulfilment of claims and responsibilities without the creation of rights and the imposition of duties – the use of financial incentives amongst them.

Only experience can tell us which approach will be the most effective, given the aim of setting the conditions under which all individuals are enabled to maximise their own potential, in a manner compatible with that of others to do the same. But this just serves to reinforce the point that state actors need to take a holistic view, particularly if we are to achieve our ends with the minimum of friction and waste.

It follows that, even though the balance between the principles we employ may vary from one decision to the next, each has to be accommodated to some extent. This may not be the distinctive agenda for a liberal state in the twenty-first century that some would seek, and it certainly does not lead to simplistic solutions. But it is one to which many of us instinctively subscribe.

Afterthought

One of the less prominent but still significant features of the debate about the future of Europe concerns its role in relation to social policy, by which is largely meant labour law. A number of politicians, including some of our own Westminster parliamentarians, would argue for its 'repatriation'. The view is that EU involvement in this area violates the principles of democratic accountability and subsidiarity. And doubts, too, have been expressed about the validity of counter-argument that repatriation would lead to social dumping.

Nick Clegg, for example, has long held the view that this area should be off limits, unless the value in collective action can be shown to be compelling. For Vince Cable the value in such action can, it seems, exist only where there is a clear cross-border issue. In his view:

> It is time for economic liberals to take a stand and assert some simple principles: that all that is necessary for trade, investment and cross-border movement of workers is for different standards to be mutually recognised and that there is merit in competition between different standards (as there is between different tax systems). In practice, the Union should not be setting legally binding social standards at all.[24]

It has to be said, however, that anything like a wholesale relocation of social policy would cause major difficulties. First, various aspects of it are entirely necessary to the free movement of persons, which like that of services, goods and capital, is fundamental to the whole EU project.

These principles were written into the Treaty of Rome in 1957 and have been reiterated in and reinforced by subsequent treaties and specific legislative provisions.

Second, there are strong arguments to the effect that the establishment of some common labour standards, at least, is as intrinsic to the completion of the internal market as is the establishment of common safety standards for products. Unless we take the view that these, too, are unnecessary – effectively that all that is required is the abolition of tariff barriers – there is a requirement to show just why the latter are required for a level playing field but not the former.

Third, there is a school of thought to the effect that the achievement of comparable living and working conditions for EU citizens is part of the project. Interestingly, whilst a number of economic liberals reject this approach in relation to social policy generally, they espouse it whole-heartedly in the context of discrimination. This seems to be because, although the discrimination relates to the workplace, they regard the issue as one of human, rather than social, rights.

To this extent, subsidiarity, like beauty, appears to be in the eye of the beholder. This is not to deny the Liberal Democrat commitment to localism – only to allow for a measure of disagreement about what decisions are best made where. Arguably, though, the issue is as much about effectiveness of input into the process as it is about finding common ground concerning the level at which it is appropriate for the decision to be made.

Notes

1   See, for example, Tony Blair, Speech at the Nexus/Guardian conference, 1 March 1997, available at www.netnexus.org/library/papers/blair.htm.
2   See news.bbc.co.uk/1/hi/uk_politics/1703322.stm.
3   See www.commonsleader.gov.uk/output/page1851.asp.
4   See speech by Jim Murphy MP, 21 February 2007 at www.dwp.gov.uk/aboutus/2007/21-02-07.asp.
5   Conrad Russell, 'Tony Blair or Uriah Heep?', The Spectator, 1 February 1997.
6   Paul Marshall and David Laws (eds.), The Orange Book: Reclaiming Liberalism (Profile Books, London, 2004).
7   Julian Astle, David Laws, Paul Marshall and Alasdair Murray (eds.), Britain after Blair: A Liberal Agenda (Profile Books, London, 2006).
8   Marshall and Laws, The Orange Book, p. 12.
9   Roscoe Pound, Social Control Through Law (Yale University Press, 1942).

10 See, for example, Robert Nozick, *Anarchy, State, and Utopia* (Basil Blackwell, Oxford, 1974).

11 R. H. Campbell, A. S. Skinner and W. B. Todd (eds.), Adam Smith, *An Inquiry into the Nature and Causes of the Wealth of Nations* (originally published 1776; Oxford University Press, 1976).

12 D. D. Raphael and A. L Macphie (eds.), *The Theory of Moral Sentiments* (originally published 1759; Oxford University Press, 1976).

13 Ibid., Book III, Ch. 4, p. 11.

14 See further on this in Isaiah Berlin, *Two Concepts of Liberty* (Oxford University Press, 1958), and the consideration of his ideas in C. B. Macpherson, *Democratic Theory* (Oxford University Press, 1973).

15 Adam Ferguson, *An Essay on the History of Civil Society* (originally published 1767; Edinburgh University Press, 1978), Part I, Section IX, p. 57.

16 See Emile Durkheim, *Rules of Sociological Method* (originally published 1895; trans. W. D. Hall and S. Lukes, Macmillan, London, 1982).

17 Liberal Democrats, Constitution of the Federal Party, Preamble, para 1.

18 Ibid., para 3.

19 Marshall and Laws, *The Orange Book*, p. 20.

20 Ibid., p. 12.

21 Ibid., pp. 24–25.

22 Ibid., p. 41.

23 Astle, Laws, Marshall and Murray, *Britain after Blair*, Chapter 5.

24 Marshall and Laws, *The Orange Book*, p. 137.

Chapter 8

Using Community Politics to Build a Liberal Society

Mark Pack

I have a secret to admit. I quite like big organisations. Of course – as you would expect of a liberal – I think power should be kept at as local a level as possible, that organisations should be responsive to individuals, and so that smaller is frequently better – and that individuals' freedom and rights get trampled on when Big Brother gets free rein.

But faced with the reality of actually trying to change the world, in however small or big a way, the inconvenient truth is that big organisations are good. Lobby Tesco or frequent my local organic food shop? Sorry to say, but doing the former is going to do more to change the world. The impact of Tesco's decisions on the production and consumption of organic food has been, and will continue to be, far greater than the efforts of clutches of organic food shops scattered around the country.

Moreover, the volume of public pressure required to change a large organisation's behaviour is, despite its size, frequently quite small compared to the scale on which electoral politics operates. Mars's abortive switch in the ingredients of Mars Bars and other confectionery to include animal extracts was derailed in spring 2007 after 6,000 complaints. For Mars 6,000 was a large number – but that is barely enough to get a mediocre third place in a parliamentary election, and indeed is not much more than the number of votes piled up by winning councillors in some of the larger urban wards in England.

But – and this is the key – while the volume of pressure required to make companies change their course is often relatively small compared with the votes needed to win in even just one parliamentary constituency, the benefits can be commensurate with the organisation's large scale. Persuading McDonalds to introduce more humane treatment of animals – as it has done in response to lobbying from thousands of people – has done far more for animal husbandry, both directly (raising the standards of their suppliers) and indirectly (encouraging those who wish to become their suppliers to also change their behaviour), than if all those thousands had simply changed their own eating habits.

This is not to say that McDonalds and Tesco are perfect or don't do many bad things, or that they aren't ever kept on their toes by seeing what smaller organisations are starting to do, but the brutal reality is that if you want to change the world, getting a big organisation to make a small change frequently has far more impact that a host of small-scale projects. Being good in your own direct personal behaviour is admirable and worthwhile, but it is not the whole story. Changing the behaviour of others usually has much greater impact, especially where the 'other' is a large organisation.

Small may be beautiful, but big gives the individual leverage to make large-scale changes to community or country. This applies particularly to organisations in Britain, for so many of them are international in their reach (influence them in one country and you may have knock-on effects on their operations in other countries too), and also to the UK government, which, with its – albeit somewhat variable – special relationship with the US, UN Security Council seat and membership of the European Union, is particularly well placed to influence others when the mood takes it.

It's not just about the size of the state

This slightly perverse relationship between an individual's influence and an organisation's size – larger bodies may be less responsive to an individual than small ones, but the results of individual pressure can be massive – gives a clue as to what normally is missing in discussions such as those about the size of the state or the growth of multinationals, or policies for devolution and subsidiarity.

If you only talk about the size of the state and other bodies, you miss the important question of how to make large bodies more responsive to individuals' pressure, and how to help people influence them. Simply talking about taking some power and influence away from them neglects an important route for individual power.

Moreover, for many issues – such as global warming, Third World poverty and animal welfare – it is only through this oft-neglected route that an individual can effectively exercise influence. Certainly, I can take good care of my pet goldfish but in the overall cause of animal welfare, the question of whether or not I can influence my local council's meat-purchasing policies is far more important. A lifetime of responsible gold-fish tending will not begin to equal the influence of the local council. Altering my individual behaviour may be morally correct, virtuous and even help set a good example to others (which in turn may effect others, which in turn …) but it has major limitations.

The answer, therefore, is not simply to think about large or small state, breaking up organisations or not, but to see the state (and other large organisations) as not only a boss but also as a tool. While most of the rest of this book is about the state and the boss side of the equation (what sort of boss? how big a boss? bossing over what?), this chapter is about the tool side of the equation: how do we help people and communities organise to make the best use of the state as a tool for bringing about the changes they want?

How people can drive the state
Influencing the state is about information, access and organisation – in other words, it is about community politics, where people organise to take power for themselves and for their communities, so that the state is a tool for people to better their own lives (rather than simply seeing the state as a repository of hand-me-down solutions).

Almost as soon as community politics became a phrase in use and debate within the Liberal Party in the 1970s, there came the complaints that it was only being seen or implemented as an electoral technique, rather than as a tool to reshape society and to enable people to have great-er control over their own lives.

Some of the behaviour it has encouraged – principally residents' sur-veys, regular local newsletters and taking up local issues through local campaigns – has certainly brought great electoral benefits, so much so that now both Labour and Conservative parties increasingly see merits in such activities too.

But that is not the whole story:

> Community politics is not a technique. It is an ideology, a system
> of ideas for social transformation. For those ideas to become a
> reality there is a need for a strategy of political action. For that

strategy to be successful it needs to develop effective techniques of political campaigning. Those techniques are a means to an end. If they become an end in themselves, the ideas they were designed to promote will have been lost.[1]

What does this mean in practice? It means helping the public to effect change themselves. The practical implications of this fall into three areas: what it means for how Liberal Democrats go about campaigning, what it means for how the state and other powerful bodies should be organised, and what it means for how we directly help people organise and take power into their own hands.

How we behave in our own campaigns

For the question of how Liberal Democrats campaign, take graffiti as an example. What does a Liberal Democrat councillor or campaigner do?

He or she can encourage people to report it to them personally, raise it with the council, get it cleaned, report back to the person and also run a story in the next *Focus* newsletter. All well and good as far as it goes; the community is cleaner, with benefits quite possibly seen the next time ballot boxes are opened.

One step beyond that is carefully to tour the area and survey residents, find out about graffiti problems more extensively and more frequently and then go through the same cycle. Again, the result is a cleaner community and a bigger vote come polling day.

But that shouldn't be the limit of our ambitions. A more imaginative step would be to find out more about why the graffiti is appearing and try to tackle the underlying causes, such as designing out features that make graffiti too easy or tempting, or improving local youth services. Again, though, this is about the public being supplicants at the foot of the state. A listening and helpful state maybe, but essentially it is saying, 'Get someone else to fix this'.

Providing people with the information to report graffiti themselves (which, particularly where the local council does not run a one-stop reporting shop, can be quite complicated, with a host of different numbers depending on where the graffiti is) is a step beyond that, as is providing graffiti-cleaning information and equipment for people who need to keep clean their own properties.

And if there is a public body that does not do enough to clean graffiti reported to it (be it the council, Network Rail, British Telecom or some other body)? Then the role is to help marshal local public opinion to bring effective pressure to bear. As for the long term, the more organised and vocal residents are, the more likely it is that all these various bodies will continue to keep on their toes in dealing with graffiti.

The risk is that the siren call of the ballot box tempts the councillor or campaigner into always wanting to do the casework directly themselves. Moreover, keeping people informed about local issues and how they can influence them can be time-consuming, and councillors and campaigners are not usually short of other things to do with their time, including fighting and winning election campaigns.

The more liberal and longer-term perspective is that the more people can take power into their own hands and deal directly with such problems, the more time the councillor and campaigner has for other issues and other actions. There is more time to keep campaigning, communicating and dealing with the council if you are not having to deal directly with each individual outbreak of graffiti – and indeed, it brings other benefits, as I have written on another occasion:

> By sharing the work with others, the workload becomes manageable and sustainable. Campaigning with the community to achieve concrete results for the local area and its residents can, if done right, not only involve far more people in campaigning – and so spread the load – but it is also the way to build a positive, personal reputation that insulates you against negative campaigning from the other parties at election time.[2]

Being the catalyst to organise a public meeting or set up a local campaign group, or simply using your local media contacts to generate press coverage all take campaigning against graffiti from being a mere secretarial funnel for individual items to helping to involve the community in organising and using its own voice.

For all of these tasks, holders of public office, or those aspiring to such, frequently have means to help out, such as having the relevant media contacts, knowing the names (and direct phone numbers!) of relevant public officials, getting notice of when key decisions are to be made, and so on.

The creation of local groups is particularly important not only because collective action gives a stronger voice to the community but also because they bring more neighbours together in a way which generally strengthens social cohesion and improves society. Therefore, the test for a campaigner is to ask, 'How many local groups have I helped create or expand in the last year?'

Organising the state and other bodies

Turning to policies for structuring the state and other organisations so that they are more amenable to public pressure, beyond simply devolving power to the lowest level practical, there is a key choice to make about how democracy should operate. Should the number of elections increase or decrease?

Adding elected posts to bodies, whether health trust boards, transport-users' committees or crime partnerships, adds an immediate veneer of democracy and responsiveness to public pressure. A plethora of different elections, though, requires an appetite from potential voters not only to cast votes but also to inform themselves about candidates and issues if the resulting democracy is to be meaningful. It is far from clear that this appetite exists at present.

The alternative is to give more power to existing elected posts. The drawback is that this bundles up a wider range of different decisions and issues into just the one vote, reducing voters' ability to fine-tune their preferences through voting in different ways for different bodies and roles.

There is no easy answer to this difficult balancing act, but giving more power to individual councillors and individual MPs (by taking it away from both the government and the unelected) seems a surer way forward than creating more elections. Having more power rest on the outcome of existing elections is likely to produce more involvement in democracy than generating more elections for people to take part in – as the low turnouts in regeneration partnership board and foundation hospital trust board elections show.

Giving individual councillors and individual MPs more powers in turn opens up more power to influence by the public. The simplest example of how this can be done is with Private Members' Bills in Parliament. They should provide MPs with a ready way of turning constituents' concerns over specific issues into legislation. Yet only a tiny handful each year have a chance of making it through Parliament, and the whole process is designed so that procedural barriers waylay nearly all of them. Whether it is with Ten-Minute Rule Bills (pre-ordained to fail) or Private Members' Bills debated on Fridays (when most MPs have conflicting engagements in their constituencies) the way Parliamentary debates are structured is heavily biased against an individual MP being able to legislate. It's a relic of big-government paternalism and the view that only the government should set the legislative agenda. It reduces the impact of an individual's voice massively because it is that much more difficult for a view that requires legislative change to triumph.

Yet, as other countries demonstrate, it is possible to structure Parliamentary business in a way which gives individual legislators a reasonable chance of making legislation. Proper scheduling of Private Members' Bills, and scrutiny of draft legislation by parliamentary committees, would – amongst other measures – easily and significantly increase the power of individual MPs.

Looking beyond Parliament, many of the other bodies with elected posts have standards of election that would cause an outcry if used for MPs or councils. A good illustration of this is the British Film Institute (BFI) – not a direct arm of the state, but nevertheless an important body with a multi-million-pound budget, a Royal Charter, a key role in the country's cultural life and indirect state funding. Yet when my ballot paper for its council elections arrive, I have had to sign it, right next to my vote. Ballot secrecy or any such old-fashioned ideals of probity? No thanks, and just explained away, when I have enquired, with a rather plaintive cry of 'It's OK, we don't misuse the information'.

The BFI is by no means unique in this rather careless approach to democracy. At least in the BFI's favour it is not biasing the results, which is not something that can be said for the financial sector, where elections for directors and the like are routinely accompanied by ballot papers with preferred candidates highlighted and lopsided accompanying publicity.

Even when the elections are more closely related to public elections – as in those for regeneration partnership boards – standards of democracy are frequently very low. Did you know, for example, that if you opt out of the full electoral register in an effort to reduce the amount of commercial direct mail that you receive, you therefore also opt yourself out of elections for many of these sorts of bodies?

The law only allows the edited register to be used in many of those elections, so only if you find out – by some miracle – and voluntarily opt yourself back in do you get to keep your vote. This is no accidental mistake in the drafting of a law, because it is a line the government has stuck to through several opportunities to revise it (I know, I've asked the civil servants several times and drawn a blank each time).

Yet it would not be that difficult to legislate to ensure that any body that receives public funding and holds elections should conduct those elections to certain minimum standards (secret ballot, fair definition of the electorate, equal publicity rules), nor to require the same of the (already heavily regulated) financial sector. Enthralling though the intricacies of the relative merits of the Meek and standard ERS ways of conducting an STV count are, electoral reformers often miss the bigger picture: standards of election are frequently alarmingly low, with the result that the public loses its voice.

Having fair elections in this wider group of bodies has become more important as, with the shrinking remit of central government, more and more power has been vested in them. Take the example of the utilities industries. Water, gas and electricity have been privatised, passing the theoretical ultimate controlling power from electors to shareholders and so putting greater reliance on the functioning – or not – of shareholder voting power. And where it fails to be exercised, the result is a ceding of power to those with the corporate lobbying and financial muscle instead.

Therefore, encouraging and ensuring high standards of democracy across the full range of elections and votes, and not just in the relatively small sphere of public elections, is an important part of a modern and meaningful form of community politics: people must be able to exercise their voices freely and effectively in whatever forums modern life offers them.

But simply having a free and fair vote is not sufficient. Effective exercise of individual power through elections and other means is most effective where it is easy for people to organise amongst themselves into order to be an effective collective advocate rather than just a collection of individual voices. This community-politics-based concept of communities organising and taking power for themselves can be fostered – or not – by the policies of the state.

How to help people take power into their own hands: giving people the tools

A simple example from the then Liberal Democrat administration on Bristol City Council illuminates this. They provided a simple online campaigning tool that made it easy for residents to run local campaigns – whether they were in favour of a council policy, against a council policy or indeed really about something else. This wasn't a big council versus small council question but one of how best to enable people to take up the cudgels successfully on their own behalf.

It can be difficult to overcome the natural (and understandable, even if wrong) instinct for councillors to think, 'why should I help people criticise me?' But in the long run an active and engaged community brings better and more effective decisions. Rushed, botched decisions result in time spent in dealing with the fallout, when a small extra investment of time before the decision had been made would have been a far better choice.

Traditionally, giving the public power in a council context has been seen by Liberal Democrats as meaning decisions such as letting individuals ask questions at council meetings, or allowing the presentation of petitions to councils. However, this is very much a top-down, one-to-one, communication – you can come and present your views to me, and I will listen, or not, as I wish.

The real power of community politics lies in unleashing peer-to-peer communication – getting people talking to each other so they can organise and lobby more effectively as an organised group. Aiding self-organisation and peer-to-peer communication is different from simply providing a few channels for individuals to directly voice their views.

This can be dressed up in Web 2.0 peer-to-peer internet jargon (and many internet developments have made creating such dialogues much easier) but at heart the idea is very simple – rather than simply having the state communicate one-way with different individuals, it should help individuals talk to each other and organise amongst themselves in order to influence the state.

Five-step plan for helping the consulted organise amongst themselves

So here are five easy small steps councils could make, three of which are based around the internet, but two of which are also applicable to anyone.

First, provide local organisations with space on the council's website. Many will have their own websites, but building up traffic (and good search-engine results) is much harder than simply setting up your own website. Providing local groups with space and links from the council's website gives a useful and immediate hand-up on both scores.

Second, run online discussion forums in parallel with council decision-making. Some councils already have some modest experiments in online discussion forums (e.g. mirroring their area or neighbourhood assemblies) but linking the council's consultation processes, and committees such as those dealing with planning and licensing, consistently with online discussion forums make it much easier for people to find others of a like mind on a particular issue.

Third, copy Bristol in providing local residents with the tools to run their own online campaigns.

Fourth, consciously encourage the use of council premises for meeting rooms for local organisations at reasonable prices. Finding appropriate venues at reasonable prices can often inhibit local groups; they need not.

Fifth, provide local groups with space in council publications, beyond the occasional phonebook-style listing, so that they can advertise their existence, build up their own audiences and memberships and engage more with the community. Large and vibrant residents' associations will cause headaches for council officers from time to time, but this is a desirable part of helping people organise themselves.[3]

None of these steps would require major policy change or major financial investment, but collectively they add up to an attitude of mind – and it is that attitude which is, consistently applied in a myriad of different ways, so important.

Applied beyond the council level, what would this mean? Take two examples. First, it would mean the widespread provision for free of an accurate postcode-to-ward-and-constituency lookup database. This matches up someone's postcode with their ward and constituency, and is therefore a key tool in matching people up with other information (which, across a whole range of data, is often provided on the ward or constituency building-block level) and also with their elected representatives. At the moment, this data has to be paid for – which immediately places an obstacle in the way of any pressure group or other organisation

that wants to make it easy to link up supporters with the relevant political unit. There is a host of different ways in which the easy marrying of
postcode to other data could be used, but by enforcing a cost the government is cutting off a stream of lobbying creativity.

Second, the petitions on the 10 Downing Street website are – currently – an unfortunately good example of drive-by democracy: I see an
issue, I take a few seconds expressing my view, and I then pass on by,
never to engage with the issue again.

The 10 Downing Street system has a few bells and whistles – such as
the confirmation email and allowing up to two replies from government
– but the system essentially allows only just this very brief and superficial
engagement with the issue.

Imagine, instead, a system designed to encourage peer-to-peer
organisation, automatically created a new online discussion forum for
each petition and providing a rich range of supporting tools and information, along the Bristol model. That would allow the petition to be the
starting point for real engagement on an issue.

Taming the regulators through organised harrying

A final consideration should be given to the role of regulators. Regulators
have huge power. The members of Postcomm, with their strong preference for free-market solutions, have had a significant impact on how the
Royal Mail performs. ICSTIS, which regulates premium rate phone lines,
has repeatedly fined Opera Telecom, but has still been willing to let them
keep running the fraudulent phone-ins for GMTV that conned people
out of their money and caused much media coverage in early 2007. In
other words, in both cases the regulators have had real impacts on people's lives. But in both cases they are, in effect, insulated from those same
people.

Where are the confirmation hearings for the senior regulators?
Where is the public questioning of their performance? Where, in fact, is
any sense of accountability?

This raises a complicated issue for politicians, as the argument for
independent regulators is that there is often good reason for providing
a degree of insulation between their decisions and politicians. Ofcom is
a good example: how comfortable would we be with politicians – whose
media coverage is vital to their electoral prospects – being intimately

involved with Ofcom's deliberations? But insulation can too easily be taken as an excuse to leave regulators to their own devices.

The impact of Postcomm's attitude to post offices or Ofcom's to local radio stations can have a huge impact on communities. The answer is to use the community politics approach once again to ensure that people can take and organise power, in this case through organised lobbying and engagement with regulators.

Using a community-politics-minded approach to help people organise themselves to have an effective voice allows this dilemma to be resolved – opening regulators to pressure without subjecting them to day-to-day political control. Indeed, by enabling more public pressure, you need to directly exercise state power – whether through law-making or through other means – less often.

The organised harrying which community politics encourages allows solutions to problems that would otherwise be beyond the reach of sensible regulation. Take the issue of food outlets at transport interchanges. Healthy eating options are only rarely available at most of them. Given the problems that unhealthy diets produce for not only the eater but for the NHS and the community as a whole, encouraging the provision of a wider range of choices is reasonable (especially as there is not an efficient free market operating here, given the limited number of outlets allowed and the intermittent allocation or removal of them from particular firms).

However, having central government regulate how many pine nuts should be on sale at Birmingham New Street on a Saturday morning is unlikely to be a productive approach. Instead, the community-politics perspective points at enabling and encouraging people to organise – and to pressurise and harry.

Conclusion: making the state a tool for people

It is very easy to slip into the 'I don't like X, so government must regulate or spend' mindset, or indeed the 'I don't like big government, so you mustn't do anything about X' mindset.

Yet there is a whole world of progress available beyond regulation and public spending. The RSPCA's Freedom Food Mark, the WWF-inspired Forest Stewardship Council certificate, and Fairtrade Coffee are all examples of schemes that have both had a significant impact in improving the world while not relying on government action, even though they cover areas that could be regulated by government.

This chapter started with the question of whether a large state (and other organisations) was beneficial or not. The argument here is that, aside from the direct issue over size, there is an important discussion to be had over how to enable people to make the best use of the state and other bodies regardless of their size. The big-versus-small, interfering-versus-regulating argument can often be sidestepped by helping people organise and lobby effectively, genuinely taking and exercising power, especially when done through voluntary organisations.

People can use their own voice, the state and other bodies to bring about change in a way that moves beyond simply always asking for more rules or more money – for you can influence and change the world without having to rely on the false choice of regulating or hoping for an invisible market hand.

Notes

1   Bernard Greaves & Gordon Lishman, *The Theory & Practice of Community Politics* (Association of Liberal Councillors, 1980).
2   Mark Pack, 'Putting community politics back into election campaigns' in *Community Politics Today* (Association of Liberal Democrat Councillors, 2006).
3   Of course the sixth point – as promoted by the Federated Union of *Focus* Deliverers – would be to use the planning system to pressure developers to provide all properties with sensibly located individual letterboxes.

Chapter 9

Status versus Friendship and the Common Good

by Lynne Featherstone

We all want status of some sort. For some, status is mostly about possessions, but for most of us it's about relationships, respect, security, experiences and opportunities – all as important for most people, if not for everyone, as what they own.

We are conditioned from birth and throughout life to strive for more – to keep up with, and preferably overtake, the Joneses, whether that is in terms of what we own, our station in life or our appearance. Unfortunately we soon adjust to our new status and then feel it not to be enough and so want more. Clearly, therefore, status is not the whole answer to making us content with our lot.

Our definition of life in terms of purchasing power has simply created internal deserts which are hungering for something more substantial, more rewarding than material goods, an 18-hour day, or being a size double zero. And if you are at the bottom of the heap, then what's the point? There is almost no hope of changing your status. There is lower social mobility now in Britain than there was thirty years ago. If you are at the bottom, society, it seems, is not going to value you for what you do, and you have very little chance of changing anything.

So, whilst it is undoubtedly more comfortable to be rich and miserable, we are all, in reality, miserable. To comfort us in our misery, or to insulate ourselves against the reality of the deficiencies in ourselves, our work, our lives, or our families, we seem to be numbing ourselves to reality by passing time anaesthetising ourselves with the quick-fix, feel-good-for-a-moment relief of retail therapy, stopping ourselves having to think about anything by watching reality TV – watching people live instead of living ourselves – or consuming excesses of food to comfort us or excesses of drink so that we don't have to think or feel the pain of reality.

Public policy on health, crime, employment, housing, education, the environment we live in and, in this government's case, foreign policy, all contribute to this downward spiral. Of course there is an underlying rationale for some particular instances of malaise and misery – for example when divorce, unemployment or ill-health come our way – but current levels of unhappiness seem excessive when set against the low levels of unemployment, a relatively decent health service and lack of income which is not generally the grinding poverty of yesteryear.

So what can be done, both by the state and by individuals, to improve our lot? The thesis of this chapter is that the balance between status and friendship has gone out of kilter. The old structures that held our society safely in place – marriage, religion, the law, class or an unwritten but universal understanding of acceptable behaviour – are far less certain, uniform or permanent than used to be the case. Consumerism rules OK – but the periods of relief provided by quick-fix solutions or the momentary glow from retail therapy are getting shorter and shorter. We seem to see our welfare in terms of our purchasing power. We value appearance rather than substance. The 'me' society is reaping its selfish reward.

So how – in this world that has moved on from those 'old-fashioned' values – can we create structures or environments that value our good human qualities more and place less importance on wealth or status? How do we rebalance the relationship between status and friendship – indeed, is possible at all? Can the genie be put back in the bottle? How do we balance what's good for 'me' with what's best for 'us' – the aspiration for the common good as opposed to selfish individual advancement?

And what role, if any, does government have in all of this? This is tricky territory to tread in; one false slip of the sentence and you open yourself up to pastiche for wanting a Ministry of Fun, or state-regulated force-fed humour courses with every meal. David Cameron's 2006 conference speech calling on us to 'let sunshine win the day' certainly did seem rather risible (though perhaps he thinks he will be running against a 'more rain now' Prime Minister at the next election).

The breakdown of us

The deal used to be that we behaved well because Church (or other religious establishments), parents, teachers, the police and our government said we should. They set an example of good behaviour (on the whole) and expected us to do the same. If we did we were rewarded with approbation from our family, friends, teachers, the community or God – depending on one's proclivity – or an inner feeling of positivity or well-being.

From our establishments and our institutions and their leaders came a code of social conduct that we all understood. There was either a penalty for deviating from the expectation of good behaviour, such as social exclusion, civil or state punishment or excommunication, or there was the simple reward of doing the right thing, fulfilling our own expectations of ourselves stemming from our innate sense of good behaviour. This was enough for most of us to keep to the rules, to put up with our hardships without resorting to crime, and to discipline our children so that our neighbours and community would approve of us. We waited for our reward, in heaven, or somewhat nearer to home.

This is no longer the case. An ordered existence has been gradually disintegrating over recent years as church attendance and belief drop, teachers' position and authority are diminished and parents do not exercise the level of control or influence over their children that they used to. The remedies we appear to have put in place to keep us on the straight and narrow of behaviour are legal boundaries rather than the old social ones, which will not work in the longer term.

Feeding upon this frenzied downward cycle – cataloguing the cataclysm – we have the media, with its emphasis on the negative and the nasty, the banal and the low-grade. And helping it along are reality TV, 24-hour news, advertising, the competitive society, the lack of social mobility, the inequality gap and the backdrop of an increasingly destabilised western democracy and political short-termism.

Some of the underlying changes do, of course, have positive outcomes as well as negative ones. People are less deferential and more free to do what they want – which is a liberal outcome. The trick is to try and work out a way of developing a new framework, a new social contract that preserves this greater freedom while restraining license, without having to resort to increasingly punitive, but ultimately ineffective ways, of keeping order.

We have seen very clearly, under an authoritarian and centralising Labour government, how very, very little is being achieved in terms of changing behaviour by ever-more stringent laws, surveillance, rules, regulations, targets and punishments. The only real solution is to create an environment where behaviour matters because of the social order, not because of a purely legalistic one. Just as the government is discovering, you cannot make people behave well by ordering them to; note the failure of anti-social behaviour orders to change the nature of the people they are awarded to.

So why, then, are the joys of life often apparently in such short supply? Status has got out of kilter with friendship, and the common good has been crushed under a stampede of selfishness. Where do we go from here?

Institutional and behavioural decline

Britain has seen a continuous decline in church attendance and belief. A report from the University of Manchester found that a parent with a religious belief had a 50/50 chance of the child continuing that religion.[1] However, non-religious parents had a much higher chance of their child following their example. Thus the inevitable decline in church attendance and religious belief, indicating the continued secularisation of British society, marches on. Religion, whilst clearly not the panacea for all the world's ills, at least has pretensions to a code by which its devotees are to live and behave.

As the inmates of Great Britain have had the temerity to become restless, object to more restriction, behave badly or simply want something different from government decree, the state has reacted with panic measures, attempting to draw ever-more restrictive circles around our lives. The never-ending stream of legislation and guidelines issuing forth from a centralised and centralising government has removed individuals' sense of ownership and responsibility for good behaviour. The increasingly authoritarian approach to almost everything moves us towards a population controlled through legal parameters rather than social ones, be that with regard to crime or health or education.

ASBOs, which were supposed to be a means of last resort applied to very wayward anti-socially behaving kids, quickly started being dished out like sweeties to the naughty kids who wore them as a badge of honour. If an ASBO is breached – and over half of them are – then the young person can be imprisoned in the university of crime, prison. The reoffending rate is over 60 per cent and our prisons are overflowing. Once again, if there is no change in behaviour there is no improvement in the crime rate. Building prisons and applying ASBOs do not make criminals behave better.

We used to think of hospital as a place of safety – now we are scared within an inch of our lives (literally) by MRSA and C-difficile. Our trust when we are admitted to this-once bastion of safety is no longer there. And why can't these bugs be beaten? Not because the government does not lay down loads of tick-boxes for hospitals to tick and staff to jump to (they do), but because the personal responsibility for immaculate behaviour has been diminished. The outsourcing of cleaning services may be one reason, but in the end making something really clean has to be about your own personal desire to reach a standard that is unimpeachable. Do most of us still expect that standard of ourselves, or will ticking a box to say something has been done replace that high expectation of our own performance? Have personal standards been diminished and replaced by measuring and monitoring, to little avail?

We used to have pillars of the establishment to look up to – doctors, teachers, police, judges. People still, to some extent, retain respect for the majority of them, but in a fast-track world, where there isn't enough time to do the job properly, we find that GPs, for example, may have no time just to listen, and are so pushed that they will write a sick note for someone who isn't really sick, or a prescription that isn't needed. (Yes, of course doctors do a wonderful job, but I am highlighting the results of pressures for some.) Relatively low-paid teachers act as referees in their classrooms; they cannot deal with disciplinary situations for fear of allegations of assault or molestation. The police fare slightly better, but are still the villains when it comes to racism or shooting the wrong person or not responding to a call. Knocking our role models is par for the course.

Our sporting heroes, who used to feature on card collections from sweet or cigarette boxes, now have feet of clay. An investigation is currently in train over football match-rigging. We find that those gifted with speed are too often found to take performance-enhancing drugs. Sport is often now less about the taking part and more about the winning. The Olympics has become less about the games, and more about the legacy. The purity of our heroes is no longer beyond question.

And the 'professions' no longer profess as they once did. In fact, employment standards in general seem to have changed. Has the quality of people doing a job fallen? Almost all appointments these days are based on qualifications. Modern-day human resources procedures make sure that boxes are ticked, rather than whether the applicant has the real talent or practical experience to do a good job, so anyone who does not have the right academic qualifications cannot get an interview – a hurdle which is probably responsible for delivering mediocrity. Anyone outside the box won't even make it to the long list, these days. Thus we see the downgrading, again, of personal application and ability in favour of just taking the Jo whose score we can point to. The emphasis is on academic ability and qualification, not on who you are as a person. And then it's a joke, really, because in the end it's often something about the person that makes that person the one for the job. I've seen and been on panel after panel where the scores awarded for applicants' answers are made to fit the person that the panel 'feels' is the right one for the job. Qualifications don't make you a person; they don't quantify natural talent and they don't deal with life experience and how you handle it.

The mix of professions has changed. What used to be the respected professions – doctors, teachers, police – have given way to business, PR and management. Architects used to command a percentage fee of a job – a professional fee. They strove to create buildings and spaces of beauty as well as of a high standard. Now a developers' charter rules the construction world. Architects are the servant to all the others whose profit motives come first and foremost, and are often the only arbiter of the required standard of the built environment. No wonder we are served with mostly developer-led dross. And so it goes on.

Why is *The Apprentice* such a TV hit? Why is Alan Sugar, at the age of sixty and not exactly blessed with the usual good looks of superheroes, someone that kids love to watch? Because, firstly, he is a real person, not a product of the sausage-machine that is now demanded by the educational and working world; and, secondly, he says what he thinks and not what is amorphous rubbish. God save us from the double-rubbish-speak that now inhabits our speech and our thought.

The nuclear family, with Mum, Dad and two kids living together, is no longer the norm. More than 40 per cent of marriages end in divorce. Now nearly one in two children in the UK are born to unmarried parents. Family break-up is sited as one of the main causes of people living in temporary accommodation. Four thousand children a day call Childline. Britain has the highest rate of teenage pregnancies in Europe and one in four children live in lone-parent families. So we're not exactly hacking it with regard to the perfect family.

David Cameron's proposal for a small tax-break to incentivise marriage and staying married is not the glue that families need. The real question is how single-parent families can be supported in ensuring that children have the right environment in which to flourish. How can we get separated or even never-actually-together parents to both take responsibility for the life they brought into the world? Yet again, the question is, how can we change behaviour?

And as for parents, we're not as good as we should be. We let our children have TVs or computers in their bedroom. Some of us don't know where our child is of an evening and some will even write a sick note for a child that doesn't want to go to school, or take them on holiday in the term time. We parents used to uphold authority if our child was told off or punished – now we hear all the time of parents berating teachers for telling their little dear off.

Nor are we the community-minded souls we once were either. Joyce Vincent, a constituent of mine, lay dead in her flat in a busy block of flats in a busy area for three years before she was found. How could that happen in a civilised, caring society? This was a big story in Italy, where because family and community are so strong they could not believe that family, friends, neighbours, or even utilities, had not called or wondered about her in over three years.

There are many streets where neighbours don't know each other and never a word is exchanged. One cause of crime (let alone unhappiness or loneliness) is anonymity. Where people move around a lot and where the population is transient, crime rates rise. One of the best predictors of crime is how many people you know within a fifteen-minute walk of your home; the more people you know, the lower the rate.

When someone fails to keep their property tidy or clean or is noisy, neighbour disputes ricochet up to explosion level and local authorities don't step in to enforce cleanliness or social behaviour, or noise complaints, until murder is threatened. There cannot be an MP or local councillor who has not encountered neighbours who were once reasonable people but who now are hysterical about each others' behaviour.

And don't get me started on health and safety. Suffice to say that it took a teacher practically a whole morning to fill in the paperwork necessary to bring two local schoolboys (aged fifteen) up to Parliament (a simple three-quarter-hour tube journey) to interview me for their school magazine. Personally, I thought a permission slip from the parents would have sufficed, and at that age they could and should have come on their own. Has our risk-averse world (or fear of being sued) now tipped the balance in favour of the ridiculous?

My own daughter is doing some voluntary work helping children in a local school with their reading. Her couple of days' training was mostly about how not to touch or hug the child and what not to say. So much so that when one of the kids she had been working with ran across to her and flung her arms around her middle with affection, my daughter had gently to disengage the child's arms and tell her that she mustn't do that any more. What a horrible, hostile, unaffectionate and distancing world we are creating. Fear of being sued or accused is replacing common sense and human reaction.

Sticking plasters for the human condition

So, there we are, feeling sorry for ourselves, unhappy with work, no one to love, separated from our children, not as slim as the magazines say we should be, our family miles away, our home too small, traffic terrible, public transport sheer hell, work too routine, trouble on the streets and nowhere and nothing to do. What is our pick-me up? How can we replace love, security, respect, status? What are our modern sticking plasters?

There's always retail therapy. Our desire to purchase our way out of gloom gets us into more trouble as we borrow on what used to be called the 'never-never'. Live now, pay later is leading to spiralling levels of debt; a record number of people became insolvent in the first three months of 2007. We just love that feelgood factor.

Sometimes retail therapy just doesn't ease the pain enough, however, and some turn to drink. One in four men drink on at least five of the seven days in the week.[2] According to Alcohol Concern, girls aged 11–13 increased their alcohol consumption by 82.6 per cent between 2000 and 2006, while for boys consumption went up by 43.4 per cent during the same period.[3]

Or we can drug ourselves with television. According to the British Audience Research Bureau, by the age of 75 the average Briton will have spent more than eleven years of their life watching television.[4] So now, instead of living our lives, we watch reality TV and observe other people living their lives.

Widening equality gap

This chapter does not address the poverty or inequality issue directly, but as Chapter 2 makes clear, there is a strong link between inequality and social outcomes. In particular, the more unequal a society, the less socially cohesive it will be, with higher rates of crime and anti-social behaviour. The underlying reason for this pervasive relationship, I believe, is the stress caused by living at the bottom of the pecking order, on the lowest rung, with all its related issues of status, disrespect and exclusion.

We are social animals, and the quality of the social relations we experience matters enormously. Feelings of shame and embarrassment are powerful, and in extreme cases can lead to violence. Questions of 'respect' – or disrespect – and status are central to the behaviour of chronically violent men, and is a large part of the knife culture in our big cities, for example. With a knife, so the twisted logic goes, you're somebody; who's going to diss you now?

Drawing out the links between inequality and social problems isn't being soft on crime – it actually gives us far more scope for action to tackle crime than just wringing our hands muttering, 'they're so evil'. What governments of both the other parties have done in our country is to allow a society to develop where inequality, exclusion, stress and low-level tension is the norm. As a report by the Young Foundation put it, looking at east London, 'mutual support and neighbourliness have declined; isolation is increasing; mental illness is more prevalent than it was half a century ago; the signs of day-to-day anger and tension are everywhere'.[5] So as a party we should be looking at policies to reduce stress and inequality, with less emphasis on status and more on cooperation and friendship.

Status and friendship have their roots in fundamentally different ways of resolving the problem of competition for scarce resources. Status is based on pecking order, coercion and privileged access to resources, while friendship is based on a more egalitarian basis of social obligations and reciprocity.

So what can the state do, and what about us?

Perhaps first and foremost, we need to re-establish trust in the state, the behaviour of the state and the nature of the state. This last Labour government has completely lost the nation's trust. Gordon Brown has a lot to do if the nation is to regain it.

We need to re-establish society and resurrect helpfulness and kindness as virtues to admire. A World Health Organisation survey showed that in the 11–15 age group the majority interviewed in England did not feel that 'most of the students in the class were kind and helpful'. In Sweden over 75 per cent said that they were, but in England it was under 46 per cent.[6] These are telling statistics.

Kindness, trust and niceness – what happened to these virtues? Was it Margaret Thatcher who began the slide away from the common good, with her 'no such thing as society' and the nation's love affair with home purchase, leaving social housing never to recover?

If one of the primary needs is to create communities where we know each other, then we, from the bottom up, and the state, from the top down, need to take action. How can we create structures and environments that value our human good qualities more and place less importance on wealth or status? There are certainly many things government and public bodies can do to make us sad or angry, so should their role simply be to minimise such actions or are there more positive steps that can be taken too?

In the grand sweep of policy, there are obvious big-picture items, including tackling poverty, reducing social exclusion and cutting crime. All help remove real causes of misery. But they are not the whole story. Just think of the number of times people say things along the lines of, 'we may have been poor, but at least we were happy ...'; so I am interested, too, in the smaller-scale measures.

Take one example: the question of how engaged someone is with their neighbours has huge knock-on effects on their participation in society, level of crime, happiness and even health. Government can hardly order people to talk to, or like, their neighbours, but at the micro scale, what about councils doing more to help and encourage the organisation of street parties, so that people get to know each other? Lots of streets already do have their own parties, which do help to create neighbourliness and bonhomie. Perhaps an annual street-party week would help to encourage all those who mutter about how nice it would be to know the people in their street to get round to it? One street near me does a great street party, where each person wears the number of their house on a badge. You hear all the time: 'Oh, you're number 46 – you're the one with the beautiful roses over your porch', or whatever. Knowing me, knowing you, is one of the answers to the common good.

Perhaps councils should be doing more to help online communities emerge in their areas? Measures such as providing easy-to-use and free website and online discussion forums can help people set up an online community for their street or neighbourhood – and of course click a link to print off some flyers to distribute to their neighbours.

Lots of social credit, or 'units of happiness', can be gained by (and this is a list from a constituent answering my call for ideas): more paved areas, to make streets pedestrian-friendly; cafes open later and easier regulations for pavement tables and chairs; neighbourhood coffee-and-cakes round the houses; street sales outside houses; piazzas; neighbour-hood involvement in local charities; proper walking and biking facilities in towns (kerbed bike lanes, safe walks for pedestrians); more open-air lidos all year round; neighbours selling produce from their houses (e.g. excess fruit from fruit trees, like allotment-holders do); more neigh-bourhood allotments; good cafes in parks; more bandstands; closing off streets from time to time for celebrations (New Year, summer solstice – anything celebratory); neighbourhood barbecues; interaction with neighbourhood old people's homes, schools, hospices, and day centres, through encouragement to visit, or go to events; local sport initiatives; fetes in parks – the list is endless!

If you look at the fastest-growing communities, they're on the inter-net. And for young people, the fastest growing part of their internet activ-ity are the social networks. Why? Because human beings crave social engagement. Websites such as Facebook are the new means to gossip, check who's talking to who and who's doing what and going where.

What are we going to do about our own parental behaviour? If our children run riot or fail to flourish, this is our own responsibility first and foremost. Clearly the government and various authorities have an important role to play – and they may fail our children, in terms of their schooling or other ways – but in the end we are the parents.[7]

A recent UNICEF report on children's well-being doesn't paint a pretty picture, placing British children at the bottom of the heap in the twenty-one rich countries that they looked at.[8] British children are more bullied, more unhappy and poorer; and we have the second highest rate of family breakdown. To me, a key issue is recognising that families do break down, and doing more to ensure the best for children in such circumstances. This includes have more and better male role models as well as more support for mothers. This is where the effort should go, and it isn't about headline-seeking legislation.

So many of our institutions, including many schools, mainly engage with the mother and rely on her to communicate in turn with the father. The result? If the mother and father don't get on, it means it is too easy for fathers to drift away, through different mixes of volition, apathy and circumstances, from proper involvement in the bringing up of their children.

Someone recently told me about 'Dads and Doughnuts' – a US initiative to get fathers involved with their children and their schools. Interpreted in different ways in different schools, the schools invite the Dads with their kids for socials, breakfasts, reading sessions, or whatever, but without the Mums. Crucially, it means that whether Dad and Mum don't get on, the Dad still gets involved – or, indeed, even if parents are still in situ it brings in the father in his own right. Since I have expounded 'Dads and Doughnuts' in the media, it has clearly resonated – Alan Johnson and ex-Prime Minister Blair have been following in my wake!

Talking to people it is quite clear that even where schools have a policy on paper of contacting both parents it isn't always happening in reality. One single-father journalist rang me to say that his experience, despite giving his details to the school, was that they never contacted him; contact was always through the mother. However, one of my colleagues, Paul Holmes (MP for Chesterfield) says that it is policy in his area automatically to contact both parents. So, there is some good practice in place that we can work to expand.

And we need to give power back to teachers to teach, and the ability to use that authority judiciously but without fear of being accused of sexual harassment if they cuddle a child to comfort it or pull it off another child it is attacking. This is a world gone mad. We, the adult population, need to learn to disapprove publicly of what we see that is not OK. We must learn to intervene. We must take responsibility to challenge unacceptable behaviour. This is not authoritarian, this is social liberalism. When an individual's behaviour adversely affects others, then freedom to behave as one wants must be curtailed – by society, i.e. by us!

And what about really tackling the disfranchised young people who get so complained about, but who have so little to encourage them into society? The local football team should be training and coaching; there should be lots of facilities for young people – but there aren't. I believe that you can engender a different energy from the negative toward crime, low achievement and unemployment.

It's time for change – the most radical change to give our young people a wider, broader and more challenging base. To teach them comradeship and bravery and the joy of helping other people – and perhaps most importantly of all, to take them away from what they know and where they know, away from their comfort or discomfort zones, and give them a new vision of how life can be. The middle classes already do it, with their kids taking a gap year. Perhaps there should be a national programme for all young people: a year out of their own environment, no young person to be with anyone they knew before, tested and nurtured through a couple of months' physical training and then voluntary work around the country or abroad?

I am all for a year in the wilderness. Our youth need help to build their status from things other than educational achievement, other than carrying a knife, away from television and computer games and free from coming from a privileged or a deprived background. We need to rebuild a great equaliser and a great opportunity to develop as individuals, not within the confines of our upbringing. Let us remove the status we find ourselves with at sixteen or eighteen, and build a new one built on friendship, effort and the common good. If we don't, then the cycle of decline will simply continue, and endless initiatives designed for headlines, rather than to really improve peoples' lives, will fail every single damn time.

Conclusion

Clearly a more equal society is vital in addressing much of the current malaise. But we also need to reward and revere our human good qualities and give them value and worth too. We need to work on creating a feel-good society rather than a feel-bad one – and that 'feelgood' needs to come more from our behaviour and less from what we own or what we do for a living. We need to rebalance 'me' with 'us' by promoting and valuing the common good through communities and a programme of youth training that takes young people out of their home comfort or discomfort zone and enables them to experience the glow from helping others and taking social responsibility for themselves. We need to look at praising the good and stop rewarding or accepting the bad. We need more time on social intercourse and less time insulated by work or stupe-fied into oblivion induced by our modern day pain-killers of TV, inter-net, booze or drugs.

It isn't necessarily the structures that can or will change. Change has to come from within and it is about the behaviour of the people who are part of those structures. This is not about morality, but about engage-ment, where consideration for others and the common good comes as high at least on our list as simply our own well-being.

If you think about what makes you happy – really happy – it isn't just about what you have. It isn't about what you do. Status isn't nothing, but it isn't everything, and we have managed to create a value system that says it is. It's not really status versus friendship – but it is about human relationships. After all, that's what makes most people's world go round!

Notes

1   *The British Household Panel Study and Key Issues in Religious Change* (2003–04), Cathie Marsh Centre for Census and Survey Research, School of Social Sciences, the University of Manchester.
2   Office of National Statistics, *Household Survey 2004–05*.
3   Alcohol Concern, *A Glass Half Empty?*, April 2007.
4   Calculation based on Broadcasters' Audience Research Board Ltd (BARB) monthly viewing figures; available at http://www.barb.co.uk/viewingsummary/monthreports.cfm?report=monthtotal&requesttimeout=500.
5   Geoff Dench, Kate Gavron and Michael Young, *The New East End: Kinship, Race and Conflict* (Profile Books, London, 2006).
6   Candace Currie, Chris Roberts, Antony Morgan, Rebecca Smith, Wolfgang Settertobulte, Oddrun Samdal and Vivian Barnekow Rasmussen (eds.), Young People's Health in Context: Health Behaviour in School-aged Children Study (World Health Organisation, Copenhagen, 2004).
7   Part of this material on parental behaviour first appeared as an article in the *Ham and High*, 12 April 2007.
8   UNICEF, *Report Card 7, Child Poverty in Perspective: An Overview of Child Well-being in Rich Countries* (UNICEF, February 2007); available at: http://www.unicef.org.uk/campaigns/publications/pub_detail.asp?pub_id=124.

Chapter 10

The Politics of Parenting: Confronting the F Word

Matthew Taylor[1]

Childhood is in crisis. British children are unhappier and more badly behaved than any others across the developed world, desperately needing more parental involvement. However, the financial pressures on parents – to find work, pay the mortgage, buy more than ever before for your children, and get them into the best childcare, nursery, and then school – are at an all-time high, undermining both the amount and quality of the time parents are able to spend actively raising their children. With 'child poverty' measured in purely material terms by government, income is the key focus of policy, with the result that a 'good parent' is largely defined as no more than a working parent, or at least one who pays the bills.

New Labour's approach has been to champion work, but to the detriment of care. Long working hours and high employment rates have not eradicated child poverty, and instead have kept parents away from their children, often for little return, fuelling rising childhood unhappiness and social breakdown. Furthermore, by calculating child well-being solely in pounds and pence, current policies, combined with an excessive political correctness that makes it harder to speak frankly about the benefits of two-parent family models, are undermining the expectation both on mothers and, especially, on fathers to engage fully with their child's upbringing.

The Conservatives, on the other hand, do little else but argue for a two-parent model. Their reasoning, however, is not based on parenting per se, but rather on the sanctity of marriage and a moralistic conception of the family proper. As has always been the case, and despite all their talk of modernisation, when it comes to the family the Conservative attitude remains rooted in traditionalism. Under David Cameron they have raised the possibility of tax breaks for married couples with children, despite the fact that these would discriminate against hundreds of thousands of children, would do very little to help married couples be better parents, and are hardly a reason to marry or stay married.

Yet at least the Conservatives have been prepared to talk about the importance of families and, in particular, fathers. For years both Labour and Liberals have shied away from any such debate for fear of gendered stereotypes and ethical impositions. As a result, any discussion of good parenting has been almost completely surrendered to the right, leaving progressives insisting – pretending – that parenting itself is no place for government comment, let alone intervention (except in the most extreme cases).

This needs to change. Historically Liberals have avoided the 'F-word', acutely aware of the tension between parents' rights and children's well-being contained within the liberal conception of the state. In recent years this silence has occasionally been acknowledged and some steps have been taken to assert a distinctly Liberal approach to the family, most notably in Steve Webb and Jo Holland's 'Children, the Family and the State' chapter in the 2004 *Orange Book*,[2] and in last year's *Stronger Families, Brighter Futures* policy paper.[3] However, the message has not been delivered strongly enough, and a set of uniquely Liberal family policies have not yet fully emerged. There appears to me to be a danger that Liberalism will not make a clear enough break from Labour's misguided belief that working parents raise happy, successful children, and that income is the sole measure of child 'poverty'. Plus, it is time for us to make clear that we, as Liberals, support a two-parent model in which both mothers and fathers are fully involved in the lives of their children – a very different approach to the Conservative obsession with marriage.

A crisis in childhood

A rapidly growing body of evidence is showing that British children are not fulfilling their potential and that their futures are being compromised. UNICEF's 2007 report, *Child Poverty in Perspective: An Overview of Child Well-Being in Rich Countries*, ranked the UK at the *bottom* of twenty-one industrialised countries for measures of child well-being. What this means is that British children are less happy, feel less secure and are making worse decisions than their counterparts across the rest of the developed world.

Many children are finding themselves trapped in self-destructive patterns very early on. According to data from the Millennium Cohort Study, which tracks the development of children born in the UK between 2000–02, an astonishing one in four are overweight or obese by the age of three.[4] Aside from health, safety is also of increasing concern as the threat of serious injury to young children is a growing reality as gang culture and the use of knives and guns are on the rise, with children as young as eight are becoming embroiled in armed violence.[5] Older children, teenagers, are smoking more, drinking more, and are taking bigger risks with their sexual health, with the UK having the highest rates of teenage pregnancy and sexual infections in Europe.[6] A great many are still not benefiting from the school system, a truth well concealed by the government focus on headline averaged improvements at ages 11 and 16. Fifteen per cent of sixteen-year-olds are still not participating in any education or training at all,[7] and three-quarters of those pupils in receipt of free school meals (a widely accepted indicator of disadvantage) fail to get five GSCEs at a C grade or above.[8] Plus, just as in 1997, over one in four nineteen-year-olds still fail to reach a minimal educational standard (NVQ2 or equivalent), leaving them ill-equipped for adult life.[9]

Predictably, the downward path on which more and more young people are entering adulthood is most pervasive amongst disadvantaged groups. Disadvantage links to underachievement very early in a child's life. Research shows that the gap between the development of those from low-income backgrounds and their more affluent counterparts emerges as early as at twenty-two months, and even if poorer children have higher cognitive scores at this stage they are likely to lose this advantage over time.[10] By the age of three it is believed that children of disadvantaged families already lag a full year behind their middle-class contemporaries in social and educational development.[11] For these children, there is no equality of opportunity.

The disparity between the development of poorer children and wealthy children is increasingly leading policy to focus almost exclusively on Britain's continuing failure effectively to eradicate child poverty. The current government is not on target to eliminate it by 2020, as promised, and has not achieved the 25 per cent reduction target set for 2005. Despite Labour's deafening self-congratulation over the 700,000 children who have been lifted above the poverty threshold, this only constitutes 17 per cent of the total; 3.4 million children still live in households surviving on less than 60 per cent of the national median household income. Child poverty is now double what it was in 1979,[12] and it is estimated that 1.3 million children live in severe poverty, in families scraping by on an average of £7,000 a year.[13]

But it is not only the extreme cases that are suffering. The present social exclusion agenda, which focuses on the poorest few and which tends to be absolutist in its conceptions of disadvantage, fails adequately to capture the nature of modern childhood. Young people alienated from the rest of society are frequently portrayed as a minority, persistent in small pockets across the country, extreme in circumstance but thankfully low in number, a final hurdle for the government to jump. This is nonsense. Social exclusion is a much wider problem in the UK, entrapping many more people – and many more young people – than government rhetoric would have the public believe. Modern alienation and detachment grips significantly more than the poorest few, sweeping across society in a growing wave. British children are now the unhappiest and unhealthiest from all developed nations – despite living in one of the richest countries in the world.

A crisis in parenting
All in all, it is hardly surprising that policy increasingly focuses on poverty, as defined by low income. But I think it is time to pause for thought. Is poverty solely the problem? The cycles of deprivation I discuss elsewhere in this book (see Chapter 4), which contribute to a growing sense of alienation in communities characterised by poverty, a lack of education and health care, drugs, and violence, help explain increasing levels of anti-social, unhealthy and unwise behaviour amongst young people. However, too frequently these phenomena are attributed to a lack of cash alone. These explanations are relevant, but they are only partial. It is impossible to understand the current crisis in childhood unless sense is made of what I believe is a crisis in parenting.

A good parent is a working parent?
In a liberal democracy the guiding premise is that, beyond the basic, fundamental laws that are in place to ensure that people cannot hurt one another, the state has no place telling them how to live their lives. The

liberal state is ultimately in place to protect the personal autonomy of the individual, based on the belief that the educated person's reason enables him or her to know what is best when it comes to their own well-being – and that of their children. Parenting is only the business of government when the basic physical needs of children are obviously not being met, or they are subject to clear physical harm.

A number of critics have argued that the New Labour nanny state has over-stepped this mark and waded well into the territory of child-rearing, pointing to overtly interventionist policies, for example support for breastfeeding, penalties for truancy, or parenting orders, showing that the state is now taking a firm stand on matters that were traditionally decided at home. These critiques, however, do not capture the full extent to which the state has appropriated the definition of good parenting, and made it equivalent to financial well-being. Regardless of the details of how you raise your children – bedtimes, diets, the type of nappies you use – the reigning dogma has elevated the things that you can buy for them, and so your income, as the primary concern. Thus parents, and so children, have been taken hostage by the drive to work, reinforced by government rhetoric and benefit sanctions.

Material security increasingly depends on any and every adult in a family going to work, whilst the state lays on ever more childcare to allow it. Employment has been the jewel in the present government's crown. They have taken credit for record high levels; currently almost three-quarters of all people of working age are employed.[14] Britons now work longer hours than any other nation in the developed world. According to research conducted by the United Nations, around a quarter of the workforce toil for over 48 hours each week.[15] Many people work over 60, and those working the longest hours in the UK are actually men with children.[16] Furthermore, while two decades ago 59 per cent of women were working,[17] this has now risen to 70 per cent.[18]

But, despite high employment rates and long hours, poverty has not been eradicated, and the current agenda fails to recognise the growing dilemma of in-work poverty. The New Policy Institute has found that '*half* of the children in poverty are in families where someone is already doing paid work'.[19] Low levels of pay and staggering housing costs – consequent on planning rules that have rationed the supply of housing despite the spiralling numbers of people needing it – mean that for many people, particularly those from disadvantaged groups with low skills attainment, it is perfectly possible, and indeed probable, to be both working and poor. The absurdness of the current tax and benefits system also means that low-income families may face disproportionately big cuts to their benefits when employed in even very low-paid jobs.

Not only is New Labour's drive to work failing to alleviate deprivation, but parents are being forced into work at the expense of essential time with their children. Over 40 per cent of children up to the age of 14 now have both parents in work.[20] For many of these parents, working means atypical hours that do not correspond with the school day. Almost half of all fathers and 40 per cent of mothers usually do shift work, or have to work in the evenings or at the weekend.[21] A survey of 1,140 working parents showed that 60 per cent feel that they do not spend enough time with their children.[22] Indeed, a quarter of the mothers and a third of the fathers polled spent as little as ten hours a week with their children, and a quarter of families where both parents were working spent on average £1,200 a year on treats to make up for time.[23]

Lower-income working parents spend less time with their children than their higher-paid counterparts as they cannot afford to take advantage of opportunities for unpaid leave.[24] It is therefore predicted that as few as 4 per cent of fathers will take the newly extended paternity leave, given that it is paid at around £100 a week – less than the minimum wage.[25] This is particularly unfortunate given the fact that increasing numbers of men are aspiring to a greater care role. Further, despite the proven value of paternal interaction in a child's development, the vast majority of working fathers still do not feel comfortable asking their employers for more flexible arrangements.[26] Gender stereotypes make men feel illegitimate, even emasculated, if they prioritise a greater role in raising their children over working every hour, while many women feel that winning the freedom to pursue a career has turned into the need to be 'super-mum', perfectly juggling work and parenting. Indeed, whereas twenty years ago social stigma stopped mothers from going to work, now this often prevents them from staying at home even if they can afford to. Many children, in turn, are deprived of more and more of the parental involvement and care on which so much of their future development is based.

In addition, many parents cannot rely on their relatives and friends for childcare support as modern communities have grown disparate and traditional social networks have been undermined. Childcare is very expensive, deepening the poverty trap. And when overtired, overworked parents are at home, frequently children are left to entertain themselves. Seven in ten children now have a television in their bedroom and six have a games console.[27] Research has also linked parents' busyness to the rise in child obesity.[28]

Meanwhile, state efforts to coerce parents into work have been particularly aggressive with lone parents. Over half of all lone parents with dependent children are already in employment,[29] but in the bid to meet the government's arbitrary 70 per cent target, incapacity benefit has been cut so as to push more lone parents to work while their children are still in primary school.

From lone and absent parents to divided families

There is a fine line between the state on the one hand showing an openness and tolerance to the many different family structures existent in modern Britain, and, on the other, endorsing a view that it is OK for dad to be entirely absent from a child's life. New Labour has crossed it. In the (perfectly correct in itself) effort to ensure that children of lone parents are not further financially disadvantaged, current government tax and benefits policy has actually disincentivised two-parent models, despite the known negative consequences for young people. Moreover, there is virtually no backlash for an absent dad taking little or no interest in their child – so long as he cuts the cost of lone parent benefit to the state by paying child support.

At this point I should be clear what I mean. There are very large numbers of mums, and in some cases dads, bringing up children on their own, in the sense that the other parent does not live in the same household. Here I talk about 'absent dads' because in 94 per cent of cases that is who the absent parent is – but also because there are still very big social expectations on mums not to leave the family home, much more so than with dads. In arguing for the benefits of having a father around I am not suggesting that children raised without paternal interaction cannot be healthy and happy and successful – a lot of lone mums do an excellent job at parenting, and raise great children – but what I am saying is that the majority would have their lives further enriched by engagement with their dad, in some cases vitally so. From the child's point of view, even though they may not know it, they are missing a major part of their lives. From the mother's point of view, raising a happy, healthy child on your own is possible, but it is hard, and should you really have to?

Research shows that children benefit from positive interaction with both their parents.[30] Progressive politicians however, in both their rhetoric and their policies, have shied away from saying so for fear of being identified with the traditionalism of the right. Meanwhile the right has confused a moralistic view of marriage and traditional family units with the very different and proven truth that two parents are better (usually) than one. But the fact is while there are many amazing single parents doing a good job at raising their children, they are doing so *against the odds,* and it is not the optimum situation for the next generation, who lose out emotionally, developmentally and materially when only one parent is engaged. The reluctance of progressive politicians to accept this is astounding when it is considered in frank and honest terms; is it really that controversial to say that a child is likely to benefit from a situation in which he or she lives in a loving home with a mother and father who both actively participate in his or her upbringing?

Of course there are situations in which couples try hard at their relationships but simply cannot make them work, and to stay together would be to subject a child to a highly dysfunctional home. Where this is the case parents should not be moralised at, and it is most certainly not the role of the state to enforce or even financially incentivise unhappy marriages. In most cases, however, there should still be a very big role for dad – and almost every birth should start with that presumption and a real imperative to work at it. Progressive politicians should not be happy to create in some communities a world in which fathers walk away with moral impunity (at least so long as they pay the Child Support Agency).

Supporting lone parents and celebrating their successes is undoubtedly important – raising a child on your own is hugely difficult financially, emotionally, and physically. But hadn't we better ask ourselves why we have the highest proportion of single parents in Europe – nearly a quarter of all families?[31] Doesn't refusing to admit that children benefit from a two-parent model fuel an attitude that absolves parents – fathers, to be more accurate – of their responsibilities? A staggering one in ten adult males in the UK are 'non-resident parents', better known as 'absent fathers', meaning those who do not live with their children, which instead live with either their mother or another guardian.[32] Many fathers who do not reside with their children are extremely supportive, both emotionally and financially, but it is a mistake to deny that many are not. Less than a third of lone parents are receiving child maintenance – despite roughly half of all children in lone parent families living below the poverty line.[33]

The shotgun father has been replaced with the quick-draw separation. Absent dads today escape the social condemnation that might once have pressured them into playing their part, because the modern political habit has been to downplay the consequences of paternal absence in the rush to comfort and support the single mum. The term 'lone parent' is itself unhelpful, as it perpetuates the misconception that the in-home parent is truly all there is, whereas in reality there is almost always another parent out there, somewhere, who often could be playing a much more major part in their child's life. A cultural shift in the way that these men (and overwhelmingly it *is* men we are talking about) and their families are understood will be needed to alter these misconceptions.

Furthermore the UK tax and benefits system has undermined the involvement of both parents, as couples with children can end up worse off than lone parent families. It has even been calculated that while a couple with two children needs to work 74 hours a week at the minimum wage to clear the poverty line, because of current welfare provision a lone parent with one child only has to work 16 hours to stay above the threshold.[34] The point here is not to argue that lone parents have it easy, but rather to show that we have eroded not only the moral but even the financial appeal of the two-parent family model, despite its benefits for children. Present policy, then, has institutionalised mechanisms that discourage the fullest possible engagement of both parents.

Good parenting does not always come naturally

If it is difficult for progressive politicians to break the taboos addressing the issues of spending time with children rather than working, and fathering rather than separating, perhaps the issue of teaching better parenting is even more of a no-go area. Here left and right have tended to unite in the view that the state should stay clear, and that people are gifted with the natural ability to raise children – that parents know best.

Yet we know this is not necessarily true. What is it that makes two children, both with natural ability, achieve so differently in school, in work, in life? What leads one to success and the other to flunk? Often as not, it is the parenting. For example, a report for the Joseph Rowntree Foundation concluded that the reason why white working-class boys are the worst performers in school is precisely that their parents fail to talk to them and don't confront the view that it is 'uncool' to learn.[35]

Take two babies, with the same inherent abilities. Which will get on better – the five-year-old encouraged to question, stimulated to discover – or the child always left to amuse themselves? It is devastatingly obvious that poor parenting leads to underachieving children, and eventually creates another generation of poor parents. Habits of bad decision-making are very often passed down from one generation to the next, worsening as time goes on. Some children do not reach their potential, or go off the rails no matter how good the parenting, and some, of course, excel in spite of the obstacles they face. But for babies born into a background of low expectation, a family history of low achievement and negative attitudes, the chances of this pattern being repeated is almost overwhelming, regardless of the amount of child tax credit they receive. On the other hand, successful parents are often repeating the successful parenting they experienced themselves – not because they are 'better' or more committed to their children, but because they imitate their own parents, as probably will their children in turn.

However, traditional communities and lifestyles helped, where modern ones hinder. Today the first baby we hold may be our own. Children are relatively isolated by long-distance relatives and scary streets. The TV entertains, where it used to be granny, or brother, or neighbour. The world has changed. We don't learn the skills of parenting as we used to. At best the training comes only when you are already pregnant, from Sure Start, or NCT classes, or from parenting books. Isn't that a little late? It therefore makes sense to replace these lost sources of education by teaching parenting in schools. The educational system contains within it the opportunity to replicate the natural development of parenting skills that used to happen in extended families and close communities.

For fierce defenders of the neutral state this will undoubtedly connote an unacceptable level of state interference, but in reality teaching parenting is no more questionable than teaching history or science. It is not about brainwashing the masses with particular parental styles or values, but is about exposing young people to the debates and issues surrounding what is probably the hardest and most important thing they will ever have to do. Good parenting simply does not always come naturally, and teaching good parenting, far from needing to be intrusive can be liberating. Crucially, it is preventive.

Teaching parenting can be as simple as engaging older children with the development of younger children, for example through reading practice or mentoring, in which they take a position of responsibility in relation to a more dependent party. As children grow older, lessons in life skills should not be confined to avoiding unwanted pregnancies, but should rather explain how to nurture those babies that the pupils will one day raise. Parenting classes could, for teenagers, involve lessons in the psychological and developmental side of child-raising, and the financial side of budgeting for a family.

These are the tools that will help equip future parents and foster a culture of interaction and engagement. Millions of parents, rich and hard-up, overworked and time-poor, still do it brilliantly. Perhaps that's why we think it doesn't need to be taught. Think again. Instead of bullying mums into work, dishing out ASBOs, offering one-off programmes and projects to parents already facing problems, wouldn't we be better off helping children grow into great parents in the first place?

The Liberal challenge: confronting the F-word

The right offers no immediate solutions to the parallel crises in childhood and parenting. It was the resounding failure of Major's 'back to basics' campaign and traditional Tory values that cleared the way for Labour to appropriate parenting and create a dominant but fundamentally flawed understanding of what children need in the first place. Attempts at centre-ground tolerance for divergent family values and models are a gimmick for the Conservatives rather than an ideological commitment, and they cannot shake their ties to dated, gendered stereotypes because for many of them those stereotypes still hold true. Hence the Conservative obsession with marriage and breakdown, rather than with care and parental involvement.

For modern Liberals, family – the F-word – has posed philosophical problems. How do we ensure that parents are as liberated as possible to raise their children and follow their lives (and relationships) in the best way that they see fit, free from the political imposition of narrow and restrictive conceptions of the good family, while still ensuring that children are protected and their well-being enhanced? Where does progressive politics step in? In other words, what elements of a parent's relationship with their children is the business of the state?

There is of course no question when it comes to the basic protection of children. The state must intervene in cases where there is clearly direct violence, either physically or emotionally. The waters are muddied, however, in situations where the actions of parents are not inflicting harm in immediately recognisable ways, but are undermining a child's ability to meet his or her potential.

What must be seen, however, is that the current government's drive to work and its unwillingness to support the family structures that better a child's situation are major contributors to the crisis in young people's health and happiness that is well under way in the UK, and are sufficiently damaging to a child's development to warrant a response.

Despite Liberal Democrats showing signs of at least being willing to discuss families, for example in the Webb/Holland *Orange Book* chapter, and the party's recent policy paper, advocating greater state intervention into parenting is a bold step for many Liberals. It still creates a sense of anxiety. But unless certain parts of a child's upbringing are guaranteed, namely that their parents are free to, helped to – and expected to – fully parent in ways that are stimulating, involved and thus beneficial for children, millions of children are going to continue to fall behind. Furthermore, for many mothers and fathers, the freedom to choose parenting over work and to choose active involvement in the lives of their children is greatly emancipating. What is more, child welfare is not simply a private matter as it impacts on society as a whole, as disaffected, alienated young people are becoming our future.

Thus, on the basis of evidence to show that children would often benefit more from time with both parents than the low pay coming in from their demanding jobs – which often does very little to alleviate hardship, and in fact can perpetuate a poverty trap given the absurd tax and benefits system – Liberals must firstly fight for an end to the short-sighted drive to work. Any proposal which would mean lone parents losing benefits if they do not work before their child is sixteen is therefore flawed and should be resisted. This is, of course, not to say that Liberals do not support high employment rates or in any way seek to devalue the importance of work, but rather that we recognise its limitations and role in resolving society's ills.

Challenging the work agenda will involve ensuring that there is genuine lifestyle choice and that it is not to the detriment of children's well-being. The first element of this is cultural and linguistic, and involves the way government talks about work. Rather than simply assume that work is the one-size-fits-all solution to poverty and deprivation, government needs to engage in debates that give credence to opposing views which show that this is not the case. Then, the state must put in place the legislation that will allow mothers and fathers to work less and care more. Primarily, this will mean removing arbitrary employment targets for parents while their children are still young, and greater flexible working arrangements, particularly for men, which must also be actively promoted in order to erode the stereotypes and stigma that prevent men from taking them. Isn't it time that maternity leave was not only extended, but that mum and dad were able to share the entitlement to full and part-paid leave, and a right to return to work? Shouldn't both mum and dad have the right to flexible and part-time working whilst their children are pre-school, or even throughout primary age and into secondary?

Alongside this must come addressing the role of parents square on. The married unit as the only good family is no answer for millions of real situations – but we should be able to address the important role of fathers for most children without alienating or stigmatising families that do not accord with conventional models, and particularly lone parent families. Liberalism must lead the shift, again in culture and language, needed to tackle this, advocating a state that openly supports the moral imperative for parents to work at their relationships for the sake of their children, and in cases where it is not possible for the child to live with both their mother and father, for both parents to be actively involved in child-raising. Families may be divided, but that does not mean that both sides should not feel under pressure to fulfil their care duties to the children. Many do, and the intention here is not to treat all non-resident fathers as bad dads, but rather to recognise that in the increasing number of lone parent families many children do not receive either financial maintenance or time and attention from the parent they do not live with, and this is not often good for the child.

In terms of policy, it is crucial that welfare provision does not punish couples in relation to lone parents, but given the advantages to children of two-parent models, the state must take pains to ensure that tax and benefits do not discourage it, and that we do not allow the idea that generally children do just as well when mum is on her own. The fact is that on average they do worse, and we need to admit it.

Finally, it cannot be assumed that when a child is born, mum and dad instinctively know what to do – or that parents or friends will provide the role models they need, let alone the practical support, 'Natural' parenting used to evolve, but that was because most children grew up looking after siblings or playing with neighbours and cousins. Socialisation skills came out of the practical need to interact. Now many children interact as much with the DVD and the video game. Bad parenting is too often passed on, and teaching child development and parenting skills to children in school is a practical necessity.

Conclusion

Not only is the counter-attack on the crisis in parenting an opportunity for Liberals, but it is also a duty. The UK's young people are faring the worst in the developed world – no surprise when we consider the barriers that policy and society are placing between them and their parents. The obsession with work amongst policy-makers in the UK has undermined the value of parental interaction with children and is placing mothers and fathers under extreme pressure to 'have it all', forcing them into an impossible balancing act between work and family where ultimately the latter suffers. Furthermore, the failure of politicians to encourage interactive and engaged involvement from both parents for the sake of an absurd political correctness has meant that the ethical expectation on many fathers is purely financial. Whichever way you look at it, many children are getting less time with their parents. And improving the quality of that time, not least by preparing every child for the parenthood that awaits the great majority just a few years later, is the least the present generation should give the next.

The path that I have proposed is a bold one for Liberals. Rather than turn on our heels and retreat from the 'F-word', we must open our eyes and look at what is happening to today's young people. The right will not save them, as it ties itself in knots over the importance of marriage and awkwardly attempts to pretend it no longer adheres to outdated values and gendered stereotypes. The Labour Party under Gordon Brown meanwhile continues obsessively to champion income and work over quality of parenting, despite the fact that solving the family finances at the expense of family time and parental involvement is throwing the baby out with the bathwater. Thus responsibility falls to us – for the sake of our children.

Notes

1   I am grateful to Zena Elmahrouki for her assistance in producing this chapter.
2   Steve Webb and Jo Holland 'Children, the Family and the State – a Liberal Agenda', in P. Marshall and D. Laws (eds.), *The Orange Book: Reclaiming Liberalism* (Profile Books, London, 2004).
3   *Stronger Families, Brighter Futures,* Liberal Democrat Policy Paper 72, June 2006.
4   'One in four children are overweight by age three, *The Guardian,* 11 June 2007.
5   'Young children being used as "gun couriers"', *Daily Telegraph,* 23 February 2007.
6   Independent Advisory group on Sexual health and HIV, *Sex, Drugs, Alcohol and Young People: A Review of the Impact Drugs and Alcohol Have on Young People's Sexual Behaviour,* 15 June 2007; available at http://www.dh.gov.uk/en/Policyandguidance/ Healthandsocialcaretopics/Sexualhealth/Sexualhealthgeneralinformation/ DH_4079794.
7   New Policy Institute, *Monitoring Poverty and Social Exclusion,* 2006.
8   Department for Work and Pensions, *Opportunity For All Eighth Annual Report.*
9   New Policy Institute, *Monitoring Poverty and Social Exclusion.*
10   Department for Work and Pensions, *Opportunity For All, Eighth Annual Report,* 2006.
11   'Harman claims study backs up her family-friendly campaign', *The Guardian,* 11 June 2007.
12   Barnardo's, *It Doesn't Happen Here: The Reality of Child Poverty in the UK,* 2007.
13   Save The Children, *Severe Child Poverty in the UK,* 19 June 2007.
14   Office of National Statistics, *Employment;* available at http://www.statistics.gov.uk/ cci/nugget.asp?id=12.
15   International Labour Organisation, *Working Time Around the World: Trends in Working Hours, Laws and Policies in a Global Comparative Perspective,* June 2007.
16   Chartered Institute of Personnel and Development, *Working Hours in the UK Factsheet,* January 2007; available at http://www.cipd.co.uk/subjects/wrkgtime/general/ukworkhrs.htm.
17   Institute of Public Policy Research, *Daddy Dearest? Active Fatherhood and Public Policy,* 2005.
18   Office of National Statistics, *Employment;* figure relates to Spring 2005.
19   New Policy Institute, *Monitoring Poverty and Social Exclusion,* 2006.
20   Written Answer to Parliamentary Question 141689, based on figures from the Spring 2006 Labour Force Survey.
21   Written Answer to Parliamentary Question 141690, based on figures from the Spring 2006 Labour Force Survey.

22 Skipton Building Society, *The Cost of Guilt,* March 2007; available at http://www.skipton.co.uk/press_office/publicity_campaigns/theCostOfGuilt/index.asp.
23 Ibid.
24 Equal Opportunities Commission, *The State of the Modern Family,* March 2007.
25 'Baby-time initiative fails most new fathers', *The Guardian,* 2 June 2007.
26 Equal Opportunities Commission, *Twenty-First Century Dad,* June 2006.
27 BBC News, 'Most kids have TVs and games consoles in their bedrooms', 01 February 2006; data taken from a poll of 1,300 families conducted by Lloyds TSB.
28 'Parents are focus of new childhood anti-obesity education campaign: report links excess weight in minors to bad parenting: 40 per cent of 6–9 year olds choose own evening meal', *The Guardian,* 15 March 2007, citing research from the Medical Research Council's Human Nutrition Research Centre.
29 Office of National Statistics, *One Parent Families Today: The Facts,* taken from the Spring 2006 Labour Force Survey; available at http://www.oneparentfamilies.org.uk/1/lx3x1olx-5001x10ix1591x1/0/0/250607/0/0/scch_2D2D8B720C1FD49D92C606A03B3770A8_scrt_facts/lone-parent-facts.htm.
30 There are many examples, including Equal Opportunities Commission, *Twenty-First Century Dad,* June 2006.
31 One Parent Families, *One Parent Families Manifesto 2006/7;* available at http://www.oneparentfamilies.org.uk/1/lx3x1olx20x10ix1354x1/0/0/270607/0/0//Manifesto_for_One_Parent.htm; Eurostat News Release, 'The Family in the EU Seen Through Figures', 12 May 2006; available at http://epp.eurostat.ec.europa.eu/pls/portal/docs/PAGE/PGP_PRD_CAT_PREREL/PGE_CAT_PREREL_YEAR_2006/PGE_CAT_PREREL_YEAR_2006_MONTH_05/3-12052006-EN-AP.PDF.
32 Written Answer to Parliamentary Question 137526.
33 One Parent Families, *One Parent Families Today: The Facts,* 30/11/06; available at http://www.oneparentfamilies.org.uk/1/lx3x1olx- 001x10ix1591x1/0/0/250607/0/0/scch_2D2D8B720C1FD49D92C606A03B3770A8_scrt_facts/lone-parent-facts.htm.
34 Patricia Morgan, 'You're breaking up families, Gordon', *Sunday Times,* 25 March 2007.
35 Robert Casson and Geeta Kingdon, *Tackling Low Educational Achievement* (Joseph Rowntree Foundation, 2007).

Chapter 11

Globalisation and the Role of the British State

David Hall-Matthews

'Globalisation' is a slippery term. It is discussed in terms of economic interactions, political relations, cultural and intellectual exchanges and even as a state of mind. It has been explained by advances in technology, political openness and the rise of multinational corporations (MNCs), including international media houses. All of these phenomena are interrelated, but can also be analysed separately. Many of the disagreements over the causes, impacts and ideal responses to globalisation therefore arise simply because commentators are looking at different things under the same banner. Even attempts to examine the big picture vary according to priorities. All discussions of globalisation – including this one – are thus normative, because there will never be universal consensus as to what it is.

This slipperiness is very useful to certain kinds of politician. Those who thrive on never being pinned down and prefer to appeal to voters' emotions rather than to win rational arguments can have a field day pontificating about ill-defined global threats or opportunities. Globalisation as a concept has far more political than analytical utility. A senior British civil servant once anonymously admitted, 'The only time 'globalisation' is used in the Civil Service is in speeches, often as an alibi in cases where it is felt that policy cannot be influenced.'[1]

The negative tone is typical: pessimism is the default position in most public discussions of globalisation. It has become the perfect scapegoat: vague, neutral and beyond control. It can be held responsible for everything from job losses and climate change to the dumbing down of television, letting governments off the hook. Not only can politicians evade blame for the impact of globalisation, some argue that they must not even try to halt its tide, because 'there is no alternative'. This creates the potential to have it both ways. Most British politicians do not profess to see globalisation as bad, even if some of its effects are undesirable. Indeed there is currently all-party consensus in favour of economic liberalisation. Does this mean that it is accepted that many issues are now outside the purview of the nation-state? Perhaps even that some ought to be beyond interference? It is not so simple. Globalisation may be used periodically to justify the lack of government intervention in the economic sphere, whether in response to specific British factory closures or concerns about labour standards in developing countries, but that does not mean that the government has stopped managing the economy altogether, nor that nation-states have lost all ability to influence international economic trends.

This chapter will therefore discuss the extent to which states retain control over their individual and collective destinies; and the ways in which Liberal Democrats would wish to see the British government use its particular powers, both to respond to globalisation and to promote it further. It will start by emphasising the need to examine the role of governments when conceptualising globalisation, particularly in debates about its historical origins. Commonly expressed fears about the consequences of globalisation will then be explored to suggest that many revolve around the perceived diminishment of state capacity and thus of democratic accountability. It will be argued that this is only true to a limited extent. Governments have exercised, and still exercise, considerable influence over the process of globalisation itself, and there is a clear desire for them to retain it in the future.

This is not an argument that the British government ought to stand in the way of globalisation. Rather, that it ought not to use it as an excuse to evade its responsibilities. The state has a key role in maximising the benefits of globalisation and there is a correlation between strong states and successful economies. A strong state does not have to mean big government. The UK is among the most globalised of the major economies and has gained immensely by being so. The Liberal Democrats have by far the closest historical and philosophical associations with free trade. They must stand that ground, not only on principle but also politically. There is a real possibility of Labour, the Tories, or both responding to future economic or political downturns by reverting to positions of economic nationalism. However, many people who are deeply concerned about globalisation are also sympathetic to the Liberal Democrats (and vice versa). There is nothing to be gained by dismissing them as naïve. On the contrary, it is possible to respond to such concerns without creating obstacles to markets, by reinvigorating political accountability at all levels, from the local to the global.

Local communities that feel secure and in control of their future prospects have nothing to fear from globalisation. Indeed they are more likely to be outward-looking. Globalisation will work if it stimulates local enterprise; if it does not, it will never be politically popular, even if it brings down prices. So those in favour of globalisation need to start at the bottom. Liberal Democrat local policy must focus on economic regeneration, not creating a semblance of choice in the provision of public services.[2]

A cautious approach is required, then, to liberal economics. First, there are other liberal goals which must not be subsumed to economic ones but will occasionally come into conflict with them, such as human rights, reduction of conflict and protection of the environment.[3] Second, more cognisance needs to be taken of the risks associated with liberal markets. There will be global recessions in future, which need to be anticipated. Individuals will have less job security and require assistance to adapt to circumstances. And, third, attention needs to be paid to the political dimensions of globalisation and the ongoing primacy of democracy. The final sections of this chapter will therefore discuss Liberal Democrat principles and policies, both internationally and domestically, with the goals of pursuing global cooperation while minimising the economic, political, social and environmental risks associated with globalisation.

What drives globalisation and when did it start?

Historians often argue that globalisation is nothing new. Movements of people and goods go back thousands of years.[4] More pertinently, there have been several periods of intensification of trade and communication since the time of Adam Smith.

There is less agreement, however, on which period is most useful to compare with the present. It depends what you are looking for. For example, many point to 1870–1914 as an era of massive expansion of global exchange, with the proportion of goods traded internationally reaching levels that were not matched again until the mid-1990s. Among others,

Chris Huhne, in *The Orange Book*, rightly identifies the importance of advances in transport and communications technology, notably the steamship, which greatly reduced transaction costs.[5] But what of 'political willingness to be open to global opportunities', which he lists as the other key determinant of globalisation?[6] The late nineteenth century was a period of economic retrenchment, following a currency crisis in 1873. Attempts to simplify trading by linking all currencies to gold resulted initially in disastrous depreciation and stagnation for those economies linked to silver, such as India, or to a 'bimetallic' system, notably Germany. The consequence was the first global recession, prompting almost all nations to re-erect tariff barriers that had been steadily lowered via bilateral and multilateral treaties during the 'era of free trade' from 1850. The only states to persist with free trade on principle after 1873 were Britain and Denmark. Colonies like India remained open in the interests of British exporters. America, significantly, had never joined in nineteenth-century tariff reductions.

Thus the period of technology-led trade expansion and the political era of free trade did not coincide. Which, if either, was the precursor to the current period of globalisation? If globalisation primarily refers to the cumulative effects of widespread economic liberalisation, the precedent was set in 1850–73. On the other hand if, as Anthony Giddens believes, modern globalisation is the result less of policy than of advances in information technology[7] – the twentieth-century equivalent of the steamship – then it is more helpful to consider 1870–1914. This has a number of implications when drawing comparisons. A technological interpretation of globalisation suggests that the current phenomenon started with the development of information technology in the 1970s – coincidentally another period of global economic crisis, recession and rising tariffs. In which case, state policy is of limited relevance, except as a response to genuinely uncontrollable and arbitrary market forces. Alternatively, if economic liberalism is to be credited with any influence, it can only have started in the 1980s with Thatcherism, Reaganomics and the Washington Consensus, then accelerated globally in the 1990s after the end of the Cold War and the partial liberalisation of China, Russia and India.[8]

This raises another aspect of globalisation. Thatcherism was more than non-interference, it was aggressive dogma. The Washington Consensus was actively pushed, particularly in developing countries, via structural adjustment programmes. Again there is historical precedent. Smith's *The Wealth of Nations* was quoted abroad with evangelical zeal throughout the nineteenth century. The over-promotion of free markets in under-developed areas was ironically carried out actively by colonial states.[9] Both historically and recently, then, powerful national governments – including Britain's – have driven the globalisation agenda, which suggests that it cannot have been designed to undermine them. Globalisation might then be seen as the global spread of ideas about trade, in which case the historical precedent was earlier still, in the late eighteenth and early nineteenth centuries. That period also saw much more sanguine discussion of the possibility of global governance than ever since as well as – or perhaps because of – a far greater role for private companies (such as the East India Company) than at any point until the 1970s.[10]

It is significant that history is usually cited comparatively. Few suggest that globalisation has been a continuous process since the nineteenth century. The Whig conception of history as endless progress has been abandoned in studies of international political economy. Historians of British liberalism know better than most that things cannot only get better by sticking to laissez-faire in all circumstances. Looking back tells us emphatically that globalisation is not irreversible. Indeed historians debate whether crises in the global economy – both purely economic (1873, 1929, 1973) and military (1815, 1914) – were the inevitable result of too much competition allied to too little cooperation.[11] Might we also now be, as David Held believes, at such a turning point?[12]

What is wrong with globalisation?

Held argues that if nations stop working together to manage global issues, they face another century of conflict like the last.[13] Few Liberal Democrats would disagree with his support for political globalisation, based on the coming together of states. International trade will neither increase nor bring benefits if governments do not actively cooperate and facilitate fair global competition. When examined closely, most of the fears of globalisation pessimists – in all parties and none – relate to the undermining of national governments. Yet, as discussed, the notion that globalisation is an inevitable and irreversible force does not stand up to scrutiny. It has been spread through the active promotion – by governments – of trade, ideas, treaties and international bodies, not passive surrender to market forces. But what states have created they can also destroy. Major trade wars between America, Japan and the European Union, or a return to Chinese isolationism, would be enough to slow the global economy as a whole.

Some fears about globalisation reflect this. It enhances the ability of strong states to dominate others. Will Hutton chimes with a large swathe of British opinion in his specific diatribe against 'globalisation as Americanisation.'[14] Disquiet about the prospect of China becoming an economic superpower is rising. Even greater fear is expressed at the power of non-state actors to dictate to governments. The most strident attacks on globalisation focus on the roles of MNCs and global finance houses.[15] There are serious concerns that poorer nations are willing to surrender taxation policy, or the ability to regulate capital flight, working conditions and pollution, in a race to the bottom to attract inward investment. Nor are wealthy nations immune. Chris Huhne reminds us that American politics is 'alarmingly responsive to specific corporate interests.'[16] A related apprehension is that the division of labour has been globalised, with wealthy elites and under-employed poor to be found in every nation. Capital is too mobile to be taxed, the bourgeoisie conceive of themselves as citizens of the world, the international proletariat is exploited by ever-more distant employers and a persistent underclass is universally ignored.

Such fears, though often exaggerated, have validity. None of them amount to an argument that global markets, global institutions or liberal trade policies are inherently bad things, but they present a challenge to governments to do more than just reduce tariffs. Although anti-globalisation protestors are rarely seen as advocates of state power, all of the fears discussed above reflect the common perception that governments can no longer control their economies, ensure social justice or protect public goods. Politics in many countries, including the UK, is harmed by this perception. People who are shopping not voting want their elected representatives to show that they have the willpower to stand against the worst excesses of global markets.[17] There is no reason why national governments should cease to oversee relations between capital and labour, for example, just because both are increasingly able to cross borders. Those who fear globalisation want to regain a sense of control over their destinies from distant, unaccountable bodies. They therefore mistrust politicians who are seen as too powerful, but respond positively to those who defend local interests against still more powerful multinational corporations or institutions.

This is consistent with Liberal Democrat philosophy, which empha- sises the importance of avoiding concentrations of power. Liberals instinctively oppose anything that stifles individual enterprise, includ- ing – but not only – centralised state interference. Nineteenth-century economic liberalism was based on opposition to the landed classes' dom- inance of the economy at the expense of industrial entrepreneurs. By the same logic today, liberals must oppose individual nations dominating the global economy, or oligopolistic MNCs dominating their sectors at the expense of local competitors. Freeing markets is one tool in the quest to free people from exploitation, but it is not sufficient. Both strong state institutions and accountable global regulatory bodies are needed to prevent excessive accumulation of wealth and power by international vested interests. Local communities need to be reconstructed to stimu- late enterprise from the bottom that will not wither in the hard glare of global competition. These require active political interventions, requir- ing us to move beyond knee-jerk concerns about recreating a nanny state, and misleading assumptions that a lone government like the UK's cannot influence global forces. It is nigh-on impossible to develop productive international enterprise in the absence of government. Global cooper- ation can only work when it is agreed and pursued by strong states, and the UK is ideally placed to lead.

Strong states in the context of globalisation

In the 1990s, it was often argued that globalisation would necessarily lead to the weakening of states.[18] To some extent this was tautological, however, because globalisation was being conceived not so much as the triumph of the free market as of free-market philosophy. One analyst suggested that it should be renamed 'denationalisation' because the widespread (but not universal) decrease in state powers was not driven by global forces so much as individual states' preference for deregulation.[19]

This suggests that globalisation does not reflect how much states can do, but how much they try to do. Margaret Thatcher and Ronald Reagan were architects of globalisation, not victims of it. Weaker states have been much less successful than strong ones at reducing their own regulatory regimes and gaining from free trade. This suggests that globalisation depends, to a great extent, on the strength of governments, rather than causing their weakness. Thus there are necessarily limits to the extent to which states can be rolled back, even if only in order to maintain the capacity to promote further globalisation. For all his attempted public sector reforms, no one thinks that Tony Blair tried to diminish the power of central government. Gordon Brown's theory of economic growth is endogenous – implying, if anything, an increasing role for the state – not exogenous. The relative success of economic liberalisation in China, India, Russia and Brazil – both until now and in the future – depends massively on the capacity of their governments to manage the impact of change.

Individual governments can still choose to intervene heavily in their economies, though others may try to persuade them not to. Serious problems arise where aid conditionality is used to force regimes to reduce trade barriers before they are ready, but this is a result of unequal international relations, not the fault of global trade per se. States that do seek to gain from globalisation have varied greatly in the timing and pace of deregulation, as Vince Cable has usefully shown.[20] Moreover, levels of international trade vary substantially, both between nations and over time, as can be seen in Table One below.

Table 1: Percentage ratio of merchandise trade (combined imports and exports) to gross domestic product (GDP)[21]				
Year	1913	1950	1973	1993
France	35.4	21.2	29.0	32.4
Germany	35.1	20.1	35.2	38.3
Japan	31.4	16.9	18.3	14.4
Netherlands	103.6	70.2	80.1	84.5
UK	44.7	36.0	39.3	40.5
USA	11.2	7.0	10.5	16.8

This confirms that the ratio of trade to production can go down as well as up. At the global level, this was most striking during the Great Depression between the world wars, but trade also fluctuates year on year, and patterns vary somewhat between different economies, suggesting that they are not only subject to global trends. This can be seen in Table Two below, giving more recent figures from the OECD. These are calculated on a slightly different basis, including trade in services.

Table 2: Trade in goods and services as a percentage of GDP[22]						
Year	2000	2001	2002	2003	2004	2005
France	28.1	27.5	26.3	25.1	25.6	26.6
Germany	33.2	33.8	33.4	33.7	35.7	38.1
Japan	10.3	10.3	10.7	11.2	12.4	13.6
Netherlands	67.3	64.4	60.9	59.9	62.9	66.1
UK	29.1	28.7	27.8	27.0	26.9	28.3
USA	13.2	12.1	11.7	11.8	12.7	13.4

It is noticeable here that the ratio of trade to GDP actually declined in several countries, including the UK, during the early twenty-first century, suggesting that recent globalisation has not been so rapid as is often argued. Trade figures picked up in 2005, however, and in 2006 the UK reverted to type with a vengeance, recording double-digit export and import growth, by far the highest of the advanced economies.[23] Regardless of fluctuations, it is also clear that levels of international trade vary considerably between nations. EU countries unsurprisingly trade more. This partly reflects the size of domestic markets and the openness of neighbouring countries (a particular issue for Japan) but also variation in trade policy, including tariffs and subsidies. It does not, however, correlate with deregulation. America was the least regulated economy from the Second World War until at least the 1980s, but a low proportion of its production was traded internationally.

Similarly, the increased interrelatedness of national economies has not, as some expected, resulted in convergence in levels of taxation or public spending. Even within the EU, the share of GDP taken in tax varies from under 30 per cent to over 50 per cent. Governments can still make policy choices and, importantly, voters can judge them. In *The Orange Book*, Vince Cable notes that high tax levels in Scandinavia eventually created economic disincentives and led to political change, and Chris Huhne that low taxes in Ireland encouraged inflation and similar democratic 'self-correction'.[24] But it was also voters' preference that justified the opposite tax strategies in the first place. The figures for public spending as a proportion of GDP are even more striking. The 2002 EU average was 48 per cent, compared with an OECD average of 41 per cent,[25] with individual figures ranging in 1995 from 68 per cent in Sweden to 33 per cent in America and 20 per cent in Singapore.[26] All three states have consistently benefited from participation in the global economy. Despite fears to the contrary, it is clear that international investors are not put off by tax or public spending per se, so long as national economies are competitive. Far from seeking out passive governments, their greatest priorities are the rule of law, political stability and the skills and flexibility of workforces – which require robust state institutions and can be enhanced by public spending.

Globalisation and British politics

Table One makes clear that the UK has historically had a strongly globalised economy relative to many of its G8 partners. International trade remains far more significant than in America or Japan. In financial terms too, globalisation is well established in the UK. Inward foreign direct investment (FDI) was 28.5 per cent of GDP in 1995, compared to 13.4 per cent in the EU as a whole, 7.7 per cent in America and 0.3 per cent in Japan, while the percentage of commercial bank assets invested abroad was 48.8 per cent in 1996, compared to 30.2 per cent from France, 12.9 per cent from Germany and 8.2 per cent from America.[27] Britain's inward and outward FDI both grew sharply in the late 1990s, led by the service sector. Total outward FDI stock rose from £200 billion in 1995 to over £600 billion in 2001, while total inward stock almost trebled to £350 billion.[28] Though rates of new investment then fell, the UK remains especially heavily involved in the global economy. Perhaps because of this, there has been almost complete agreement between the major political parties for the last decade or more in favour of its continuation. It is unusual, even in rich nations, to find only fringe parties on the populist anti-globalisation platform. There are scenarios, however, in which it is possible that Labour or the Conservatives might again turn inwards in the not-too-distant future.

As has been argued, anti-globalisers' fears about loss of state control are exaggerated, but have political significance. On the other hand, the far more serious threat of future global recession, as part of normal – if unpredictable – economic cycles is arguably not discussed enough in political treatises on globalisation. An economy like the UK's, which is tied to the global economy to a great extent, is necessarily more exposed to global risk and liable to be more severely affected if and when the next global downturn comes along. History shows that many states respond to balance-of-payments difficulties by reintroducing tariffs to reduce imports, no matter how much they preach free trade. This makes life hard for economies that are heavily dependent on exports, particularly in the service sector, like the UK's. A global recession may not seem to be on the horizon, but it is conceivable that the next American President will seek to address chronic US trade deficits, causing a global downturn, and the current impasse in World Trade Organisation (WTO) negotiations looks dangerously permanent.

Before the start of the Doha Development Round in 2001, the WTO was widely seen as 'the prime agent of all the negative aspects of globalisation',[29] yet anti-globalisation campaigners like Will Hutton and George Monbiot now see it as the best hope of reining in powerful states and ensuring trade justice.[30] However, the failure of the ministerial meetings in Cancun and Hong Kong has shown how hard it is for fairness to be achieved through negotiation between unequal partners. EU Trade Commissioner Peter Mandelson still refuses to make any concessions without reciprocation from other major players – including Brazil and India as well as the US – even on agricultural subsidies. Yet the case for support for poor farmers in less developed countries is as strong as that for maintaining the EU's Common Agricultural Policy (CAP) is indefensible.

The likely collapse of the Doha Round will emphasise deep flaws in the negotiation process. The creation of voting blocs by developing countries in Cancun has prevented them from being bounced into unfair deals, but it is no coincidence that nothing has been agreed since. It is not impossible that either the disillusioned G21 group led by India, Brazil and China or, unilaterally, the much-criticised US, will abandon the WTO in frustration.[31] That would accelerate the existing trend back towards bilateralism (giving strong economies much greater capacity to bully weaker ones) and slow growth in international trade, harming the export-oriented UK alongside developing countries. If the WTO collapses completely, global recession would be a likely outcome.

How might the UK respond to such events? It is hard to imagine the current government turning against trade, but if a period of economic hardship coincided with one of opposition, there might well be a resurgence of dirigiste tendencies in the Labour Party. The political clamour to protect jobs could supersede the economic rationale for non-interference. The Conservatives have consistently undermined their free-market message through the nastiness of their objections to economic migration (which true economic liberals should positively encourage). The party's long-standing petty nationalist philosophy makes it likely that they would return to protectionism under pressure. Indeed the debate has already started, with calls from the right wing of the party for withdrawal from the EU. Worldwide, one response to globalisation has been the reassertion of national (and sub-national) identities, often with positive effects for local communities. It is important, however, to distinguish this from economic and cultural exceptionalism, as displayed by the Scottish National Party as well as little-England Tories.

Another unhelpful response to globalisation – or to the perception that globalisation is weakening nation states – has been the demonstration of government power in the non-economic realm. Just as in the eighteenth and nineteenth centuries, the growing inter-connectedness of states and markets has been accompanied by fears of global terror that are based on real crimes but also exaggerated. While terrorist attacks in New York, Bali, Madrid and London were linked, it is questionable whether they were responding to globalisation. By contrast, the drastic response of many governments, including the curtailment of their own citizens' civil liberties, appears in part designed to reassure themselves of their value to society in an era when the pursuit of wealth is no longer perceived to fall within their remit. The extent to which they have achieved this – and thus proved how far we remain from the borderless world predicted by hyperglobalisers – is, if nothing else, greater than their success in combating terror itself.[32]

Liberal Democrats, then, must resist the tendency towards macho posturing by the state in response to both economic cycles and security fears. But they must also recognise real risks and the validity of many people's fears about globalisation. Canadian academic Mark Brawley warns that liberals must get the balance right between economic benefits and social costs or face an economic and political backlash[33] – akin to that which sank Margaret Thatcher. As David Laws concedes, economic liberals today are at least as much her heirs as the nineteenth century Liberal Party's, yet the differences between the Thatcherite and Liberal Democrat conceptions of the role of the state remain stark.[34] While she went little further than defence of the realm, Liberal Democrats believe that government should provide adequate welfare safety nets, defend public goods and stimulate communities, in the best traditions of David Lloyd George and John Maynard Keynes.

Social liberalism should neither be seen as opposed to economic liberalism, nor as an adjunct to it, but as central to the party's raison d'etre. It is not enough to speak 'the *language* of fairness'[35] and still less to assume naïvely that, post-Thatcher, 'society is more at ease with itself.'[36] Fairness must be actively pursued. Governments able to respond to global threats by radically increasing surveillance of all their citizens and visitors are more than capable of ensuring their social inclusion too. The final section of this chapter suggests some ways to achieve a balance between promoting global trade and protecting people and the environment, both internationally and domestically.

International policy

Globalisation has been achieved by the actions of strong states, rather than at their expense. It has been successful when cooperation has triumphed over sectional or national interests. The difficulty of achieving this can be seen in the economics game called the prisoner's dilemma. Two prisoners in adjoining cells discover that one has bread but no water and the other water but no bread. They agree to pass half of what they have, simultaneously, through separate holes in the wall. If they both do so, the optimum outcome will be achieved. But if one withholds his share while the other passes hers, he will end up even better off. If neither keeps to the deal, nothing changes. Thus it would be rational not to pass, even if that means an ideal scenario cannot be reached. So it is with states that believe in complete free trade but do not practice it, or groups who will not sacrifice their interests for the greater good. Liberal prisoners, by instinct, would pass their share and hope for the best. It was a Liberal government that stuck to free trade on principle in the late nineteenth century when all around were putting up tariffs, just as Liberals argue against EU subsidies and tariffs today, without expecting reciprocation from poorer nations.

In the context of uneven cooperation between unequal economies, it is tempting to see global governance as the best way to ensure that international goals like poverty reduction and environmental protection – as well as freer trade – are achieved. While social democrats like David Held are optimistic about 'the emergence of democratic transnational forces anchored in [the] thriving sphere of global civil society',[37] others fear that global government would be captured by interest groups. The Liberal Democrat view should be determined by clear principles. First, power should be as localised as possible, so global control can only be considered on a few specific issues where national cooperation or regional governance has demonstrably failed. Second, all institutions must be fully transparent and democratically accountable; the more so, the bigger they are. In other words, the approach to organisations like the World Bank, International Monetary Fund and WTO must be the same as current policy towards the EU. Democratising the European Commission, for example, would be likely to create a stronger impetus for reduced protectionism. Mandelson's tit-for-tat approach in WTO negotiations has not only been unhelpful, it has contradicted the stated views of his erstwhile Cabinet colleagues in the UK who, like all member governments, have no say over the EU's stance.

It is self-evident that the EU must not behave like the kind of distant, unaccountable institution that liberals have always opposed. It must be responsive, helping to solve problems that cannot – or do not – get solved locally. It is therefore legitimate to move beyond trans-border issues such as pollution and crime into aspects of social policy where the setting of minimum standards does not restrict reasonable national or local government. The EU should also work for the greater good rather than defending particular sectional, national or even purely European interests. Britain – which has a closer natural affinity with the wider world than many of its European partners – has a leading role to play in encouraging the EU to look beyond itself. Just as Liberal Democrats argue for the UK to be more European, they should press Europe to be more global, starting by showing leadership through unilateral reductions of tariffs and subsidies affecting Third World farmers.

The EU cannot afford to be a safe haven, buffered from external shocks in the global economy – though the euro may well prove to be a useful stabiliser for its members. Academics are divided over whether regional trade agreements are building blocks for the global economy, or stumbling blocks.[38] From the inside, the EU – uniquely built from already open economies, before the term 'globalisation' and the anxiety it induces were in circulation – looks very much like the former. In many ways Britain's membership *is* its experience of globalisation, and it has been an exceptionally positive one. For all its flaws, the EU has been a beacon of successful international cooperation, both economic and political. Until global institutions are better designed to cooperate in formulating constructive policy, without structural biases or endless vetoes, the EU is the closest there is to a template for global governance. This makes it all the more important that internal reforms continue, to make it into an example others wish to emulate, and that it seeks to engage more openly with the rest of the world.

There are several arenas in which greater power for international institutions could help, so long as it is democratised. The WTO will persistently fail so long as decisions can only be made by absolute consensus. At the least, a clear qualified majority voting system is required. Better still, a neutral and fully accountable board could be given executive powers to demand the removal of specific obstacles to trade, such as the CAP, and mandated to ensure that the poorest benefit. Similarly, the existing Liberal Democrat policy to call for the establishment of an International Financial Authority to oversee and, where necessary, regulate capital flows, should be pursued with greater vigour.[39] This is an area where effective state insurance mechanisms have on occasion been undermined by both commercial and bilateral pressures, away from international scrutiny. The World Bank and IMF have been complicit in this and themselves need to be democratised to ensure that they act in the interests of all nations. The World Bank's remit as a development agency has become opaque through lack of accountability to its clients. It should focus on enhancing the competitiveness of developing economies, less through market reforms than through institutional, democratic and human capacity-building. A strong state and a well-educated workforce are prerequisites for economic take-off and poorer governments need support in developing them.

Foreign Direct Investment, like global trade itself, attracts much criticism when it is not properly competitive. The solution is therefore to encourage more competition and thus more investment by MNCs, as well as encouraging developing country governments to introduce robust but transparent regulation. It is unsurprising that markets fail most regularly – whether in commodities or labour – in poorer, less globalised, regions. Global regulation of MNCs is therefore counterproductive – and also unnecessary because even now it can be achieved by states. No matter how widespread their production chains, almost all MNCs have clearly defined headquarters that they would be loath to abandon. The UK should therefore set an example by demanding that its domiciled companies meet minimum environment, safety and labour standards in their overseas operations, as America does for its corporations on accounting matters.

Protection of the environment has long been a Liberal Democrat concern. Notwithstanding the recent signs that America has started to take climate change seriously, the need for a global body with executive powers similar to those proposed for the WTO remains apparent. The environmental lobby itself is interesting because it represents a response to globalisation. It has reflected on global politics and economics and proposed both local and global solutions in a way that marks it out from traditional political ideologies centred on the nation-state.[40] Such simultaneous commitment to local communities and the global commons bears similarities to much recent Liberal Democrat rhetoric. 'Think global, act local' could easily have been a party slogan. This natural sympathy can be built upon to develop a bottom-up globalisation agenda to which green activists can also subscribe. Inevitably, there will be occasional clashes between environmental priorities and others (vide the Soil Association's opposition to excessive 'food miles', resulting in its unfortunate refusal to classify African meat and vegetables as organic), but empowerment of local community sustainability – environmental, economic and political – requires global oversight and is achievable within the context of global exchange.

Domestic policy

The primary role of a liberal state in a globalising economy is to maintain stability. This requires it to oversee capital movements, liberate and encourage entrepreneurs, insure workers against the impact of economic fluctuations on their career paths, and ensure that no citizens (or poor nations) are left out of the global economy entirely. Liberalism is not, by nature, a purist creed; it is all about mediating between conflicting needs. As John Ruggles suggests, 'reconciling the tensions of government interventions in the domestic economy with liberal practices internationally' is not impossible; it is precisely the task of 'embedded liberalism'.[41] The assumption that governments cannot or should not continue to enable the economic activities of their populations and provide social insurance should therefore be tackled head on.[42] The most strikingly successful economies of the last decade – India and China – have liberalised in stages, with the state actively managing the transition. After poor workers and farmers combined, unusually, to defeat the government at a time of economic boom in 2004, the new Indian regime introduced strong welfare measures, including 100 days of guaranteed employment per person per annum, while maintaining high growth.

Increased openness will necessarily require some workers to move from inefficient sectors to efficient ones. It takes robust and focused government to facilitate such transitions, but not centralisation. Encouragement of enterprise development within local communities, for example through micro-credit or alternative currencies, has considerable under-explored potential. Above all, there is little dispute that improved education and life-long training opportunities are required in the UK. Economic liberals from Adam Smith onwards have recognised the necessity for the state to enhance competitiveness in the labour market, while social liberals emphasise its responsibility for helping workers to adapt to changing circumstances. They are two sides of the same coin. This is now urgent, with the demand for unskilled labour in the UK predicted by the government to fall from 3,000,000 to 600,000 in the next decade. The social and political costs of the economic exclusion of a significant proportion of the population would be unsustainably high.

Adequate welfare provision – focused on equipping beneficiaries to return to work – is also an economic imperative. Other nations that have highly internationalised economies, such as Denmark and Holland as well as India and China, have tended to maintain high welfare spending which serves, in Paul Hirst's words, 'to cushion the domestic economy against internationally induced shocks and [enable] domestic economic actors to remain competitive by giving them aid and time to adapt'.[43] By contrast, nations with traditionally small welfare buffers, such as America and Japan, are less exposed to global economic trends, as seen in Tables One and Two. As Nicholas Stern showed in his analysis of the impact of climate change, it is possible – and politically necessary – to estimate the economic costs of failing to spend now to prevent future calamity. Calculating what is needed to maintain a motivated and adaptable workforce should therefore take priority over the desire to cap public spending, as proposed by Vince Cable.[44] Though keeping costs down is desirable, self-imposed boundaries between the public and private sectors are neither an appropriate response to globalisation, nor a logical component of economic liberalism.[45] It is no more nanny-statist to anticipate economic problems for individuals – and the economy as a whole – than to be prepared in advance for disease epidemics.

Conclusion

Those who oppose globalisation fall into two categories. Some are xenophobes, like the BNP or UKIP, who seek to keep all relationships with other countries and peoples to a minimum. Unable to blame what they falsely perceive to be an emasculated British state, they rail against the most visible manifestations of international interaction they come across, be they immigrants, call centres or the EU. Others, however, are motivated by a progressive desire for both global and local economic justice and environmental protection. Economic liberalism can contribute to this to some extent, but it is not naïve or illiberal to recognise where it cannot, and where globalisation can have detrimental effects.

Liberal Democrats stand four-square against the protection of powerful industries or nations – including those within the EU – whether by tariffs, subsidies or bilateral trade deals. But there is a strong case for allowing developing countries some infant-industry protection. Free trade can reduce living costs for the poor, but it can also contribute to excessive intensification of production and global warming. International relations are improved by increased economic and cultural exchange, but over-exposure to global economic cycles creates risks that must be anticipated. Reinvigorating local communities would be the best platform for sustainable globalisation, both economically and politically. So long as globalisation is seen as harmful to localism, it will provoke resistance, and economic and social liberals will fail to find common ground.

Globalisation is still a long way from overwhelming states, however. Governments need to be strong in order to facilitate international economic cooperation and fairness. Many have already demonstrated their capacity to respond robustly – and not always positively – to global phenomena in the economic, political and social realms. Strong and effective regulatory governance does not put business off in any country – it attracts it. There are circumstances in which international institutions are still necessary, but they can only be relied upon to ensure just outcomes if they are fully transparent and accountable to states. Similarly, the British government has to retain responsibility for helping those who are least well-equipped to benefit from global economic growth, and for checking its negative impacts. To argue that this is no longer possible would be dishonest and unwise. Not only would it expose the UK to unnecessary risk, it would further alienate thousands of very politically engaged citizens who are turning their backs on democratic politics.

Notes

1 Recorded in the discussion section of Paul Hirst, 'How "global" is globalisation? And where does the UK fit in?' (Goldsmiths Public Policy Seminar Series, London, 1998), pp. 31–32.

2 Ed Davey, 'Liberalism and localism', in Paul Marshall and David Laws (eds.), *The Orange Book: Reclaiming Liberalism* (Profile Books, London, 2004), pp. 43–58.

3 See Stanley Hoffman, 'The crisis of liberal internationalism', *Foreign Policy* 98, 1998, p.175.

4 For a review of different historical perspectives, see Manfred Steger, *Globalization: A very short introduction* (Oxford University Press, 2003), pp. 18–36.

5 Chris Huhne, 'Global governance, legitimacy and renewal' in Marshall and Laws, *The Orange Book*, pp. 104–05.

6 Ibid., p. 104.

7 Anthony Giddens, *Runaway World: How globalisation is shaping our lives* (Profile Books, London, 2002).

8 See, for example, Meghnad Desai, *Marx's Revenge: The resurgence of capitalism and the death of statist socialism* (Verso, London, 2002).

9 See, for example, David Hall-Matthews, *Peasants, Famine and the State in Colonial Western India* (Palgrave Macmillan, Basingstoke, 2005), pp. 57–91.

10 Emma Rothschild, in 'Globalisation and the return of history', *Foreign Policy* 115, 1999, pp. 106–16, focuses on 1770–1820.

11 Ibid.

12 David Held, 'The crisis of globalization' in David Held, Anthony Barnett and Caspar Henderson (eds.), *Debating Globalization* (Cambridge University Press, 2005), p. 3.

13 Ibid.

14 Will Hutton, *The World We're In* (Little, Brown, London, 2002), pp. 200–07.

15 Among others, Teresa Brennan, *Globalization and its Terrors* (Routledge, London, 2003); Noreena Hertz, *The Silent Takeover: Global capitalism and the death of democracy* (Arrow Books, London, 2002); Naomi Klein, *No Logo: Taking aim at the brand bullies* (Picador, New York, 2002).

16 Huhne, 'Global governance, legitimacy and renewal', p. 111.

17 Hertz, *Silent Takeover*, Ch. 6.

18 Most notably by Kenichi Ohmae, *The End of the Nation State: The rise of regional economies* (Harper Collins, London, 1996).

19 Michael Zurn, *Regieren Jenseits des Nationalstaates, Globalisierung und Denationalisierung als Chance* (Suhrkamp, Frankfurt, 1998), cited in Mark Brawley,

The Politics of Globalization: Gaining perspective, assessing consequences (Broadview Press, Peterborough, Ontario, 2003), p.18.

20   Vince Cable, *Globalization and Global Governance* (Royal Institute of International Affairs, London, 1999), p. 20.

21   Paul Hirst and Grahame Thompson, *Globalization in Question: The international economy and the possibilities of governance* (Cambridge University Press, 1996), p. 27.

22   *OECD Factbook: Economic, environmental and social statistics* (OECD, Paris, 2007); available at http://oberon.sourceoecd.org/vl=7246579/cl=15/nw=1/rpsv/factbook/data/03-01-01-T01.xls.

23   International Monetary Fund, *World Economic Outlook: Financial systems and economic cycles* (IMF, Washington, 2006), p. 220.

24   Vince Cable, 'Liberal economics and social justice' in Marshall and Laws, *The Orange Book*, pp. 164–65; Huhne, 'Global governance', p. 125.

25   *OECD Economic Outlook 74* (OECD, Paris, 2003), p. 163.

26   Hirst, 'How "global" is globalisation?', p. 17.

27   Ibid., pp. 19–20.

28   UNCTAD, *FDI in brief: United Kingdom* (UNCTAD, Geneva, 2003); available at http://www.unctad.org/sections/dite_fdistat/docs/wid_ib_uk_en.pdf.

29   Duncan Brack and Nick Clegg, *Trading for the Future: Reforming the WTO* (Centre for Reform Paper 23, London, 2001), p. 48.

30   Hutton, *The World We're In*; George Monbiot, *The Age of Consent: A manifesto for a new world order* (Flamingo Books, London, 2003).

31   See Amrita Narlikar and Rorden Wilkinson, 'Collapse at the WTO: A Cancun post-mortem', *Third World Quarterly* 25 (3), 2003, pp. 447–60.

32   Steger, *Globalization*, p. 63.

33   Brawley, *The Politics of Globalization*, p. 40.

34   David Laws, 2004, 'Reclaiming liberalism: A liberal agenda for the Liberal Democrats' in Marshall and Laws, *The Orange Book*, pp. 32–33.

35   Cable, 'Liberal economics and social justice', p. 132 (emphasis added).

36   Paul Marshall, 'Introduction' in Marshall and Laws, *The Orange Book*, p. 2.

37   Steger, *Globalization*, p. 67; Held, 'The crisis of globalization', pp. 25–34.

38   Hirst and Thompson, *Globalization in Question*, are pessimistic; Ohmae, *The End of the Nation State*, and Held, 'The crisis of globalization', see regionalism as complementary to globalisation.

39   Liberal Democrat Policy Paper 65, *Wealth for the World: International trade and investment* (2004), pp. 10–12.

40   Brawley, *The Politics of Globalization*, pp. 50–51. Another exception would be Marx, who wrote in direct response to global imperialism.

41   Cited ibid., p. 117.

42   See, for example, Dani Rodrik, *Has Globalization Gone Too Far?* (Institute for International Economics, Washington DC, 1997), p. 53.

43   Hirst, 'How "global" is globalisation?', p. 17.

44   Cable, 'Liberal economics and social justice', pp. 164–65.

45   As argued in Laws, 'Reclaiming liberalism', p. 33.

Chapter 12

The Economy and Climate Change

Chris Huhne

No government has yet taken the measure of the economic restructuring that will be necessary to tackle climate change. The effort to
decarbonise the world economy – to run our lives on renewable energy
rather than oil, gas and coal – will rank among the most far-reaching
technological changes ever undertaken since the dawn of industrialisation. Although there have been great changes in the past – from gas to
electricity, and from steam to the internal combustion engine – these
have always been driven by some advantage to the end consumer. For the
first time, we have now to take account of the unsustainable side-effects
of most of our economic activity. That means driving change through
policy rather than the incentives that come about from consumer reward
in the marketplace. Moreover, the changes will have to sustained over
decades. This is a formidable challenge at global and national level.

The response to climate change must be global. The problem cannot be resolved in Birmingham if it is not also tackled in Bangalore. It is
also a cross-cutting issue at home. It involves most government departments in a way that is unprecedented in peacetime, and requires strong
and coordinated leadership and teamwork to deliver change. This chapter summarises the key responses needed, at international and domestic
levels. It advocates a package that can be constructed without hurting the
poor or even compromising on redistribution. This chapter will argue that
the effort to decarbonise the economy requires a new long-term vision
wholly at odds with the short-term preoccupations of recent politics.

Liberalism and eco-Marxism

The crisis of climate change represents a challenge to conventional
thinking in all political philosophies, including liberalism. The threat
of global warming – of storms, rising sea levels, drought, crop failures,

mass migration – is so severe that many extreme greens have argued that we must jettison the objective of economic growth. Indeed, the Green Party's leadership itself describes the party as 'eco-Marxist'. Since growth is, in one view, the end result of so many other actions freely undertaken by individuals and companies, albeit within a framework set by government, this implies that we must abandon the principle that we are free to do as we will so long as the activity is not forbidden by law. It implies a process of licensing and permission that is deeply antithetic to liberal values. It would, indeed, be reminiscent of the Soviet Union's economic planning by Gosplan.

This chapter argues that no such extreme solution to global warming is workable, necessary or desirable, but that economic instruments that work with the grain of the market offer the most efficient solution that also preserves the maximum of economic freedom. The solution is efficient in the sense that it discovers the least costly ways of achieving our decarbonising objective. Moreover, such a framework can be progressive in that it can be constructed while protecting the poor from its impact. Most importantly, it can preserve the choice of consumers about their own behaviour and how they decide freely to 'spend' the carbon that they can emit.

The modern liberal approach preserves basic economic freedoms while setting a framework of incentives to ensure sustainability. We already forbid many activities (such as dangerous driving that would lead to car crashes and repairs) that would boost gross domestic product, and we merely need to ensure that environmentally harmful activities are contained enough to ensure sustainability. In some cases, activities such as the use of chlorofluorocarbons have proved so damaging that nothing short of prohibition will do, which was the end result of the 1987 Montreal Protocol and its amendments. But in the case of the activities that lead to global warming – the burning of fossil fuels and the destruction of carbon sinks like rainforests – sustainability can be attained through a mixture of economic instruments that work by changing the market's incentives.

Economic instruments and their practicality

The best example of economic instruments – and potentially the most effective mechanism in principle – is the European Union's Emissions

Trading Scheme (ETS), modelled on the cap-and-trade scheme pioneered in the United States to curb sulphur emissions and acid rain.

Under the ETS, businesses are allocated a quota of carbon based on past use, which they can sell if they cut their actual use below the quota. If they use more than their quota, they have to buy. The allocations add up to national totals that are designed to tighten gradually in line with international commitments, and thereby generate increasing incentives to cut emissions through a higher price for carbon.

Until now, the ETS has been ineffective. This is largely because the caps have not been binding enough, and because it has failed to create enough long-term certainty to produce more investment in lower carbon technologies. The price of a permit to emit a tonne of carbon in 2007 had sunk as low as 25 eurocents at the time of writing (June 2007), which is negligible. But the allocations in the 2008–12 phase are a lot tighter, and were reflected in a price of €23 per tonne. In addition to a tougher allocation properly policed by the EU Commission, it would make sense to curb permits even further and sell the remainder by auction. At present, the directives allow up to 10 per cent to be auctioned.

The advantage of the ETS is that a company can generate ever-increasing cash by curbing its emissions. (This is superior, for example, to the incentive effects of a tax, where a company can only save the tax rate on the activity or lack of it.) Because permits are tradable between companies both in Britain and across the EU, the ETS also seeks out the emissions that are easiest to curb first: companies that can cut emissions at lowest cost will do so and sell their allocations onwards. In this sense, the ETS promotes the most efficient – least-cost – carbon reductions. This type of scheme should be generalised as widely as possible so that the costs of curbing emissions are cut to the minimum necessary. There is no merit in a hair shirt for the sake of it.

Nevertheless, the ETS still covers less than half of the UK carbon emissions in big energy-using industries like electricity generation, steel and chemicals. Even if it is extended to other industries – to aviation, road freight and shipping – it will still leave substantial carbon-creating activities untouched. Indeed, the two most substantial growth areas of carbon emissions in the UK are domestic energy and private transport. Neither is fully covered by the ETS, nor can be fully covered. The biggest gap would be personal carbon use when driving a car.

REINVENTING THE STATE: SOCIAL LIBERALISM FOR THE 21st CENTURY

In theory, this gap could be filled by a scheme of personal carbon allowances, under which each individual would have an annual allowance that would be slowly used up whenever she or he used a carbon-emitting service. You would enter, for example, the garage and swipe your carbon card as well as your credit card. If you had no carbon allowance left, you would have to pay extra at the current carbon price over and above the petrol price. An attractive feature of such a scheme is that big carbon emitters – drivers of large saloons – would theoretically run through their allowances rapidly and would have to buy surpluses from others with no car or a more modest vehicle. The scheme potentially has both environmental and redistributive consequences and is worth examining closely as a policy option.

There are potential difficulties with personal carbon allowances if they are to include domestic fuel, as there is an enormous variation in fuel use quite unrelated to income. Among the poorest 10 per cent of the population by income, fuel use varies by a factor of six.[1] Poor pensioners in draughty homes with old boilers might find themselves running out of personal carbon allowances too quickly. They would then either fall victim to cold and hypothermia, or they would become a charge on the welfare payments of the state. Moreover, the technology is not yet ready to deliver even a modest scheme of personal carbon allowances. Similarly, the option of a national road user charge based on congestion and fuel use is unlikely before 2012 at the earliest. These are, realistically, second-generation policies rather than practical means of delivering the first wave of serious carbon cuts.

If we are to tackle the problem of climate change on a ten-to-fifteen-year horizon, as leading scientists such as James Hansen suggest we must, we need to use existing technologies and policy instruments. This effectively means the ETS for larger businesses, and other measures for the activities of individuals and small businesses. In the hierarchy of liberal economic instruments, cap-and-trade schemes are closely followed by green taxes designed to put a higher price on environmentally damaging activity. By using the price mechanism, those carbon-emitting activities that are least expensive to stop – or to which customers are most indifferent – are hit first.

This is the case for green taxes: you can tax pollution, not people, in a green tax switch that changes the way taxes are raised. There is currently a whole panoply of such green taxes – landfill tax, aggregates levy, vehicle excise duty, air passenger duty, fuel duty – but fuel duty raises two-thirds of the total revenue. Due to the government's retreat in the face of the fuel duty protests in 2000, the pressure exerted by green taxes has steadily fallen. Green taxes then raised 3.6 per cent of GDP – the best measure of any tax burden – but this had fallen to 2.9 per cent of GDP by 2005.[2]

Of course, it is theoretically possible for green taxes to fall because they are being successful in choking off carbon emissions. However, it is disingenuous of ministers to argue this case when carbon emissions have risen since 1997 and a key reason why Britain is meeting its Kyoto Protocol targets is a switch from coal to gas as a fuel by the power generation sector for reasons other than a concern about climate change. Gas produces about a quarter less of the carbon emissions than coal for a given amount of electricity.

The use of green taxes to change personal behaviour is most appropriate in situations where the number of actors is so large that an emissions trading scheme is implausible. A classic example is transport, where carbon emissions have risen 18 per cent since the Kyoto base year of 1990, in contrast to every other sector of the economy, which have seen absolute declines in emissions.[3] One cause is the steadily declining cost of motoring compared with the real rise in the cost of bus and rail travel. Given that there are easy substitutes for high-carbon-emitting vehicles, the declining pressure from green taxes cannot be sensible policy. In effect, all the fuel efficiency gains brought about by technological improvement have been wiped out by changing consumer tastes towards large sports utility vehicles (SUVs). Households too could make very substantial gains in energy use through simple substitutions such as compact fluorescent bulbs for incandescent bulbs, more efficient boilers and installation of the minimum recommended twelve inches of loft insulation – for which the payback period is just a year, but more than a third of households are still under-insulated.

There are, though, constraints. It may make sense eventually to extend the climate change levy – based genuinely on emissions rather than energy use – to households but this is, as we have seen, not fair in the short term because of the enormous dispersion of energy use among the income-poor. A much more radical policy of improving energy efficiency is necessary for those in fuel poverty, and at risk of fuel poverty, before the price mechanism can be vigorously used in the household sector. There is also a question mark over whether the price mechanism is effective in this area, since energy usage depends so much on the vintage of the boiler and of the home. Energy and carbon are now also very cheap relative to disposable incomes for the great majority of households, so such taxes would have to be very high if they were to bear the burden of dissuasion from carbon emissions.

Transport is another matter. Transport taxes are not inherently regressive, despite the conventional wisdom. Some 28 per cent of UK households have no access to a car, and so are not affected by fuel duty or vehicle excise duty. Moreover, any scheme that targets the purchase of new cars with a steeply graduated vehicle excise duty will also bear down on richer parts of the income distribution. VED is a high-profile 'lumpy' tax, which is much more likely to make people think twice before deciding to buy a fuel-inefficient car than merely ratcheting up fuel duty, where the responsiveness of behaviour to more incremental price changes has been modest because of rising incomes.

The evidence on air travel is that demand is responsive to price in the leisure area: typical estimates are that a 1 per cent rise in prices leads to a 1 per cent fall in demand if other things are equal. The sharp fall in prices is one of the principal reasons for the explosive growth in flights. Nor are distributional concerns a block. With flights, growth has been fuelled more by the more frequent short breaks of the prosperous middle classes than by the foreign holidays of the less well-off. Just 20 per cent of leisure flights are taken by those in the bottom half of the income distribution.[4] The average income of those taking leisure flights from UK airports recently surveyed by the Civil Aviation Authority was nearly £50,000 – more than double the national average.

This is also the firm conclusion of the most thorough study yet undertaken into green taxes as they have been pioneered among the Nordic countries. Commissioned by the Nordic Council, the study's conclusion on regressivity is as follows:

> Wherever a tax is introduced there are likely to be concerns about the distributional implications – environmental taxes have not escaped this tendency and they have often been proclaimed as regressive. Research results from Sweden, Norway and Denmark,

reviewed in the report, unveil more carefully the precise distributional effects and, in fact, come to more balanced conclusions. These studies take into account both the direct and indirect effects of taxes on equity, as these effects also occur as a result of changes in consumer prices. The findings show that rural areas are disproportionately burdened by environmental taxes. Another main result is that while energy taxes tend to be distributionally regressive, taxes on transport fuels and pollution are, respectively, progressive and neutral. Lower income households tend to spend a larger share of their disposable income on heating, electricity and water than high-income households – while the opposite is the case for vehicle and transport consumption. To put it simply, richer people drive bigger cars, and for longer distances. In Denmark, the regressivity of energy taxes is more or less similar to the regressivity of Value Added Taxes (VAT) when measured through the Gini index. However, compared with alcohol and tobacco taxes, energy taxes are less regressive. These findings are subject to any subsequent redistributive efforts. A Swedish analysis which incorporates mitigation efforts introduced to neutralise the distributional impacts shows that a change in the personal allowance (standard deduction) was sufficient to neutralise the regressive impacts.[5]

There are, of course, competitive constraints that mean some green taxes have effective national limits. Aviation is very lightly taxed, paying neither value added tax on tickets nor any fuel duty on kerosene use. However, the European Union would probably be the minimum sphere of action for either tax if there were not to be an encouragement for passengers to evade the tax by flying long-haul from other European cities instead. The Liberal Democrats' judgement has been that the national element of aviation tax – the air passenger duty – can nevertheless be reformed and raised substantially before serious evasion sets in. The obvious change is to base the duty on the emissions of the flight – emissions that increase with the inefficiency of the aircraft and the length of the flight – rather than the headcount of passengers. This would provide the airlines with an incentive to fly full rather than half empty.

There may also be competitive constraints on fuel duty, certainly for the haulage industry. Our fuel duty is already relatively high within the EU, but should certainly not be allowed to fall further. Moreover, there may be occasional opportunities at times of falling oil prices to raise the real value of fuel duty. However, the experience of the fuel duty protests suggests that operating on the purchase of new cars may be a more sustainable route.

Our proposal on VED is similar to the proposals tested by the Energy Savings Trust and the Department for Transport, and could be expected to lead to 72 per cent of car buyers shifting to a lower emission model (and of course also to a shift in the models offered by manufacturers).[6] Our proposed top rate on cars emitting more than 225g of carbon per kilometre (this compares with an emission rate just above 100g per kilometre for a Toyota Prius) would be £2,000 a year.

The role of direct measures and regulation

The appropriate approach to decarbonising our homes has to be different precisely because of the potentially regressive effects of using prices, but also because of the sluggish response to price signals as households are locked into old technologies. This splits into two areas: electrical products, and heating, light and hot water use. The EU is clearly the right place to reset product standards to save electricity, as this will maintain the integrity of the single market and the efficiency gains of scale economies. That means curbing the appetite for electrical power by banning expensive stand-by devices, and legislating for the use of dynamic demand fittings that will switch off inessential appliances at surge times of high demand use (such as breaks in popular televised football games). It also means an extension of the already successful energy efficiency labelling scheme for white goods to other appliances.

The second area is improvements in household energy efficiency and the encouragement of micro-generation: new domestic housing should be far more ambitious. Our building regulations are 65 per cent less energy efficient than those now being applied in Sweden.[7] They could and should mandate German-style *passiv haus* standards with much higher insulation (triple and e-glazing) and pressure testing for effective leakage. Moreover, testing should be independent and verifiable with the possibility of pursuing house-builders that have failed to meet agreed standards.

A parallel set of commitments needs to be undertaken on new commercial buildings, with offices mandated to have light- and movement-sensitive area switches for their lighting. The zero-carbon house, office building and even factory is within reach using existing technologies, but with a modest increase in the building cost, and the argument for high standards is particularly compelling given the long life of the assets, the substantial externalities in the decision, and the difficulties of measurement and enforcement in any scheme that employed pricing (such as cap and trade or tax).

Even more crucial is improvement of the existing housing stock, since new build represents less than 1 per cent of the housing stock in any given year. As a result, some three-quarters of the homes we will be inhabiting in 2050 have already been built. But the government's WarmFront scheme for improvement is both unambitious and slow: at the present pace, it would take 125 years to upgrade the existing housing stock. Here voluntarism has clearly failed either because of lack of information, or because the individual gains that households stand to make from energy efficiency investments are relatively small. For example, 43 per cent of households still do not have more than four inches of loft insulation, compared with the recommended 12 inches. The cost of full loft insulation is typically £230 and the payback period is just over a year since the savings on the annual energy bill are £180–220.[8]

The cumulative effect of such individual ignorance or indifference is enormous. We need a scheme that improves British housing as systematically as the suggested scheme in Germany, under which 5 per cent of the pre-1978 housing stock is being upgraded each year. The WarmHomes proposal would encourage comprehensive upgrading of existing homes at a potential cost typically of £5,000 to £12,000, the vast majority of which is worth undertaking on a purely commercial basis. The funding would be partly from an energy mortgage paid back through the utility bill, and partly from a grant from the utility. The energy company would in turn have an incentive to give such grants because it would face a legislative requirement to cut sales from one year to the next: a cap-and-trade scheme for energy utilities sales to households would give them the incentive to sell less energy through energy saving.

Such packages could also involve the funding of micro-generation as an option: wind power, solar thermal and photovoltaic roof cells, and the combined heat and power boilers that are now available for larger homes, and should soon be available for smaller ones. These should be the next generation of boiler, as they generate electricity from the process of heating water and rooms. Such decentralised electricity generation now accounts for less than 5 per cent of UK output, whereas it has reached 40 per cent in the Netherlands. A simple incentive – such as a commitment to buy surplus power at four times the rate at which customers import power from the grid – has worked well in Germany and elsewhere to encourage micro-generation. We should abolish the complicated grant schemes and go instead for a simple incentive of a high feed-in tariff to the grid.

Towards zero-carbon transport

Any climate change programme has also to plan for a big shift from road and air to rail. For years, there have been successive proposals for new investment in rail – for a north–south high-speed line, for dedicated freight lines, for incremental improvements to existing tracks to relieve bottlenecks such as Reading junction – yet proposals are repeatedly sidelined essentially because transport is seen as a lower public spending priority than health or education. The key issue therefore is funding, which is why we should look at new sources of finance such as a motorway freight toll that could endow a future transport fund for rail improvements. A freight motorway toll modelled on the existing German scheme could raise £600 million a year, Together with a charge on domestic flights, that could raise a capital sum of some £12 billion if the revenue flow were securitised and sold. This would be a substantial catalyst for schemes that are near to commercial viability.

Encouraging the use of public transport is also an important part of the green agenda. Local congestion charges combined with national tax pressure should provide increasing incentives for the use of public transport, but there is a continuing market failure in the under-provision of infrastructure schemes in urban areas, such as Crossrail in London or the Metrolink in Manchester. We know that such infrastructure spending creates substantial value for private landowners – the Jubilee Line in London is estimated to have raised capital values along the line by £13 billion.

Yet there is little individual incentive for landowners to make a contribution to the funding of such projects because the benefits accrue to all landowners – a classic 'prisoner's dilemma' incentive structure. In the case of the Jubilee Line, the contribution from the private sector (the owners of Canary Wharf, just one development that benefited) was only £180 million.[9] If, though, the business rateable values were revalued to reflect the rising value of land created by such infrastructure developments, and if the business rates were returned to local authority control, councils would be able to generate rates income to fund the interest and debt repayment costs of infrastructure spending. If they could show a likely revenue gain, they would be able to issue bonds or raise bank loans.

Such a scheme would also have incidental benefits in encouraging development where planners would like it to happen. If the business rate were based on the land value, rather than the value of the whole development including the buildings on the land, each owner would have an incentive to build to the maximum use allowed by the planning authorities.

Such an incentive has worked well in the United States, Australia and Denmark. It helps to ensure that parcels of land do not fall into disuse and under-use in urban areas, which can rapidly spread to blight a whole street and more. It is therefore a more pluralist and liberal solution to regeneration than state-led planning agencies such as the London Docklands Development Corporation. By making blight less likely, and by encouraging rapid regeneration when a site falls into disuse, it would ensure a pattern of diverse development that most people prefer.

Land value taxes are therefore also a substantial answer to one of the structural problems of the British economy, which is the need to maintain high real interest rates (and hence to depress investment) in order to cap wealth effects and inflationary pressures from the housing market.

Adaptation: preparing for the inevitable

It is also crucial that the government does not merely tackle the threat of future climate change by reducing carbon emissions – but also adapts to the climate change already under way. The floods in Yorkshire and the Midlands in the summer of 2007 were another example of the extreme weather events that are forecast to become far more frequent with global warming. Coastal and fluvial flooding are serious problems, and are augmented by flash flooding that arises due to the inability of old rainwater and combined sewerage systems to handle the high short-term rainfalls that seem to be a feature of the new world environment. Given the impacts of climate change, the government needs to adopt a comprehensive programme of adaptation that deals with the full range of likely impacts, such as tougher roofing standards to protect against extreme wind and rain, larger storm drains, flood defences, and reservoir and other water investment.

Institutional reform to sustain change

It should be clear from the complexity, political difficulty and sheer number of the measures discussed above that the process of decarbonising the economy will not be easy to sustain over decades. It is for precisely that reason that it makes sense to legislate for a climate change act. This should set up an independent body of experts – a climate change committee – to report annually on the progress towards a carbon-neutral Britain. Because it should report annually as soon as the economic and other figures are published – in March following the year in question – the committee should set an annual target against which progress can be benchmarked. That target should be varied to take account of the business cycle, temperature and energy price spikes.

Although the act would in theory allow ministerial failures to be scrutinised by the courts in cases of judicial review, the real leverage is public opprobrium. By raising the political costs of short-termism, such a policy could help governments to stay on track. Targets in themselves do not solve problems – if they did, this would be the best-governed country in the world. You cannot reproach this government for a failure to set targets. But targets can help provide an overall framework and sense of direction for the policy measures that must be taken. As such, they should help concentrate the debate on practical action and away from overblown rhetoric.

The international context

The above discussion shows that domestic decarbonising policy instruments can work with markets, but it begs the question of what international action is needed to deal with the problem of global warming. With Britain responsible for just 2 per cent of global emissions, it is crucial that there is an international successor to Kyoto, which extends serious carbon constraints not just to the United States, but also to major developing economies such as China and India. The United States alone accounts for more than a quarter of global emissions, but the shift in US politics symbolised by the mid-term elections in 2006 suggests that federal emission limits are not far off. In Australia, a former climate change denier (and refuser of Kyoto) like Prime Minister John Howard has become the first Western leader to ban conventional light bulbs. In Canada, a Conservative administration elected with support from Albertan oil interests has performed a U-turn on meeting its Kyoto commitments.

Most crucially, the European Union is gearing up to perform the same role that it performed during Kyoto, when the Protocol was only ratified because of EU pressure on the key signatory, the Russian Federation. German Chancellor Angela Merkel is a former environment minister who negotiated Kyoto, and understands both the urgency and importance of the issue. The EU's promises and targets at the March 2007 Brussels summit – not least to negotiate a successor to Kyoto, hopefully by the end of 2008 – were a vital launch to the process that continued at the G8 Heiligendamm summit.

China and India are more problematic, both because they see no reason why they should not have just as much development as the developed world, but also because they can plausibly argue that the world's carbon problem has been created by the developed countries. After all, carbon stays in the atmosphere for a century once it is emitted, and 70 per cent of all man-made carbon in the atmosphere comes from the present developed countries.

One interesting proposal from Professor Jagdish Bhagwati is that the developed world should recognise its historical responsibility for the problem by committing to a 'superfund' that could help the developing world.[10] The role of this fund might include the underwriting of the continued existence of rainforests, and research into and subsidy of technologies that would allow developing countries to leapfrog old carbon-generating activities, moving straight to zero-carbon ones; an example would be the development of photovoltaic-based generating systems for rural villages, which would no longer require expensive connection to a grid.

Perhaps the most crucial role of such a superfund – or leapfrog fund – would be to allow developing countries to leapfrog carbon-emitting technologies entirely, rather as they leapfrogged the need for land-line based telephony by moving straight to mobile telephony. Only when it is cheaper to electrify villages through renewables than through coal-fired generating plant will the dilemma of climate change versus prosperity be removed. It is in our interest to ensure that the research is undertaken to reduce dramatically the unit cost of renewable electricity.

Preventing future climate change, and adapting to that which has already occurred, needs to become the central theme of modern government simply because of the millenarian impact on poverty, inequality, public services, crime and migration it will have if it is not tackled. It touches most departments of state, cutting across Whitehall and beyond: the Treasury on green taxes, the Department for Transport on vehicle regulation and aviation, the Department of Communities and Local Government on building regulations, the Department for Environment, Food and Rural Affairs on energy saving and the emissions trading scheme, the Department of Business and Enterprise on power generation, the Department for Children, Schools and Families on public awareness, the Foreign and Commonwealth Office on the international framework, and the Department for International Development on the impact on the poorest in the world.

It is extraordinary that a progressive government cut back on flood defence maintenance budgets last year before finally agreeing a rise in the wake of the June and July floods. It is mad that it encouraged the building of 108,000 new houses on floodplains, installed high-energy-use coolers in new government office buildings, and cut research into the impact of climate change on biodiversity at the Centre for Ecology and Hydrology, or into climate change itself at the Hadley Centre of the Meteorological Office (which, bizarrely, falls under the Ministry of Defence). The government needs a high-powered cabinet committee on climate change, chaired by the Prime Minister, able to insist that it is a priority throughout Whitehall. Instead, Gordon Brown has downgraded the energy and environment committee.

Climate change is the most serious threat to our national prosperity and security, and requires a coordinated response across the private and public sectors unlike any other policy challenge that we have faced in peacetime. That effort needs to be led from the top with an understanding and commitment that can deliver serious change. There are no short-term fixes, but there are plenty of hard political choices. We have the technology and the policy framework. All we need is the most difficult element of all to muster: the political will to tackle a long-term problem in a political system known best for its short attention span.

Notes

1   S. Dresner and P. Ekins, 'Economic Instruments to Improve UK Home Energy Efficiency' without Negative Social Impacts', *Fiscal Studies* Vol. 27 no. 1 (2006), pp. 47–74.

2   Office for National Statistics *Environmental Accounts* (ONS, London, 2006).

3   Environmental Audit Committee, *Reducing Carbon Emissions from Transport* (Ninth Report, Session 2005–06, HC981).

4   Civil Aviation Authority *Passenger Survey Report* (CAA, London, 2004).

5   S. Speck, M. Skou Andersen, H. O. Nielsen, A. Ryelund and C. Smith C, *The Use of Economic Instruments in Nordic and Baltic Environmental Policy 2001–2005* (National Environmental Research Institute, Denmark, 2006).

6   MORI and Department for Transport, *Assessing the Impact of Graduated Vehicle Excise Duty: Quantitative Report* (unpublished, 2003).

7   S. Eppel and N. Eyre, *Putting Climate Change at the Heart of Energy Policy* (Energy Saving Trust, London, 2002), Appendix 2.

8   Energy Saving Trust, *Domestic Energy Primer – An introduction to energy efficiency in existing homes* (EST, London, 2006).

9   D. Riley, *Taken For A Ride* (Centre for Land Policy Studies, London, 2001).

10 J. Bhagwati, 'A global warming fund could succeed where Kyoto failed', *Financial Times*, 16 August 2006.

Chapter 13

The Limits of the Market

Paul Holmes

The market rules unchallenged – or so we are told, by a whole range of voices from Adam Smith in the eighteenth century through to the neocons of today.

This view was most succinctly formulated by Francis Fukuyama in his 'End of History' article, published in 1989 after the fall of the Berlin Wall and expanded into a book in 1992. He argued that the collapse of Soviet Russia and its Eastern European satellites marked the final success of political and economic liberalism against rival forms of political and economic organisation such as feudalism, hereditary monarchy, fascism and now communism. History had come to an end, not in the sense that events would no longer happen, but that the model of the liberal free market coupled with liberal parliamentary democracy had once and for all triumphed over all possible rival models for the organisation of society.

In 1989 I was a history teacher, and immediately incorporated Fukuyama's thesis into my A-level methodology classes, alongside other theories of history such as Christian, Whig, Tory, Marxist, and the Annales School. In many ways Fukuyama's thesis was a modern updating, from the US perspective, of the Whig interpretation of history, which had seen the world through the prism of English parliamentary democracy at the centre of the largest empire in history and fuelled by a mixture of the 'white man's burden', God's will and the prosperity of the Industrial Revolution and 'free trade'. The parallels with the modern US's perception of its dominant world role hardly need spelling out.

The Whig interpretation of history as inevitable, although not always smooth, progress, on the lines of the English model, hit the buffers of two world wars, concentration camps and Hiroshima. Might Fukuyama's view, I asked my students in 1989, also be a little lacking in both humility and historical perspective? Might the (then) slowly growing environmentalist movement have a different view about the benefits of unfettered capitalist growth? Might the Muslim world-view provide a different perspective? Nearly twenty years later the democratically elected Hugo Chavez has a different viewpoint too.

These are not abstract intellectual discussions and Fukuyama was not 'just' an academic. He was also a State Department adviser to the first President Bush and an affiliate of the Telluride Association, where he rubbed shoulders with Paul Wolfowitz; he was also active in the Project for the New American Century. After the 9/11 attacks in 2001 he was a signatory to this group's letter calling on the second President Bush to remove Saddam Hussein from power 'even if evidence does not link Iraq directly to the attack'.[1] Bush and Blair duly did so, dodgy dossiers and all, with the disastrous consequences that we are all preoccupied with now.

This is not an essay about foreign policy, ethical or otherwise, but about the limitations of what we should expect from the free market. Fukuyama's triumphalist neo-con thesis about the end of history serves to illustrate the dangers of unquestioningly adopting a Holy Grail – any Holy Grail – which purports to be the one and only answer, a limitation which he belatedly recognised when in 2003 he called for Donald Rumsfeld's resignation and criticised the Bush Administration for being overly optimistic about the success with which social engineering of Western values could be applied to Iraq and the Middle East.

None of this is to question the basic premise that, as Fukuyama puts it in the introduction to his 1992 book, 'Liberal principles on economics – the free market – have spread and have succeeded in producing unprecedented levels of material prosperity'.[2] The free market, however, is not in itself an automatic or unfettered good, as global warming, pollution and the misuse of scarce resources show today.

In the nineteenth century Britain, as the first industrial nation, enjoyed historically unparalleled wealth. In part this wealth was pump-primed by the slave trade and was bought at the cost of exploiting the subject nations of the Empire. In India, for example, the previously extensive manufacturing of cotton cloth was forbidden so that raw cotton could be shipped to British factories for manufacture and then sold back. In even greater part this wealth was earned at the expense of the vast bulk of the working population. As contemporary studies by Rowntree in York, Booth in London and even Engels in Manchester showed, large sections of the working class lived lives of appalling poverty and exploitation in environmentally degraded conditions. Even the Conservative leader, Disraeli, recognised this at the time and wrote of a Britain divided into two nations. His 'one-nation' Conservative philosophy was regrettably abandoned a century later by Thatcher and has yet to re-emerge despite Cameron's media spin.

The key driver of Adam Smith's 'invisible hand' is the profit motive based upon success or failure in cutthroat competition – not motives of fairness, humanity or the common good. Two centuries later this is still apparent – look at Bhopal, look at the record of oil companies in the developing world, or even in the Gulf of Mexico, and look at the way they fund climate-change deniers in the US. Examine the sorry story of the tobacco companies and their fifty-year campaign to suppress the evidence on the link between cigarettes and cancer, or their current efforts to expand into less well-regulated Third World markets. Look at the drive to privatise the water supply in such countries, where Western companies leave large slum areas devoid of clean water because slum dwellers, as in Bolivia, cannot afford to connect to the privatised mains. For that matter, look at Detroit, a major city in the wealthiest country in the world, where over 40,000 poor households have been disconnected from the water supply. Here in the UK, private equity companies seek short-term profit via methods including asset stripping and dangerously high company borrowing before selling the company on. A purely profit-driven privatised energy market embarked upon the 'dash for gas', leaving the UK with an unstable future source of energy supply as UK gas reserves start to dry up. Even look at the nonsense of commercial companies providing sports equipment for schools in return for tokens obtained from buying chocolate, crisps or fizzy drinks.

Free-market zealots are quite simply wrong if they believe that all will be well if you just leave everything to Adam Smith's invisible hand. In the US the top fifth of households 'earn' 50 per cent of the national income while the poorest fifth lives on just 3.5 per cent. The number of Americans living in severe poverty has expanded dramatically under the Bush administration. The number simply classed as living in poverty stands at 37 million (12.7 per cent of the population), the highest percentage in the developed world. Forty-four million Americans have no health insurance and, while wealthy Americans enjoy the best health care in the world, the nation as a whole has the worst pre-natal death rates in the developed world and poor areas match Third World mortality rates. Even in Britain the gap between rich and poor has grown under Blair and Brown, while the share of income paid in tax is greater for the poorest 20 per cent of earners than for the top 20 per cent.

It is only political regulation that offers the option of choosing to put protecting health and environment before the greater short-term cash profit to be found in dumping pollutants into air, water or landfill. It is only political regulation that can offer the option of ensuring workers' rights, health and safety legislation and moves towards fair pay. It is only taxation that provides the quality of public services that avoid the 'private affluence and public squalor' that J. K. Galbraith warned of. It is only tough political regulation that can tackle monopolies and cartels who abuse the market; dairy farmers, among other producers, certainly question how effectively this is being done with regard to the dominance of just two or three major supermarket chains. The hidden hand of the profit motive in the free market, left to itself, will deliver the opposite of all these outcomes.

Of course, this struggle to prevent abuse by dominant economic groups is not a new preconception. As early as the fourth century BC, Rome passed the Licinian-Sextian law to try and limit the growing menace of a dominant class of large-scale agricultural capitalists. In the twenty-first century the struggle to contain the excesses of the market and concentrations of power and money continues, with globalisation and the dominance of multinationals making the process both more urgent and more difficult than ever before.

Liberal Democrats and their predecessors have always been at the forefront of this debate. In the crudest terms the last two centuries saw practical political philosophy in the Western world divided between two extremes. Right-of-centre 'conservative' thought defended the interests of those with wealth, power and privilege derived variously from inheritance, land, trade and industry. Left-of-centre Marxist/socialist thought, with an emphasis on state control and planned economies, fought for the poor majority who laboured in field and factory. At the start of the nineteenth century the 'moral liberalism' of the Whig party in Britain (opposed to the over-mighty power and privilege of state, monarchy and Established Church), enjoyed a natural affinity with economic liberalism and ideas of maximising individual freedom and enterprise. As the Whig party morphed into the Liberal Party this marriage of ideas can be clearly seen, from Gladstone to Grimond.

However, as early as the 1830s social liberalism too played a major part in the development of the Liberal Party. Radical or social Liberals were a driving force behind the 'decade of reform' which, from the 1832 Great Reform Act onwards, ushered in long-overdue social reform, starting with the first Factory Acts. Edwin Chadwick fought a long battle to persuade the establishment that spending taxpayers' money on public health measures made good sense. Later in the century municipal Liberals like Joseph Chamberlain led the way in introducing public-service provision of everything from gas to trams. By the twentieth century Lloyd George was putting into practice the ideas of Hobhouse and Hobson. The first council houses were not long behind the 'People's Budget' and the first old-age pensions and unemployment pay.

By 1924 the Liberal Party had imploded; historians still debate how much this was due to the divisions over how to fight the First World War, tensions between Lloyd George and Asquith, or the inability of the Liberal Party to appeal to an increasingly class-conscious electorate. There were also tensions within the party over the economy and the state, but nobody seriously attributes the Liberal split to these, and in any case the social liberal tradition continued to be very influential. That influence ran from the Liberal William Beveridge's plan for the creation of the NHS and the welfare state through to the post-war implementation of the Liberal John Maynard Keynes's blueprint for Western Europe's full employment from the 1950s to the early 1970s.

At the start of the twenty-first century a reinvigorated Liberal Democrats has its largest number of MPs since 1922, following three record-breaking general elections in a row. Recent years have seen experience of government in the Welsh Assembly, the Scottish Parliament and across a wide range of local councils. The largest Liberal vote in Europe gives us a strong presence in the European Parliament. Putting aside legitimate debate about how the Liberal Democrat tradition should adapt to face the changing needs and circumstances of the new century, one thing is clear. Anyone who wanted to adapt a purist economic liberal approach would simply have joined Thatcher rather than devoting their political careers to fighting against her and her legacy. Neither, of course, is there any evidence of any real change in Conservative Party policy or prejudices, despite David Cameron's warm words and media spin. New Labour, having abandoned socialism, is now left by Blair confused and divided over what it stands for. Liberal Democrat philosophy and policy – liberalism, environmentalism, internationalism, devolution of power from London, community politics – are all in tune with the needs of this century. However without the narrative, the cement or unifying theme of social justice, of social liberalism, each of these remains an isolated strand to which both Conservatives and New Labour could and do try to lay claim – albeit with varying degrees of enthusiasm and little credibility.

What value community politics and devolution if only the elite of society exercise their rights? What value environmental policies if only the less well-off make the necessary sacrifices? What is the value of economic liberalism if it simply means that the rich, educated or well-connected flourish at the expense of others? As R. H. Tawney famously observed 'The freedom of the pike is the death of the minnow'.[3] Not happy with the words of a socialist? Then, like my good colleague David Laws in *The Orange Book*, try those of Lloyd George in 1908:

> Let Liberalism proceed with its glorious work of building up the temple of liberty in this country, but let it also bear in mind that worshippers at that shrine have to live.[4]

The Liberal Democrat 2002 policy paper, *Its About Freedom*, said that:

> Wealth creation is often best encouraged through markets which liberate the energies and talents of individuals. We believe that in the economy, markets are generally the most effective way of giving individuals more control over their lives and delivering higher living standards ... At the same time we recognise that markets are subject to major flaws and dangers. Where these occur, government action is needed to safeguard people's freedoms ... Liberal Democrats seek tough legislation to prevent monopolies, cartels and other market distortions.[5]

More importantly from my perspective as a social liberal is the next passage of *It's About Freedom*, which clearly distinguishes us from the more gung-ho economic liberalism to be found in Conservative Party thinking:

> Markets on their own will not provide some of the requirements that are fundamental to the liberty of present or future genera- tions. They do not take account of the way in which individual consumption may affect others.[6]

The Huhne Commission on public services also reported in 2002, and its product, *Quality, Innovation and Choice*, was debated and adopted by the Brighton Conference that autumn. The report noted that:

> The areas which are described as public services share one overall characteristic: society has decided that, left to its own devices, the market will fail to provide such services adequately, and that gov- ernment intervention will result in a better outcome.[7]

What are these areas that the market cannot adequately provide – although with regulation and/or subsidy they might have a valid role to play in helping deliver?

Clearly making and marketing consumer items such as lingerie, mobile phones or widgets can happily be left to the free market. This is the well-proven route to delivering quality, innovation and consumer responsiveness. Did I care or society shudder when Marks & Spencer drastically lost market share to some other high-street retailer? No. Is it a matter of fundamental justice or injustice that Marks & Spencer have – prompted by profit and loss pressures – recovered their market share at someone else's expense? No. Does it really matter if the average consumer does not actually have perfect knowledge of the market, as required by the economic theory of perfect competition, and as a result spends a bit too much on a particular, and perhaps slightly inferior, brand of car or jeans or washing machine? No.

Did it actually make sense to have such nationalised industries as Amersham International, British Airways, British Aerospace, Thomas Cook, British Leyland (what a success story!) or BT? No – other than the fact that the introduction of choice and competition into Directory Enquiries has been an expensive and confusing failure. Does it matter if your bins are emptied by directly employed council staff or instead by a national refuse disposal company whose economies of scale have saved Chesterfield Council Taxpayers £140,000 per year since the Liberal Democrat council outsourced the service in 2003? No, as long of course as savings are not made by slashing service quality or staff conditions of service to detrimental levels, as was done in many instances under Thatcher's compulsory competitive tendering, with the emphasis on taking the cheapest bid regardless of quality of service or delivery. This was particularly seen in the impact that CCT had on hospital hygiene, as demoralised staff implemented cuts in cleaning schedules.

In December 2005 the Public and Commercial Services Union held a conference on the future of the civil service, and in a paper I presented I asked:

> In looking at civil service reform we have to ask, firstly, are there some functions which must be delivered by public servants for reasons such as impartiality, accountability, equity of service delivery or state and public security? In short, are there areas which require a public service ethos rather than a profit motive – in the way the police or armed forces clearly do?

Now there are of course a variety of considerations and possible answers that open up in response to such questions about applying the market to public services of one kind or another. Should we – must we – maintain a high-quality public-service broadcaster such as the BBC? In Parliamentary debate I have made it clear that I think we should because of the impact its high-quality output has on other commercial providers both with regard to news output here and abroad, as with the World Service, and with regard to other programming. The experience of expanding the commercial market has not been one of relentlessly expanding quality. For example, despite the appearance of over twenty children's channels (pay and free-to-air), spending on original children's programmes has declined in real terms, and ITV has announced it will not commission any new children's programmes. Award-winning author Philip Pullman told the *Observer* newspaper in May 2007 that,

'The ideology of profit before everything in children's television is toxic … when young children are regarded as customers to be separated from their money as quickly and efficiently as possible there is no chance for life-enhancing work to flourish.'[8] Others would disagree and argue that a universal tax such as the licence fee is no longer justifiable, gives the BBC an unfair advantage in funding and cannot be maintained in the future in a rapidly expanding digital world. To lose the quality and experimentation allowed to public-service broadcasters by the licence fee would, however, be a disaster.

What of public transport? Can you actually have any such thing if it is left entirely to the market? Since deregulation of buses in 1985, fares nationally have risen by over a third and bus use has dropped by over a third. London has bucked this trend but London, of course, was not deregulated and Mayor Ken puts a large subsidy into the city's very good public transport services. In London the congestion zone can and has worked because there actually is a good public transport alternative, as there was once was in my home city of Sheffield before dear old Margaret ended South Yorkshire Passenger Transport's subsidy. A retired senior police officer who now lives in my Chesterfield constituency told me how the graphs of bus use and car congestion in Sheffield rapidly passed each other, in opposite directions, in the years immediately following that economically liberal policy decision. Modern concerns over carbon emissions plus the rapid growth in car use and congestion make revisiting the whole question of free markets and public transport a priority. As for the experience of Network Rail/Railtrack …

What of privatising prisons and the Probation Service and introducing the benefits of the market to the administration of justice? A massive 80 per cent of prison costs are accounted for by staff, so how might a private provider look to make a quick profit? In fact private custody officers are paid less than prison officers, and staff turnover is higher in private prisons. Paul Tidball, President of the Prison Governors' Association, argued in *The Guardian* in April 2007:

> … that it was essential that internal judicial processes in prisons were conducted without an eye to costs and profit … that the worst recent prison inspection reports had all involved private prisons …. That [unlike private prisons] no public sector prison

had been caught out failing to provide prisoners with toilet seats and pillows or with a body of staff so inexperienced and lacking competence that they were in fear of the prisoners.[9]

Special pleading from an interested party, or legitimate concerns? If private profit motives have led to an inferior prison service in private prisons, is the 'saving' worth the effect on prisoners, most of whom are short-term inmates and will be released in a more 'damaged' psychological state than when they entered prison. Certainly both the current (2007), and the previous Liberal Democrat Shadow Home Secretaries (neither generally regarded as committed social liberals) have expressed grave reservations about privatising both prison and probation services and so risking sacrificing the administration of justice on the altar of profit.

What of Post Offices? Even the most economically liberal of Liberal Democrats have argued that, because of their vital role in isolated communities, they are a special case rather than just another commercial outlet that should be left to sink or swim according to the fortunes of the market place.

Health and education both have chapters elsewhere in this book so I will not trespass too much on them. These two are, however, for me the absolute lodestones of my social liberalism. In all the current national debate on this we must remember two key points.

First, the chronic under-funding of both sectors, from the IMF cuts of 1976 through Thatcher to the cuts still being imposed by New Labour up to 1999, should make us wary of crass comparisons with other Western European systems. Britain has 1.7 doctors per thousand of the population compared to 2.9 in France and 3.4 in Germany. Pupil–teacher ratios are among the worst in comparable European countries, as is higher education funding as a share of GDP. All the 'massive increases' in public investment in these sectors from 1999 to 2007 mean that by 2008 we will reach average Western European levels of investment in health for the first time in a quarter of a century or more. In education we achieved the average level of investment in 2006. It takes a lot more than a year or two's average levels of investment to turn around twenty-five years of cuts. As a teacher for nearly all of those twenty-five years, I can give you enormously detailed chapter and verse if required!

Secondly, the market-based choice agenda is a dangerous diversion from the need to establish quality of access and opportunity for all patients across the NHS and for all pupils across the education system. The top 200 academically performing schools in Blair's league tables serve school populations with significantly lower intakes of children with special needs and/or who qualify for free school meals. Schools put into special measures almost universally take significantly higher levels of such pupils. Counties with selective grammar and secondary modern systems, like Kent and Lincolnshire, achieve less academically across the whole school population than comparable counties with comprehensive systems.

City Technology Colleges established in inner-city areas have seen significant changes in their intake over the years as a backdoor selection process kicks in and the most supportive parents clamour to get their children into these schools. What happens, though, to those children who cannot gain entry to over-subscribed schools and whose parents do not care about education or who do care but do not have the knowledge or means to 'work' the system? The Academies are already showing evidence of the start of the same process. We must not be satisfied with a market-based system that selects the best and ignores the rest – as used to happen in the 'good old days'. Those who hanker for the golden age of grammar schools, for example, seem to forget that 70 per cent or more of the nation's children were excluded from them, just as the gold standard of O-levels were designed only to be only taken by at most 40 per cent of children and passed by less, whereas 55 per cent gain the equivalent qualification today.

However, I promised not to stray too much into other chapters' territory so let me finish with three more detailed case studies.

Social housing

The obsession of the current New Labour and the previous Conservative government with market solutions means that the UK is sleep-walking into a social crisis of massive proportions over social housing. Forty years after 'Cathy Come Home' shocked the nation, waiting lists are soaring and social housing is in sharp decline. Since 1997 council waiting lists have increased by half a million (from 1 to 1.5 million) which, not entirely coincidentally, is the same as the number of council houses that have been sold off in that period under right-to-buy legislation. In some areas the situation is worse – and contrary to government preconceptions, that is not just in London. In Chesterfield and Sheffield, for example, waiting lists have not increased by 50 per cent, they have actually trebled In Bolton they have more than quadrupled, from 5,000 in 1996 to 23,700 today. In 2003 the Royal Institution of Chartered Surveyors told the government that unless more was spent on subsidised rented accommodation, Britain would see a housing underclass develop. The government failed to act; the free market will not provide for this group, and political dogma must urgently give way to practical necessity.

There is, too, a structural imbalance in the social housing that remains, with too many flats (built in the 1960s and '70s for a young population), and too few OAP bungalows for today's ageing population. Meanwhile right-to-buy meant that family houses in the best areas were snapped up first, and today there is a severe shortage of such accommodation for young families in the rented sector.

All this represents a human crisis for those involved – who I see weekly at my constituency surgeries. It also represents an open goal for racists and xenophobes from the BNP to UKIP. Even in Chesterfield, which is 97 per cent white, I am often told that 'they' are taking our council houses – when in fact the small non-white population in my constituency mostly live in privately owned property. This crisis also extends to the private (to rent and buy) sector where the dearth of decent, affordable social housing to rent is helping ramp up prices in an already grossly overheated private market.

The answer to all this? The Conservatives talk only of letting private house-builders solve the problem. New Labour say much the same but do at least see a limited role for housing associations – though little, if any, for councils who have had the system rigged against them in an attempt to force the privatisation of all remaining council property.

Yet the private sector failed to meet the challenge in both the nineteenth and twentieth centuries. Yes, they produced model estates in places – Port Sunlight, Arkwright's village at Cromford, Strutt's housing in Belper – but the majority product was the cheap, disease-ridden slums of Sheffield, Manchester, Leeds and London. That is precisely why far-sighted politicians in the twentieth century began to clear the slums and build council estates in their place. Remember too that this particular legacy of market failure, many of these slum private rentals, were still with us on a large scale as late as the 1950s.

In the twenty-first century private builders may no longer be allowed to build slums, but how many of you have ever compared cramped 'family' accommodation in so called 'town-house'-style dwellings with the substantial family houses and gardens of the traditional council estate? With land in the cities at a premium, what private developer wants to provide 'affordable' housing when so much more profit can be made from more up-market properties? Above all, do we really believe that with 71 per cent home ownership already, the highest in Europe, that the remaining 29 per cent can easily move on to the property-owning ladder? Even key workers in well-paid steady jobs like teachers, nurses, police and fire officers cannot afford to buy in many areas, so what hope is there for the low-paid or the unemployed, the single parents, the sick and the elderly?

Ruth Kelly's obsessing with selling a 10 per cent stake in their home to the poorest in society, shows just how out of touch with reality this government is. Yes, rent to buy, golden shares and all the other schemes have their value. Right to buy? – fine if the money goes back into building new social housing, but it doesn't. No, I do not want to return to the vast impersonal council estates of the 1960s and '70s – although the one I grew up on in Sheffield was a good place to live. Yes, we need to tackle sink estates starved of investment throughout much of the last thirty years. But the prevalent truism, that we can leave it to a benevolent profit-driven private sector to resolve these problems, is dangerous wishful thinking.

Without public sector investment we are simply not going to tackle the desperate crisis in social housing that is rapidly developing. One quick start for any government would be to let the 140 housing authorities like Chesterfield (over a third of the total), where tenants voted to remain with the council, plus the 60 ALMO authorities, operate on a level playing field in comparison to housing associations or PFI landlords. Chesterfield's 10,000 council tenants saw Gordon Brown cream off £3.2 million of their rents every year – a sum which will rise to £5 million per year as the government forces up council rents by more than inflation. Let Chesterfield keep that money – and the 75 per cent of right-to-buy proceeds that the government takes each year – and Chesterfield could massively improve its housing estates *and* start building new family houses and OAP bungalows too. The biggest insult of all is that if

Chesterfield's tenants had voted to 'privatise,' their new landlord *would* be allowed to keep all this money.

The housing green paper of July 2007,[10] despite the advanced spin, does little to move us forward from this stance. All the talk of affordable housing largely ignores the fact that key workers and first-time buyers cannot get on the housing ladder at all in 94 per cent of urban areas, and that even an 'affordable' house rapidly becomes completely unaffordable. Only by allocating at least 25 per cent of the new housebuilding land to community land trusts can we ensure that enough affordable houses are provided and that, above all, they remain affordable further down the housing chain. The small print of the green paper also seems to confirm that all but a chosen few of the 140 councils retaining their own stock are still to be in effect excluded from tackling the social housing crisis. Even the sixty arms' length management organisations will continue to be severely restricted. It is a perverse and dogmatic hatred of the public sector by Blair and Brown that has put privatisation and failed market-driven solutions before the interests of the poorest sector of society.

Local economic regeneration: a case study

Chesterfield, like many, many, areas, has been very badly hit by the economic events and policies of the last two decades. In 1981 Chesterfield employed 20,000 people in coal-mining and heavy manufacturing. By 2004 this figure had fallen to 7,000. Chesterfield has now reinvented itself and is once again a thriving town, with employment at 49,000, approaching the 51,000 of 1981.

Neither government policies nor the private sector offered much help to begin with during the free-market recession of the 1980s and 1990s and the government-imposed pit closures of 1992. The cost of reclaiming the numerous derelict sites was deemed uneconomic by the private sector at a time of severe economic recession. The provision of high-quality business space, designed to attract new business activities to an economically depressed area, formerly based on traditional heavy industry, was also considered high risk by the market.

Despite limited budgets, further compressed by national rate-capping threats and cuts to local government budgets, Chesterfield Borough Council embarked on a property-led strategy. All the council-provided sites, including sixty-five low-rent starter units, more than seventy industrial units, five serviced sites and two technology innovation centres, are now fully occupied, which is a measure of the success of this policy. Another success marker is the example of firms such as Knight Warner Ltd, a process control engineering company, or of Image Sound, both of whom began with two or three employees at the Council's Tapton Hi-Tech Innovation Centre, and now employ eighty people between them at other larger sites.

This process continued in 2006 with newly opened high-specification office/workspace such as Venture House and Prospect House. The council is also now placing emphasis on making the town in general more attractive, with major investment in the historic open air market and the town centre, as well as a state-of-the-art coach station in place of the eyesore previously lambasted in the national press. A number of companies are now locating their offices in Chesterfield because of its combination of excellent communications links, lower property prices and attractive environment.

In a more buoyant economic climate the council's earlier pump-priming (aided by development agency, single regeneration budget and European matched funding), has now attracted a high level of private-sector interest. Over the next few years major redevelopment of derelict industrial corridors is set to transform Chesterfield further with a combination of retail, offices, housing, a new canal basin and a new football ground. Derelict sites near the town centre are now snapped up for private-sector house-building – where twenty years ago, as a then newly elected councillor, I was told no one was interested in such sites.

Without the far-sighted efforts of a small borough council, operating against the prevailing climate of the 1980s and 1990s and with tightly limited resources, the groundwork for the private-sector interest of today would not have been provided. The local council was also, of course, much better placed to know what the local economy needed than remote civil servants in London planning Heseltine's grandiose garden city festivals.

If local government in the UK had the flexibility of operation I have seen in the US or Europe, so much more could be achieved. Instead we have the most centrally controlled system in the Western world, with 90 per cent of taxation raised by No. 11 Downing Street and handed out with many strings attached by central government. Local government is completely distrusted – indeed, emasculated even more by New Labour than it was by the Conservatives. Liberal Democrat policies are committed to devolution but to work, the iron grip of the Chancellor has to be removed. The Huhne Commission report, *Quality, Innovation, Choice*, examines how this can be done along the lines successfully used across Europe and in the US. It recommends that local authorities and regions should be able, within a national stability pact (as applied, for example, in Germany), to borrow for investment in their own name or by issuing bonds secured against assets and revenue flows.

PFI

The latter point leads us on to the controversy surrounding the Private Finance Initiative which, for the last ten years, has been the only show in town where public infrastructure such as hospitals, schools, prisons or transport links is concerned. PFI, and private–public partnerships like that imposed on London Underground, we are told from No. 11, brings the benefits, drive and efficiencies of the market into otherwise sloppy, over-budget and over-schedule public sector projects.

Unfortunately for this argument, as early as 2003 the Audit Commission provided evidence to the contrary.[11] That report compared seventeen of the first twenty-five PFI schools, completed in 2001, with twelve constructed by traditional public finance. The report concluded that schools designed and financed by the private sector were no cheaper, better or completed more quickly than those that were built by councils. All the PFI schools were significantly worse for light, space, heating and acoustics. A report commissioned by the Audit Commission from the Building Research Establishment observed that:

> The best examples of the type of innovation that can improve fitness for purpose and minimise running costs came in traditional schools within local education authorities with a long-established track record of excellence in school design.[12]

Four years later the Commons' Education and Skills Select Committee has been examining the Building Schools for the Future and Academies programmes – all delivered by PFI – and we have found much the same story.

The Institute for Public Policy Research, normally seen as New Labour's favourite think-tank, also published a report in 2003 which looked at several hundred PFI projects and found little evidence of better value in schools and hospitals building.[13] In 2007 a research team at Edinburgh University investigated the Treasury claims that 88 per cent of PFI projects were delivered on time and within budget while 70 per cent of publicly funded and run projects were late and 73 per cent were over budget. The team looked into the data used to justify these claims and found they had been based on interviews with the managers of PFI projects – hardly objective sources! Professor Allyson Pollock reported the university team's findings as showing that 'It would appear that comparisons are rigged in favour of PFI and that Treasury policy is not evidence-based'.[14]

PFI schemes do not, of course, bring 'new money' into the equation as is often misleadingly claimed. The private sector borrows, at higher cost than the public sector, and the taxpayer then pays back this higher cost, plus private profit margins, through a mortgage of around thirty years. During this mortgage period the taxpayer is locked into paying for the ongoing management fees and maintenance of an expensive capital asset as well as the mortgage cost. In 2007 the Association of Schools and College Leaders reported:

> Unacceptably high management fees for what is often mediocre service are taking away money that should be spent on improving resources for learning. In many cases, PFI contractors have shown that they are more interested in their profit margins than the welfare of students and communities.[15]

The latter point, of course, should not come as a surprise – after all, profit margins, not the public interest, are the whole point of the free market, as I noted at the start of this chapter. The ASCL report to the Department for Education went on to list problems such as long delays in taking action on basic maintenance and repairs, normal wear and tear being charged to the school and shoddy fittings that were not fit for purpose when they were installed. Access to buildings after normal school hours could often be difficult or too expensive to obtain.

As pupil numbers fluctuate over the thirty-year mortgage period, so a PFI school's income might fall, yet it will still be locked into the same high level of 'mortgage and management' fees. The same applies to PFI hospitals, as patient numbers vary but inflexible thirty-year PFI contracts have to be paid. *The Times*, on 11 May 2007, reported an economic analysis produced by the NHS in London which argued that relatively expensive PFI hospitals could not be closed (in favour of more cost-effective older hospitals), to stem a £65 million deficit in south-east London because the debts and management contracts incurred would still have to be repaid.[16]

If PFI and the market are not, after all, the wonder solution to providing public-service buildings such as hospitals and schools, why does the government – above all a Labour one – still persist in closing down traditional public sector provision? The answer is, of course, the very simple one of the public sector borrowing requirement straightjacket. The Treasury says that around 50 per cent of PFI schemes are on the books as part of the PSBR (although others claim only 20 per cent), but that still leaves a large number that are not. This is straight voodoo economics. Cheaper public sector borrowing for capital investment in public services is public debt and so is a 'bad thing'. More expensive private sector borrowing is off the books, counts as economic growth and so is a 'good thing'.

Conclusion

The winners-and-losers process of the competitive market works well in providing manufacturing and consumer goods and many services (such as hotels, restaurants professional sport and entertainment, for example). There are, however, areas where cut-throat competition and denial of service – or provision of vastly inferior, even inadequate service – to those who cannot pay is not acceptable; as witness the law which, without legal aid (and even with it?), would be like the Ritz Hotel, open to all as long as they can afford it. A Liberal Democrat approach should not be the dogmatic ideological one of purist economic liberals, epitomised by Thatcher, who see almost all public provision other than law and order and the armed forces as inherently inferior. Social justice has to be the key thread that distinguishes the Liberal Democrat approach.

As the PFI debate shows, the market is not always the most efficient method of providing a public service. The Huhne Commission analysed this further, identifying four reasons that each or together could make market solutions inappropriate – access, public good, merit good and market inapplicability.[17]

Social justice is about much more than efficiently providing a service and much more than about any attempt to achieve a fairer distribution of income and wealth, as the Liberal Democrats are attempting to do in seeking to end the current New Labour tax policies that see a widening gap between rich and poor, while the lowest paid pay a larger percentage of their income in tax than do the highest paid. Social justice requires fair access to essential services such as education and health, and an ideological pursuit of a 'choice' agenda must never be at the expense of this.

If the Liberal Democrats are to maintain their unique identity in British politics over the last two centuries then the major – even, I would argue, historically dominant – contribution of social liberalism must not be sacrificed on the altar of purist economic liberalism and the market.

Notes

1   Project for the New American Century, open letter to President Bush, 20 September 2001; available at http://www.newamericancentury.org/Bushletter.htm
2   Francis Fukuyama, *The End of History and the Last Man* (Hamilton, London, 1992)
3   R. H. Tawney, *Equality* (George Allen & Unwin Ltd., London, 1931)
4   David Laws, 'Reclaiming Liberalism: a liberal agenda for the Liberal Democrats', in David Laws and Paul Marshall (eds.), *The Orange Book: Reclaiming Liberalism* (Profile, London, 2004)
5   Liberal Democrat Policy Paper 50, *It's About Freedom* (Liberal Democrats, 2002)
6   Ibid.
7   Liberal Democrat Policy Paper 53, *Quality, Innovation, Choice* (Liberal Democrats, 2002)
8   'Children's TV is social poison, says top novelist', *The Observer*, 27 May 2007.
9   'Ministers plan to let private prisons discipline inmates', *The Guardian*, 17 April 2007.
10 *Homes for the Future: More affordable, more sustainable* (Cm 7191, July 2005).
11 Audit Commission, *PFI in Schools: The quality and cost of buildings and services provided by early Private Finance Initiative schemes* (2003)
12 Audit Commission, *Buildings Research Establishment, Client Report: Design quality of PFI schools* (2002)
13 Paul Maltby, *In the Public Interest? Assessing the potential for public interest companies* (IPPR, London, 2003)
14 Allyson M. Pollock, David Price and Stewart Player, 'An Examination of the UK Treasury's Evidence Base for Cost and Time Overrun Data in UK Value-for-Money Policy and Appraisal', *Public Money and Management* 27:2, April 2007.
15 'Ongoing PFI problems must not recur in BSF, says ASCL', news release 11 May 2007.
16 'Bankrupt or sinking under debt, the new hospitals too costly for cuts', *The Times*, 11 May 2007.
17 Liberal Democrats, *Quality, Innovation, Choice*.

Chapter 14

Repoliticising Politics: The Case for Intervention

Tim Farron

If Tony Blair is a third-rate Bill Clinton, and David Cameron is a third-rate Tony Blair, how much further into the depths of convictionless spin-driven drivel must we descend before those involved in politics are prepared to believe in something again? Shouldn't the role of the Liberal Democrats over the next few years be to repoliticise British politics?

I hope so.

Just to clarify for a moment, repoliticising politics does not, to me, mean creating a new cadre of desperately earnest ideologues reminiscent of the newspaper-selling Trotskyist who used to stand outside your students' union. Repoliticising politics means having hard opinions and a clear set of beliefs that make people sit up and take notice. It means offending people, but it also means inspiring many others to flock to our banner.

We'll inspire no one if we simply try to develop our own interpretation of the Clinton/New Labour/Cameron Tory phenomenon. Let's call the phenomenon 'I can't believe it's not politics' (ICBINP – catchy!).

ICBINP is essentially all about appealing to the largest number of voters by presenting them with enticing images, playing the counterintuitive card in order to neutralise negative images (e.g. David Cameron posing as 'green') and causing offence to the smallest possible number of people.

Minimising the causing of offence is the most dismal element in this unholy trinity. The best way to cause offence is to have policies, the best way to avoid causing offence is not to have policies. Once you have got to the stage where not having policies is no longer sustainable (because the media start to make you look silly because you haven't got any policies) the crucial thing is to have policies that don't upset people. In order to be successful at developing your own ICBINP brand, you need to be particularly careful not to offend anyone powerful. So, don't upset big multinationals and don't ever upset anyone who owns lots of newspapers and television stations, for instance … These people have the power to influence millions of people and get them to vote for another variety of ICBINP.

The whole point of going down the ICBINP road is to win elections and run the country. Not because you believe the country needs running differently, but because you believe the country needs running by different people (i.e. you and your mates). Your conviction lies in the firm belief that the current administration is not administrating as well as you would.

If that is a fair analysis of the whole Brown v. Cameron situation (New Labour v. Blue Labour?), then what is our angle? How do we get cute enough to challenge this depressing state of affairs?

We start by looking at what Labour and the Tories agree on, and then providing a simple and effective critique of the whole lumpen mass. Despite Cameron's botched attempt at a 'Clause Four moment' over grammar schools, both Labour and Conservatives agree that there should be greater selection in school education, they both actively support the premature replacement of Trident, and they share a desire to see what is euphemistically termed 'reform of the public sector' (which simply means hiving off large amounts of public sector work to the private sector). Both parties are now committed to retaining student tuition fees and neither party has policies that will remove the threat to personal dignity and financial security entailed by the requirement that older people and disabled people have to pay for personal care out of their own pockets.

Fundamentally, they also agree on a non-interventionist approach to the market and are opposed to anything more than a gesture in the direction of redistributing wealth. Given that the redistribution of wealth is a precursor to evening up the distribution of power and thus the distribution of freedom, it is fundamental to a social liberal philosophy that we should seek to enhance freedom by ensuring a fairer distribution of resources. Freedoms are not worth the paper they are written on if citizens don't have the power to exercise them. Freedom without power is no freedom at all. It is here that our chance to flush out the menace of ICBINP lies.

People fear poverty, especially in their old age. They also fear the loss of dignity, financial independence and comfort should they need care when they become elderly. As Liberal Democrats we already have the kernel of excellent policies in these areas – we need to be bold and provide an answer to these fears.

Traditionally, the majority of Liberal Democrat-held parliamentary seats and target seats have involved close contests with the Conservatives. There is an argument put about by some that this means that we should therefore ensure that our message is sufficiently Tory-friendly not to frighten the horses. I take issue with this because being inoffensive is not going to be enough to win us any election. What we do need is a clear message which is authentic and comes from our Liberal convictions and which gives people a strong and distinctive reason to vote for us. In simple sales parlance, we need to identify the need and then meet it. My suggestion is that both the real need in our country and the perceived need amongst the electorate is for appropriate, bottom-up intervention.

Nowhere is this need more clearly evident than in rural communities such as those that I represent in South Cumbria.

In my part of the world, whole communities are dying out because of the unfettered growth in the second-home market. For example, Satterthwaite is a village near Hawkshead with around eighty houses. It used to have a school and a post office. Now it has neither. The fact that half of the properties in the village are second homes is the defining factor – because this removes from the village a full-time population of sufficient size to create the necessary demand for schools, post offices, bus services and the like. Dozens of villages in rural Britain are now lifeless collections of houses where once upon a time there was a thriving community. It is entirely possible to prevent this decline, but to do so would involve rigging the market, changing planning law and upping taxes on some of the wealthiest people in our society. The ICBINP response to this is to wring our hands, express regret and do nothing. Our response must be to intervene.

Of course, second-home ownership and the concentration of resources in the hands of a minority is not the preserve of rural Britain. Throughout urban areas the growth in the buy-to-let market is leading to a new property polarisation. The ability of some to own more than one home helps to fuel a market situation where others will never be able to own any home at all. Liberal Democrats were critical – though not critical enough at the time – of Mrs Thatcher's right-to-buy programme, which led to the loss of the majority of social rented housing in this country. We should now be clearer about ensuring that certain social rented properties can never be bought. And why should we not ensure that the reverse is also true and consider placing restrictions so that certain categories of property cannot be transferred from owner-occupied to the rental market?

No doubt this approach would be riddled with difficulties and many would say that it would be intolerable interference. However, the alternative is to allow a new class divide to open up between the property-owners and the property-renters, where a proportion of the former category are multiple property-owners, exploiting their capital advantage at the expense of the latter category, most of whom could never hope to switch categories as the gap between average earnings and average house prices widens by the year in all but the most undesirable of neighbourhoods.

In public services too, the approach of this government – which sits happily with Conservative philosophy – is to make judgements about the distribution of services on a private-sector, free-market basis. Consequently, we see the ever-increasing involvement of private companies in the provision of NHS services and local council functions. We also see the policy in the NHS of ensuring maximum efficiency by concentrating resources in 'centres of excellence'. On this basis, the government speculates about the possibility of closing down up to half hospitals' accident and emergency units in order to consolidate and improve provision. In my area, the NHS trusts seek to close down the local heart unit too, in order to concentrate provision at a site twenty miles away.

A social liberal, interventionist, approach should be to acknowledge that centres of excellence and concentration of services bring efficiencies, but to choose to ensure that fair access to quality services wins the day. If the government's ambition of ensuring that each A&E unit serves 450,000 people is realised, then we're looking at a journeys of an hour and a half in order to get seriously injured people to hospital. Our approach is not to shrug and accept the rule of the market, but to intervene and to ensure that everyone lives within a safe distance of key services.

There is an enormous level of affection for the NHS, and even people who traditionally support the Conservatives are deeply suspicious about creeping privatisation from within. Liberal Democrats should feel particularly uneasy about the increased role of the private sector in the NHS for these reasons. At present operations carried out in-house attract a charge which comes from the purchaser (e.g. the Primary Care Trust) and go to the provider (e.g. the Hospital Trust) – thus keeping the money within the NHS. Operations carried out by a private-sector provider under the aegis of the NHS (such as those provided under contract by Capio) see funds being transferred not from one arm of the NHS to another, but from the NHS into the pockets of shareholders. Private-sector providers are understandably driven by the need to provide a return to their shareholders, which means that a proportion of the purchasers' costs will always be earmarked in this way. Consequently it stands to reason that PCTs will get fewer operations for their money from the private sector than they would from paying for operations within the NHS, because the private sector carries the additional cost of having to provide a shareholder return.

This flies in the face of the normal assumption that private-sector providers within the public sector are able to be more efficient, more fleet of foot and offer better value for money. Indeed, these are the reasons given for involving the private sector in the first place, but the practice is very different.

The company Netcare has recently been given preferred-bidder status by the NHS to provide clinical assessment, treatment and support (CATS) service centres. CATS centres aim to tackle the thorny issue of excessive waiting lists and waiting times, but there is no certainty that the centres will have sufficient numbers of patients referred to them to make an impact or, indeed, to make the centres themselves financially viable. This is where Netcare comes in. You might expect that what the government is seeking is a private provider who will take on the risk in return for a reasonable return if they are successful. You would, however, be wrong. In Cumbria and Lancashire alone, Netcare will receive a minimum-income guarantee of around £6 million a year for five years, irrespective of whether they meet target patient numbers. This is sadly typical of the way that governments treat the private sector, to the extent that private firms like Netcare and Capio must rub their hands together with glee each time a public-sector contract is unveiled.

When it comes to the provision of services for local authorities, we increasingly see key areas of work from highways to human resources operations being hived off to the private sector, often in the form of Capita. Capita is part of a huge multinational outfit. The notion that this powerful entity is working for and under the direction of your local council is absurd. Last year, Capita underperformed on one of the key items in its service-level agreement with Cumbria County Council. There was a £1 million penalty clause payable as a result. It was never paid. I'm not sure it was even called in, but it proves a point – that huge firms like Capita simply have too much influence, direct or indirect, over local authorities. In no way can we look at these relationships as being advantageous to the taxpayer, or helpful in bringing market efficiencies into an otherwise leaden-footed public sector. This is Thatcherite fantasy. The reality is shareholder gain at taxpayers' expense, with no improvement in service.

I suspect that the average reader of the *Daily Telegraph* or the *Daily Mail* would not find this line of reasoning hard to follow – in fact my belief is that these are winning arguments with people who feel that they and their families are being dealt a poor deal.

Adam Smith was a great economist and Mrs Thatcher's hero. His strong belief was in the inbuilt checks and balances within the free market and that any imperfections in the market would always be rectified by the 'invisible hand'. This is, of course, a load of old guff. The only natural force within the market is gravity, i.e. power and wealth accrue to those already possessing power and wealth, thus enabling them to accrue even more power and wealth, allowing them to liquidate their competition and merrily exploit their workers, suppliers and customers. Just look at the state of British farming, or the outrageous exploitation in world trade to see the consequences of this natural phenomenon. Smith was right to observe that the market needs a hand, but it has to be the highly visible hand of the community, or state, if the inequalities and unfairnesses of the market are to be removed.

Despite the high numbers of people leaving the farming industry, farming communities (which includes not just farmers but all those who see themselves as being economically dependent on, or culturally influenced by, the agricultural sector) make up a very significant section of the electorate. Traditionally, those communities are supposed to be great supporters of the Conservative Party. However, if you look at their marginal economic position and at the way in which they are victims of an insufficiently fettered free market, you will see that their interests are not at all represented by the Conservatives and that, actually, it is the Liberal Democrats who can best serve their needs and meet their aspirations.

Rural Britain has traditionally supported the Conservatives only by default. The Liberal Democrats, however, are in touching distance of having a narrative which could produce a crucial shift, but we will need to be bold and risk offending a few people – a few powerful people.

Take dairy farming as an example. At the time of writing the average price a farmer receives for their milk is 17p per litre. The average cost to the farmer of producing that litre of milk is 21p per litre. Farmers have no choice but to take this price because otherwise they would lose their contracts and would have to kiss goodbye to any longer term hopes they might have of receiving a fairer price. At the same time as farmers are enduring a margin of –4 per cent, retailers are enjoying a margin of +30 per cent on average. Bear in mind that there is a significantly larger amount of input and value added to the product by the farmer than by the retailer, and you will begin to get a sense of the enormous injustice in this situation. We should also note that in 2002, the retailers' margin averaged 11 per cent. There has been no significant move in the market (such as oversupply) over the last five years in order to justify that tripling in retail margins, just as there is no market explanation for the reduction in farmgate prices. Let's be clear, retailers (and I mean, of course, very large retailers i.e. supermarkets) have tripled their margin and impoverished their producers simply because they can. Supermarkets are immensely powerful. They behave entirely legally, but nevertheless they seriously abuse their market position. Liberal Democrats already have strong policies in support of a market regulator and so our position on this doesn't need strengthening so much as proselytising. I have heard Conservative MPs from rural constituencies speaking enviously of our policy in favour of a supermarket regulator but of course, their party would never let them indulge in such a heresy!

Farmers are not free-marketeers – so let's get out there and loudly proclaim that neither are we and that, better still, we have policies that will lead to intervention in the market to ensure that British farmers become the beneficiaries of a home-grown fair trade movement.

Rural Britain is not, on the whole, a wealthy place. The people who visit their second homes for the occasional weekend may be wealthy, but the people who live there the rest of the time face serious struggles, and they are mostly struggles caused by the free market. The way to win in these areas is to be bottom-up interventionists where appropriate.

Market principles demand that your post office should go, that the cottages in your village that could provide a home for a local family should be sold to the highest bidder, even if that highest bidder only spends five weekends a year there and contributes nothing to the community before selling it at vast profit to another second home-owner, who in turn will use it as his or her bricks-and-mortar pension. The market dictates that small farmers have no future, and that therefore our uplands will no longer be farmed – so think carefully about any future holidays in the Lake District, because with no farmers, there'll be no sheep, and if there are no sheep then there'll soon be unkempt wilderness through which you will not be able to ramble. There'll be no attractive drystone walls, no drainage to keep footpaths passable, no one around to implement Natural England's ecological priorities. There'll be no heritage, there'll be no environmental schemes, and there'll be no UK-based meat or wool production.

National Parks came into being after the Second World War not for the benefit of rural communities – quite the opposite. They were established in order to provide recreation, relaxation and access to landscape heritage for occupants of urban Britain. If I walk through Bowness, Ambleside or Coniston on a Saturday, the majority of people I see will be residents of urban Britain who visit the Lake District because of its natural beauty, but also because of its synthetic culture (not a pejorative term – by definition, all human culture is synthetic), which includes the beauty of the managed landscape, the accessibility of the fells (without management by farmers there would be barely any passable footpaths) and the presence of living communities.

Now, there may be some arch libertarians who take the view that if the market dictates that the managed landscape of rural Britain should return to scrubland, and that village post offices should close and become second homes, then so be it. However, the residents of urban areas – in whose interests the National Parks were established – surely don't want to see these national assets allowed to go to rack and ruin as a result of an unfettered free market.

For Liberal Democrats there is an important political angle here too. Rural England has traditionally supported our opponents but surely the interests of residents of rural areas are better served by us than by the Conservatives? Indeed, they will be even better served if we are prepared to be bold in our assertion that we are an interventionist, social liberal party with a down-to-earth, practical and scathing critique of the free market.

This is a message that is just as powerful in urban communities. All communities recognise that while efficiency in service provision is important, the quality of those services and fair access to them must be of greater concern.

The Conservatives have no answer to this. They exist to champion the very causes that threaten the future of our communities. This is the window of opportunity for the Liberal Democrats.

When tackling the challenges facing our public services, the Conservatives are locked in an embrace with Labour over the need to 'reform the public sector' – although David Cameron confuses things by then unconvincingly opposing the consequences of these reforms, such as the closure of A&E units or maternity services. The government refers euphemistically to the need to 'reform' the public sector which, mostly, means bringing in the private sector to do work that had previously been done by the public sector in order to ensure that market principles apply within a public-sector setting.

It is interesting, isn't it, that almost two decades since Mrs Thatcher left office, her legacy is alive and well and dictating strategy to both the Labour and Conservative parties?

The right to have a home, to enjoy family life, to have fair access to quality health care are all compromised if we leave the provision of these to the market. Of course, my view of these matters is coloured by the experience of the communities that I represent in Cumbria, communities that are often isolated, where well-paid work is rare but where demand for housing from people from outside the area is such that market prices are pushed up and beyond the reach of the majority of local people.

The consequences of the near-total absence of affordable housing and the inadequate supply of social housing are social disintegration, mass migration and the isolation of the elderly. A countryside where only the wealthy can afford to exist is most definitely not the intended outcome of the socialist idealists who established the National Parks. Nevertheless, this is becoming a reality. It serves as a stark picture of the failure of the marketplace to preserve viable communities which applies to urban areas as well.

Intervention is the only course of action open to a true liberal who values practical freedoms as opposed to those which are merely theoretical. The wonderful opportunity that presents itself to Liberal Democrats is that we have within our grasp a highly political message that stands out as principled and (dare I say it) ideological in contrast to those two indistinct brands of ICBINP. We can also – via a sweet irony – make unexpected inroads against Conservatives by attracting their traditional supporters with an unashamedly interventionist platform.

Chapter 15

The Case for Localism: The Liberal Narrative

Chris Huhne

The argument of this chapter is that the British state is failing to deliver much of what British people want, and has become a toxic source of disillusion with the entire political process.

Since progressive politics is about changing and reforming society, and since the state is an essential instrument of much of that change, there is no more corrosive or potentially conservative development in our politics than cynicism about state failure. The task of reviving faith in the political process is therefore urgent, and this essay argues that a key part of that revival must be localism: the decentralisation not just of management decisions but of political responsibility to a human scale where voters can once again identify – and complain to, or praise, or boot out – decision-makers in their community.

Localism is crucial to reviving faith in collective decision-making. It is vital in reviving world-quality public services, and is a key element of the explanation of why the Labour government's vast increase in money spent on public services has failed to deliver commensurate increases in quality. It is also a essential part of the Liberal narrative about what has gone wrong with the state. Just as important for progressives, this paper argues that those who distrust localism for fear that it will lead to greater inequality are mistaken. It gives international evidence to demonstrate that there is no relationship between the degree of decentralisation of political power in a society and income inequality.

Liberal philosophy and localism

There has been a lot of recent commentary about the need for the Liberal Democrats to have a narrative, which is something between a slogan and a philosophy. This is really a quest for an answer to the age-old problem of any political party: what on earth are we for?

That should be simple. The Liberal Democrats are for liberalism, which is essentially a doctrine about the individual and power. Liberals want to create a society that puts people first and enables them to thrive. That means that the undue exercise of power over individuals must be curbed, whether it is private or state power. People must be allowed to make their own lives and choices so long as they do not harm others. But liberalism is also a positive commitment to enable people to thrive, from whatever background they come and in whatever unfortunate circumstances they find themselves. That is the social liberal element that was introduced by the Edwardian New Liberals, such as L. T. Hobhouse and T. H. Green, but whose early stirrings are discernible in the work of classical liberals such as J. S. Mill (such as in his essay on the subjection of women).

Classical liberalism is against concentrations of power, whether private or public. It is associated, for example, with the Sherman Act in the United States against monopolies, cartels and abuses of dominant position. It is also associated with Gladstonian frugality in the public finances and the defence of civil liberties and the rule of law. Classical socialism is a bastard child of liberalism, as socialists are merely concerned with the abusive exercise of private power and remove their critical faculties when they look at state power. Like socialism, social liberalism is a progressive creed. It believes not just in removing oppression but in putting in place support for the individual. It has moved far beyond laissez-faire. It therefore embraces the need for an active and empowering state. But it combines the social concern of socialism with the critique of power of classical liberalism: it sees the accountability of the state as a central part of the progressive argument.

In common with classical liberalism, social liberalism remains a doctrine concerned about the excessive exercise of power by the state. If the state is to be powerful enough to ensure essential tasks – national defence and policing, providing people with help when they are sick or old, maintaining a cohesive and just society, and giving chances to the young through education – it is bound in the modern world to spend – indeed, redistribute – a substantial part of our national income. The most striking feature of British political life is the relative stability of public spending as a share of gross domestic product – usually around 40 to 42 per cent – despite furious ideological battles between Labour and the Conservatives about tax and spend versus rolling back the state. Since 1970, public spending has never been lower than 37.2 per cent of GDP and never higher than 50.1 per cent. Social liberals believe that the really important question is how to make state power accountable and answerable to the people. The boundary between public and private is less important than the argument about how to manage the inevitably large publicly determined expenditure that a modern developed country needs and wants.

Indeed, it is this perception – the need to make the state accountable – that is so crucial to understanding the Labour government's failure since 1997. Labour came to power in 1997 committed to a radical improvement in public services. There has already been a 38 per cent increase in real terms (over and above inflation) in public spending, from 1996–97 to 2006–07. The equivalent real-terms increase in education spending is 55 per cent, and in health is 72 per cent. And there is more in the pipeline. We in the Liberal Democrats rightly backed those increases. Alone of all the major parties, we were even prepared to say that taxes had to be raised to pay for them. Except in Labour–Tory la-la land, you do not get something for nothing. We won that battle after the election, if not quite before. Money was an essential part of the solution.

Yet it is now clear that there has been no corresponding increase in quality. There have been improvements, but not improvements commensurate with the extra resources. We remain behind other countries in the provision of world-class public services, especially in health. We now have some of the highest paid doctors in the European Union. Indeed, they are so richly rewarded that German doctors (from a society as rich as ours) travel to Britain to provide locum services for ours at the weekend. Yet we continue to have fewer doctors per thousand population than almost any other EU country, a contrast that suggests that someone in central government believed that you only had to pay doctors more to get more of them. A better planned increase in training might have been more advisable.

But the unfortunate split in extra money between pay and more staff is only symptomatic of a deeper problem. There is something wrong with the way we are attempting to deliver public services. Any MP knows how powerless his or her own constituents are in holding local decision-takers to account. If you complain locally, the odds are that managers will blame Whitehall. If you attempt to hold Whitehall to account, ministers or officials are likely to say that the information is not held centrally or that local bodies are responsible. The most pervasive feeling in the British public sector is of the enormous difficulty of change and responsiveness to new circumstances. It is like treading treacle. Even those parts of government that are theoretically most local – under the control of local authorities – have increasingly found their own discretion removed. School budgets are determined largely by Whitehall. Discretionary spending has been steadily reduced. Tax powers are severely limited. Pay deals are often nationally negotiated.

The fork in the road: localism or markets

There are two broad schools of thought on what we should change in the public services. The first is that we should introduce more markets and quasi-markets, allowing individual choice to determine successful providers in the public sector as it does in the private sector. The second is that we should introduce more local democratic decision-taking. The two are not always in contradiction, but there are important contrasts.

Let us take marketisation first. Nobody should be against choice, as long as it does not limit the choices of others. But there are dangers in zealously pursuing market and quasi-market solutions to the lengths suggested by Labour's Blairites or by the Tories. I have considerable doubts about whether there is really such a close parallel between markets in the private and public sphere: if you buy more or fewer oranges, you are unlikely to affect in any material way anyone else's options. But if you take your child away from a failing school, you may worsen the outlook for the children left behind. One person's exercise of choice may limit another's.

Many education authorities such as my own in Hampshire provide very high degrees of choice for parents: 96 per cent get their child into the primary school of their choice, and 92 per cent into the middle school they want. A change in the system that undermined the ability of the local authority to act as ringmaster might well reduce the number of children going to the schools their parents chose. Indeed, in extreme circumstances marketisation could mean schools determining their own admissions policies. The result would be schools choosing pupils, not pupils choosing schools. That would be a curious sort of market, as if the supermarket chose its shoppers rather than the other way round.

In their obsession with marketisation, the government has been drawn to some pretty rum solutions. For example, a thirty-year hospital building private finance initiative (PFI) does not provide the most obvious benefit of normal private sector involvement, which should be to increase flexibility. On the contrary, such contracts lock in the same service provision, and merely increase potential liabilities when the contract has to be renegotiated to reshape services for a change in needs. The failure of Gordon Brown's London Underground schemes are a clear example of the long-term public liabilities.

Moreover, the choice of marketisation as a national policy removes the possibility of competing solutions tried in different places as a way of learning how best to proceed. If marketisation does undermine the provision of public goods in a particular field of activity, the entire national system would have to be scrapped. How much better it would be if there were an ongoing means of trying out changes in response to new circumstances, with the continuing possibility that successes will be copied and failures shunned. Localism provides a model by which we can gradually discover the best ways of tackling problems in conditions of great uncertainty.

I believe a more compelling explanation for the failure of services is not the lack of markets or quasi-markets but the extent of local accountability and control. This is an old Liberal Democrat theme. Let me repeat: the issue is not the size of the state, with Labour wanting more and the Conservatives less, but the accountability of the state's power and the checks and balances operating on it. The problem is that public services have in recent decades been provided in this country in a top-down manner determined by the man or woman in the ministry in Whitehall, who is at best wholly ignorant of the conditions determining the delivery of public services in each locality of this country.

The problem is the same as with all excessively centralised systems. You apply the same solution regardless of circumstances: one size must fit all – and too often fail all. There is inevitably a lack of creativity, innovation and experimentation. There is merely the dead hand of the Whitehall directive depriving local decision-takers and professionals of choice and initiative. In the health service, for example, there are now more than

1.3 million employees. The only bigger organisations in the world are said to be the Indian Railways and the Chinese People's Liberation Army. Yet there is just one democratically elected politician – the Secretary of State for Health – held to account for every success and failure, regardless of the impossibility of her or him knowing about, let alone being responsible for, delivery in Hampshire, Cornwall and Cumbria.

The problem with Britain's public sector is that it has not developed systematic ways in which it can come up with new ideas to respond to new challenges. There is no parallel with the power of the private market-place to reward genius and punish indifference to the customer. Indeed, too often ministerial failure is ignored entirely. One of the largest recent administrative cock-ups was the abject failure to pay single farm payments on time. The minister responsible – Margaret Beckett – was promoted to the Foreign Office. Her successor at the Department of Environment, Food and Rural Affairs – David Miliband – then bizarrely cut flood defence budgets (a decision that was reversed by his successor Hilary Benn). Yet Miliband too was promoted to the Foreign Office. It is as if we are implicitly admitting that the system is so big and so complex that it would be unfair to hold anyone to account for its failures.

Our centralised public service system leads to absurdities of target-setting: we have a target for carpet cleanliness in hospitals, as if they were quite incapable of working that out for themselves. We set a target for patients to be seen within 48 hours of ringing their GP for an appointment; the result was that many GPs then only booked appointments 48 hours in advance. Target met, but welfare lowered. Contrast this system with the private sector, where it is natural to experiment, to try something new. If businesses fail in some effort, they stop and try something else. If they succeed, they try more. There is a constant process of change and improvement – or the business dies.

The only solution to the problem of preserving public goods while introducing the possibility of innovation is local decision-taking. This allows local decision-takers to innovate, be creative and experiment just as much as the private sector. Those who succeed in setting new standards will be followed by others. Those who fail can and should be booted out by their local electorates.

Please note that this will also allow local authorities to experiment with different types of provider: with traditional public-service providers, with mutuals, cooperatives and social enterprises, and with private companies. At all stages of the welfare state, all types of provider have been involved; Nye Bevan used the private sector to build hospitals. But the right mix and balance should surely be a matter of discovery best left to the judgement of local circumstances, not arbitrary Treasury fiat.

In this model, the role of national government is necessarily limited if it is not once again to begin arrogating power to itself. Central government must analyse success and failure, spread best practice through reporting and comparisons, and ensure that local electorates are informed about the relative success of their authority. This is a crucial task, but it is essentially to help local electorates maintain informed accountability.

Think of this problem another way: who best knows whether a service is being provided well or not? Surely the best placed people are those who are using it, not people miles away in an office in Whitehall. That is why putting local people in the driving seat through elected local authorities or elected public boards is the best way forward. Who is the best person to judge the success of a restaurant in providing meals? Is it the customer who actually eats there or a civil servant in DEFRA who sits in an office hundreds of miles away relying on reports of the restaurant's food quality, hygiene and staff relations?

The disease of giantism

In my view, the failure of the British state is essentially a failure of giantism. Look at the money flow to appreciate the enormity of the issue, because money determines power. Those who pay the piper call the tune, as Gordon Brown well understood when he struck the deal with Tony Blair that not only gave him the Treasury but also put him in the lead on domestic policy. And money in Britain's public sector is uniquely and extraordinarily centralised. Some 94.4 per cent of tax revenue in this country goes through central government, according to Eurostat figures for 2005. Only one other EU country puts more through central government: Malta. Malta, of course, has a population only a little larger than the London Borough of Croydon. It is hardly a suitable comparator for a country in the G8 group of leading industrial countries of the world. (See Figure 1.)

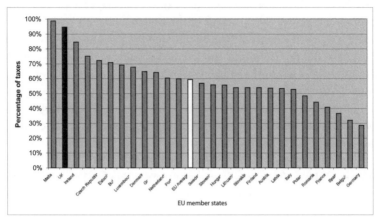

Figure 1: Share of tax revenue paid through central government[1]

On average, a little more than half of taxation – 51.8 per cent in 2005 – goes through central government in the EU, and a little less than half through lower levels of governance. That is an extraordinary and damning contrast with our own centralisation, and is the measure of the change that we need to bring about in Britain.

In Britain, we chronically underestimate the sheer scale of our political units. Only one English region – the North East – has a population smaller than that of the Republic of Ireland, one of Europe's most successful economies. The South East of England is bigger in population than more than half of all the twenty-seven member states of the European Union. Hampshire – a large county, but not the biggest by any means – has a population of 1.6 million. This is bigger than the population of four EU member states (Estonia, Cyprus, Luxembourg and Malta). We are a big, big country still attempting to pretend that we are a small one. With the exception of devolution to Scotland, Wales and Northern Ireland, we in England are still making do with a centralised system that our forebears would have recognised during the Napoleonic Wars, when we had a population half that of France.

Tackling the problems of localism: national standards
If we were to have a substantial decentralisation, what would be the problems that we would have to face?

The first is the issue of national standards. People are attached to the notion that we should all be able to access a similar standard of public service – schools or hospitals or police – wherever we live in the UK. People rightly want to be sure that if they are involved in a car crash while on holiday in Cornwall they will be as well looked after as if they were at home in Colchester.

However, many decades of trying to deliver such a standard have lamentably failed, as the recurrence of the postcode lottery – most recently over the prescribing of Herceptin – shows. Our centralised system cannot deliver common standards for the simple reason that the levers in Whitehall are not connected to the real world. Pull as ministers may, the trains do not run on to the designated lines.

It would be far better to have accountable local decision-taking units where the standard of service is at least designed for a purpose and stands some chance of being delivered to plan. If there are differences, they will be designed and meant, and those responsible can defend their choices. At present, differences are the random effect of a dysfunctional Whitehall bureaucracy and a historic pattern of provision owing as much to private philanthropy as good national design. The real choice is between planned differences or dysfunctional differences.

We should also recognise that we can have national minimum standards without them being imposed from on high. Central government should not on its own set minimum national standards, as that would again introduce leverage for central Whitehall bureaucracies to pre-empt local decision taking. The way to agree national standards is between the authorities that each have responsibility, as consensus ensures that none feel that their own room for manoeuvre has been restricted. This is the model that is followed in many industries, where standards are reached by agreement. It is also the model for EU-wide standards.

Competition at local level

The second condition if local decision-taking is to work is that there have to be contested and contestable political units. Here the way has been pioneered by the Scots, with their introduction of the single transferable vote system of proportional representation for local councils from 2007. For the first time since Keir Hardie, the red central belt of Scotland has become a real political battlefield. Voters can award politicians the order of the boot in areas where the boot was unknown. Competition works in politics as much as in the economy. One of the reasons for the destruction of the powers of local government by both Conservative and Labour governments was the unrepresentative nature of many council groups; think of Red Ted Knight in Lambeth or Ken Livingstone sparking the abolition of the GLC in London. The sheer irresponsibility of extremist Labour politicians was protected by the residual loyalties of Labour electorates and the unresponsiveness of the first-past-the-post election system. Similarly, some dyed-in-the-wool Tory authorities have persisted with poor levels of services for far too long but have been shored up by the electoral system.

The case for proportional representation in local government is as strong as the case for PR at Westminster, and it will allow a substantial decentralisation of power in the knowledge that local people will be able to hold to account and discipline those who exercise it.

Money is power, so finance must be local

Thirdly, local authorities have to be able to raise their own finance. At present, they raise about a quarter of their spending, which means that they are not financially responsible for most of their spending (see Figure 2).

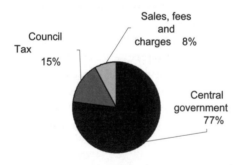

Figure 2: Share of local government revenue[2]

They need to be able to raise much more of their own resources if there is to be genuine accountability. At the same time, this will reduce the pernicious gearing effect, whereby a decision to spend 1 per cent more on local services leads to the need for a 4 per cent rise in local taxation because local taxes raise so little of local spending.

The fourth condition for local decision-taking is that there has to be a system of reallocation of central funds to take account both of the difference of needs from one area to another and the difference of resources or of the tax base.

Such equalisation is not rocket science: it is done in many countries with more federal and devolved constitutions than ours, both on the continent and in English-speaking countries such as Australia and Canada.

In principle, such equalisation could involve payments from rich and less needy authorities to poor and more needy ones while raising all local spending from taxation. But it may be realistic to maintain a central government block grant raised from central taxation instead, just so long as the criteria on which it is allocated – fairness in needs and resources – are both clear and settled and are not subject to ministerial whims from one year to another. As soon as there is ministerial discretion over the system, there will be ministerial gerrymandering to deliver cash to favoured authorities.

Localism and inequality

The question raised by the debate is whether such decentralisation would lead to less or more social cohesion and solidarity. My answer is that it is entirely irrelevant to the question of equality. Local decision-taking has no consequences for equality or social justice one way or the other, which is why the degree of centralisation should be decided on other grounds.

In the United States, you can see the results of a decentralised system where the left has always championed federal government, and the right has championed states' rights. And the US is of course marked by appalling inequality. However, the Scandinavian countries and Germany offer precisely the opposite model: substantial decentralisation combined with a much greater commitment to equality than here in Britain.

Let me here display some compelling evidence to reassure those acquainted with the American debate that localisation does not mean inequality. Figure 3 plots income inequality against a measure of centralisation. Income inequality is measured by the Gini coefficient, and is based on the Luxembourg income data series for countries where individual surveys were completed at the end of the 1990s and beginning of

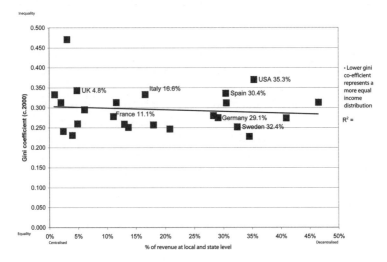

Figure 3: Equality versus decentralisation?[3]

this decade. The measure of centralisation is the amount of tax revenue going through central government on the public finance figures of the OECD (so that the United States and other non-EU countries may be included).

What it shows is that, if anything, there is a very modest trend to associate decentralisation with greater equality. If I am totally fair, I would say that there is no obvious relationship between the two. (The coefficient of determination – the R^2 statistic – is extremely low, suggesting that these two factors are almost unrelated to each other.) This in turn undermines any notion that decentralisation causes inequality. There are countries with a high degree of centralisation and high inequality like Britain. There are countries with a low degree of centralisation and high inequality like the United States. And there are countries with a low degree of centralisation and low inequality like Germany or Sweden.

In short, the international evidence is abundantly clear. You can have decentralisation, with all its advantages for quality and productivity, with no attendant disadvantages in lack of solidarity. We can have all the advantages of localism without fear that there is a hidden US-style agenda of cuts in public services or devil take the hindmost.

The democratic argument for localism

I have so far put my argument in terms of efficiency, but I think there is a deeper case for localism. I believe that the roots of much disillusionment and disenchantment with our political system lie in the destruction of the powers of local government and local governance. A political system that ensures that local people know a local figure who matters in their community, and who has the power to change things for the better (or the worse), is a political system which makes itself immediately relevant to people's lives. It is a system that is perceived to engage people and do things for people, and not merely to do things to people. In such a system, political engagement is likely to be far higher than in a system where voters regard a far-off national choice about leaders with little more enthusiasm than their choice of breakfast cereal.

The steady erosion of the power and prerogatives of local government in this country under both Labour and Conservative administrations has destroyed the vital first rungs on the ladder of electoral participation. Sadly, Britain is by no means the only country where central government has increasingly arrogated powers to itself. The Norwegian study of power and democracy – a Royal Commission – found that the centralisation of powers in Oslo had undermined the link between the voter and the political system, because local politicians were increasingly unable to deliver what local people wanted. Since those local politicians are the eyes and ears of the political system ward by ward, the consequences for disillusion are profound.

The exercise of power and discretion at local level is probably the single most important change that we could introduce to ensure that people reconnect with the political system. That reconnection is vital not just to progressive politics but to the health of the national community. Single-issue organisations, however noble their cause, cannot trade off one issue against another, prioritise one spending project rather than another, decide on the general direction that a society should choose. When a single-issue organisation like the Royal Society for the Protection of Birds has more members than all of Britain's political parties put together, the warning signals for our democracy are clear. Nothing less than a reinvention of the British state will do if we are also to revive the roots of Britain's democracy.

Conclusion

In this chapter, I have set out to argue that the British state is failing because of its sheer scale combined with its extraordinary belief in centralised decision-taking. The decentralisation of powers is crucial if local decision-takers are to be held to account by those who use public services, which is in turn a necessary condition for their long-term improvement. None of the commonly expressed objections – such as a possible variation in standards, or the growth of inequality – are based on evidence. Moreover, decentralisation is a wider issue merely than the efficiency of public services. It is also about connecting the electorate back to the political system by ensuring that they know someone locally who can deliver undoubted improvements.

Notes

1 *Taxation Trends in the European Union*, June 2007, Table B.1 T.
2 Source: House of Commons library.
3 Source: House of Commons library from OECD tax statistics (for tax revenue) and the Luxembourg income study (for price-adjusted income).

Chapter 16

The State and Education

John Howson

It is not the job of the state to educate its citizens, but rather to see that they are educated.

Adapted from J. S. Mill, On Liberty

When Labour came to power in 1997, their battle cry was 'education, education, education'. At the time, everyone thought this heralded a new dawn for education. However, it can now been seen for what it really was: a slogan that was so typical of New Labour, almost entirely devoid of any values and designed just to catch the headlines. What education, for whom and to what purposes, were the questions a savvy journalist, not blinded by the media hype surrounding the triumph of New Labour, should have asked.

Historically, England came late to the view that schooling its citizens was a key responsibility of the state. The view that dominated much of early nineteenth-century thought was that it was the responsibility of individuals to invest in their education and not of the state to provide it. That still strikes a chord in modern British society. Elsewhere in the Western world the involvement of the state was, and often is, unchallenged. However, over the past quarter-century the old orthodoxy has been confronted in some of the Nordic countries, elsewhere in Europe, and in parts of the US, as well as in England. Where should Liberal Democrats find themselves in the debate about the role of the state in education?

As Britain emerged from the post-World War II ideology of large-scale planned enterprises into an era where greater wealth for some became more acceptable than the creation of a fairer society for all, so education inevitably became caught up in the changing zeitgeist. The distributed management of the school system that had been crafted during the first three-quarters of the twentieth century, often described by commentators as 'a national system locally administered', gradually gave way to the present era of central direction and local site management. In making these changes, politicians at Westminster ensured that local communities were effectively ruled out of the practical involvement in the planning of their local education provision. So today, a secondary school governing body can vote on becoming a Foundation School against the wishes of elected councillors; the operation of any new secondary school must be put out to tender, probably with a presumption that the council will not be expected to win the tender; an Academy can be inserted, like a cuckoo in the nest, into a community school system, even one facing significant reductions in overall pupil numbers without any regard to long-term planning; and communities no longer have any real control over the financing of their local schools.

However, underneath these ideological shifts there exists a school system that remains, as ever, dependent for its success upon four basic factors: adequate resources, suitable and well-maintained buildings, sufficient well-trained staff and an appropriate curriculum. Without these, the system cannot function effectively. To some extent, the ideological changes have been the product of failures by politicians to provide for one or more of the four basic needs facing schools. One might describe the algorithm as Performance = Pounds (for resources) + People (sufficient appropriately trained staff) + Places (school buildings fit for purpose) + Pedagogy (an appropriate curriculum and learning methods). To these might be added a fifth, Parents, whose attitudes and those of their offspring can seriously affect schools. This would include the state itself, where it is acting as a corporate parent for children in care.

However, before looking in detail at the role of the state in supporting these basic needs, it is worth reiterating that state education is not compulsory. It remains, as it has ever since Gladstone's government instituted a requirement for schooling for all, the default model; the state assumes responsibility for provision when parents either can't, don't or won't make other arrangements. From the start, possibly because of economic caution and a reluctance to increase public expenditure unnecessarily, together with a concern not to upset the established church, the state took over the funding of church schools, but did not buy out the asset base. What may have seemed like an astute move then has come to bedevil education in England many times during the years since 1870.

Education for whom?

So, if education has been shaped by its historical roots, how has the state responded, and what mistakes has it made? And is the current investment both fit for purpose and in line with the beliefs of Liberal Democrats over fairness, equality and justice?

To answer these questions it is also necessary to decide to what extent education is a private or a public good: investment for the individual's benefit or for the common good? The debate about this issue is fundamental to current issues such as the introduction of tuition and top-up fees for university students, and the Chancellor's announcements over paying teenagers to remain in education, just as it was in the early part of the twentieth century over fees for secondary education.

I would contend that a fair system is one that seeks to offer the same high quality of education for all. In accepting this goal, the issue of choice then becomes a second-order question. The aim of the state for its citizens must be choice *for*, not choice *from*; this might be bad news for house prices, but good news for many parents. At the most basic level, this means treating the notion of equality not as one of 'the same for everyone', but as 'what education is needed' by individual learners to reach their goal. This is the idea behind the notion of a pupil premium, first espoused in my 2002 Commission report for the Liberal Democrats, *No Child Left Behind* and developed further by Sarah Teather MP and David Laws MP in their roles as education spokespersons.

There can be arguments about how to operate the mechanics, but the approach is simple to understand: the cash follows the needs of the learner. This vision of fairness has all too often been corrupted even at school levels, where cash for younger pupils has propped up expensive and uneconomic sixth forms, or funds for special education are spent on other parts of the budget. At the most basic level, this tension between fairness and the allocation of resources confronts every teacher every day in their classrooms, just as it does anyone who has to allocate scarce resources. How much time do I spend with this learner compared with that one? Education is not a value-free activity for anyone, and especially not for governments. Thus, a pupil premium is really a needs-based funding system that aims to ensure that resources reach the pupils who most need help. In that sense it operates in the same manner as a tax credit system, by supporting those who do not have their own resources to make the most of their children's education.

This notion of fairness and equity has been used by the government to mask what seems to me sometimes to be deeply unfair actions. The development of Academies, the Labour derivative of the Conservatives' City Technology Colleges, has been projected as a move to improve the education chances for some of the most deprived in society. But by giving these schools control over their admissions policies and freeing them up from controls over staffing and the curriculum, they can become not servants of their local communities, but rather determinants of who may access their abundant resources.

The same lack of fairness could be seen in the policy over specialist schools. Where is the rationale for a coherent strategy that meets both the needs of communities and their learners? Why are many science specialist schools in the South East selective schools, and often single-sex schools? Does society not need technicians with science backgrounds to work alongside our future Nobel Prize winners? Or is science only for the most able in society? The same arguments about rationality can be made for the new breed of Trust Schools announced in the 2006 Education and Inspections Act. At a time of falling rolls, such as those faced by many secondary schools in England over the next ten years, to privilege some schools above others is to risk paralysing the development of the system in the same way that the Conservatives' grant-maintained schools initiative did in the early 1990s. The fear of schools 'opting-out' both blighted local planning in some areas and meant that longer-term planning in places like London ground to a halt. The result was a shortage of school places in many parts of the capital in the early years of this century, when increased pupil numbers had not been planned for. Such folly deprived many of access to their local community schools, as those with more social capital used the appeals system to their own advantage.

Staffing

The early years of this century saw other examples of Labour's lack of underlying vision and managerial incompetence that stand as stark warning for Liberal Democrats when in government. One example of this was in the policies developed to staff schools. Both Labour and the Conservatives have been deeply suspicious of the university training departments, and have sough to rein them in. Although the original Teacher Training Agency was a creation of the Conservatives, the present

Training and Development Agency has seen its role develop significantly under Labour. However, it is not the creation of the Agency that by itself affects how schools are staffed; rather, it is the various mechanisms by which the government created a teacher supply crisis on the back of the introduction of tuition fees after 1997. Labour's initial involvement with teacher supply was a welcome one; the capping of class sizes for pupils at Key Stage 1. However, even this laudable policy failed the test of equality used earlier: larger classes at Key Stage 1 in 1997 were often to be found in authorities run by the Conservatives. The blunt tool of a policy initiative reducing all class sizes at Key Stage 1 to a national maximum effectively risked transferring funds to these areas, where literacy might already be high, and away from areas where the need was greatest. What was needed was a policy, such as the pupil premium described earlier, that encouraged the allocation of resources where they were needed to aid those most at risk of falling behind during their crucial early years.

If the class-size reduction policy was at least founded on good intentions, Gordon Brown's attempts as Chancellor in his 2001 budget to be both a tax-raiser and spender apparently demonstrated no such inherent values. Handing large cash sums directly to schools, based solely upon their size and irrespective of their needs, is not only by itself a policy based upon a simplistic notion of equality, but one that risks in its execution the chance that it will go further and 'deprive the deprived'. Indeed, that is what happened. Not surprisingly, many schools went off on a staffing spree that would have not seemed out of place from a lottery winner, after they had survived a period under the Conservatives and the first two years of the Labour government when staffing resources had been under pressure, and class sizes, especially in the secondary sector, had been rising. Sadly, the Treasury's – or to be more accurate the Chancellor's – attempts at being a spending department had not been backed by the provision of a pool of teachers looking for jobs; indeed, most teacher-training courses were experiencing their worst recruitment levels for many years, particularly in some of the so-called 'shortage subjects'. The Treasury money was like adding petrol to a bonfire; the demand for extra teachers rocketed. The results were a massive churn within the system, as teachers found job opportunities more plentiful. An influx of overseas teachers with no training in the National Curriculum and little long-term interest in the schools they were working in were sucked in to fill the gap. At one time, there were more overseas teachers working in the London Borough of Tower Hamlets than in the whole of the North East government office region. Was it the suburban schools that suffered the most? Most likely not – more likely the unfair outcome of this ill-judged interference was to disadvantage the most challenging schools. Without stable teaching staff such schools cannot make progress, and it is not surprising that many such schools, in both the primary and secondary sectors, struggled. Test scores, so beloved by the government, either failed to improve or even fell, and several cohorts of children were left floundering for the remainder of their education careers.

More than any other resource, a shortage of qualified teachers has long-term effects upon the generation of pupils that encounter them. Failures in teacher supply are one of the main causes of educational failure, as the rebound in results over the past few years has demonstrated. Not that the problem has been entirely solved. The government may be sleep-walking into another crisis, as it fails to train staff properly to teach the new diplomas. Indeed, the current subject categories under which secondary school teacher-training places are allocated reads more like the curriculum of fifty years ago than a modern system providing education for all.

This is one area where a regulated market might operate better than the current centralised planning model. Secondary schools could hire 'interns' who would be trained against the national standards to attain Qualified Teacher Status. Most of the training could continue to be delivered, as at present by higher education staff working with both trainees and current professionals learning together at the interface of training and research. Schools would be able to meet their needs for teachers, as they do with all other staff, and trainees would be salaried and more likely to be offered a post where they live than under the present system that, particularly for mature students who can only work in particular locations, represents something of a career gamble.

Central direction v. local initiative

As in so many different areas, Labour's continued tinkering with the education system has barely let a policy have time to be initiated before it is often overtaken by another new idea. Education Action Zones, Sure Start, specialist schools, Academies, Foundations, Trusts, and many other initiatives have come, and some have gone. Most have been imposed from Whitehall through a one-size-fits-all model, with little or no room for local communities to tailor the proposals to their own needs. Such central direction can hamper communities from developing their own solutions, and is a central flaw in Labour's concept of the state.

Nowhere has insecurity toward education policy been more visible than in the government's attitude to the education of 14–19 year olds. Mr Blair's swift rejection of the Tomlinson Report in 2005 masked an even deeper issue of whether the present break at eleven, crafted to meet the needs of the raising of the school-leaving age to fifteen after the Second World War, provides for a system where many now stay in education until eighteen, and all are encouraged to remain as learners – and indeed may be required to remain in formal education until nineteen – under the latest government thinking.

The fall in the birth rate that will reduce the secondary school population over the next decade may free up the resources to make the target of learning until eighteen for all a reality, but it surely needs more thought than just articulating the desire. The present school curriculum is not fit for purpose for most of those who do not already remain in education. The problem is not, as it was when the school-leaving age was raised from fifteen to sixteen in the 1970s, the large number of able children who were forced to leave school to start work. Many who leave school at sixteen today have in reality 'left school' much earlier, disengaging from a 'grammar-school-for-all curriculum' that seems irrelevant to them and is often delivered by a generation of teachers whose own schooling was several lifetimes away from that of their current pupils who have grown up in a world of computers, mobile phones, the internet, e-Bay, YouTube and Myspace. This is not an area where the outcome can realistically be left to the market. Neither does the present model of the distribution of funds for 16–19 education from a central quango to individual institutions inspire confidence.

The role of local communities, through a decentralised state of locally elected representatives, should have a key part to play in the development of appropriate learning frameworks, whether for those destined for university or those who seek to 'earn and learn'. Indeed, rising tuition fees for university students may force many eighteen year olds to seek to study closer to their homes rather than to commute long distances to university campuses in distant cities. If that happens, then the role of civic leaders in both developing and promoting education should once again become a core responsibility, as it was when the so-called 'red-brick' university colleges were developed by an earlier generation.

However, the involvement of the state in education through active participation at both the national level and by local communities is not to deny individual families any rights within the system. It is just to place these rights within a context that recognises the right of all citizens who accept the state's offer to provide education to demand high-quality provision and to call government to account when it is not provided.

Sadly, too often since Clause 6 of the 1980 Education Act formally legislated for parental choice, the driving motivation has been to satisfy the wishes of the individual or the minority, sometimes even at the expense of the majority. This can be easily illustrated by the confusion over the role of primary schools run by the Church of England. Many of these are found in rural locations, and often they are the only school in the area. As I suggested earlier, when schooling became compulsory, the state took on the burden of running these schools, but did not take over the original assets. Nevertheless, since 1870, most of these schools will also have received considerable capital funding to repair or extend their buildings. The recent changes to the admissions code still leave adherence to the teachings of the Church of England as a key criterion for admission. With only a small proportion of the population regularly practising as Anglicans, the minority have advantages that are not open to the majority, even though the school is basically funded by the state.

Indeed, the present vogue for anyone with the money being able to start a new school – regardless of whether or not they have any educational values – comes perilously close to the marketisation of education. Was this the view of education that nineteenth-century thinkers wanted liberals to embrace? The state viewed as the provider of funds, and the individual as the purchaser of education? In its extreme form this results in the creation of vouchers that transfer the funds into the hands of the individual to decide what education to purchase. The state regulates the provision, and presumably steps in where there are no providers willing to enter the market.

This model seems wonderful in theory, real liberalism at work. It has also seemed attractive to some modern Conservatives, often those who have little or no experience of the business world. Apart from the practical problems that such a system might create, however, there are two economic arguments that make it an unrealistic proposal. The first of these can be seen clearly in the special school sector. Indeed, this is an area where the state has always been prepared to make the most use of private, and more often charitable, provision. However, recently the cost of purchasing places at some of the more specialist types of provision seems to have spiralled out of control, with providers able to name their prices. This is not to deny that high-quality special education provision is expensive, but to suggest that the state has no mechanism to ensure it is able to obtain value for money. There are ways that this can be overcome, through price controls and competition strategies, although the recent price-fixing inquiry into school fees amongst schools in the private sector has demonstrated the power of the provider to determine the market price.

There is, I believe, an even more persuasive argument against the state abrogating the use of its funds to individual purchasers. This is an argument that relates to the way in which state education was founded. As I suggested earlier, state provision is the default, you can educate your child at home or pay for someone else to educate then for you. Under the state-as-funder model, there is the likelihood that all those parents who currently pay for the education of their children would expect the state to contribute a share. In effect, this would transfer the sum of several billion pounds each year from tax revenues to fund expenditure currently financed out of private resources. In a society where political parties are striving to keep down tax levels, such an increase in the tax burden would be suicidal in electoral terms.

Higher education

Of course, it can be argued that this is the way in which the state funds tuition for higher education, through a regime that is basically the same for all but with help to the most needy. Liberal Democrats have argued that control of this funding is best and most fairly achieved by the state bulk-purchasing places and allowing them to be funded free at the point of delivery. Such a bulk-purchase model should allow for proper discussions about the appropriate level of funding for the activity which is required: tuition of undergraduates. However, it takes away responsibility from the consumer to become involved in what they are purchasing. As individual students are in a weak position, wanting something they cannot do without (a degree), their power to demand a better experience can easily be frustrated by providers who only have to claim that 'this is the best you will get for the money'. The fact that the present system emerged without serious debate about whether the existing structures of higher education were fit for purpose shows more about the unintended consequences of making the polytechnics into universities, and not realising that they would go on a recruitment spree that was possible under the funding model in use in the early 1990s during the Conservative government. Once such a policy of expansion became endorsed by government, with the target of approaching half the age cohort going on to higher education, there was no real public debate about how this was best achieved given the different types of provision available. That debate has still not occurred and in the distance, as the rolls of sixth forms start to fall, is the spectre of unplanned contractions, mergers and even the threat of financial deficits leading to enforced action to prevent an institution going into receivership.

One consequence of the present market-based model is the freedom for individual universities to cut courses that are uneconomic to operate. Does it matter that courses in areas like music, and more frequently the sciences, are abandoned by individual institutions? After all, the consumer has other choices. They may be more expensive for some consumers, but that's not the issue for the provider in a market. Such a view is simplistic and seems to assume that higher education is merely located in, but not associated with, a community. To take but two examples, cutting science undergraduate courses may endanger the provision of science teachers in a particular area, particularly as many graduates go on to teacher training in the same university where they studied for their first degree. More generally, graduates often want to settle where they went to university, and can make a real contribution to the local economy. Will new science- and technology-based jobs be created in areas where the university has dropped such courses, and what might the consequences of such unplanned actions be if repeated across the country?

Such outcomes are the consequences of a university system that seems all too often not to understand the changes that have taken place in education over the past decades. The school curriculum is no longer designed to create just the intellectual high-flyers of tomorrow, ready-groomed for undergraduate life. One example is the manner in which examination have changed over the past half century from school certificate, with candidates expected to study only six subjects – in other words, 'to know a lot about a little' – to the modern schema where many more subjects are studied to GCSE, and candidates might be said to 'know a little about a lot'. Such change in the scope of learning has affected A-levels, and the levels of knowledge new undergraduates bring to university studies. In a mass secondary education system, there is no going back to the former system.

There is, however, a debate to be had about whether the present models of study are fit for purpose. Do university lecturers want to work with undergraduates whose knowledge and skill bases are less than before? Could not a new system be devised that allowed the first two years of degree study to be undertaken locally as an extension of school, in either expanded sixth-form or further-education colleges, with progression after two years to honours courses in universities? Teaching such undergraduates might be more meaningful for those who also want to do research, and the preparation stage could help develop the skills necessary for accessing such courses. There could also be a period of reflection that would help those progressing to honours degrees to make the appropriate course choice, a matter of concern for many who ether drop out or change courses under the present system; a wasteful and expensive process for both students and providers alike.

Schools

If there is room for a radical re-think on higher education, what of the government's plans for the schools sector? Two areas currently under development by the government are the notion of extended schools and the personalisation agenda. Both should be attractive principles for Liberal Democrats. However, the extended day is another policy that risks being handed down from on high rather than being developed through community involvement. Apart from the strain that the policy can place upon school leadership resources, especially in the primary sector, there must be some anxiety that the policy is more about providing somewhere for children to go whilst their parents are out at work rather than necessarily about improving their educational chances.

Personalisation is a more complex issue. Liberal Democrats have long argued that Labour's league-table mentality hindered the progress of some children, when schools just taught to the tests; so concentrating on the needs of individual children seems not just sensible, but also a way of focusing on the development of every child. However, as discussed earlier, unless the funding follows the need, schools will be asked to make the difficult decisions about resource allocation. As the gifted-and-talented programme has shown, not all schools seem willing to make this step. Without a programme that focuses on individuals, any national strategy for school improvement must rely too much on school-level data.

School buildings

Improvement is clearly linked to resources, but the algorithm cited earlier contained a number of different elements. The importance of staffing has already been discussed, as has the need for an appropriate curriculum and pedagogy. The issue of resources and their allocation is obviously also of great importance. The other two elements are the buildings and the parents and pupils.

As far as the physical spaces for learning are concerned, central government has once again taken the key role, with capital funding through schemes such as the Private Finance Initiative that will potentially affect the manner in which some authorities will be able to respond to the challenge of falling rolls. Long-term debt might make it sensible to keep some schools open for financial reasons when there were sound reasons for them to close on educational grounds.

The progress of the present Building Schools for the Future programme also seems to be top-down. There is not enough encouragement to develop local solutions. At the present time, with growing concern about the environment, schools, along with other public bodies, should be taking the lead in areas such as renewable energy use. The present method of capital allocation does not always encourage solutions that could cut the use of fossil fuels and potentially save on expensive fuel bills. One radical solution would be the use of community energy bonds to fund capital developments associated with both energy saving and the adoption of renewable supplies. If the capital from bonds to invest in schemes provided a 10 per cent saving on current energy costs, a return of 5 per cent might allow the bonds to pay for themselves over a twenty-year period. They would have the additional advantage of communities directly investing in their own development instead of allowing such investment, and any profit, to be made by the private sector.

Such developments might also act as local showcases for new technology, since schools are very visible public buildings. These schemes would also help in the education of future generations about the need for responsible stewardship of our planet.

Education and society

When the National Curriculum was being designed in the late 1980s, issues such as education for sustainable development (or environmental education, as it is was then known), citizenship and life skills were largely dismissed, resulting in a curriculum that produced a generation that was rich in knowledge but low in skills and attitudes. Fortunately, this is changing, but there is still a need for a real debate about the purpose of education beyond the development of key skills, such as those associated with literacy, numeracy and oracy. How should education contribute to the kind of society we want to live in? Can education do anything to help remove Britain from the upper reaches of too many of the league tables, such as those for teenage pregnancy, addition to drugs and alcohol amongst young people, and a general culture of self-centredness? To do so, we have to accept a level of values that are agreed by all. For Liberal Democrats, the recent UNICEF Report that appeared in the spring of 2007, and was critical of the problems faced by young people growing up in Britain today, encapsulated many of our concerns over the failure of both Labour and Conservative governments to understand the role of schooling beyond the acquisition of knowledge.

To be a Liberal Democrat is to recognise that living together in society creates limitations on personal freedoms, but to work towards ensuring that such limitations are reduced to a minimum by understanding the needs of those around us. These were easy issues to cope with in the days when schooling first became mandatory. Today, schools are competing with a mass media that requires little or no skill to access beyond the flick of a switch. Success and glamour are all too often shown as not resulting from skills acquired at school, but through being chosen for a reality TV show or some other form of instant gratification, such as winning the lottery.

Throughout this chapter I have referred to my belief that local communities still have a key role to play in the direction and delivery of education services from early years to life-long education. This is despite the more mobile society in which many of us live. Changing jobs and taking families to new locations are commonplace these days and the education service must recognise this movement. However, there are still many people, and especially young people, for whom even a visit beyond the boundaries of their own community remains a great adventure. Their lives are as rooted in their communities as were those of their ancestors. To them education is a vital public service that is best controlled locally but within a national framework. To try to do everything centrally is the wrong approach.

Today the challenges remain enormous: to provide an education service that is both efficient and effective, and that meets the needs of every child, and not just those whose parents are articulate enough to demand their rights. It should not be necessary to have to fight for sufficient trained staff, for proper buildings or for a curriculum that genuinely meets the needs of all learners, and not just those destined for higher education in traditional subjects.

The overriding need, however, is to re-engage in the relationships between individuals, their communities, and the state as a whole in the planning and delivery of education. For too long, under both Conservative and Labour governments, there has been a sense of ambivalence or even antagonism from Whitehall about the role of local government in education. What is clear is that to provide for a system that is responsive to the needs of both individuals and the local community, a top-down system with central government working with the private or not-for-profit sectors cannot work. The community element is too vital to be abolished: its role must be properly agreed by all concerned.

An independent and properly functioning local democracy can help strengthen democracy at Westminster; a local democracy that is hamstrung by direction from the centre risks weakening not only itself but also our parliamentary democracy. Labour's centralising attitude to education is wrong: Liberal Democrats need to put local communities at the heart of decision-making on this vital public service.

Notes

1   UNICEF Inocenti Research Centre, *Child Poverty in Perspective: An Overview of Child Well-being in Rich Countries Report Card No 7*, Spring 2007.

Chapter 17

Reforming the NHS: A Local and Democratic Voice

Richard S. Grayson

The democratic deficit in the NHS

Of all issues in public policy, health care is the one in which the public is consistently most committed to a major role for the state. The basic principle of the National Health Service – a tax-funded state-run system free to all citizens at the point of use – is a hugely popular one. Even the most pro-market politicians are reluctant to challenge it. Of course, the principle of tax funding was undermined as early as 1951 when the Labour government introduced prescription charges for false teeth and spectacles, and charges were then expanded further under the Conservatives in 1952. However, charges make up a tiny percentage of the NHS budget today, and the core of the tax-funded system remains unchallenged in party programmes.

Is that a problem? Some believe that funding through taxation has meant that the level of financing the NHS has been too low compared to other European countries. Michael Portillo made that case in 1998, saying that the necessary money could not be found through taxation: 'The gap between what we spend on health care today and what we 'ought' to spend is large, and no party is going to make it up from taxation.'[1] However, the record of the Labour government since 1997 has suggested that this analysis is wrong. They have put billions more into the NHS; one of Labour's proudest claims is that 'Investment into the NHS has doubled since 1997 and is set to treble by 2008 to over £90 billion.'[2] The funding of health care in the UK now compares favourably with other European health systems, whether publicly or privately funded.

This suggests that it is possible to fund the NHS through general taxation at levels which compare with other countries, and that Liberal Democrats should not be seduced by arguments that more funding means private funding. Moreover, Liberal Democrats should recognise that tax-funding is the surest way to ensure socially just funding. Such funding is socially just on two grounds. First, it is redistributive, in that the wealthiest in society pay the highest share of the costs. Second, and most important, access to health care is not limited (at least in principle) by an individual's ability to pay charges, whether on a one-off basis or through an insurance premium. For these reasons, this chapter does not propose any alteration to the basic funding regime of the NHS.

In contrast, decision-making within the NHS needs radical change. Despite the increased levels of funding under the Blair government, if only from 1999, there is no sense in which the public believes that all is well with the NHS. In particular, despite the extra money, the cumulative deficit of NHS trusts has risen past £1 billion. Consequently, some hospitals are faced with losing services or even closing altogether. The case has been particularly marked in the author's own constituency, Hemel Hempstead. In July 2006, Liberal Democrat research found that sixteen hospital trusts, running twenty-seven hospitals in England providing acute services, were under strong pressure due to their deficits. The research identified the West Hertfordshire NHS Trust, which runs St Albans City Hospital, Hemel Hempstead General Hospital and Watford General Hospital, as being under the most pressure. Others at high risk included West Middlesex University Hospital NHS Trust, and Surrey and Sussex Health Care NHS Trust. The list suggests that deficits appear to be greatest in the south-east of England.[3] The deficit means that trusts are obliged by the rules to make cuts, albeit after going through public 'consultation' exercises. Despite the huge public support for keeping all hospital services, trusts find they cannot do that because they do not have the money. But because they have little real meaningful independence from central government, and no power to raise extra public funds locally, they are unable to have a meaningful debate with local people about how local aspirations can be met. The end result is that after nearly a decade of increases in NHS funding, all that some local people see is the closure of wards. They understandably fear for the future of entire hospitals.

The situation in West Hertfordshire is admittedly an extreme example of the problems faced by today's NHS. But it flows from a political failure at the heart of the NHS throughout England: the inadequacy of the current decision-making structure for any kind of rational debate about the cost and shape of health-care provision in local communities.

The NHS is enormous. As Patricia Hewitt pointed out in June 2007, 'If the NHS was a country, it would be the 33rd biggest economy in the world, larger than new European Union transition economies like Romania and Bulgaria … The NHS is four times the size of the Cuban economy and more centralised.'[4] Within this massive bureaucracy the ability of local people to influence decisions is extremely limited. In the current system, ministers are able to claim that any local closures have followed public consultation and that decisions have been made locally. Yet the unelected bureaucrats who make such decisions pay scant attention to local wishes for two reasons. First, they do not have to: they are unelected and their jobs do not depend on any form of public satisfaction. Second, they are not able to act on most local demands because they work within tightly defined budgets and central rules, which do not allow them any flexibility in the amount of money they spend on local services.

It is argued in this chapter that it is this absence of a democratic authority which can take decisions based on meaningful local debate that is the greatest barrier to satisfying public demands on the NHS. Without such a body, it will always be possible for everyone to blame somebody else without taking responsibility. Ministers can blame local bureaucrats, when those ministers have given the bureaucrats very little independence. Health care bureaucrats can point to rigid central controls, but can also blame the public for making supposedly unrealistic demands, when the bureaucrats have little incentive to engage with the public. The public can blame 'them' – usually the government or bureaucrats – despite the fact that the system allows the public to make demand after demand for high levels of local services without ever having to face their real cost. Meanwhile, without local power, demands for higher quality are difficult to balance with fairness, as only the better off can access the 'more' or 'quicker' health care which is so often what people mean by quality.

In place of this current system, the NHS in England needs radical reform. We need a radically different system which puts elected local people in charge instead of the plethora of unelected bureaucrats currently in power, and the remote national ministers who set targets. Crucially, these elected local people need to have the power to raise funds for the NHS so that any demand made by the public for higher quality can have a real price attached. Only in that way can there be a rational public debate about local health-care provision in which those making the demands also pick up the tax bill.

The danger of not reforming the NHS is that its noble concept will lose public support. In 1970, the economist Albert O. Hirschman wrote a classic study of what happens to organisations faced with difficulties: *Exit, Voice, and Loyalty: Responses to Decline in Firms, Organizations, and States*.[5] This study has relevance for the NHS today. Hirschman argued that in any organisation which is failing to deliver a satisfactory service, its users have two choices: exit and voice. In the NHS today, exit is an option for the wealthy, but it is not a real choice for the many. Meanwhile, the ability to have a voice is extremely limited. Democratic reform can provide that voice.

Counties and cities, not regions

Although the NHS is notionally UK-wide, and is certainly funded as such, the system in England post-devolution to Northern Ireland, Scotland and Wales is unique to England. So although an English parliament would stop MPs from the devolved parts of the UK voting on England-only matters, it would do nothing to decentralise decision-making in the NHS, as the Parliament in Westminster already makes decisions on English health matters. But the problem with the NHS in England is not that Jo Swinson, Alun Michael or Ian Paisley can vote on English-only matters, but that the NHS in England is too vast. The challenge is therefore not simply to remove Scottish, Welsh and Northern Irish MPs from decision-making in England, but to devolve power below the English level that already exists.

As part of a model for a federal UK, the Liberal Democrats have long argued for regional devolution. The regional dimension was a particularly important aspect of the 2002 Liberal Democrat public services policy paper, *Quality, Innovation, Choice*. This was the report of what was colloquially known as the 'Huhne Commission', named after the working group's chair. The paper proposed that where elected regional authorities existed in England, current unelected Regional Health and Social Care Directorates and Strategic Health Authorities should be scrapped. Instead, regional assemblies would take responsibility for the strategic development of health and social care services. Crucially, these regional bodies would be able to vary taxation (specifically, a proposed earmarked NHS contribution) to supplement funding received from central government. Meanwhile, Primary Care Trusts would be scrapped, with their powers given to whatever tier of government in the area had responsibility for social services. In such a system, regions would have agreed collectively on setting minimum health care standards across England. The role of central government would be limited to public health, regulation, medical research, and medical, nursing and other professional training, while a new Finance Commission for the Nations and Regions would allocate central funds to each region based on need.[6] There was no alternative proposed for regions without an assembly because implicit in the policy was the belief that in time, regional assemblies would cover all of England, and those which did not initially want such a body would be encouraged to adopt one through the promise of more control over the NHS in their area.

I was closely involved in developing these policies as the party's Director of Policy at the time, and I still believe that given the assumptions of the time, they were the right policies for us to develop. However, it now turns out that one of our key assumptions was wrong. The context in which we operated was a shared belief, held in both the Labour Party and the Liberal Democrats. We believed that regionalism in England offered the only way in which England could have the same measure of democratic devolution as that enjoyed in other parts of the UK through elected bodies in Belfast, Edinburgh and Cardiff. It was assumed that there would be a rolling process of devolution across England, with the North East being the first to adopt a regional assembly. However, those assumptions were faced with a reality check when the North East decisively rejected such a body in 2004. It had always been known that some 'regions' (notably the South West, which has always had strong county identities) were resistant. But from the south of England, the 'Geordie nation' looked like exactly the kind of region that could blaze a trail for regional devolution.

With even the North East rejecting a regional assembly, that chapter in progressive plans for devolution is now closed. The Labour Party rapidly shelved further plans, and even the Liberal Democrats downplayed the proposal in the 2005 election. Three lessons came out of the North East case which need to be learned by anyone who wants to see decentralisation in England. First, people are inherently sceptical about additional layers of government or bureaucracy. There is always a fear that such a body could be a gravy train for politicians who had not quite made it to Westminster. Second, there is no appetite for 'talking shops' as bodies with minimal powers tend to be called. This was a major problem with the type of regional body proposed by Labour in 2004. However, it is not at all clear that people would have opted for a more powerful body, for the third problem that emerged from the North East is that regions, even in the North East, are not natural communities. For all that there is a 'Geordie nation', it is easy to forget that such a label does not apply to the people of Sunderland, Middlesbrough or Durham, and within each region there are often major divisions. Put simply, regions are just too big and too recent a creation for people to feel any emotional affinity to them.

So anybody who wants to decentralise within England has to look for alternative natural communities. These must be ones through which people will consent to organise services and with which people will feel some community of interest. They must also be large enough in which to take strategic decisions. Do they exist already? The simple answer is yes: they are counties and cities. Crucially, although county identities are not as strong as they once were, people already understand them as legitimate political entities because they exist in the form of county councils, and the same can also be said of England's major cities which have their own authorities.

The task therefore becomes to prove that they are large enough units to take on strategic health care functions, or that in the cases of very small counties, there is a way of pooling responsibilities with neighbours. Part of the evidence lies in another part of the UK. Northern Ireland manages to take strategic decisions for its share of the NHS with a population of around 1.5 million. That is significantly below the populations of the current ten strategic health authorities and more in line with the size of many of the twenty-eight strategic health authorities that existed in England between 2002 and 2006. The NHS in Northern Ireland is also the part of the NHS with integrated decision-making on, and provision of, health and personal social services. Does it work? Mortality rates per 100,000 of the population (standardised for age) are about 2.4 per cent higher than for the United Kingdom as a whole. However, the direction of this figure is downwards, and at a faster rate than for the rest of the UK. Between 1996 and 2001, for example, overall mortality in Northern Ireland fell by nearly 14 per cent, which was faster than for the whole United Kingdom, at 9 per cent.[7]

However, further evidence of such a scale of decision-making can be found from another country: Denmark.

Danish lessons
In the early part of this century there was a vogue for examining public services in other parts of Europe – and indeed outside Europe – in order to see what can be learnt. The think-tank Civitas has carried out extensive research on health care. Conservative spokesmen were dispatched to the continent, prompting wry smiles from those who had grown used to the Conservatives being at best wary of the supposedly pro-state solutions of the French, Germans and, not least, the Scandinavians. Liberal Democrats took part in this exploration too, first on education, and then on health. Within the party, some of this research had an impact on policy. The Dutch model of funding schools, set out in a pamphlet by myself and Nick Clegg, found its way into the party's policy in 2002.[8] Meanwhile, the Centre for Reform's work on comparative systems of health funding offered strong arguments against health insurance schemes at a time when the party was looking at all options and ended up not choosing insurance.[9]

However, the party skirted round the need for radical devolution. That was despite the fact that Denmark, the country with the most radically devolved health system in Europe, was cited as a model of good practice. The 2002 public services paper said, 'Although Denmark has a population of just 5.3 million, its popular and tax-funded health service is run by its 14 counties and two cities. Denmark spends modestly more than we do as a proportion of national income – about 1.2 per cent – but has the highest satisfaction ratings in Europe.'[10] Having failed to follow this approach through in 2001–02, it is now time that the Liberal Democrats revisited the Danish model as one that could be transplanted to the NHS in England.

The Danish system is now even more appropriate for England than it was in 2002. At that point, as the policy paper said, it was run by fourteen counties and two cities (Copenhagen and Frederiksberg). These bodies were responsible for both GPs and hospitals and they funded them mainly from county taxes, used primarily for health. Below the counties were local authorities (273 of them) which had responsibility for matters such as school health care. At a national level, the government played a hands-off regulatory role, for example on parents' rights.[11] However, even though the Danish public were very satisfied with health care at that point, there was a sense that the system was not as efficient as it could be. Moreover, in a relatively small area, there were difficulties in coordinating between a large number of decentralised authorities.[12] Even the counties were often very small compared to England. The smallest, Bornholm, had a population of 43,245 in 2006. The largest, Aarhus, at 661,370, was smaller than most English counties. Several were smaller than all English counties except Herefordshire, the Isle of Wight and Rutland.

As a result, the Liberal Minister of the Interior and Health, Lars Løkke Rasmussen, pushed a series of proposals through the parliament, the *Folketing*, in 2005. These measures, a total of fifty acts under a broad 'Agreement on Structural Reform', abolished the counties (including the two city authorities) and replaced them with five regions, ranging in population from about 600,000 to 1.6 million, thus making them analogous in size to English counties rather than regions. The 273 municipalities were replaced with 98 on revised boundaries.[13] The powers of the new levels of government, which came into being on 1 January 2007, are now as follows:

- Municipalities:
  - Preventive treatment, and non-hospital care and rehabilitation, including that at home; and
  - Treatment of alcohol and drug abuse.
- Regions:
  - Hospitals;
  - Psychiatry; and
  - General practitioners, specialists and reimbursement for medication.[14]
- State:
  - Planning for specialist treatment; and
  - Follow-up on quality, efficiency and IT usage.

The argument here is this: if Danish counties, which were smaller than English counties, could deliver a health care system, funded from general taxation, that was the most popular in Europe, why cannot English counties do the same? Moreover, why is this model not even more appropriate now that it has been established on a working basis in units that even more closely match the English counties in size? The arguments against are only those about whether the units are to small for strategic thinking, but the Danes have shown that a radically devolved system can work, and work well.

The argument about exactly what a Danish transplant would mean for England in terms of organisation is developed further below. However, one other issue from Denmark needs to be discussed before that: funding. Under the pre-2007 model, most of the money for health care in the counties was raised in the counties. In the new scheme, approximately 80 per cent of each region's funding comes from a national health contribution, amounting to a rate of around 8 per cent on income tax. That is part of the replacement of county taxes which had been, on average, over 30 per cent, and which were completely scrapped in the 2007 reforms, so it is not an additional tax. The minimum national health contribution per year is 1,000 Danish *kroner* (about £90) and the capped maximum is 1,500DKK (about £140). That represents only a small amount, but it can provide useful extra funding at a local level, and can be vetoed on a vote of two-thirds of the municipalities. The final 10 per cent of the regional health budget comes from a basic contribution payable through municipalities, but set by the regions, described as an 'activity-related contribution'. Since the municipalities have a non-hospital care role, the amount they pay through this final contribution is reduced as they make relatively low demands on hospitals, thus rewarding effective preventive treatment care.[15]

As with decentralisation, the funding aspect of the Danish model is similarly capable of being transplanted to English counties without being rejected by the host. At its core are concerns for equalisation and redistribution, to ensure that the very different tax bases of the regions and municipalities do not result in disparities in funding. As the Danish government said:

> If each municipality were to finance its own expenditure, the service level and tax burden of the municipalities would … vary considerably. The purpose of the equalisation system is to

> ensure that the same service level involves the same tax percent-
> age regardless of the income of the inhabitants and any demo-
> graphic factors … [T]he grant and equalisation system means
> that money is transferred from the rich municipalities to the less
> affluent ones.[16]

However, the system also allows local flexibility in funding should more funds be needed *and* rewards attention to preventive measures. That makes the Danish funding system compatible not only with the prin-ciples of a *National* Health Service, but also with the Liberal Democrat commitments to localism.

The absence of democracy: the NHS in England today

To determine what could be devolved in England, the starting point has to be an analysis of the situation as it currently is. There are two main levels of the NHS which ministers regularly describe as 'local' and are concerned with commissioning services: Primary Care Trusts (PCTs) and Strategic Health Authorities (SHAs). Yet neither are democratic in any meaningful sense, as local councillors have very limited powers of scrutiny. Meanwhile, the Strategic Health Authorities are hardly local, as they operate on a regional basis. There are also other bodies, such as acute trusts, which will be discussed briefly.

The Primary Care Trusts are the key building blocks of the NHS. Created in 2002 following the government's 2001 *Shifting the Balance of Power* initiative, they are responsible for 80 per cent of the NHS budget. PCTs can provide services but their main role is to commission services from GPs, hospitals and other parts of the NHS. Their role is officially described as to 'make sure there are enough services for people within their area and that these services are accessible'.[17] The boundaries of PCTs are often counties, but they can be smaller. For example, in the East of England region, there are fourteen PCTs. There are two for Hertfordshire and five for Essex; four nominally cover whole counties (Norfolk, Suffolk, Beds and Cambridgeshire), but a further three cover parts of these coun-ties: Luton, Peterborough and Great Yarmouth & Waveney. Although these PCTs match local government boundaries in some cases, they do not always do so, and one result is a confusing array of mechanisms for accountability to local people.

The Strategic Health Authorities were created in 2002, to replace existing health authorities. They are the link between the Department of Health and the local NHS, ensuring that national targets are incorporated into local health service plans. They also develop strategic plans for health services across the region and monitor performance. There were originally twenty-eight of them, based on a city or one or more counties, with London divided into five. Most covered an area containing 1.5–2 million people. However, in 2006, they were reduced to ten: London, South East Coast, South West, South Central, East of England, West Midlands, East Midlands, Yorkshire and the Humber, North East, and North West. They range from a population of 2.2 million in the North East to 7.4 million in London, with most in the 4–5 million range (that is, as large as Denmark as a whole).

In addition to PCTs and SHAs there are other bodies which aim to make the administration of the NHS more local. Acute trusts manage hospitals and are sometimes regional or national specialist centres. They employ those who work in hospitals and thus have a crucial role in spending the money that comes from elsewhere in the NHS (for example, from PCTs), while those attached to universities have a role in training professionals. The acute trusts often have boundaries which come close to those of PCTs, but not always; for example, the East of England's fourteen PCTs are joined by eighteen acute trusts. Some of the acute trusts have become the controversial foundation trusts, of which there are fifty-four across England. Other types of trusts include ambulance trusts (which largely match SHA boundaries), care trusts (covering only thirteen very specific parts of the country), and mental health trusts (MHTs). As regards the latter, their boundaries can match those of other trusts, but not always. To take the East of England as an example again, its fourteen PCTs and eighteen acute trusts are joined by eight MHTs. The result of this is a confusing mish-mash of overlapping boundaries which can bemuse any member of the public who is trying to work out who runs which part of the NHS. But all these bodies have one thing in common: democratic accountability, and the ability of local people to make meaningful choices about levels of service, is extremely limited.

Theoretically, the Secretary of State for Health can intervene in decisions made by trusts, but they have been reluctant to do so, sometimes deploying the argument that local decisions should be made by local people. That is right, yet it is not what happens, because local people have very little power or meaningful voice over decisions. There are plenty of ways for the public to make their views known about the NHS and to scrutinise its work. Not only can they lobby politicians, but they can currently get involved in Patient and Public Involvement (PPI) Forums. These Forums monitor each NHS trust (including SHAs) and monitored bodies are obliged to respond to their reports. However, the government is in the process of abolishing PPI Forums and replacing them with Local Involvement Networks (LINks) which will be organised in such a way as to match social service boundaries.

In addition to this, since 2000, local authorities (both counties and boroughs) have had powers to scrutinise the NHS in their area, and councillors have been vocal in criticising all types of NHS trusts. However, they can only challenge trusts over whether procedures have been correctly followed.

Consequently, the central political problem of this system in the NHS in England is that there can be mass consultation on local health care, but there are rarely the means to implement local people's wishes on the most controversial issues such as keeping hospital wards open. Those running trusts are able to respond to local demands by saying that they would like to do as the public wishes but simply cannot. They can say that they are unable to act because they do not have the money within existing budgets and do not have the power to raise extra funds. Moreover, because local people are never faced with a real choice – such as having to pay higher taxes for the services they went – they end up feeling profoundly powerless and dissatisfied. The only way to change that is to introduce radical democratisation of the NHS at a local level.

A democratic and local NHS

One option for democratising the NHS in England is simply to elect Primary Care Trusts, replacing them with elected Local Health Boards. The attraction of this option is that it would not involve any reorganisation of the current NHS management, and would recognise the extent to which people see the NHS as separate from other parts of government. With all the change that there has been in the NHS in recent years, such an approach has huge practical attractions and may be necessary as a first step to further reforms. However, in the long term, more radical democratic decentralisation is necessary if we are not only to devolve decision-making in the NHS but to create the kind of devolved government in England that is enjoyed in the rest of the UK. Such radical reforms should be centred upon counties, which are historic units of England, and many of which encourage strong feelings of local identity.

Creating a democratic NHS at a county level will mean revisiting the boundaries of existing trusts. As part of that, the distinction between PCTs and SHAs should end, with their commissioning powers given to elected local people who are in touch with local needs and have the ability to raise extra funds to meet local demand. That will mean centralising some functions which currently take place at a level below that of counties (or a similar level of government), and decentralising those which are dealt with at a regional level. But it will mean democratisation all round, giving real power to elected local people.

The last thing the public wants is another level of government. Indeed, in many places, the number of levels is already being reduced with the introduction of unitary authorities. So instead of creating regions, the powers of SHAs and PCTs should be given to more local levels. The most obvious boundaries, very much in line with the Danish model, are those of the thirty-four counties, six metropolitan counties, or forty unitary authorities across England. London is a special case which is discussed below.

There are two options for the way in which such devolution could be achieved to provide local people with the voice that they lack. The quickest and simplest way might be to give PCT and SHA commissioning powers to existing county-level authorities. The great advantage of this approach is that it could have positive effects on the quality of government beyond the NHS. By giving county councils significant powers over the NHS, counties would become more directly comparable to the devolved bodies in Belfast, Cardiff and Edinburgh. This would help to answer the 'English question', which is increasingly a factor in debates on the power of Westminster. If an effect of that was that people who are ambitious to wield power in their area stood for county councils rather than Westminster, the overall quality of decision-making at a county level would be greatly increased.

An alternative option would be for each county-level local authority to choose whether to run the local NHS itself, or to create a Local Health Board with powers to vary local taxes in much the same way as unelected police authorities do. Such a Board would be directly elected by local people at the same time as local elections, on the basis of manifestos put forward by local parties or independents. The advantage of this approach over the more timid measure of simply turning PCTs into Local Health Boards along current boundaries is that county boards would reflect well-understood community boundaries and reduce confusion about where decisions are made and by whom. Meanwhile, the advantage of such an approach over submerging NHS functions into wider county-council matters would be that there could be a very clear focus on NHS-related issues at election. All the evidence suggests that this is the primary concern to voters, so why not give them a chance to have a separate debate over how to run the NHS? This would allow clear choices to be made over, for example, additions to the NHS budget in return for maintaining a local hospital ward, rather than confusing health matters with the broad range of issues tackled by local authorities. It would also allow those with specific expertise of the health service, such as retired doctors or nurses, to get involved in the running of the local NHS, having put their case to the electorate. Their expertise could greatly inform manifestos and invigorate local debates on health care.

County-level devolution – whether to councils or Local Health Boards – would be a significant development of Liberal Democrat policy. As regards the powers of PCTs, this approach is already in essence party policy in the proposal to give the commissioning powers of PCTs to local government at the same tier as social services.[18] But the proposal goes much further on SHA powers because it assumes not only that regional assemblies *do not* exist and are *unlikely* to, but also that they *should not* exist, as they are far too remote from local people. Overall, this proposal will mean the devolution of commissioning powers from ten regional SHAs, and the centralisation of power from 151 PCTs. So the wide-ranging but unaccountable decision-making bureaucracies of 161 bodies will be scrapped and their powers given to around eighty existing county-level councils.

Underpinning these changes in decision-making must be one crucial change on funding. Core funding has to remain at the national level, as it does in Denmark, to maintain fairness across the country and so that poorer areas do not have under-funded health care. Yet local decision-making cannot be effective unless there is local flexibility over funding. So aside from having the power to make those decisions currently made by PCTs and SHAs, local authorities must have the ability to support those decisions with necessary funding. Only by having the ability to raise extra funds can authorities truly respond to local needs because more often than not, local demands for services will have a price attached. Thus, authorities should be empowered to raise funds for the NHS through additions to the NHS Contribution discussed in the next section. That will give them the power to meet public demand, while at the same time showing the public that their expectations have costs.

There should not, however, be wholesale change of all structures in the NHS. Although the commissioning powers need radical reform, there are three reasons why it does not make sense to make such major changes in the provision-side of services, as regards the role of acute and mental health trusts. First, those working in the NHS are already demoralised by government targets and consistent reorganisation. Second, giving powers over provision to politicians rather than clinicians would fly in the face of the strongly held Liberal Democrat belief that professionals should be allowed to get on with their jobs. Third, if one wants to retain the advantages of the purchaser–provider split in the NHS, which can promote value for money, then it is necessary to retain separate acute trusts so that the commissioning arm of the NHS can make real choices between them. There is the danger that acute trusts will continue to make decisions which are unpopular with local people. For example, a trust which runs the same service at more than one different hospital (perhaps in two different towns), may decide that it wishes to centralise a particular service in one hospital. Such decisions are usually driven by financial limits, and so negotiations will have to take place between the acute trust and the locally elected commissioners. If the latter are convinced that there is no case for retaining services at both hospitals, then they will have to defend that at election time. However, if they believe that it is essential for services to remain at both, they will be able to raise money locally to pay for that.

There is one important caveat to the proposed radical democratisation of the NHS in England. We need to recognise that some local authorities may feel that they are not the right size for taking sole responsibility for health care because they feel themselves to be too big or too small. It may be that larger counties wish to split the geographic areas they cover into two or more units. If so, they should be able to do that. But smaller counties may wish to work with others. So they should be given the opportunity to collaborate with other authorities by agreement. Two smaller counties may decide to commission hospital services together, and that may well make sense. In such a situation, they would have the option of making decisions either through joint meetings of the county councils or through a joint health board. But the crucial democratic accountability element should remain, so that at elections, council or health board candidates put a health programme to voters and can be held to account on their NHS-related decisions.

The precise nature of boundaries is a problem that will be faced by Londoners in particular. The current London SHA covers a population of over seven million people. It may well be that Londoners would wish to run health on a city-wide basis, and if so, the Greater London Authority and Assembly already exist. However, to ensure that the potential benefits of devolution and genuine local accountability can be enjoyed across the city, London boroughs should be offered the same powers and choices as counties, or the chance to pool their powers with other boroughs. The result may be London-wide decision-making, or the city may be split into smaller units, but that will be for Londoners to decide.

Maintaining national guarantees

The Liberal Democrats have a clear position on how the national level of the NHS should be reformed and that approach is consistent with the model advocated here, though with no role for regions.[19] The starting point should be a reformed Department for Health. Its current role in defining national NHS targets should end, as they have consistently distorted clinical priorities. Instead, the Department should focus on matters such as ensuring standards of professional training and competence, inspection and audit, and coordinating the agreement of minimum standards for quality of care and patient experience.

Funding for the NHS should come from an earmarked NHS Contribution, based on National Insurance, and distributed using current formulae. When this policy was first developed by the Liberal Democrats in 2002, the amount raised by National Insurance Contributions (NICs) conveniently matched the NHS budget. This meant that the revenue stream from NICs could easily be diverted to the NHS. However, the

NHS now consumes more money than is raised by NICs. This is not a problem if five steps are taken. First, all NICs should be diverted to the NHS. Second, the shortfall should be made up by money from general taxation. Third, a rate should be set for an NHS Contribution which will provide enough revenue to maintain the current NHS budget. Fourth, the basic rate of income tax should be reduced by the difference between the NHS Contribution and the old level of NICs. Finally, there should be an exemption from part of the NHS Contribution for those pensioners who pay income tax (since they do not currently pay NICs) so that they do not pay more under the new system. The overall effects of these steps will be that the NHS Contribution will be higher than the NICs rate, but the basic rate of income tax will have been reduced, and pensioners will not have to pay the full NHS Contribution, so that the overall level of taxation remains the same. The amount of money coming into the NHS will remain the same, but the cost of the NHS would be much more transparent, greatly aiding political debate and decision-making.

Conclusion: the need for voice

Within such a national framework, a reformed local NHS can flourish. But it can only do so if the existing bodies are scrapped and given to democratically accountable local people with wide-ranging powers. Those could be existing local authorities on a county or city basis, or they could be new Local Health Boards. There may also be more short-term attractions in simply transforming PCTs into health boards, as already proposed by the Liberal Democrat health spokesman. But without one of these reforms, people will not have a voice over the local NHS and will be continually frustrated about their inability to influence decision-making in the areas of the NHS that most affect them.

Without local power, local people will be continually asking for health care that is not on the menu, and for which they have not been given a price. Without local power, people have no chance to pay for the quality they want, and monitor the quality of local services. Radical devolution has happened in Denmark, and it works. The challenge in England is to sweep away swathes of unaccountable local bureaucracies and give their powers back to the people through elections in which local health care can be thoroughly debated. As regards the NHS, that does not mean reducing the overall size of the state, but relocating it.

Notes

1   Michael Portillo, 'The Bevan Legacy', Kathleen A Raven Lecture given at the Royal College of Surgeons on 10 June 1998; available at: http://www.pubmedcentral.nih.gov/articlerender.fcgi?artid=1113449.

2   http://www.betterwithlabour.co.uk/nhs/Made_by_Labour#top10.

3   Liberal Democrat press release, 'Lib Dems highlight English hospital trusts most under pressure', 25 July 2006; available at: http://www.libdems.org.uk/news/story.html?id=10674&navPage=news.html.

4   Patricia Hewitt, 'The NHS: The Next Ten Years, Speech at London School of Economics, 14 June 2007; available at http://www.lse.ac.uk/collections/LSEPublicLecturesAndEvents/pdf/20070614_Hewitt.pdf.

5   Albert O. Hirschman, *Exit, Voice, and Loyalty: Responses to Decline in Firms, Organizations, and States* (Harvard University Press, 1970).

6   Liberal Democrats, *Quality, Innovation, Choice* (Liberal Democrats, London, 2002), pp. 50–51.

7   Angela Jordan et al, *Health Systems in Transition: the Northern Ireland Report* (World Health Organisation, Copenhagen, 2006), pp. 1, 6.

8   Nick Clegg and Richard Grayson, *Learning from Europe: Lessons in Education* (Centre for European Reform, London, 2002), pp. 19–21; *Quality, Innovation, Choice*, p. 57.

9   Nicholas Bromley, *Universal Access, Individual Choice: International Lessons for the NHS* (Centre for Reform, London, 2002).

10 *Quality, Innovation, Choice*, p. 21.

11 Ministry of Health and the Interior [Denmark], *Health Care in Denmark* (Ministry of Health and the Interior, Copenhagen, 1997, revised August 2002), pp. 8–10 and 15–17.

12 Ministry of the Interior and Health [Denmark], *The Local Government Reform – In Brief* (Ministry of the Interior and Health, Copenhagen, 2005), p. 7.

13 *The Local Government Reform – In Brief*, pp. 53–56.

14 Note that this category is described as 'health insurance' in the English translation of the Danish documents. However, this is misleading as the 'insurance' is simply funded by taxation, and is not a form of insurance as understood in the UK.

15 *The Local Government Reform – In Brief*, pp. 36–39.

16 Ibid., pp. 36–37.

17 Details of the scope and roles of trusts are available at: http://www.nhs.uk/England/AuthoritiesTrusts/Default.cmsx.

18 Liberal Democrats, *Healthy Communities, Healthy People* (Liberal Democrats, London, 2004), p. 25.

19 Ibid., pp. 23–29.

Chapter 18

Rebuilding Trust in the Criminal Justice System

Tim Starkey

Nowhere are Labour's controlling, centralising habits more evident that in the management of the criminal justice system.

First there is the sheer volume of legislation. Since 1997 a staggering 3,000 new offences have been created. During that time there have been over fifty criminal justice bills, representing a far faster rate of legislation than any previous government. Too much of this legislation has been a knee-jerk reaction to events, a badly thought-through bid to win headlines. The inevitable consequence has been confusion, with the agencies of the criminal justice system barely able to catch up before the next raft of legislation, the next plethora of initiatives comes along. Leaked documents between Tony Blair and his polling guru Phillip Gould back in 2000 showed clearly what was driving policy. 'Find me an eye-catching initiative on crime' was the message.[1]

Next there is the assumption that 'Whitehall knows best', with this government's obsessive setting of targets. This has seriously distorted the way the police work, with the pursuit of targets forcing them to make arrests for petty offences. Ludicrous recent examples include a man from Cheshire who was cautioned for being 'found in possession of an egg with intent to throw', a West Midlands woman arrested on her wedding day for criminal damage after her foot slipped on her accelerator pedal and her vehicle damaged a car-park barrier, and a child in Kent arrested after throwing a slice of cucumber at another youngster.

Excessive pursuit of some targets can result in neglect of other types of work. Commenting on the points system given for arrests by North Wales police, Richard Eccles, North Wales Police Federation Secretary, said:

> We have got grave concerns about what sounds like a crude scale
> for measuring an officer's work. Imagine if an old lady has been
> burgled, and an officer stays with her for two hours while she
> waits for relatives, or a locksmith to fix the door. You would not
> get any points for that, but most people would agree it would be
> a good piece of community policing. An officer should be judged
> on what they actually do over the course of a shift, not how many
> points they can rack up.[2]

Likewise, fewer officers are now available to respond to 999 calls. Indeed, some crimes such as burglaries and car thefts have had to be reclassified as 'non-emergencies' due to lack of manpower. The conclusion of Jan Berry, chair of the Police Federation, is that:

> As a result of government diktats the service has been reduced to
> a bureaucratic, target-chasing, point-obsessed arm of Whitehall;
> debasing what was once a sensible police service.[3]

Furthermore, there is the continuous undermining of judicial independence. A persistent trait of legislation on sentencing since 1997 has been an attempt to tie the hands of judges. The rationale is clear: the government does not trust judges to pass the 'right' sentences; they must be told what to do. In this way a series of mandatory sentencing provisions has been introduced, with minimum penalties and presumptions for judges to follow. The purpose of such legislation must be to force judges to pass sentences that they would not otherwise pass.

Liberals believe that the government should do less, better; that the government should trust professionals 'on the ground' to get on with the job; that it is the judge dealing with a particular offender, with all the facts in front of him, who is best placed to determine how he should be sentenced; that the local council is in the best position to decide how to tackle local anti-social behaviour; that professionals in the probation service or the police should be set free of targets that distort the way they carry out their work.

Behind much of Labour's controlling, centralising approach is a desire to be seen to be taking tough action. For many years the debate on crime has been reduced to a banal tough–soft divide. In recent months the Liberal Democrats have sought to redefine this debate by identifying the real issue as one of effectiveness. As Nick Clegg wrote in *Britain after Blair:* 'Competence is now the most precious of all political commodities in the market for ideas in strengthening our criminal justice system.'[4]

This shift in focus is timely. The criminal justice system is at breaking point. In some courts delays of months or even years have become the norm in dealing with simple, minor offences. Prisons are desperately overcrowded, with the result that little meaningful work on rehabilitation can be done and recidivism rates are appallingly high. Research from the Howard League has shown that 70 per cent of young men reoffend within two years of being released from prison.[5]

A further focus of Liberal Democrat thinking in recent months has been the need to restore trust in a criminal justice system from which many people feel alienated. The recent policy paper *Together We Can Cut Crime* stated as underlying principles: 'Involving the community in justice, prevention and rehabilitation' and 're-engaging the public with the criminal justice system and improving support for the victim'.[6]

The paper is full of concrete ideas for achieving this, from giving the public a say in what forms of unpaid work should be carried out as part of community penalties to greater use of 'community justice panels' to speeding up the process by which victims of crime are compensated. Another important way of restoring public confidence is to make sentencing more honest, with sentences meaning what they say and making sense to the public.

In this chapter I shall explore some of these themes and set out some of the foundations to a liberal approach in rebuilding trust in the criminal justice system.

Policing

The most urgent change to the way we are policed is to end the 'target culture'. The power of the Home Secretary to set objectives and performance targets for police authorities undermines their freedom to set their strategy in accordance with local conditions and local people. Liberal Democrats therefore support shifting the balance away from the Home Secretary and towards the police authority.

There is also a real need to ensure adequate police accountability. To this end Liberal Democrats are committed to giving local communities a greater say in how their neighbourhood is policed. Minimum levels of service would be clearly set out in a local policing contract, which will require Chief Constables and police authorities to come to an agreement with local authorities on how the policing element of Council Tax is spent – a minimum service guarantee. Another way to foster links between police and communities is to give every community a named local police officer with whom local people can build a relationship of trust. This is vital to maintaining the tradition of 'policing by consent'. It is vital too for getting intelligence information, which is the key to all police work, from tackling anti-social behaviour to terrorism.

Policing is also about numbers. Many rural communities feel ignored by the police, with people frequently complaining that 'you never see the police around here' or 'even if you ring them they never come'. It is always far more effective to deter crimes from happening than to try and deal with them after the damage is done. This was clearly demonstrated by the success of the taxi marshal scheme in Liberal Democrat-controlled Newcastle. Four city-centre taxi ranks were identified as flashpoints for violence and public order offences. Police officers were put on duty there between 9.30 pm and 3.30 am on weekend nights, and the trouble stopped.

Liberal Democrats are committed to increasing police numbers through savings made from scrapping the misguided ID card scheme. Increasing police numbers provides a good opportunity to consider the balance in the force between full officers and police community support officers (PCSOs). Whilst Liberal Democrats supported their introduction, there is growing concern that they are being used as a cheap alternative to ordinary officers rather than to supplement them, as was the stated intention. Since their introduction overall numbers of fully trained officers have actually gone down. PCSOs are frequently hampered by their lack of powers and goaded by youths who know they can't do anything. An urgent review is needed of the way in which they are deployed.

Liberal Democrats also want to make better use of existing officers. Patrol officers make up about 56 per cent of police staff, but a large part of their time is not spent on the beat. Reducing bureaucracy and equipping police with the latest technology would free officers to spend more time on the street.

The police service has suffered, like many components of the criminal justice system, from reform for reform's sake, as demonstrated by the botched attempt to amalgamate police forces. In despair the Police

Federation has called for a Royal Commission on Policing. However, Liberal Democrats prefer a standing conference on policing, a permanent advisory body bringing together all the relevant interested parties. In this way, a measured approach can be taken to reform rather than one motivated simply by a desire to be seen to be doing something.

Anti-social behaviour

In *Britain after Blair*, Nick Clegg wrote that:

> … there is no simple, off-the-shelf solution to the dispersed, varied, low-level and highly disruptive anti-social behaviour that is prevalent in so many British towns and cities. Any sustainable approach will necessarily involve a diverse cast of actors, from local and central government, the voluntary sector, community groups and schools, and from families themselves.[7]

In the year since, this common-sense approach has been vindicated by reviews of anti-social behaviour interventions carried out both by Camden Borough Council and the National Audit Office.[8] The evidence suggests that Liberal Democrats were right to support the introduction of ASBOs, but right too to regard them as a weapon of last resort. Labour's relentless focus on ASBOs has reduced them to being a 'one-trick pony', judging councils by the number of ASBOs issued. In contrast, Liberal Democrat councils have been innovative in creating a variety of tools for tackling anti-social behaviour. For Liberal Democrats the issue of large numbers of ASBOs is not a sign of success, but of the failure of earlier types of intervention.

One successful form of earlier intervention pioneered in Lib Dem Islington is Acceptable Behaviour Contracts. Young people identified as having been engaged in persistent anti-social behaviour are invited, along with their parents, to an interview with the housing department and police. The aim is to discuss the problem and to identify a series of behaviours that the young person would agree not to engage in over the coming six months. The family are informed at the interview that if the contract is broken and they hold a council tenancy the housing department may initiate possession action against it. In addition, the young person may become subject to an ASBO.

Home Office research shows that this has been an effective form of intervention, normally dealing with the problem before an ASBO is even needed. The scheme is quicker and easier than applying for an ASBO. In addition, it obliges the young person to consider and take responsibility for their behaviour. As the National Audit Office report shows, these measures have been copied nationwide.

One of the most important ideas to have come out of Camden's review of ASBOs is the idea of putting an 'anti-social behaviour ladder' at the heart of the council's approach. The review found that interventions work best when a person causing anti-social behaviour is given a clear ladder of goals and expectations that must be met – alongside providing them with information on support programmes available and consequences about what will happen if the agreement is broken. The review recommended extending the existing yellow and red-card-style system, already in place for young people with Acceptable Behaviour Agreements. In this way the consequences of their actions are clearly spelt out.

A key element of the 'anti-social behaviour ladder' is that the threat of punishment is accompanied by an offer of help. A vital part of tackling anti-social behaviour is engaging young people. A frequent complaint from youngsters themselves is that they don't have enough to do. Boredom and frustration is behind a good deal of petty crime. Improving recreational facilities is part of the answer and *Together We Can Cut Crime* identifies the need not just to consider 'designing out crime' in planning new housing developments, but also 'designing in alternatives to crime': giving youngsters places they can gather without seeming a threat to other residents, creating sport facilities and so on. But facilities alone are not enough. Most important of all are adults taking an interest in and guiding young people's lives. It is impossible to overestimate the importance of the voluntary sector in diverting young people away from criminal activity: people giving up their time to coach football or cricket, run youth clubs or Scouts. As well as the need to 'give young people something to do' is the need to give them supervision and guidance. First and foremost this should come from parents. Anti-social behaviour interventions designed to support parents can be as useful as those focused on the offender.

In addition, mentoring schemes can make a real difference to young people's lives. Often simply showing an interest in a young person can be a source of great encouragement. Once a relationship of trust has been established, a mentor can try and help with specific problems such as helping to write a CV or preparing for job interviews. Where appropriate, the mentor can provide guidance and assistance in rebuilding relationships with family and friends. Mentoring can sometimes 'get through' where organised youth programmes are dismissed as patronising or uncool.

In Chiltern District, Chiltern Lighthouse mentoring has recently been set up. The scheme works on a referral basis in association with the police, social services, anti-social behaviour units and other youth volunteer groups. Its purpose is to:

> ... intervene early, to support and redirect young people who may be at risk away from more serious and long-term problems. Our mentors help them identify their own goals and support them through a difficult period in their lives.[9]

Two important themes emerge from the evidence of how anti-social behaviour has been tackled. First, the best solutions have not come by Home Office diktat, but from local councils or voluntary bodies coming up with ideas to sort out problems in their area. Second, it is clear that government, local or central, cannot do everything. Building partnerships between local government and the voluntary sector is the key to success. On a small scale, Chiltern Lighthouse Mentoring is an illustration of that. It is often beneficial for mentors not to be associated with authority figures such as police, teachers, social workers or probation officers. Yet through referrals from precisely those authorities this group can complement all their work. It is just one example of the many partnerships that can be forged between government and the voluntary sector.

Community justice panels and restorative justice

A significant cause of the breakdown in trust in the criminal justice system is the inefficiency of the courts. Most magistrates' courts have a hefty backlog of cases that can result in delays of several months before even the most minor, straightforward trials are dealt with. This has been an important factor in the trend towards dealing with offences outside court, through fixed penalty notices.

Undeniably, fixed penalty notices have a plus side – they are a quick and cheap way of dispensing justice – but they are hardly a satisfactory way of dealing with an offence. An FPN does not attempt to rehabilitate the offender and does nothing for the victim.

An alternative is community justice panels. In *Together We Can Cut Crime* this is precisely what is proposed under the brand 'Responsible Behaviour Panels'. It is envisaged that these would be made up partly of professionals from the youth offending team or the probation service and partly of members of the public. Offenders might be referred to these panels by the police, housing associations or local authorities after a minor crime or an act of anti-social behaviour has been committed. The panel would then invite all interested parties to meet, crucially bringing the offender and victim face to face, providing mediation and facilitating an agreed course of action that it could then monitor.

To take a simple example, imagine a youth has been caught spraying graffiti on someone's fence. He would be made to apologise, clean it up and promise not to do it again. The advantages to the victim are numerous. Often he will have no interest in the matter going to court: he can do without the hassle, he can do without the delay. What he really wants is an apology, the problem put right and an assurance that it won't be repeated. This approach also makes the offender take responsibility for his actions in a way that the conventional court system very rarely does. Bringing an offender face to face with his victim can be a powerful way of making him realise the upset he's caused.

The evidence suggests that this restorative justice approach works. In Chard a community justice panel was set up by the Liberal Democrat council after the closure of the local magistrates' court. Reoffending rates for those dealt with by the panel are as low as 5 per cent.

Naturally, such panels have limitations. They could never act as courts and will never decide on guilt. Offenders will only come in front of them voluntarily and if they accept responsibility for their behaviour. The alternative – in most cases – would be taking the matter to court where the offender risks a conviction or ASBO. Presented with that choice I believe a far greater number of offenders would be prepared to admit their guilt at an early stage. In particular, tactical 'not guilty' pleas might be substantially reduced.

The argument for rolling out community justice panels across the country is compelling. In doing so there is no need to reinvent the wheel. A framework already exists with youth offender panels, made up of a mixture of members of the public and the youth offending team. Currently these administer 'referral orders', a penalty designed for first-time offenders under eighteen who have admitted their guilt. Typically, an offender will be required to meet the panel, whose members will talk to him about his behaviour and set out a programme for him to follow over the length of the order. This may involve reparation work, writing a letter of apology to the victim, or sessions with team workers to address particular problems such as drug abuse.

I believe that these panels could provide the foundations for a nation-wide network of community justice panels. Their role would be expanded beyond simply dealing with referral orders to include the court diversionary work set out above. In addition to working with youths, they would deal with adults too. The mix of lay and professional membership of these panels should lead to a strong community element assisted by expert guidance. A faster, more informal system of restorative justice would be in the interests of offenders and victims alike.

Sentencing

Public confidence in sentencing has been damaged because sentences do not mean what they say. On average, a prisoner serving a life sentence will be released after just eleven years. Furthermore, prisoners are automatically released halfway through their sentence, so a four-year sentence really only means a maximum of two years in prison.

Public confidence is also undermined by constant attacks on the sentencing decisions of judges. It is cheap and short-sighted of the government to blame the judiciary for failings in the criminal justice system, when usually responsibility lies with the politicians. Again, this smacks of a central government assuming it knows best, rather than trusting professionals on the ground.

The Liberal Democrat approach is to restore honesty to sentencing. Life sentences should only be given when the intention is that someone will actually spend the rest of their life in prison. In the case of other dangerous offenders a sentence of imprisonment for public protection with release once the offender no longer presents a danger is more appropriate.

Automatic reductions in sentences should also be ended. Instead judges would announce a minimum and a maximum term for the sentence. This policy represents a radical change of approach to sentencing. The sentence that someone would actually serve would not be determined just by the crime they had committed but by the progress they make after sentencing. This would shift the focus to rehabilitation, something which is easily forgotten in our overcrowded and under-resourced prisons.

For me, current Liberal Democrat policy does not go far enough in this direction. Minimum and maximum sentences could also be applied to community penalties. Take the example of someone sentenced for aggravated bodily harm on his partner. He receives, say, a minimum sentence of a one-year community penalty with supervision and 100 hours' unpaid work, and a maximum of two years with 200 hours. The order progresses well, he's brought back for regular reviews in front of the sentencing judge, who is told that he is making a real effort to address the problems behind his offending and that he turns up on time for the unpaid work and works hard when he's there. He would serve the minimum. Other offenders making less satisfactory progress would serve longer. This would provide a necessary carrot-and-stick approach to community orders, short of revoking a poorly attended order and re-sentencing the offender to prison. All orders would be subject to regular review, and judges would continue to take an interest in the offender's progress long after sentencing. A precedent has already been set for this in relation to drug rehabilitation programmes, where offenders regularly come back to court for the sentencing judge to review the progress they are making. This works well and should be expanded to other types of orders.

A further principle behind Liberal Democrat policy on sentencing is ending the obsession with prison. At over 80,000 prisoners Britain has the highest prison population in the EU. Many of these are serving short custodial sentences, with some 53,676 people given sentences of six months or less in 2004, each serving an average of less than two months. Such a short sentence provides precious little protection to the public and allows for no work towards rehabilitation. However, if Liberal Democrats are to advocate community penalties as an alternative the public must be given confidence that these are not a soft option.

Naturally, better enforcement is one part of the answer. Another part is giving the public a say in what work is done. This could happen through local referendums. Local people might choose to have a new play area built or a pavilion refurbished. In this way offenders would be visibly paying the community back for their crimes, and the public would be engaged in the process.

The state and criminal justice

Looking back over Labour's handling of the criminal justice system, two traits emerge. The first is a centralising tendency, the second is macho posturing. This posturing comes from a core New Labour belief that to win elections they must sound tougher than the Tories on crime. It led David Blunkett to dismiss 'airy-fairy civil liberties'[10] or Tony Blair to claim at the Labour Party conference in 2005 that the central problem with the criminal justice system was that 'the whole of our system starts from the proposition that its duty is to protect the innocent from being wrongly convicted'.[11] It has also led to repeated rhetoric from both Tories and Labour about 'rebalancing the system away from the defendant and in favour of the victim'. However seductive the slogan, the logic behind it is false. Taking away the rights of defendants does not automatically improve the situation of victims of crime. In practice 're-balancing' is normally not about doing anything positive for victims at all but is a pretext for removing the safeguards of defendants at trial. In this way, and by sleight of hand, it is not the power of the victim that grows, but that of the state.

What is really needed is not tough talk, but efficiency. Victims of crime often express frustration at the sheer slowness of the process, with cases taking months or even years to conclude. Yet tackling this has nothing to do with 're-balancing' the system – excessive delay is unfair and oppressive to victims and defendants alike.

The solutions put forward in *Together We Can Cut Crime* are practical and realistic. One idea is to cut back on unnecessary court hearings. Preliminary hearings in the crown court often serve no useful purpose. Committal hearings could be abolished, saving time by allowing cases to be transferred directly to the crown court, thus making sure trials are heard sooner. Any perceived inadequacies with the evidence could be dealt with by an early dismissal hearing.

Another idea is to allow many pre-trial hearings to be conducted by video-link. This is common practice for incarcerated defendants, appearing by video link from the prison. Video-link could cheaply and easily be used for lawyers too, thus ending the nonsense of barristers and solicitors driving long distances to court, only to make appearances lasting a couple of minutes.

Further policy proposals aim to make sure that victims of crime are always quickly paid a proper level of compensation. At present how much an offender will be ordered by the court to pay in compensation to a victim can seem like a complete lottery. The compensation is also often never paid, as the offender ends up in prison or cannot afford to keep up with payments, meaning that the victim loses out. Establishing a common fund would enable courts to pay victims up front, recovering the money from the offender later, if need be taking it from their wages or benefit payments.

These proposals may not make good copy with tabloid newspapers, but it is exactly this type of practical measure that will make a difference to people's experience of the criminal justice system.

Liberals have good cause to be alarmed by Labour's centralising and authoritarian streaks. Liberals are naturally suspicious of the centralised state and believe that crime is often best tackled at the most local level. Liberals also believe that involving the public in the criminal justice system is one of the best ways to build trust in it. It is for this reason that Liberal Democrats have always stood firm against any proposals to limit jury service, an aspect of our legal system that has always exercised a healthy check on the power of the state. Moreover, jury service connects citizens to the legal process and gives them an important stake in it. It is for this reason that Liberal Democrats have looked to ways of extending jury service. In *Together We Can Cut Crime* a proposal is made for jurors to sit alongside district judges in trials in the magistrates' court. This will put a stop to one person alone deciding on a defendant's guilt. This policy could be extended for jurors to sit alongside lay magistrates, bringing greater diversity to a magistracy that is still overwhelmingly white, middle-aged and middle-class.

Community justice panels are another way of giving the public a role in helping make offenders take responsibility for their actions. So too are proposals to give the public a say in what work is carried out through community penalties. Whitehall must also learn to trust more in local government. Councils should have a greater say in the activities of local police and be free to tackle anti-social behaviour in a way most appropriate to the local community.

The state will always be at the centre of the criminal justice system. The debates about public versus private provision that rage in other areas of public services have little application here. The challenge is to make the workings of the state more efficient, more decentralised and more democratic.

Notes

1   Cited in Helena Kennedy *Just Law* (Chatto and Windus, London, 2004), pp. 21–22.
2   BBC News, 'Criticism of arrests points plan', 30 August 2006; available at http://news.bbc.co.uk/1/hi/wales/5298208.stm.
3   Speech to Police Federation Conference, 15 May 2007.
4   Nick Clegg, 'Crime and Anti-Social Behaviour: A Liberal Priority', in J. Astle, D. Laws, P. Marshall and A. Murray, *Britain After Blair: A Liberal Agenda* (Profile Books, London, 2006), p. 193.
5   Howard League, *Out for Good: Meeting the resettlement needs of young men* (May 2006).
6   Liberal Democrats, *Together We Can Cut Crime*, Policy Paper 78, March 2007, p. 5.
7   Clegg, 'Crime and Anti-Social Behaviour, p. 202.
8   Camden Borough Council, 'Report of the Anti-Social Behaviour Review', January 2007; National Audit Office, *Tackling Anti-Social Behaviour*', December 2006.
9   Chiltern Lighthouse Mentoring, Information Memorandum, 2005.
10 Patrick Wintour, 'Blunkett rejects 'airy fairy' fears', *The Guardian*, 12 November 2001.
11 Tony Blair, Speech to Labour Party Conference, 27 September 2005; available at: http://news.bbc.co.uk/1/hi/uk_politics/4287370.stm.

Chapter 19

Tackling Terrorism: A Liberal Democrat Approach

Nick Clegg

> Although a democracy must often fight with one hand tied
> behind its back, it nonetheless has the upper hand.
> *Israeli Supreme Court ruling on illegal practices by Shin Bet, the*
> *Israeli security service, 1999*

The national debate on Britain's response to al-Qaeda-inspired terrorism is still in its infancy. Much of the early government response, as the shock waves of the 9/11 attack crossed the Atlantic, focused on the need to pass new anti-terror legislation. Governments always reach for the statute book to reassure themselves, and the public, that something is being done to meet new, hitherto unknown, challenges. Notwithstanding the illiberal excesses of the government's early legislative reactions – prolonged detention without charge, control orders and so on – a fair amount of the new laws nonetheless enjoyed strong cross-party support, notably the creation of the new offence of 'acts preparatory to terrorism'.

At the same time, much of the public commentary surrounding the country's anti-terrorism policies developed an increasingly polarised character. On the one hand, a number of commentators focused on the role that the UK/US invasion of Iraq had played in aiding and abetting terrorist extremists. The political inconsistency of a Prime Minister keen to prosecute a 'war on terror', when the war in Iraq was proving to be such a powerful recruiting sergeant for tomorrow's terrorists, has remained a subject of repeated critical comment. At the same time, an increasingly vocal group of commentators viewed such a link between the Iraq conflict and terrorism, especially the advent of deadly home-grown terrorism after the 7/7 suicide attacks in London, as dangerously apologetic. Notably, the Conservative MP and *Times* journalist, Michael

Gove, and the *Daily Mail* commentator, Melanie Phillips, developed a stinging critique in which, they asserted, 'Britain has been consumed by a loss of cultural nerve that has all but destroyed its belief in itself as a nation'.[1]

According to Gove and Phillips, far from seeking to identify reasons why Britain has provoked such loathing in others, the key priority should be to identify the warped Islamist ideology which seeks to destroy both mainstream Islam and liberal western values. This allegation was reinforced by the work of think-tanks such as Policy Exchange, which published a series of papers purporting to demonstrate 'Whitehall's love affair with Islamism'.[2] This critique married a condemnation of the relativist weaknesses of multiculturalism with a forensic analysis of the extremist credentials of a variety of British Muslim groups to whom it was felt the British government had for too long conferred an unwarranted degree of legitimacy.[3]

In recent months, the debate has developed further. Importantly, the new Brown government appears to have taken a decision to pursue the anguished arguments about new anti-terrorism powers in a more measured manner. Much has been said by ministers about the need to seek a new cross-party consensus on anti-terror powers. Since, at the time of writing, the rhetoric has not yet been transformed into any meaningful process for cross-party consultation, and Gordon Brown himself remains wedded to pushing through controversial new measures, it remains too early to tell whether this change of heart will be pursued in earnest. But, in tone if nothing else, it is an important departure from the habit of Tony Blair and his Home Secretaries to move with indecent haste to create points of party-political difference on anti-terrorism policy in the wake of each new terrorist attack at home or abroad. Importantly, it may reflect a belated respect for the view, widely shared by the intelligence services, that belligerent political rhetoric risks making it all the more difficult for the intelligence services to get through to the young men who may be susceptible to the call of extremist terrorists.

This, in turn, highlights a major new political preoccupation: the so-called 'battle for hearts and minds'. Slowly but surely, the initial military and legislative reactions to the 9/11 attacks – the invasion of Afghanistan to thwart the Taliban, the ongoing hunt for the al-Qaeda high command in the mountainous tribal regions of Pakistan, the development of a raft of new national and international anti-terror powers – is giving way to the grim realisation that neither military action nor new laws will ever be enough to stem a terrorist threat of such potency. The mindset of Islamist extremism, both within individuals and within whole communities, must be tackled if al-Qaeda terrorism is not to become a self-perpetuating phenomenon passed from one generation to the next.

This chapter identifies six principles which must be adhered to if the battle for hearts and minds is to stand any chance of success. It suggests that this poses a particular challenge for liberals, since it requires a more aggressive assertion of liberal values, and a rejection of the relativist tendencies in some liberal thinking, in order to build a meaningful platform from which to appeal to hearts and minds. It seeks to move beyond the infantile stand-off between those who see terrorism exclusively as an expression of multiple grievances and those who regard any engagement with extremists as a form of appeasement, towards a policy of 'critical engagement'. It also suggests that the emphasis on the need to promote integration between different communities must be coupled with a focus on the absence of inter-generational integration within certain communities. Finally, it proposes a number of reforms both to the law and to police and intelligence structures, including the creation of a National Counter-Terrorism Service spun out of the Metropolitan Police Force, to further strengthen our ability to pursue prosecutions against terrorist suspects, a fundamental objective if terrorism is to be successfully defeated by the rule of law.

The limits to liberal tolerance

Liberalism is optimistic. It is rooted in the belief that individuals and communities should, wherever possible, be left to their own devices. If given the freedom to decide what is best for themselves, individuals and communities are more likely to fulfil their potential for harmony, creativity and contentment. It also trusts in the power of rational argument, in the genius of democratic debate in sifting through competing claims to reach a settled view of what is best for society. It celebrates diversity, and promotes the right of all citizens to express their own views uncensored and unhindered by authority. It abhors excessive concentrations of power, especially unaccountable power. It has an obstinate faith in the rule of law and due process, both nationally and internationally.

In short, it could be said that liberalism is peculiarly ill-equipped to deal with the contemporary threat of global terrorism. For this is a threat in which the perpetrators sacrifice their individual identity wholly to a hateful and irrational ideology. It is a threat the response to which, by necessity, is often covert and hidden from public scrutiny. Above all, it is a threat which infuses the political debate with fear and pessimism, the very opposite of liberalism's keen sense of hope.

So does the al-Qaeda terrorist threat require an abandonment of liberalism? Are quaint notions of individual rights, accountable government, due process and reasoned debate simply unaffordable luxuries at a time of heightened insecurity? Is liberalism simply not up to the job of defending the nation from such implacable enemies? Can liberalism only ever thrive at times of unruffled tranquillity?

This chapter argues forcefully to the contrary – that liberalism is the very essence of what the terrorists are seeking to destroy, and so must be the starting point in the design of our own defences. Liberal values are the antithesis of the theocratic intolerance espoused by Islamist extremism. (The term 'Islamist' is not without its problems. It refers to a theocratic form of Islam which insists on the unity of secular and religious power, and respect for sharia law. Clearly, it is possible to hold Islamist views without espousing violence or terrorism. But all al-Qaeda-inspired terrorists seem to advocate the virtues of an Islamist state, or new caliphate. Thus the use in this chapter of the term 'Islamist terrorism', or 'Islamist extremism', as distinct from mainstream Muslim thought.)

A belief in the universalism of civil rights, in the merits of rational inquiry, in gender equality, in the virtues of democracy, in the rule of secular law, in constrained government, in the non-violent contest of ideas, in the liberating potential of science, and in the separation of church and state – all of these are rejected by a purist, medieval Islamist creed which regards almost all contemporary liberal achievements as decadent failures which need to be purged in favour of the theocratic rule of strict Islamist government.

All religions based on a promise of salvation tend to spawn purist schools of thought which seek to strip away what they regard as the corrupt misinterpretations of the original faith in favour of a self-appointed version of the true faith. Religions have long been shaped by the tensions which arise between a settled institutional order and challengers who contest the self-regarding nature of that order. This is not necessarily negative. Martin Luther was one of the greatest religious revolutionaries, espousing a purer relationship between God and the individual, liberated from the interference of a politically corrupt Catholic church. He was, in the strictest sense, a fundamentalist, returning his religion to what he regarded as its fundamental roots. There are Christian fundamentalists active in the United States today who advocate a literal, unbending interpretation of the Bible contrary to the teachings of mainstream Christian churches. Christianity has been invoked down the ages in violent conquest of other religions and cultures. No religion is immune to the deadly appeal of fundamentalism, and occasionally violence.

Today, however, the focus of attention is understandably on the role of fundamentalist movements within Islam because of the advent of al-Qaeda-inspired terrorism. The Wahhabi movement in Saudi Arabia, founded in the eighteenth century by Muhammad ibn Abd al-Wahhab, also espoused a return to religious fundamentals. Wahhabists believe that life should be lived in accordance to the strict dictates of Islam, by which they mean the way in which the prophet Muhammad and his followers lived during the seventh century in Medina. Wahhabism later combined with the anti-colonial fervour and religious fundamentalism of ideologues such as Sayyid Abul Ala Maududi (instrumental in turning Indian Muslims away from a united India and towards a separate Muslim state in Pakistan) and Sayyid Qutb (the principal thinker of the Muslim Brotherhood founded in Egypt in 1928 by Hassan al Banna) to create the ideological framework in which contemporary Islamist extremists operate. These different strands of thought are united by a vitriolic rejection of Western values, and a belief that true Islam, and the might of a theocratic Islamic state, have been suppressed down the ages by Western imperialism.

The power of this ideological motivation has been given a significant boost by the internet, which one analyst has called the 'turbocharger' of jihadi radicalisation. Stephen Ulph of the US Jamestown Foundation claims that at least 60 per cent of the material on jihadi websites deals with ideological questions, not current affairs or practical bomb-making tips. According to Mr Ulph, the internet has become the leading tool in 'a civil war for the minds of Muslim youth'.[4] The internet, a quintessentially modern method of communication, is being used by Islamist extremists to trawl the past for any support in their ongoing ideological mission. The Combating Terrorism Centre at the US military academy in West Point discovered that Ibn Taymiyya, an Islamic scholar who lived at the time of the medieval Mongol invasions, now tops the bill as the most cited figure on Islamist internet sites.[5] Unsurprisingly, Ibn Taymiyya advocated a return to a purer Islamic faith, a violent rejection of the Mongol invaders, and an unforgiving attitude towards all non-Muslims. That his views should now resonate several centuries later with modern Islamist extremists shows the potency of the internet in facilitating ideological time-travel.

The greatest loathing in the pantheon of hatreds harboured by Islamist extremists is reserved for those Muslim regimes which are perceived to be mere supplicants to Western imperialism – thus Osama bin Laden's well-documented aim to topple the House of Saud in Saudi Arabia, or the growing threat of unrest in Pakistan against General Musharraf's pro-Western government. The terrorism aimed at Western powers such as the United States and the United Kingdom is, therefore, a consequence of an internal power struggle within Islam itself. And our most important allies in this struggle are not other Western powers, but those in moderate Islam who do not wish to see their religion captured by medievalism.

Liberals must be aware of this ideological and historical background to the current terrorist threat in order to understand their place in it. There can be no accommodation between liberalism and Islamist terrorism. They are mutually exclusive, and represent value systems which are diametrically opposed to each other. In other words, liberalism must be forthright in its own defence, in protecting the principles of liberalism which have become caught up in the struggle between mainstream Muslims and extremist Islamists.

That, in turn, demands greater clarity about the limits to liberal tolerance. If liberalism is to win the ideological battle against violent prejudice and theocracy, it must be self-confident in insisting on the inviolable nature of core liberal values. A belief in diversity, a commitment to freedom of speech, should never collapse into lazy relativism. To win the battle of hearts and minds, to drain the swamp of warped ideology in which terrorism thrives, liberals must be forthright in asserting the merits of their own values. If the long-term success of any anti-terrorist strategy depends in large part on the contest of ideas, liberals must be prepared to engage and win that contest on their own terms.

The power of critical engagement

This is not merely of esoteric interest. The most pressing challenge today is to work out how to stop more individuals – usually but not exclusively young men – from transforming their widespread sense of grievance into a pursuit of jihadist violence. A strong, inclusive liberalism must provide *both* mainstream Muslim citizens and those of other faiths and none with the ideological tools to counter the madness of violent theocracy. In short, liberalism must be compelling enough to keep people on side, to hold them back from resorting to violence as a weapon for religious purism and revenge. This challenge is not specific to al-Qaeda-inspired terrorism. It took almost forty years after Bloody Sunday for confidence-building measures in Northern Ireland's Catholic community to bear fruit. But the IRA could not have been defeated without that painstaking work. Terrorist movements all over the world are not defeated until the communities in which they operate are won over.

According to some academics, we are in danger of accepting a myth of Islamist religious extremism, first expressed by Lord John Stevens in the wake of the July 2005 London bombings, that about one per cent of Britain's Muslims are involved in serious forms of religious and political extremism. Whilst even this estimate amounts to a fairly large number of people (16,000 out of a total British Muslim population of 1.6 million), academics such as Shamit Saggar believe that the focus should, instead, be on 'a long tail of soft, unintentional acts of omission within and across Muslim communities that can serve to support men of violence'. In other words, by focusing only on a comparatively small number of men of violence, we have 'taken our eyes off those who surround, and tacitly support, violence and its perpetrators'.[6]

Saggar cites extensive opinion-survey evidence to suggest that the levels of grievance in many Muslim communities – grievances against UK foreign policy in Iraq and elsewhere, grievances against economic and educational underachievement, against poor housing, against the police, even against the imposition of what is perceived to be excessive secularism – provides a natural buffer zone for the activities of violent extremists. Those who might be aware that something is amiss with their friends, neighbours, husbands, brothers, and sons but do not, or cannot, act upon their misgivings, Saggar labels as 'fence-sitters'. They provide a tacit, invisible layer of camouflage in which it is easier for violent extremists to plot their acts. Saggar states baldly: 'the 7 July London suicide team, in preparing to execute their mission, did not operate in a vacuum'.[7] Again, these insights can be applied to other terrorist movements, present and past, too. The IRA never operated in a vacuum either. Other than a few exceptional examples of lone attacks, few terrorists have ever existed in complete isolation from the communities in which they operate.

Needless to say, this characterisation, if it is valid at all, will not apply to all Muslim communities. Indeed, the description of 'fence-sitters' providing an unarticulated protection for extremists – because of inaction, rather than any deliberate course of action – will rightly be considered offensive by the significant majority of British Muslims who are perfectly capable of separating their own individual sense of grievance from the criminal plots of terrorists. Nonetheless, it is an analysis which casts fresh light on one of the greatest public-policy dilemmas we face: how to divorce the widespread grievances of large numbers of British Muslims from the activities of Islamist extremists, in order that the former can actively help to expose and defeat the latter?

One thing is for sure, an approach based solely on the wish to condemn any Muslim individual or organisation who has ever flirted with fundamentalist views is doomed to failure. Yet that would be the consequence if policy-makers were unduly swayed by the polemic of writers such as Melanie Phillips or Michael Gove. They should take credit for pioneering a powerful insight into the current terrorist threat which others were slower to acknowledge: that it has a strong ideological component which must be responded to in ideological terms. But winning an ideological battle is not possible if battle is not engaged in the first place. That is why it is so curious that those who have rightly sought to delineate the nature of the ideological threat have then advocated a highly introverted strategy in which the sole purpose of public policy appears to be to ignore, exclude and ostracise those individuals and organisations who might provide some insight into the threat we face.

There is a simple test whether an individual or an organisation should be excluded, banned or prosecuted: do they espouse the use of violence to pursue their ideological ends? If they do, the full force of the law should be brought to bear, as is already the case in the growing number of terrorist organisations that have been banned under British law. However, crucially, we have every incentive to confront and engage critically with those groups and individuals who harbour views which we may find utterly unacceptable – such as the imposition of sharia law and a theocratic Islamist state – but do not do so through the use of violence. Indeed, given the need to develop as much intelligence as possible on the forces which aid and abet the radicalisation of young Muslim men, we are duty-bound to do so to protect our own security. Such engagement must be based on a number of simple principles.

First, as Rachel Briggs has persuasively argued,[8] the whole approach must be rooted in specific communities, not on a misplaced and wildly inaccurate reference to 'the Muslim community'. There is no such thing. There are only Muslim communities, all of them existing within the specificities of their own local circumstances. In the end, there is no replacement to the hard graft of bottom-up engagement. Central government must make resources available to local authorities and to grassroots organisations to adopt innovative approaches to boosting the involvement of local Muslim groups, individuals and families. It should also provide funding for new public policy research into a 'mapping' exercise of the enormous ethnic, religious, linguistic and geographical diversity of our Muslim communities. Too many policy-makers remain largely ignorant of the scope and complexity of the communities with whom they are hoping to engage. Importantly, a particular effort must be made to reach young men, and women of all ages. The former are more often than not the cohort where the process of radicalisation is most likely to take place. The latter are, in some communities, almost entirely locked out of wider social and political participation. A sense of greater empowerment amongst the former, and emancipation amongst the latter, would over time go some way to help provide the natural checks and balances within families and communities to halt the process of radicalisation before it is too late.

Second, government must accept that a large part of engaging critically with the so-called 'fence-sitters' in our Muslim communities involves listening seriously to the widespread grievances shared in those communities. An unholy alliance of Tony Blair's stubborn refusal to admit any errors in his decision to invade Iraq, and the breathless accusation of appeasement bandied about by hardline commentators against anyone prepared to acknowledge community grievances, has led to a self-defeating defensiveness in government. Instead, a self-confident government should have the strength of purpose to listen and, where justified, refute the economic, social, cultural and policy grievances of many mainstream Muslim communities. Acknowledging a grievance does not mean legitimising a grievance. What is essential is that there is a process, a channel of communication, which allows those grievances to be expressed in a non-violent manner. This is crucial to the overarching objective: to separate the grievances of mainstream Muslim communities from the violent intentions of Islamist extremists in order to ensure that the latter can find no tacit succour or refuge amongst the community at large.

Third, policing strategies need to be reviewed and, where necessary, changed in order to foster as much trust between the police and Muslim communities as possible. Senior police officers understand very well that if the police are viewed as nothing more than enforcers of an increasingly intrusive state, then the long-term battle for hearts and minds will be lost. Anti-terror officers remember well the boost provided to the IRA and INLA when the state imposed harsh 'anti-terror' measures; internment in Northern Ireland was immediately followed by a substantial increase in violence. As Bob Lambert, head of the Metropolitan Police's Muslim Contact Unit (MCU), has observed 'terrorist actions intend to provoke over-reaction from governments, security services and the police' in order to strengthen their appeal to new recruits to their cause.[9] That is why the police must work especially hard to develop relationships of trust amongst the most distrustful communities. The experience in London of Operation Trident, where Met police officers have sought to win the confidence of black Londoners in order to reduce black-on-black gun crime has served as a model of sorts for early attempts at confidence-building between the police and the capital's Muslim communities. That is why the Met's MCU has focused on developing relationships with regular worshippers at mosques such as those at Finsbury Park and Brixton, even though both have been the setting for extremist preaching and retain a reputation for radicalism. The Met's MCU should be emulated in each police authority with significant Muslim communities, and the ability of officers to demonstrate a real commitment to community engagement should be fully recognised within police career structures.

Fourth, the political class itself must learn to act with greater intelligence and subtlety in stemming the process of Islamist radicalisation. In large part, as already described, this must involve a willingness to move beyond an obsessive focus on new legislative powers. While, as explained below, there is undoubtedly a case to revisit some of the powers already on the statute book, there remains an unhelpful tendency for government ministers to intervene in the public debate only when seeking to introduce sweeping new powers.[10] The language used is also important. The government's apparent decision to abandon Blairite references to the 'war on terror' is a significant, and helpful, change of political language. It is now widely accepted that constant references to such a 'war' can have the unintended consequence of legitimising terrorist activities by implying that somehow their criminal actions are that of legitimate combatants in war.

Nonetheless, politicians and political parties could still do more to bridge the gulf that exists between those parts of our Muslim communities who have developed deep suspicions of the political process and themselves. It has been suggested, for instance, that the government should launch an ambitious shadowing programme for young Muslims to allow them to gain an insight into the work of MPs, peers, local councillors and political party officials, and that the policy working groups of all political parties should make greater efforts to open up their deliberations on security policy to the direct input of young Muslims who feel disaffected by the political process.[11]

Fifth, we cannot duck the crucial role played by religious leaders. Much rhetoric, not all of it by any means helpful, has been thrown at the question of 'radical imams'. While it is clearly unfair to imply that imams coming from abroad are generally liable to spread a radical perversion of Islam, there is an issue associated with the lack of supply of imams in the UK. The problem has been recognised by some within the Muslim community for several years, and highlighted as far back as the 1980s. It is instructive that, when asked in opinion polls, the overwhelming majority of Muslims indicate that religion plays a very important role in their lives – but only a minority go to mosques on a regular basis, if at all. One of the reasons for this is the lack of fully-trained imams.

In principle, a fully trained imam should have spent at least ten years in training and study, but in Islam there are no actual minimum requirements. In practice, since many mosques cannot afford such an imam, many rely on volunteers. The result is that many – perhaps most – imams have only a basic knowledge of some elements of Islamic law, only know enough Qu'ranic texts to lead in prayers, and have no training for living in or guiding a community living in Europe. The result of this is that many, particularly young, Muslims have come to see mosques as irrelevant – as evidenced by the falling-off in attendance from the first year of secondary school.

There is, therefore, a real issue here – and attempting to help solve it could be of considerable benefit to local mosques as well as to the wider community. In June of last year, four key Muslim organisations established the Mosques and Imams National Advisory Board (MINAB), with a view to helping to train imams and to reduce the need to 'import' them from abroad. There are of course practical concerns – the Netherlands experienced considerable difficulty in ensuring that training programmes met reasonable standards in Islamic terms – and, in particular, there is a risk that 'home-grown' imams might be seen as coopted by the state. In this context, the fact that MINAB was set up partially because the organisations concerned felt the government was taking an overly high-handed approach may prove helpful.

Finally, all public policy prescriptions must make a clear distinction between the need to boost integration between communities and the importance of relationships within those same communities. In particular, it is now becoming obvious that a common driver for radicalisation amongst young Muslim men appears to be a breakdown of respect towards their own fathers and grandfathers. A recent analysis of the motivations of Mohammad Sidique Khan, one of the 7/7 suicide bombers, suggests that his radicalisation started with a growing sense of anger about what he viewed as the supine, conformist values of the first-generation immigrant elders of his community. In particular, he appears to have been galvanised at a fairly early stage by the scourge of drug-dealing in his own community in Beeston, Leeds, to which he felt the older generations did not put up a sufficiently strong challenge.[12] Inasmuch as Islamist extremism appears to be a rejection of conventional, mainstream forms of Islam by the angry fundamentalism of younger Muslim men, it is clear that it is tensions between different generations within one community which are as important as, if not more important than, the lack of integration between communities. At the very least, this analysis underlines the pressing need for local authorities and governments to do all they can to provide community leaders with the tools to deal with challenges which their own communities face lest they are viewed as powerless or redundant by their own children and grandchildren.

These six guiding principles for engagement are by no means exhaustive. A whole chapter could be devoted to the way in which foreign policy, or schooling, or housing policy can impact on relations within and between our various Muslim communities, yet they have barely been touched on here. Nonetheless, these principles seek to provide a conceptual framework for the policy of critical engagement which is indispensable to the fundamental objective of starving terrorist extremists of all tacit or explicit support from non-violent members of the communities in which they live.

Structural reform

We rely on the work of the police and security services both to pre-empt attacks, such as the alleged plots which were halted in August 2006, and to secure the necessary evidence for prosecution. The work of both has been absolutely essential and has served to prevent several attacks. Nonetheless, we need to consider whether the structures of our intelligence agencies and police, developed over a long period of time and before the emergence of the present terrorist threat, are still appropriate. I believe that we need to go further than the government has so far through its creation of a streamlined Home Office focused more tightly on anti-terrorism strategy.

At present, there are three principal intelligence agencies in the United Kingdom – the Security Service (MI5), the Secret Intelligence Service (MI6) and Government Communications Headquarters (GCHQ). In principle, the division between MI5 and MI6 is geographical: MI5 is responsible for domestic threats, while MI6 operates abroad (GCHQ covers signal intelligence and information assurance). This rigid geographical division of functions is dissolving fast as the resources of MI6 are overwhelmingly being devoted to countering al-Qaeda-inspired terrorism, for which the lead remains with MI5, and MI5 itself now has some operations of its own abroad. Events have rightly propelled this increasing operational convergence between MI5 and MI6 forward: it is generally agreed that the 7/7 bombers' travel to Pakistan had a motivational effect at the very least, although the precise extent remains unclear. Al-Qaeda is also believed to have regrouped in the border region of Pakistan and Afghanistan – with direct implications for counterterrorism in London or the North of England. The contemporary terrorist threat makes a mockery of any neat division of labour between domestic and foreign operations.

Three questions emerge from the evolving institutional response of our security services: first, should the example of the joint section of MI5 and MI6 which was formed at the height of the Northern Irish terrorist threat be emulated now on a larger scale? This would have the benefit of making explicit a blurring of MI5 and MI6 responsibilities which is already taking place. Importantly, it would also allow those parts of MI6 which are not subsumed into the MI5-led anti-terror operations from continue their valuable work promoting British interests, and gathering vital intelligence, abroad. Crucially, this includes the sensitive work of bringing covert political influence to bear in precisely those countries where we want to see moderate Islam strengthened, not weakened. The danger of drifting towards a wholesale takeover of MI6 priorities by work undertaken by other agencies is that MI6 itself would lose the capacity to do the work abroad, which extends well beyond the current al-Qaeda threat, for which it was designed. Creating an anti-terror capacity able to act seamlessly at home and abroad, answerable to the Home Secretary, by folding the relevant parts of MI6 into MI5 would free up the remaining parts of MI6 to continue with its core functions, answerable to the Foreign Secretary.[13]

Second, are the procedures for parliamentary accountability and scrutiny of the security services strong enough? When the Intelligence and Security Committee was first set up, there were widespread concerns – which Liberal Democrats shared – that it was not a select committee of Parliament but a body appointed by the Prime Minister and reporting to him or her, and that it would perform the work of a select committee with fewer powers. It cannot be right, for instance, that the Prime Minister has the right to determine the timing of the release of an ISC's report. Similarly, if a witness fails to appear before a select committee, it can go to the House of Commons to request it to summon the individual concerned;

the ISC has no such power. Statute law would clearly have to provide for a degree of secrecy unparalleled in other select committees, and its members would need to continue to be Privy Councillors, but it is surely wrong that such an important function as scrutiny of the security services should be performed with fewer powers than those of a normal select committee.

We would, subject to appropriate safeguards in legislation, change the ISC into a select committee of Parliament with the same powers and with members drawn from both Houses. In opposition, Labour shared these concerns. It is promising that Gordon Brown, within days of becoming Prime Minister, finally agreed too. It can only be hoped that he will now act fast on his change of heart.

Third, and finally, the intelligence services must give urgent priority to building up the resources to engage in the propaganda battle which is increasingly being played out on the internet and on satellite broadcast stations. As described earlier, the internet is the pre-eminent tool by which radicalisation occurs, and the instant means by which terrorist atrocities are communicated around the world for maximum political and presentational effect. Obviously, any attempt to engage in this 'invisible spectrum' must not collapse into the dark arts of some of the Cold War propaganda operations which eventually led to them being disbanded in Britain's security services. But that experience must not prevent us now from undermining and disrupting the sophisticated al-Qaeda-inspired propagandists who are using new technologies to such devastating effect. Their messages of violence should not go unchallenged.

Policing

At present, the United Kingdom has no policing body at a national level with responsibilities in the field of counter-terrorism. This fits with our practice of local policing and with the traditional opposition to the idea of a national police force. It does, however, also place the UK in an anomalous position in comparison with other countries in the Western world – even the most decentralised states in Europe, such as Spain and Germany, also have some kind of national policing body whose responsibilities include areas of counter-terrorism.

Aside from the recent establishment of the Serious Organised Crime Agency, SOCA, in the area of serious organised crime, Britain's approach has been to make use of the idea of 'lead police forces' for a number of areas of criminal activity. In the case of counter-terrorism, this has meant that the Metropolitan Police has had 'lead responsibility'; in cases where terrorist crime is involved, local Chief Constables can (and invariably do) call the Anti-Terrorist National Coordinator (one of the top police officers in the Met) into the area.

So far, this arrangement seems to have worked reasonably well. However, it presents some serious potential problems. The events of 7/7 made it clear that we need to be gravely concerned about radicalisation and terrorist activity outside London – particularly in the North and Midlands – and that, as MI5 has recognised, we need to develop a 'rich picture' of terrorist activity at local levels. Clearly London faces the greatest threat, but are we comfortable in these circumstances with such an overtly London-focused body having counter-terrorist responsibility for the whole of the UK? Furthermore, the current arrangement creates issues of accountability; the Met is primarily London's police force, and scrutiny arrangements are inevitably London focused.

Liberal Democrats have, in the past, supported the principle of bodies such as SOCA when there is a clear need for a UK-wide approach on aspects of countering crime, preferring targeted national bodies to centralising control of local forces. We should extend this to supporting the creation of a National Counter-Terrorism Service along similar lines. As the Met's counter-terrorist capacities will always be far larger than those of any other police force, an NCTS would be able to adopt a specifically regional focus, bringing specialist expertise to bear upon the development of terrorist networks and the activities of sympathisers in areas of the North and Midlands where this is an increasingly acute concern.

Similar problems of lack of clarity and overlap currently affect Britain's policing of its borders – obviously a vital part of counter-terrorist efforts, given the international nature of the threat. Local Special Branches, Her Majesty's Revenue and Customs, the UK Immigration Service and (to some extent) port police and MI5 share responsibility in this area. Liberal Democrats have called for an integrated UK border force for several years now. We welcomed the Home Secretary's statement on this matter last year, and Gordon Brown's support in principle in July of this year, but we are concerned that the government's proposals as they have now emerged involve little more than a redeployment of existing officers. A new force will require new resources and police powers; the government itself has admitted that it would cost £104m to secure every port in the country. Such expenditure would certainly be far more helpful to our security than the billions of pounds due to be wasted on identity cards.

Legal reform

It is too often forgotten that the UK already possesses some of the toughest and most extensive counter-terrorist laws in the democratic world. The Terrorism Act 2000 was intended, following the effective end of the Troubles in Northern Ireland, to bring British anti-terrorist legislation into one statute and to set it on a modern footing. The Terrorism Act already allowed for seven days' pre-charge detention, an extremely broad definition of terrorism and of terrorist offences and a power to search without reasonable suspicion in zones established by the police under Section 44. Following 9/11, however, legislation was passed in 2001, 2003, 2005 and 2006 – four times over a five-year period – affecting the counter-terrorist framework and extending its reach dramatically. Since 2001, we have seen:

- Indefinite detention without trial of foreign suspected international terrorists, later ruled incompatible with the European Convention on Human Rights by the House of Lords;
- A system of control orders, imposing draconian restrictions on liberty on the basis of 'reasonable suspicion', on evidence unavailable to the suspect and on charges which are not disclosed;
- The extension of pre-charge detention in terrorist cases to 14 days (already the longest in the liberal democratic world) and subsequently to 28 days – reduced from the government's original attempt to extend detention to 90 days.

While many of these measures were rushed through Parliament in an ad hoc fashion, there are clearly elements common to them all. In particular, they display a consistent – and striking – lack of faith in the capacity of the criminal justice system to address or thwart terrorism. Detention without trial, control orders and 90-day pre-charge detention all represent means of imposing controls upon – or outright deprivation of – liberty for extensive periods without providing for fair trials. This approach amounts to a very serious abandonment of basic due process.

Labour's approach has very real disadvantages, both from a perspective of liberal principle and from the point of view of anyone concerned to address the terrorist threat. In any free society, measures which amount to the deprivation of liberty on the basis of mere 'reasonable suspicion', often with minimal or no judicial oversight and without the ability of a suspect to know why he or she is held, must be regarded with grave concern. Furthermore, such deprivation of liberty is vulnerable to legal challenge and unlikely to be compatible with our human rights obligations. In 2001, the UK was the only state in the Council of Europe to derogate from the European Convention on Human Rights in the name of the terrorist threat; do we really believe that, unlike every other country in Europe (many of which face serious terrorist threats of their own), we cannot operate within our international commitments?

However, if we are to reject the government's attempts to circumvent our legal system through devices such as control orders and extended pre-charge detention, we need to be prepared to look at the law and to reform it. If the Crown Prosecution Service faces severe difficulties in prosecuting terrorist suspects within the present legal framework, Liberal Democrats should put forward means of enabling such prosecutions. This is emphatically not a means of undermining our civil liberties by another route; where possible, the best method of dealing with terrorist suspects is through fair trials. Our proposals seek to do just that.

Threshold test

When deciding whether to charge a suspect, the Crown Prosecution Service usually requires there to be a 'realistic prospect of conviction'. This is defined as being a greater than 50 per cent chance of conviction on the evidence available at the time of charging, the 'full code test'. This represents a considerably higher threshold than in most continental legal systems – which helps to explain why pre-charge detention has historically been more extensive in the UK. However, this poses significant challenges in terrorist investigations. The need for the decryption of data from PCs, and the analysis of forensic evidence and records of mobile phone conversations, often means that, even though a great deal of investigation will of course take place before arrest, there may be difficulties in meeting the full code test.

This is why the CPS is also able to apply a 'threshold test' in cases where a suspect presents a substantial bail risk but where much of the evidence is not available when the decision on charging has to be made. The test requires Crown Prosecutors to decide whether there is at least a reasonable suspicion that the individual has committed an offence and whether there is a public interest in charging him or her. It also requires consideration of a number of factors:

- the evidence available at the time;
- the likelihood and nature of further evidence being obtained;
- the reasonableness of believing that evidence will become available;
- the time it will take to gather that evidence and the steps being taken to do so;
- the impact the expected evidence will have on the case; and
- the charges the evidence will support.[14]

As matters stand, the threshold test is usually employed in terrorism cases. It has been argued by senior policemen that it is of little use in addressing the question of pre-charge detention, on the grounds that in their view the test requires a clear indication that particular evidence is likely to become available. The wording of the test seems to be considerably more open than this, and organisations such as JUSTICE and Liberty have interpreted it rather differently; but as there is doubt, it should be clarified. We should make it clear in the code for Crown Prosecutors that, in terrorism cases at least, the threshold test falls rather closer to a threshold of 'reasonable suspicion' – which is already explicitly cited – than it does to the full code test.

Post-charge questioning

The issue of questioning suspects after charge was also raised by the police when arguing for 90-day detention, and goes to the heart of their case. In principle, questioning is supposed to cease when charges are brought. However, exceptions already exist in the Police and Criminal Evidence Act Code of Practice C, allowing post-charge interviews if they are judged necessary:

- to prevent or minimise harm or loss to some other person, or the public;
- to clear up an ambiguity in a previous answer or statement; or
- in the interests of justice for the detainee to have put to them, and have an opportunity to comment on, information concerning the offence which has come to light since they were charged or informed they might be prosecuted.

Organisations such as Liberty have suggested that it might be possible to widen the grounds for post-charge questioning to terrorism cases. This might allow the gathering of further evidence or information after charge, putting new evidence together with continued questioning – and fitting neatly with the use of the threshold test to charge with lower levels of evidence than would be possible under the full code test. Again, if there is ambiguity, liberals should have no objection to clarifying the position.

There is, of course, a need to ensure that oppressive questioning is not permitted – obtaining more information must not be allowed to shade over into attempts to 'break' suspects, not least because the evidence might well be deemed inadmissible in court. We would recommend that suspects be able to challenge repeated requests for post-charge questioning before a judge where there was a risk that this might be oppressive.

Plea-bargaining

It has long been accepted that a timely guilty plea, along with providing evidence for the prosecution in other cases, has benefits for the legal system and that this can affect a defendant's sentence. Until relatively recently, however, this was a purely informal process; prosecutors and the defence could agree, for instance, that some charges would be admitted and others dropped, but no indication of the likely reduction of sentences by judges could be sought. Recent legislation has changed this position in England, Wales and Northern Ireland – prosecutors now have the formal power to offer immunity from prosecution or guarantees that testimony will not be used against a (voluntary) witness.[15] Courts are now also allowed formally to take cooperation into account when passing sentences, while prosecutors may refer sentences for review.

These changes have significantly increased prosecutors' powers in respect of organised crime, but they are legally applicable to any offence. We believe the time has come to make it clear that they should be seen as available tools in terrorism offences. Understandably, such a move will arouse controversy, but – as with organised crime – one of our greatest failures in counter-terrorism has been our inability to apprehend key figures in terrorist networks. Needless to say, work would need to be done to ensure the maximum reliability of evidence obtained as a result of plea-bargaining. The experience of Northern Ireland in the early 1980s, when the testimony of some thirty 'super-grasses' resulted in the charging of over 300 people with terrorist offences, is indicative of the potential risks; nearly half of the super-grasses subsequently withdrew their statements, and many of those convicted were cleared on appeal. If evidence derived from plea-bargaining is to become more prominent, arrangements to make it clear that this is the source of such evidence will be central.

Intercept evidence

Liberal Democrats have long called for the removal of the current prohibition on the use of UK telephone intercept evidence in court. Although they did not take this view in government, the Conservatives have come to adopt the same position. Gordon Brown has confirmed that he will convene a committee of Privy Councillors from all the political parties to examine the issue anew, reporting its conclusions before Parliament resumes in October 2007.

The UK's blanket ban is highly anomalous – the Republic of Ireland is the only other state which shares it, and other democratic states find our reticence extremely hard to understand. Furthermore, the ban does not extend to foreign intercept material, or to intelligence evidence such as a bug in a room, or even to allowing UK intercepts to be used in foreign courts – rendering it even more illogical.

However, we also need to recognise that the intelligence agencies have a legitimate interest in preserving necessary secrecy with regard to their methods and operatives. This extends particularly to questions of disclosure – and it is important to recognise that by making intercept evidence admissible in court, we not only increase the amount of evidence available to prosecutors in trials; we also increase the rights of the defence to demand disclosure of evidence in the interest of a fair hearing.

There is currently a framework which allows for the non-disclosure of evidence where the judge agrees that the public interest in non-disclosure outweighs the defendant's interest in having full access to the relevant material. (In any case, there is no obligation to disclose information which is not actively helpful to the defendant.) The production of edited and summarised documents or an admission of facts which the evidence would tend to prove against the prosecution, in place of full disclosure, can also be approved by the judge. However, the law in this field is covered by several different statutes, is also defined by court decisions, and has had to be fleshed out in codes of practice.

Irrespective of intercept evidence, there are good arguments for instituting a clearer statutory framework for public-interest immunity. Other jurisdictions, such as the United States and Australia, have statutes explicitly designed to govern the rules surrounding the disclosure of classified information in criminal proceedings. The Australian framework, in particular, makes it clear in statute that the full range of 'partial disclosure' options are available to the court. It is important to note that this does not represent an erosion of defendants' rights, but a codification and bringing-together of the present legal framework which should help to encourage prosecutors to make more use of partial disclosure in terrorism trials and to reassure the intelligence agencies that safeguards will be adequate.

Our four key proposals in this field will serve to strengthen and clarify the framework of criminal law in respect of terrorism. Rather than circumventing due process, they are intended to make it work. These proposals will also reinforce each other – for instance, the admissibility of intercept evidence, which often leads on to further, firmer evidence, will make the clarification of the threshold test more effective. The overall result will be more a more structured and effective approach to terrorist trials – allowing effective prosecution without compromising basic liberties.

The fact that the government has confirmed its support in principle for one of these innovations (post-charge questioning) and its willingness to look at the case for another (admissibility of intercept evidence), and given that two others represent a clarification of existing codes of practice rather than wholesale legislative change (plea bargaining and the use of the threshold test by the CPS), the opportunity for greater cross-party consensus on the government's latest Terrorism Bill is considerable. This opportunity should not be squandered by a fruitless, and evidence-free, push to reopen the anguished debate about the specific issue of the length of time of pre-charge detention.

Conclusions

No measure, or package of measures, will be able to eradicate the threat of terrorism altogether. It is likely that Britain will continue to face a significant terrorist threat for the foreseeable future – potentially for decades. It is therefore vitally important that Britain's response is intelligent, proportionate and targeted at the specific ideological nature of Islamist terrorist extremism.

This chapter has sought to explain how Islamist extremist ideologies are a direct affront to the most basic liberal values we hold dear, and to mainstream Islam. We must be unqualified in our assertion of our own liberal values, not least to strengthen the bonds with Britain's mainstream Muslim communities. Divorcing the widespread grievances than exist amongst mainstream Muslim communities from the world of terrorism, blocking the path towards rapid radicalisation, remains our single most important policy objective.

This chapter has set out a number of steps – including the need to abandon any reference to a single British 'Muslim community', the vital importance of intergenerational relationships within Muslim communities, the crucial role of the police in promoting a policy of engagement, the need to boost the training and qualifications of Imams practising in the UK, and the influence of political language – which must be taken if a policy of critical engagement with our Muslim communities is going to be successful.

It has also set out radical proposals for the reorganisation of our security and policing capacity – including the creation of an integrated anti-terror intelligence capacity which covers both foreign and domestic intelligence gathering, a focus on internet-based propaganda, and the creation of a National Counter-Terrorism Service – in order that resources are used in the most effective and targeted way possible. Finally, proposals for incremental changes to the law in order to strengthen our capacity to detain and prosecute terror suspects have been set out in detail.

In short, a policy of critical engagement with our Muslim communities, organisational restructuring of our intelligence and police capacity, and a strengthening of the law to facilitate anti-terror prosecutions, represents a three-pronged approach to the unprecedented terror threat facing the nation today.

In the past, the government has appeared too hasty in side-stepping due process in a rush to meet the new terror threat, whilst overlooking a host of practical reforms which would strengthen Britain's response to terrorism whilst not sacrificing the very liberal principles that terrorists seek to undermine. As the national debate on terrorism matures, our aim should remain steadfast and simple: to protect both our lives and our liberties, and to refuse to accept that one requires the sacrifice of the other.

Notes

1   Melanie Phillips, 'The Londonistan Mindset', *New York Post*, 4 June 2006.
2   Martin Bright, *When Progressives Treat with Reactionaries* (Policy Exchange, London, 2006).
3   See, for instance, Munira Mirza, Abi Senthikimaran, and Zein Ja'far, *Living Apart Together: British Muslims and the Paradox of Multiculturalism* (Policy Exchange, London, 2007).
4   'Internet Jihad: Briefing', *The Economist*, 14 July 2007.
5   Ibid.
6   Ibid.
7   Shamit Saggar, 'The One Per Cent World: Managing the Myth of Muslim Religious Extremism', *Political Quarterly* 77, 3 (2006), pp. 314–27.
8   Rachel Briggs, *Bringing It Home* (Demos, London, 2006).
9   Bob Lambert, 'Reflections on Counter-Terrorism Partnerships in Britain', *Arches* (Cordoba Foundation), Jan–Feb 2007.
10   The public comments of the new Security Minister, Lord West, instantly supporting the off-the-cuff suggestion from the head of ACPO that a limitless period of detention without charge should be introduced with new judicial safeguards (BBC Radio 4's *Today* Programme, 16 July 2007) was a classic example, notwithstanding the new government's stated intention to take a more deliberate, low-key approach to anti-terror proposals.
11   Briggs, *Bringing it Home*.
12   Shiv Malik, 'My brother the bomber', *Prospect*, June 2007.
13   GCHQ's role in signal intelligence is distinct and would therefore remain separate from any new unified structure. The ambiguous division of labour between the Home Secretary and the Foreign Secretary which has arisen as a result of the recent creation of an integrated cabinet committee on security, as well as the potential for turf wars in the as yet unidentified functions of Gordon Brown's proposal for a National Security Council, would also be alleviated with the greater clarity which this proposal would provide.
14   Code for Crown Prosecutors.
15   Serious Organised Crime and Police Act 2005.

Chapter 20

To be a Briton: The Citizen and the State

William Wallace

Liberals are instinctively internationalists and individualists, opposed to the closed communalism that nationalism encourages, with its sharp distinctions between 'us' and 'them', between nationals and foreigners. Nationalism goes with war and mercantilism, and liberalism with peace, free trade, open frontiers and international understanding.

For libertarians, consideration of the relationship between the individual and the state need not extend much further: the state should play a minimal role, interfering as little as possible in individual choices, providing only those elements of security and order that require collective action. Social liberals face a more difficult set of choices. They insist that communities – built on mutual trust and social capital – provide the essential broader framework which individuals need to realise their full potential.

Social liberals need a strong state; and a strong state needs a live political community to underpin it. Political communities, in their turn, rest on shared identities, shared memories and myths. It is a central paradox for social liberalism that the open and liberal international order which we support undermines the coherence of the territorial political communities that we also recognise we need.

Liberty, for social liberals, requires fraternity: not in the sense of blind commitment to group loyalty, but of recognition of common values and common interests. Much as libertarians have wanted to deny it, emotional ties and feelings of mutual commitment – not just of shared interests – hold communities together. People obey the law not simply through rational calculation but because they implicitly recognise that they share in the community that the law protects. If they reject that sense of shared community, they become 'anti-social'. If they identify with an alternative imagined community, they may even be moved to violent action against the society and state within which they live.

For John Stuart Mill, who recognised the importance of the emotions and social ties that his father and Jeremy Bentham had pushed aside, the natural and preferred level of communal solidarity was the local. But he – and all those who have followed him – also recognised the necessary larger context of the national community, which in a stable political society parallels and underpins the state. Law, external security, taxation, and later redistributive taxation, depend upon the territorial state. Locke and Montesquieu depicted the bond between individual and state as a 'social contract', in which property-owners gave their loyalty in return for domestic order and protection from external disorder. But that was not a strong enough bond to hold mass societies together, or to persuade those without property to accept that the legal order the state imposed also benefited them. For the New Liberals, following T. H. Green, the state was a more positive force, which represented shared values – and educated its members to share these values.

The French Revolution had swept Europe's established states away by claiming to represent 'the people' and 'the nation': powerful ideas which mobilised the masses, and even to some extent bound rich and poor together. Liberals have struggled to balance the rational politics of limited government with the emotional politics of national community ever since. Pride in Great Britain moved Joseph Chamberlain from municipal radicalism to Liberal Imperialism. The Boer War split the Liberal Party between 'patriots' and 'pro-Boers', and the war of 1914 split it further. In Germany, Liberals disappointed by the failure of the 1848 'revolution' attempted to ally with nationalism as a mobilising force, and ended up supporting the authoritarian Prussian state.

State, community, welfare, democracy

Democratic government, in which those who control the state are held accountable to the citizens who elect them, operates within the boundaries of an imagined national community; if that community divides or shatters, the state collapses. Anglo-Saxon liberals in the eighteenth century did not believe that all those who lived within those boundaries were entitled to full citizenship rights; that revolutionary idea, bubbling up in the English Civil War and again in the French Revolution, threatened their concept of property and social order. Citizenship for all members of a territorial society was the outcome of nineteenth-century reform and twentieth-century mobilisation for war.

Mass democracy and national welfare emerged together, demanded by the newly enfranchised and pressed forward by the New Liberals of the 1890s and 1900s. Yet a welfare state, with high taxation and significant redistribution, depends far more upon a shared sense of national community than the minimalist state that libertarians prefer. It's rational for the wealthy to hide their wealth in offshore financial centres; their willingness to declare their income, and to pay progressive taxes, depends on acknowledgement of social ties to fellow-citizens less successful than they. The poor in their turn claim entitlements as citizens on the strength of the contributions they (and their parents and grandparents) have made to the common good; their welfare entitlements give them a continuing stake in the established order.

National solidarity, however, depends upon shared memories and myths, shaped for these imagined communities above all through war. The high point of British national solidarity was the experience of the Second World War, which mobilised the entire nation, women as well as men, under rationing imposed on rich as well as poor. It was therefore easy for the 1945 Labour government to maintain high taxes for post-war reconstruction, to introduce a National Health Service, and to expand the social safety nets of pensions and unemployment pay; the shared sense of national community was strong enough to support such redistribution.

Solidarity and diversity, assimilation and loyalty

The long-term success of the liberal international order which Roosevelt's administration designed and post-war American hegemony implemented has, however, undermined the national solidarity that 200 years of war and empire had built up. Sixty years of peace have left faded memories of past wars, and a residual pride in Britain's armed forces, as pale echoes of the solidarity of 1945. The abolition of universal male military service, fifty years ago, weakened the sense of national citizenship as a contract between rights and obligations, and of welfare for the poor as a long-term investment in national security. Open frontiers and the communications revolution (which have brought cheaper and easier mass travel) have transformed the 'national community', as more and more British citizens work and live abroad, and as successive waves of short-term and long-term immigrants have arrived in Britain.

In 1945 there were, it is true, many refugees from the European continent, who had earned their place in the British community by serving in the forces during the war. Second World War memorials nevertheless refer to 'our island race' as a coherent body. A post-war wave of 'displaced persons' from Poland, Czechoslovakia, the Baltic states and Ukraine transferred their loyalties to Britain because it appeared impossible ever to return home. Britain today, in contrast, contains a rising number of people with multiple loyalties, even multiple passports – from bankers in London to taxi-drivers in Sheffield – still closely in touch with their other national communities, often owning property in both countries, travelling between the two regularly and often.

In addition to its Caribbean and South Asian minorities, London has 300,000 French residents and 50,000 Dutch, as well as significant American, German, Nigerian, Ghanaian, Arab, Somali, Russian, Cypriot, Turkish (and Kurdish) communities. In the Midlands and north of England, Afro-Caribbean and South Asian communities plan their retirement 'back home', and marry their daughters to cousins 'from home'. 'Their' High Commissions stir them up on aspects of British foreign and development policy; politicians 'from home' seek their support, and on their fringes criminals 'from home' smuggle drugs, weapons, and even children and young women. Two hundred and fifty thousand British citizens live (and pay taxes) in Spain, though many continue to vote in Britain; as many have second homes in France, while others have retired to Tuscany or Florida. Nicolas Sarkozy came to London in January 2007 to canvass for votes in the French presidential election. British political parties struggle to make contact with registered voters in Andalucia, Gibraltar and Provence.

North American colonists fought their war of independence under the slogan of 'no taxation without representation'. The situation today is far more complex. There are British citizens abroad who pay no national taxes but retain the right to vote in British elections, EU residents in Britain who pay British taxes and can vote in local and European (but not national) elections, tax-paying Americans who have no voting rights, and wealthy 'non-domiciled residents' from more exotic states who pay little or no taxes in return for the benefits of the well-managed state and society in which they live. Priority in social housing goes to large families of recently arrived non-citizens, to the deep resentment of the children of British 'natives' who claim a greater entitlement. Social provision for refugees and asylum-seekers is a sensitive and contested political issue. Welfare, taxation and citizenship, closely linked in the twentieth-century model of the nation-state, have thus begun to separate.

The story of England: who do we think we are?

The United Kingdom was created in 1801 out of the single kingdom of England and (long-conquered) Wales, the Anglo-Scottish union of 1707, and the union of Great Britain and Ireland forced by Irish rebellion and French subversion during the Napoleonic Wars. It was from the outset a multinational state, held together by English domination, Scottish access to English markets and the British Empire, immigration from the other three parts of the union into England, and Scottish and Welsh prosperity in the shared Industrial Revolution. Active policies of assimilation spread English across Wales, the Scottish Highlands and Ireland, suppressing the Gaelic languages. It was bound together, too, by the overlapping narratives of the different Protestant churches, providing language, music and imagery common to middle-class Anglicans, working-class Methodists, Welsh Congregationalists and Scots Presbyterians.

The Catholic religion proved harder for the Protestant English to assimilate or suppress. The First World War reinforced ties between England and Scotland, but provided the chance for the alienated Irish to break away. A century later, the Welsh language is experiencing a remarkable revival, the Scottish National Party rides high in the polls, and the divided loyalties of Northern Ireland are increasingly divorced from the British mainland. Identification with Britain, the multinational state and community which the English created, is weakening. In response to strengthening separate identities in Scotland and Wales, the English flag has become a more popular symbol of group identity, and both the 'British' National Party and the 'UK' Independence Party are acting as channels for English nationalism.

The foreign policy of a democratic state rests not only upon dispassionate calculations of national interests; it is also shaped by self-perceptions of 'national role' and place in the world, of 'natural' friends and enemies, of 'who we think we are'. British identity has been shaped

by repeated conflicts with France, more broadly with (Catholic) continental Europe from the Armada onwards, and in the twentieth century
with a German-dominated European continent. A sense of separation
from the European continent runs through English history and classical
English literature. Gordon Brown, in the 2004 British Council annual
lecture, declared that 'it has been a lack of confidence about what Britain
stands for that has made it difficult for us to feel confident about our relationship with, and our potential role in, Europe'.[1] But his government
has so far made no effort to create a national narrative that might replace
the old story of England standing firm against a hostile continent. The
history taught in English schools offers little on Britain's European context beyond the rise of the Nazis and the Second World War: not a good
foundation for popular understanding of European commitments or of
multilateral cooperation.

The nation we are losing

The British nation rose with the British state: an eighteenth-century
concept that tied England to Scotland, and separated these two
Protestant countries from Catholic France and continental Europe.
Britain was repeatedly at war with France from 1689 to 1815. France was
the dominant power in Europe throughout this period, with a population over twice as large as that of the British Isles. The French monarchy fomented rebellion in Scotland and Ireland, recruited Catholic Irish
regiments into the French army, and trained Catholic priests to preach
their dissident messages to congregations in the Scottish Highlands and
the towns and villages of Ireland. The superiority of the British navy succeeded in capturing most of France's first overseas imperial possessions;
but the French, in return, provided crucial support to Britain's rebellious
American colonists in their fight for independence.

'Time and time again,' Linda Colley writes in the Introduction to
Britons: Forging the Nation, 1707–1837, 'war with France brought Britons,
whether they hailed from Wales or Scotland or England, into confron-
tation with an obviously hostile Other and encouraged them to define
themselves collectively against it. They defined themselves as Protestants
struggling for survival against the world's foremost Catholic power.'[2]
Adopting Benedict Anderson's image of a nation as an imagined community that transmits memories and myths from one generation to another,[3]

she adds that '*we can plausibly regard Great Britain as an invented nation superimposed, if only for a while, on to much older alignments and loyalties*',[4] (emphasis added) held together by the common experience of war, the acquisition of empire which the Anglo-French wars provided, and the symbols and myths that gathered around them: the monarchy, the army and navy, the supremacy of the Westminster Parliament.

The imagery of a free Britain against an authoritarian France was built into the developing British state, from its patriotic songs to its capital city and its palaces. London has Trafalgar Square and Waterloo Station. The Queen at Westminster processes through the Royal Gallery to open her Parliament past heroic depictions of these two battles. When in the twentieth century the threat of a rising Germany came to displace France, the imagery of a threatening continent was generalised further. Paul Gallico's classic *The Snow Goose*, one of the most familiar patriotic stories of the Second World War, identifies the Nazis with the Normans, and the English with the Saxons, resisting yet again the alien threat from across the Channel in defence of their ancient freedoms. Patriotic Englishmen were unsurprised by the fall of France in 1940; as Alderman Roberts told his daughter (the future Margaret Thatcher), Catholic France was rotten to the core.[5]

Britons, in this imagined self-image, were free, while those who lived on the continent were unfree; the Royal Navy ensured that 'Britons never shall be slaves'. Laws, not an arbitrary state, governed Britain. The patriotic song which during the 1745 Jacobite rebellion was taken up in London theatres, later to become the 'national' anthem, declared conditional support for Protestant monarchy: 'may he defend our laws, and ever give us cause to sing with heart and voice' – but not if the King ceased to defend the laws, and slipped back (like James II and the Stuart pretenders) to imitating the absolute monarchy of Versailles.

Yet there was no concept of British citizenship as providing political rights. The beef-eating Britons were free because they had freedom *from* religious persecution and arbitrary government, allowing them to pursue their commercial and personal interests; the vast majority of them lacked the freedom *to* take a more active part in electoral politics than rioting. Citizenship in France swept in with the *levée en masse* which filled the revolutionary armies; Britain faced the threat of French invasion, in 1803, by raising only regiments of volunteers (though naval press gangs imposed an arbitrary form of compulsory service). The idea that every British subject had the right to take part in the political life of the nation and state came only with the mass mobilisation of labour through the industrial unions, and with the prudent realisation that Britain would need mass armies of fit and loyal men to meet the military challenge of Germany – and to defeat the popular challenge of socialism. Mobilisation of women, during the First World War, made an unanswerable case for extending political rights to them, in return for the obligations to the security of the state they had undertaken. The British state granted political rights to its citizens reluctantly; but the national myth asserted that they were already free.

There was no legal definition of British citizenship until the 1981 Commonwealth Immigration Act; and that focused on exclusion rather than inclusion. Sephardic Jews established synagogues in London from the mid-seventeenth century, living in Britain but holding their community somewhat apart from Protestant English culture. Huguenot refugees had poured into England after 1685, settling (like the Jews and like later refugee and immigrant waves) in Spitalfields and across East London, and rapidly assimilating into English life. English courts outlawed slavery on British soil, so making the black communities in British cities and seaports British subjects. Protestant dissenters were excluded from political life (and from England's two universities) until the nineteenth century; Catholic emancipation was reluctantly granted in 1829; the Jewish Relief Act, which allowed Jews to take the oath to sit in Parliament according to their own religion, was not passed until 1858. Each extension of political rights came as a response to particular campaigns; at no point was an explicit doctrine of the rights and duties of citizenship formulated. Pragmatism, after all, was at the heart of the English tradition; grand declarations on 'the rights of man' were French.

Part of the English/British myth was that we did not need a written constitution, because we had been free ever since the Saxons, with their largely unwritten common laws and their councils to advise their kings, had settled across Britain. Less fortunate countries needed their fragile rights written down, to protect against a return to their natural authoritarianism. There were, of course, some constituent documents – Magna Carta, the 1689 Bill of Rights – but it was the flow of British tradition, encapsulated in statute and common law and in evolving constitutional conventions, that, for Edmund Burke and for so many others, constituted Britain's 'political genius'. What held all this in place was the acceptance by Britain's polit- ical class – the landed gentry and the politically responsible aristocracy – that limited government was held in place by gentlemanly self-restraint and political compromise. The great nineteenth-century Prime Minister and Tory leader the Marquis of Salisbury set out in successive speeches his understanding of this necessary compromise between the old political class and the rising representatives of the enfranchised masses; his grand- son's negotiation of the 'Salisbury-Addison Convention' developed these unwritten rules further. Such myths still underpin assumptions about the structure of the British state. The opening paragraph of the Command Paper on Lords Reform, published in February 2007, states that the British Parliament is directly descended, through centuries of adaptation, from the Anglo-Saxon Witan.

The end of the Napoleonic Wars, fought across several continents from the Battle of the Nile to naval skirmishes in the West Indies, left Britain dominant outside Europe, and France still the leading continen- tal power. Twenty-five years of war with a continent that the British Navy blockaded and the French controlled turned British society away; the wealthy and the intellectuals no longer travelled on 'grand tours', and their families discovered the Lake District and the Scottish Highlands as substitutes for the romantic French and Swiss Alps. Detachment from the continent allowed the British to avoid military conscription, while France, Prussia (and Prussian Germany) mobilised their mass troops. In 1914, and again in 1939, we sent a 'British Expeditionary Force' across the Channel, using the same terminology as previous expeditionary forces sent to the Sudan and Afghanistan.

In 1954, after much anxious debate within the government and the General Staff, the UK at last accepted a 'continental commitment', agree- ing under the Western European Union Treaty to maintain six divi- sions in Germany so long as the Soviet threat remained – though these were rapidly reduced to four after the 1957 defence review. One German minister remarked in the mid-1980s, when the 'British Army of the Rhine' had been in Germany for over a generation, that it was still encamped on the north German plain as if it were on the north Indian plain, with as little contact with the locals as possible. When President Mitterrand visited French forces in Germany he took part in joint military parades and ceremonies, out of which grew in time the Franco-German Brigade and then the Euro-corps. When Margaret Thatcher went to Germany she preferred to be photographed with 'our boys', without a German politician or soldier in sight.

One other deeply ingrained image of England contrasted with the continent runs through English literature and national tradition: of England (and the Anglo-Saxon world) as representing progress and modernity, with the continent symbolising decline and decay. For those who were teaching the Whig interpretation of history in the mid-nineteenth century, when Britain was 'the workshop of the world' and British government and administration newly reformed, this seemed self-evident. (Charles Kingsley, who was Cambridge University's first professor of modern history from 1860–69, wrote these images into books that children grew up with, from then until the 1960s: *Westward Ho!*, *Hereward the Wake*, *The Water Babies*.)

By the time that J. R. Seeley published his best-selling classic *The Expansion of England*, in 1883, German technological progress, industrial, military and administrative organisation, represented a painful challenge to the English sense of superiority. The demonisation of Germany between 1914 and 1918, and again from 1939 on, and the destruction of the German economy, restored the established English self-image. America, Britain's other industrial and intellectual challenger, could be coopted into the rising image of an Anglo-Saxon world, in which the English-speaking peoples and their countries represented the future and the European continent the past. That comfortable myth still remains embedded in the British conventional wisdom. Anglo-Saxon economists cannot explain the continuing resilience of the German economy, which does not follow the rules that they teach; Gordon Brown contrasts the inward-looking continent with globally oriented Britain, sweeping aside figures that show German trade with China and South America, and investment in their economies, as far ahead of the UK. British ministers habitually travel to North America in search of lessons for social and economic innovation; they travel across the Channel not to learn, but to preach.

Footnotes to Churchill

The high point of national community, of pride in the British state and popular identification with it, came in and immediately after the Second

World War. The Edwardian period, it is true, had fostered mass nationalism, sufficiently successfully for working-class men to volunteer en masse after war broke out in 1914. Lloyd George's reforms had included the welfare of the working poor within the accepted responsibilities of the British state; the Labour Representation Committee had successfully brought trade-union MPs into the conventions and institutions of the political class. The burial of the Unknown Warrior in Westminster Abbey, 'among the kings' as it says on the tomb, marked a symbolic acceptance that all British subjects could claim the same rights and privileges in return for the responsibilities they shouldered. Yet before the war the Conservative Party and the House of Lords had bitterly resisted Lloyd George's 'People's Budget', and after the war militant trade unionists came close to violence against state authorities on repeated occasions between 1919 and 1926.

The 1939–45 conflict was much more 'the people's war,' in which almost the whole country was mobilised, and much of the country – under bombing raids as well as under rationing – shared in the suffering. The turning point in the British narrative of the conflict came with the Battle of Britain, in which Britain stood alone against the threatening continent – fighter pilots and their supporting maintenance crews, women interpreting radar signals and manning searchlight batteries, ARP wardens and the WVS, all contributing to the common cause – and survived. (The overwhelming contribution that others made to later victory – Americans and Russians above all, but also Indians, Poles, East and West Africans and many others – is thus set in context by making the fighting over England in 1940 the fulcrum of the war.) The monarchy, a unifying symbol under Queen Victoria but slipping towards disrespect between the wars, was triumphantly re-legitimised by a king and queen who stayed in London during the bombing, and a daughter who maintained military vehicles. Most evocatively, the country had a Prime Minister who was both a historian and an orator, who conjured up the myths of national character and national history in Shakespearean imagery.

After the war, while out of office, Churchill turned his talents to reshaping the national myth, publishing in 1954 a two-volume history of *The English-Speaking Peoples* that brought the Whig interpretation of history up to date, linked Britain and North America together as the enlightened democracies of the world, and separated them from the unenlightened continent that they had – twice within less than thirty years – saved from dictatorship. Better than most others, Churchill understood how wide was the gap between image and reality in what he was portraying. Behind his story of the Anglo-Saxons and the colonial peoples they had enlightened, with Britain and the United States as partners at the centre of this world-wide web, lay British dependence on the US – economic, political, military – and a sharply contested process of decolonisation in Asia and Africa. But in the early 1950s, with British troops gallantly fighting in Korea (with Australians and Canadians, in the UN's Commonwealth Division) and holding back communist insurgency in Malaya, with post-war economic recovery, new roads and new housing, and with the Conservative government accepting and adopting Labour's social-welfare innovations, it was plausible enough. The coronation of Queen Elizabeth II in 1953 brilliantly staged the British myth of long continuity and confident adaptation. The 'new Elizabethan age' was presented as a blend of technological advance and stable democracy, with the UK leading both 'the British Commonwealth and Empire' and the fragile but recovering democracies of Western Europe in a natural partnership with the United States.

Much of this fell apart during the fifteen years that followed. The Suez intervention exposed the weaknesses of Britain's economy and military forces, and the depth of British dependence on American support to maintain its pretensions to world-power status. The scramble towards decolonisation in Africa and South-East Asia that followed transformed the Commonwealth from an asset to a burden, with the new leaders of the 'multicultural Commonwealth' attacking British ministers for their inaction on white rule in Central and South Africa. The people of the British Commonwealth were also arriving in Britain in rising numbers, as cheap air travel shrank distances. The refusal of India and Pakistan to share responsibility for accepting the Asians expelled from East Africa, in 1968–69, left the government facing the prospect of a succession of refugees from lost empire, clutching their British passports.

The German economy passed the British, in terms of size and dynamic growth, in 1958; the French economy followed in the early 1960s. The de Havilland Comet, suffering from metal fatigue, lost out to the Boeing 707, while successive military aircraft and missile projects fell short of expectations and ran over budget. The UK was forced to depend on the Americans to supply the missiles for its 'independent' nuclear deterrent, and on cooperation with the French for its proposed supersonic airliner. Successive governments hesitated over cooperation with their integrating neighbours on the European continent, applying half-heartedly and late to join the European Economic Community, and succeeding only at the third attempt.

Furthermore, the deferential culture, high church attendance and social cohesion that marked British society in the 1950s broke down as the 1960s progressed. Satirists poked fun at politicians, judges and bishops. Rehousing schemes broke up old communities. Affluence, and the accumulation of possessions, provided alternative attractions to Sunday School outings and trade-union meetings. The younger generation had at best a dim memory of war and of post-war deprivation, and – after the phasing out of National Service between 1958 and 1960 – no common experience of enforced responsibilities to the state. University expansion was raising a confidently critical group of young professionals. Intellectual radicals in old and new universities unpicked the story of England that their predecessors had taught, leaving history teachers, without a narrative to pass on to their students, to focus on 'skills' and multiple interpretations instead.

After 1979 Margaret Thatcher wanted to return Britain to the moral and historical certainties of the lost 1950s – her moral golden age. She even set up, in 1989, a working party on history in the (English) National Curriculum, with the clear intention of reconstructing a narrative of the story of Britain for state schools to teach. The working party, however, came up with conclusions she rejected. It pointed out that English schools had never taught British history, and that a coherent narrative of that history required a wider European context, since explaining the relationship between the three kingdoms of England, Scotland and Ireland necessarily brought in France, the Netherlands, Scandinavia, Germany and Spain. After a visit to schools in Birmingham, the chair of the working group also recommended that a new national history should aim to explain to every child in an English school how they came to be British, thus including the conquest of India, the slave trade and the opium wars. The final report was published after six months' delay, and never implemented.

So we are left with a discredited narrative of national history, appropriate to a society and culture that dissolved 30–40 years ago, and without any consensus on an alternative. Timothy Garton Ash has described attempts to reshape British foreign policy and national symbols over the past half-century as 'footnotes to Churchill', without any political or intellectual leader having the courage to propose a radical reformulation. The most visible annual ceremony of national solidarity is Remembrance Sunday, a British occasion little changed since the 1940s, in which the High Commissioners of Commonwealth countries play marginal roles and the contributions of other peoples to the common victory is marked only by small groups of elderly Poles and US Marines at the very end of the march-past of veterans. Gordon Brown's suggestion that we should adopt a second national memorial day, to be called 'Veterans' Day', would reinforce this focus on past military sacrifice as the unifying national symbol.

Right-wing historians, much favoured by Conrad Black and the Murdoch press, have attempted to reinforce the cult of Churchill and the British Empire; Andrew Roberts has even published an updated history of the English-speaking peoples. Tony Blair's incoming government attempted instead to sideline traditional images of Britain, focusing relentlessly on 'modernisation', even flirting with rebranding 'Cool Britannia'. The Murdoch press disliked, and diminished, the monarchy. The Thatcher government did introduce the concept of 'active citizenship', it is true; but its interpretation of the term emphasised less dependence on state welfare and a greater role for non-governmental organisations, rather than any greater engagement in political life. Her centralisation of government, at the expense of local democracy, made political decisions more remote from ordinary citizens.

Do we need to know who we are?

The nation-state is past its prime. Economic globalisation, instant cross-border communication and mass migration all act to dissolve coherent national communities and to weaken the authority of the states that control them. Successful global citizens live and work across state boundaries, little constrained by parochial loyalties or inherited traditions. Economic liberals happily predict the demise of the nation-state model, with its welfare provision and economic regulation, to be replaced by a less constraining 'market state'. 'The fundamental idea of the market state', Philip Bobbitt writes in *The Shield of Achilles*, is 'that equality means treating those equally endowed in an equal way … a conception quite different from the egalitarianism of the nation-state, where equality meant treating all citizens equally because citizenship was granted equally to all'. Bobbitt, one of the many Americans who have made the round of Westminster and Whitehall in recent years, sees the United States as the model for the future, and European states as the discredited model of the past. He notes that the United States more easily welcomes immigrants as citizens, on the basis of a social contract that includes little welfare and a strong emphasis on opportunity for all. He glosses over, however, the strong and exclusive national myth that instead holds the US together, the language and patriotic symbols to which immigrants are expected to assimilate. Without the patriotism that holds together national communities within secure and stable states, and the market regulation that those states provide, economic liberalism would slip into anarchy.

It matters that Britain rediscovers a sense of shared community, for several reasons: legitimacy, foreign policy, taxation, redistribution, order and social cohesion. The rich and successful are confident enough to live across national boundaries; the poor and less self-confident need a sense of place and of communal identity to provide their lives with social meaning. Without a sense of shared citizenship within an inclusive national community, acceptance of government and its laws as 'representative' breaks down. If the world of Westminster and Whitehall draws its self-legitimation from a view of British constitutional tradition of which the mass of the population are unaware, it becomes increasingly remote from those it claims to govern. The contemporary debate about constitutional reform in Britain uncomfortably balances between adherence to the myths of parliamentary supremacy, monarchical prerogative and ancient liberties and a realisation that these neither resonate with most voters nor serve the purposes of effective governance in an increasingly complex society and economy.

In the day-to-day conduct of international policy, British interests intertwine ever more closely with our European neighbours. On climate change, the densely populated countries of Western Europe share interests and assumptions that contrast with those that appeal in the wide open spaces of North America. Cross-border policing has proved far easier to operate on mutually agreed rules within Western Europe than across the Atlantic. Commitment to multilateral cooperation is stronger among European governments than in Washington. But the echoes of Churchill that resonate through British foreign policy and across the Atlantic hold European cooperation back, and incline successive governments and prime ministers to follow Washington rather than negotiate common European action. The British public have become sceptical and suspicious about European engagement, and are now becoming disillusioned with the transatlantic 'special relationship'. We need a new narrative of Britain's place in the world and international role in order to align our foreign policy more closely with our underlying interests.

Corporate taxation is now escaping the state, taking refuge in offshore financial centres. Personal taxation for the rich is following. London's wealthiest stratum includes many 'non-residents', both British and non-British, who benefit from the legal and social order the United Kingdom provides without making an equitable contribution in return. Rich British feel far less obligation than their parents and grandparents to contribute to the common good; acceptable top tax rates have fallen, while accountants assist top earners in devising tax-avoidance schemes. The well-to-do increasingly resent their taxes being spent on what they see as the undeserving under-class, let alone on newly arrived asylum-seekers or immigrant families. The scale of financial transfers between southern England and the north, and between England and Scotland, have become contested questions. Redistribution becomes harder to justify as the sense of shared community weakens.

Recognition of common loyalties and common interests also matters for the 'undeserving under-class' and those recently arrived. Support for the BNP derives partly from the sense that the political classes no longer share the same values as the native working class; that 'they' have forgotten what 'we' think Britain (or England) stands for. Second- and third-generation immigrants, uncertain of their identity and loyalties, cannot easily identify with a society and state that is itself confused about what values and symbols it wants to convey. The young Disraeli warned that a state that was divided into 'two nations' of rich and poor would risk social breakdown – and therefore supported the improvement of the working classes. Policies both of social inclusion and of 'national' education are needed, for similar reasons, now.

How do we build British citizenship?

Recognition that Britain needs to recreate a national narrative, a sense of a community of shared values, now spreads across the political spectrum, from David Cameron to Gordon Brown, and from David Starkey to Tristram Hunt. A loosely defined agenda is emerging from political speeches and think-tank reports: to reshape the teaching of history, to teach 'citizenship' both to new citizens and to schoolchildren, perhaps even to introduce some form of 'national' service for young people. Yet there is little understanding of how radical an agenda is needed if an effective national community is to be recreated. We cannot rebuild on the old symbols and myths, as Margaret Thatcher attempted to do; we have to *define* citizenship, and British values, and political and civil rights and obligations, and the underlying principles of our unwritten constitution. To do this successfully, moreover, we need to build a cross-party national consensus; otherwise the concept of national community will become a focus for political disunity.

The Labour government introduced a new citizenship curriculum in 1998. But the absence of any accompanying reconsideration of what 'citizenship' means left teachers confused; most lessons on citizenship have so far been included with classes on drugs, personal health, and social and ethnic diversity. Further centralisation, and post-2001 reductions in Britain's traditional liberties, have made it more difficult to teach the 'political literacy' the Crick Report prescribed; Tony Blair as Prime Minister questioned many of the principles of the unwritten British constitution – a limited state, local self-government, habeas corpus, trial by jury, assumption of innocence until proven guilty. Labour's new citizenship ceremony suffers from similar limitations in its attempt to adapt outdated concepts of Britain to new requirements. New Britons pledge allegiance to the Queen, but not to British values, and are then invited to sing a national anthem which mentions neither Britain nor liberty nor democracy.

We need, therefore, to reconsider not only the teaching of history and of school civics, but also a much wider agenda: the core values that Britons from diverse backgrounds are expected to share, the British 'constitutional settlement', the symbols and ceremonies that constitute and transmit national memory, the monarchy. Political values cannot be taught persuasively, furthermore, unless the state is seen to embody them, through the actions of its government, the workings of its parliament and local authorities, and the procedures of its courts. Successive reports on citizenship education in schools have urged that participation in school councils will help teenagers to understand 'the practice of citizenship'. But if they emerge from school into a society in which their lives are governed by centrally imposed targets and remote administrative agencies, they will – rightly – conclude that citizenship is a fraudulent concept.

British values *are* – or were – liberal values. The national debate we now need on those values would force the other parties to address the gap between their declared principles and their policies. Gordon Brown declared in his 2006 Hugo Young lecture, for example, that 'our long-held commitment to liberty demands … that we break up any centralised institutions that are too remote and insensitive, devolving and decen-tralising power'[6] – a demand that ten years of Labour government has failed to address. Political citizenship can only be exercised through democratic institutions, starting with each local community. It means much more than the 'active citizenship' that New Labour ministers have promoted, which encouraged participation in voluntary organisations and unpaid work while removing more and more areas of government – schools, social welfare, primary health provision, planning, transport – from local accountability. The sharpness of the contrast between voter turnout in recent national elections in Britain and France indicates the greater degree of disillusion with political participation here; but in the Nordic countries the turnout in *local* elections is often higher than in national elections in the UK.

A new constitutional settlement in Britain must therefore strengthen political citizenship against our over-centralised, executive-dominated state. Any consensual new narrative of British history would focus on the development of an open and inclusive society within the British Isles, the many obstacles in the path of that development, and the uncompleted agenda of building a democratic constitution with full rights for every citizen. The reshaping of national symbols and ceremonies may prove a more delicate task, including redefinition of the role of monarchy as a unifying symbol, while removing the 'prerogative' powers that prime ministers now wield on the monarch's behalf. It will not be easy to reach a consensus; but the direction of change would most probably be towards reasserting the liberal tradition.

The coherence the British nation achieved under the pressures of war with France, 200 years ago, has loosened after sixty years of peace and rising international integration. The sense of national community still needed to support democratic government and redistributive welfare can be maintained only by a transmitted commitment to shared institutions and values, rooted in shared understandings of their origins and rationale. Those shared institutions, values and understandings are at present confused, even contested. It is a Liberal task to clarify them.

Notes

1   Available at http://www.hm-treasury.gov.uk/newsroom_and_speeches/press/2004/ press_63_04.cfm.
2   Linda Colley, *Britons: Forging the Nation, 1707–1837* (Yale University Press, 1992), p. 5.
3   Benedict Anderson, *Imagined Communities* (Verso, London, 1983).
4   Colley, *Britons: Forging the Nation, 1707–1837*, p. 5.
5   Cited in Hugo Young, *This Blessed Plot: Britain and Europe from Churchill to Blair* (Macmillan, London, 1998), p. 307; his precise description of France was 'corrupt from top to bottom'.
6   Available at http://www.hm-treasury.gov.uk/newsroom_and_speeches/press/2006/ press_72_06.cfm.

Chapter 21

A Rational Defence Policy

Tim Garden

The evolving international system

All governments claim that the security of their citizens is a prime responsibility of the state. Yet defence, foreign policy and intelligence must all fight for their resources against many other competing domestic concerns. The difficulties of producing a coherent defence policy have increased in recent years. In a time of publicly recognised state-based threat, most recently during the Cold War, there was cross-party consensus on the need for appropriate investment in defence. With the end of the Soviet threat, the priorities for security have become more uncertain. Many of the potential threats to state security no longer come from other states. The 'enemy' is more amorphous and difficult to define. This has been true for the international institutions as well as at the national level, and means that there is a need to reassess how far state-based policies are appropriate. A crucial question is this: how far can we organise our defence as a nation-state when so few of the threats we face come from other states?

The obvious alternative to a defence policy solely organised by nation-states is collective security, whether through global institutions or regional security arrangements. Ever since the end of the First World War, the UK has been notionally committed to global collective security, first through the League of Nations and then the United Nations. But the record of the UN in promoting stability and reducing conflict around the world since the end of the Cold War has been mixed. For some states, particularly the United States, this has caused a move away from reliance on global UN-based solutions, first towards regionalism, but more recently towards unilateralism and reassertion of the authority of nation-states. The 1999 crisis in Kosovo saw the members of NATO willing to undertake a military intervention in a sovereign state for humanitarian reasons without UN approval. NATO has subsequently expanded its area of interest beyond its treaty boundaries, and the strains within the organisation have been severe, particularly over Iraq and Afghanistan. Progress in the development of a Common Foreign and Security Policy (CFSP) within the EU has been halting and has also been affected by recent conflict experience.

In the last decade, the New Labour government has been more will-ing to use military force for interventions than any post-war British administration. While keen to obtain the legal cover of UN author-ity, it has shown a preparedness to operate without clear internation-al approval. This has been as the loyal ally of the United States. The Conservative Party has been even more supportive of the US approach to international security. While it also extols the virtues of NATO, this is often only to enjoin the organisation's European members to fall in with US wishes.

Liberal Democrats have argued strongly that the emerging security problems need to be dealt with by more effective international organisa-tions instead of unilateralism on the part of nation-states. In particu-lar, the United Nations is the appropriate forum for conflict prevention, humanitarian action and stabilisation. However, recognising the limi-tations of the P5 veto, Liberal Democrats supported the intervention in Kosovo to prevent a humanitarian disaster, given that the democracies of NATO were all prepared to undertake such a mission. The intervention in Iraq was a different matter, where divisions among Western demo-cracies were very apparent, and there was no UN authority for military action.

We have also argued for much greater development of the military and foreign policy security aspect of the European Union. The new enlarged EU must be able to contribute to international security as a major global player. Uniquely, it is able to bring together the economic, political, diplomatic and military aspects of conflict prevention. We supported the early moves by Tony Blair to speed up development of a European defence identity , but regret that the adventure in Iraq has made this much more difficult. The Conservatives have strongly opposed all development of greater EU cooperation on defence matters. Thus in the defence context, reinventing the state primarily means developing greater collaboration between nation-states.

The Liberal Democrat approach

For a rational Liberal Democrat defence policy, we must first consider our foreign and security policy priorities, and then look at whether the consequent costs are affordable. These costs extend beyond the defence budget into diplomacy, overseas aid and non-military security areas. If the prospective costs are unaffordable then we need to consider why this is so, and explore different ways of meeting our essential security needs. Once the essential structure of the armed forces is determined, they must be funded in a manner which can sustain their capability over time, and give an appropriate quality of life for the members of the three armed services.

All governments have a primary responsibility to provide for the defence of British national territory and the security of our citizens, and also for that of UK dependent territories. We recognise and welcome our various responsibilities to the United Nations, to the European Union and as a member of the NATO alliance. We also have special interests in the prosperity of other members of the Commonwealth. We believe in promoting international law, good governance and stability. We have an obligation to counter the abuse of human rights whether it occurs at home or abroad. We see a need to help any human being in danger or distress, whether the cause is man-made or natural.

In furthering these aims, we recognise that the military may often have a role to play. However, there is little evidence to show that military interventions can produce rapid, low-cost, effective transitions to better governance. The Balkans have shown how long it can take to promote democracy even in Europe's backyard, particularly when there are deep ethnic divisions. Far more successful have been the transitions in central and eastern Europe, where economic and political development have led the way. The military played an important, but non interventionist role, through the 'Partnership for Peace' arrangements in NATO. However, the ultimate success was achieved through the changes required to qualify for EU membership.

Nevertheless, when we look at post-Cold-War military interventions using British forces, Liberal Democrats have supported all of them, with the exception of Iraq in 2003. We have also lamented the lack of more effective military action in several African conflicts. Nor can we argue that the current problems in Iraq should now be ignored. While we would not have intervened in 2003, the British government of the day did; and this leaves any future government with a responsibility to the people of Iraq. Following major natural disasters such as the tsunami of 2005, or the Pakistan earthquake the following year, we also expect the British military to be able to offer prompt and sustained specialist help.

In constructing a coherent defence policy, we must consider how we handle the dilemma that we want to meet commitments that are not greatly different from those currently causing the British military over-stretch, and also solve a declining capability problem caused by ever-increasing defence costs.

Future risks and threats

In planning for the future, some broad assumptions need to be made about the medium- to long-term global security environment, and how it may generate risks and threats to UK and wider interests. We can be fairly certain that climate change will have increasingly serious environ-mental consequences, and that this could lead to more conflict. Energy security may also be a growing security concern, and may also have led to wider availability of nuclear material. Populations will continue to increase for much of the twenty-first century, with India overtaking China, but Europe in decline. The future of Russian democracy is also a security factor which is of importance. What this means for balance of powers is conjecture, but is likely to mean a very different kind of world. It is impossible to discount the re-emergence of more traditional territo-rial threats in the longer term, although a strengthened European Union could do much to counter such risks to its members.

The terrorist attacks of 9/11 in America, and the subsequent Madrid and London bombings, are central to current security thinking. Yet the numbers who have died in these events are, relative to traditional conflicts, small. However, events in Iraq have shown how unfettered ter-rorism, coupled with extreme violence, can grow to levels that are more normally associated with war. Future developments in Iraq, Israel, Iran, Palestine, Lebanon, Afghanistan and Pakistan over the coming years will have profound implications for the wider region and beyond in terms of political Islam and religious extremism. Other parts of the world in Africa and Asia are also vulnerable. There are scenarios which forecast the spread of endemic terrorist violence into Europe.

In this catalogue of security concerns for the future, the spread of nuclear weapons adds a further dimension. The states currently with a known nuclear weapon capability are China, France, India, Israel, Pakistan, Russia, UK and US; North Korea appears to have demonstrated a rudimentary nuclear capability. Some of these capabilities affect regional stability. Israel's neighbours are concerned to be threatened by nuclear capability without their own ability to deter. This gives a strategic rationale for Iran, Syria, Saudi Arabia and Egypt to pursue such capabilities, as Iraq and Libya have done in the past. Similarly, we can see the effect of the concerns raised by the India–Pakistan–China nuclear weaponry on each other, and on neighbours. A North Korean nuclear capability has implications not just for South Korea, but also for Japan and beyond. Nuclear proliferation remains, therefore, a major future security concern.

Natural catastrophes are also presenting challenges to governments. They have much in common with the man-made problems which stem from conflict. As climate change increases the intensity and frequency of some environmental disasters, governments will be under pressure to provide more reliable responses than the current ad hoc arrangements. Emergency on-call responses are likely to continue to depend on military capabilities.

Security policy priorities

This analysis of future security challenges does not mean that armed forces are necessarily the optimum answer to any threat. Nevertheless, it is important to list our security policy priorities to determine how defence policy fits into the wider security picture. In broad terms, they are threefold:

1. Defence of United Kingdom territory and its citizens;
2. Contributing to the enforcement of international law;
3. Contributing to humanitarian relief.

Of these, the first is an absolute requirement of government, while the second and third will always be contributions on a scale which reflects available resources. In the days of the Cold War, the provision for the defence of the UK was large enough that other calls on defence capabilities could be provided with little difficulty. The problem today is that, given the much lower immediate threat to the UK, provision for the enforcement of international law and humanitarian relief become the more significant force-size drivers. Yet the most expensive equipment is primarily related to the need to preserve a capability for high-intensity war-fighting, even though this is rarely needed.

This effect is also seen when defence is compared to the budgets for the other two main agencies for influence abroad. By far the largest share of resources (2.3 per cent of GDP) goes to Defence to fund the Army, Royal Navy and Royal Air Force. International Development has yet to meet the UN target of 0.7 per cent of GNP. Diplomacy, through the FCO, is smaller still. In resource terms, the MoD:DfID:FCO budgets are in the ratios 32:5:2.

The rational approach

The major problem with constructing any rational structure for military capabilities is that it is always a work in progress. The planners in the Ministry of Defence know that a more appropriate assembly of forces might be designed if they could start with a blank sheet of paper and be given unlimited time and resources to tailor the capabilities to foreign and security policy needs. In the real world, most of the armed forces depend on people and equipment that were recruited and procured in the distant past. A decision to reduce recruiting of sailors in the early 1990s is now, fifteen years later, giving rise to a critical shortage of experienced nuclear watch-keepers. The RAF is just taking delivery of Eurofighter/ Typhoon, an aircraft that was conceived in the depths of the Cold War. Despite best efforts, procurement timescales mean that much equipment will be in service twenty, thirty or forty years after it was first conceived. Nor can experienced soldiers, sailors or airmen be created in an instant; they also take decades to develop and train.

Yet if we are to have military forces, defence planners must make decisions about future needs as best they can. This was perhaps more straightforward in the long stasis of the Cold War. The threat from the Soviet Union and the Warsaw Pact was agreed by NATO member states. It could be quantified, and logical pseudo-scientific arguments were deployed to justify particular defensive counter-capabilities in terms of quantity and quality needed. Yet given that NATO strategy ulti- mately relied on maintaining the credibility of nuclear deterrence, the conventional capabilities could safely vary over a considerable range of effectiveness. The threat was also well understood by the British public, and underpinned the willingness of successive governments to support defence expenditure at levels in excess of 5 per cent of GDP.

Since the end of the Cold War, defence planners have had to build their future structures on uncertain scenarios. There is now no prospect of a direct threat of military action against the United Kingdom. Britain engages in 'wars of choice' under different international banners. Workers in the Ministry of Defence thread their identity cards with lanyards bearing the slogan 'Force for Good'. Yet in the last fifteen years, British forces have conducted two major high-intensity campaigns using land, sea and air capabilities. Both were against Iraq; the first, in 1991, under UN authority to free Kuwait; and the second, in 2003, under US leadership to counter an illusory nuclear, biological and chemical threat. In 1999, the RAF contributed to an intense air campaign for humanitarian reasons in Kosovo, and that was followed by a peacekeeping operation to add to the other such commitments in the Balkans. Smaller, but nonetheless challenging, peacekeeping actions have included East Timor and Sierra Leone. While the immediate US response to 9/11 required little British assistance beyond some air support for the attacks on Afghanistan, the subsequent reconstruction project has involved an increasing commitment of UK forces in a very hostile environment. Nor has the situation in Iraq become any easier as stabilisation and reconstruction efforts stall. To all of this must be added a continuing defensive presence in the Falkand Islands, which has now been maintained for a quarter of a century since the original conflict. Only in Northern Ireland has there been the prospect of political success leading to disengagement of military forces.

In an ideal world, the tasks required would determine the capabilities needed, which in turn would be provided in the most cost-effective manner. Yet this is not the way defence policy is determined. In time of low threat to national survival, defence is treated like any other public-sector activity. It must fight the Whitehall battle for funds. It has few friends in Parliament beyond those with industrial constituency interests or those with a military background. After so many major procurement disasters, the MoD is seen as profligate with public money. When it comes to reducing costs, it is more vulnerable than other sectors in that the armed services have no trade union to make a fuss; and they also have an astonishing history of success in action however parlous their funding.

Yet the defence budget is subject to similar cost problems as affect other public-sector areas. The armed forces are a labour-intensive activity. Their staff costs must keep pace with growth in the economy. Pay is set by the Armed Forces Pay Review Body using civilian comparators with an additional percentage, known as the X-factor, for the extra dimension of risk in service life. Therefore, if average national pay rates increase faster than inflation, as they do when the economy is growing, so the pay bill for the military will also grow at a rate higher than domestic inflation. The commercial approach of balancing the books through greater productivity is not easily achieved by the armed forces, particularly when they are used on manpower-intensive peacekeeping, stabilisation and reconstruction operations. On top of these personnel costs is the need to address a large number of long-standing welfare, housing and quality-of-life issues for people in the services.

Rising salaries are not the most crippling aspect of the defence budget. The equipment budget suffers to an even greater extent from cost inflation. Price changes of defence equipment are more complicated to analyse than the rise in manpower costs. The life expectancy of a particular item is often a matter of choice, and may itself be determined by budgetary pressures. Some equipments may cost very much more than their predecessors, but fewer of them may be required to do the task. For example, each Lancaster bomber in 1945 cost some £45,000, or about £1 million at current prices. The Tornado bomber is its lineal successor, carrying a similar bomb load over similar distances. When the Tornado came into service in 1980, it cost the same as twenty Lancasters in real terms. Subsequently, the Tornado underwent a mid-life update to extend its time in service, which cost another £10m per aircraft. Each generation of combat aircraft has been significantly more expensive in real terms than the one it replaced. Each Eurofighter costs around £60m.

Defence programmers have had to balance their budgets by reducing the fleet size with each new generation of equipment. This causes an uncomfortable rise in the relative support costs of fleets, as smaller frontlines still require the full range of maintenance, logistic and training infrastructure to sustain them. Planners use a similar technique for weapon stockpiles. Weapon costs show a high cost rise with each new generation. There is a temptation to keep the old stock and bring in the new weapon more slowly. We see this effect in the current unwillingness of the MoD to phase out its stock of cluster munitions early. In the case of both weapons and platforms, the reducing numbers of units procured further forces the unit price higher still as research and development costs have to be recovered over smaller orders. In the 1950s, the UK could contemplate procuring four different aircraft designs just for the strategic nuclear bomber role. There were many different fighter and conventional bomber aircraft types. Today, all the air defence and offensive combat tasks are covered by the Tornado, the Harrier and the Eurofighter.

Surprise is sometimes expressed that military computer and other high-technology equipment have not experienced the falls in price and increases in capability that have been seen in the commercial computer industry and in consumer appliances. There are three reasons for this. The production runs are very short, and often spread over a long time. The technologies needed are often very specific to military usage, and have limited application beyond. The period of time from conception to deployment is typically ten to twenty years and it is difficult to take advantage of technical innovation, which is at a much faster rate. The stark contrast between the successful development of the commercial global mobile phone network and the difficulties with procuring a modern personal communication system for the Army graphically illustrates the nature of the problem.

Most military equipment costs rise at more than 5 per cent above inflation, and in certain areas the rate may be much higher than this. Attempts are made to offset this problem by increasingly looking to buy off-the-shelf solutions. Such an approach does help, but for many military needs there is no ready solution on the commercial shelf. There is no doubt that pressures will remain to exploit cheaper civilian products; computing and communications would appear to be a particularly good area for such an approach. Yet the demands of military ruggedness and security, coupled with a need to interoperate with allies, seem to have prevented much progress so far.

After staffing and equipment costs, the remainder of defence expenditure includes the costs of maintaining the support for the armed forces. Most running costs will be fairly closely aligned to normal inflation in the economy. Fuel, accommodation, food, transport, maintenance and logistics support activities have no reason to be out of line with inflationary pressures more generally. Indeed, there are often opportunities to undertake some of these activities in ways that take them out of some of the extra costs incurred by military operations. Contractorised, civilian-ised and out-sourced support should be sustainable with level funding in real terms. However the long-term nature of contracts under the Private Finance Initiative reduces the flexibility to put resources where they may be most needed. In a time of declining forces, it is possible to realise some of the value of the defence estate by selling off land. Short-term spend-ing regulation is also possible by reducing the activity levels of forces, and this has historically often been used to compensate for rising costs elsewhere in the defence programme. If used too extensively, such meas-ures affect both combat capability and personnel retention. These lead to steeply rising costs in later years.

We have, therefore, in the UK defence programme an inflationary problem. Personnel costs rise at a rate slightly above inflation; equipment costs rise much faster than retail price inflation; and running costs rise in line with inflation. The combined effect is that level defence spending in real terms inevitably leads to decreases in force levels year on year. In fact, level funding in real terms has been the exception since 1985, and the resultant decrease in force levels has been even more severe. The Defence Review in 1991 under Tom King reduced the combat front line by around 30 per cent with only limited reduction in defence spending. This reflected how badly overheated the programme was at the time. In 1995, Malcolm Rifkind cut the running-costs side of the budget to make the books balance, and this has resulted in some of the subsequent overstretch for the front line. In 1998, George Robertson cut tanks and aircraft to keep the capability for rapid deployment. While his strategic defence review was widely welcomed, the defence inflation effect rapidly made the plans unaffordable. In each case, the Defence Secretary of the day argued that there were good strategic reasons for the review. But the underlying fact was that without such force level changes much more money would have been needed.

Some attempt was made from 1987 to square this circle by imposing on the armed forces year-on-year efficiency savings of up to 3 per cent to compensate for this pervasive defence inflationary effect. What passing improvements were made have long since been absorbed, and such an approach suffers from diminishing returns as the years pass. The propor-tion of GDP devoted to defence in the UK has declined over the past twenty years from 5.3 per cent in 1986 to 2.3 per cent in 2005. A continued approach of defence budgets that are broadly level in real terms will call for difficult decisions on priorities in the future, just as it has in the past. Force levels, equipped as today, cannot be maintained with such an approach.

Affording the defence programme

If we start from a position that only the defence of the UK and its citizens is core to provision for the armed forces, we can then make a judgement as to how much can be afforded beyond that to meet the additional international contributions, and how they might be provided most cost-effectively. This would be a radical approach to defence planning.

The elements for direct national defence are surprisingly limited in the current strategic environment. A minimum nuclear deterrent, with its associated defence, provides adequate reassurance against threats from other nuclear powers, now or in the future. The airspace over the UK needs to be policed and defended to preserve national sovereignty. This can be achieved with a relatively small number of air-defence fighters such as Eurofighter. Maritime security requires a mix of air reconnaissance and armed surface vessels. Again the numbers for the UK could be relatively small. Land forces today have only a limited role in direct tasks on UK territory. However, it is clear that when natural or other disaster strikes, the army is necessary to provide a rapid emergency response, as has been seen in recent years during strikes, floods and farming catastrophes. Again the numbers needed are relatively small, but they must be equipped properly and have the means to respond rapidly.

Having provided for the necessary forces to defend the country and its citizens, we then have a range of options for the optional contributions to international tasks. These might be characterised as:

a. Punching above our weight;

b. Matching national commitments to resources;

c. Sharing the burden more equitably internationally.

The current national approach is to punch above our weight. The effect on the armed forces is described in shorthand form as 'overstretch'. The reality is more complicated. It is always possible for the military to surge effort to meet emergency circumstances. The problem comes when that surge is maintained for year after year. Retention declines as repeated deployments become more frequent. This increases the recruiting and training costs, while at the same time depressing overall experience levels. Equipment is used at a higher than planned rate, and needs earlier replacement or refurbishment, with associated unplanned costs. Over time the quality of the armed forces declines. This is the worry that has caused senior officers to voice their concerns in public for the first time. Punching above our weight is not a sustainable position.

If we were to make a serious attempt to match commitments to the resources available, we would need to scale down virtually all major overseas commitments for a period of perhaps two years to recover the armed forces. This is not possible given the current commitments in Iraq and Afghanistan. However, planning could be undertaken to achieve a progressive decline in commitments over a period of time. The longer it took, the greater the reduction that would ultimately be needed to allow a recovery in training and expertise. Yet for Liberal Democrats, this would be a difficult option. We would want to contribute to UN-sponsored operations undertaken for humanitarian reasons. We would not wish to have to ignore the pleas for help from the poor and dispossessed peoples of the world.

This means that we have to seek a way to make our contribution proportionate to our economy, while at the same time doing our best to ensure that the many international tasks are undertaken. In every case, we will undertake these tasks as one of a number of nations. It may be under UN auspices, or a NATO operation, or as part of the emergent EU military capabilities. In Iraq, and initially in Afghanistan, we found ourselves as part of an ad hoc coalition led by the United States. Indeed, Donald Rumsfeld suggested that this was to be the model for the future: the mission would define the coalition. Current UK defence policy also assumes that major war-fighting will only be undertaken as part of an operation which includes the US.

Sharing the burden

There are two problems with the current arrangements for multinational military operations. First, there is no incentive mechanism for nations to provide equitable shares of capability. Second, there is no effective way to benefit from the economies of scale that the larger force should generate. In fact the total effectiveness of such coalition forces is often less than sum of their parts.

Each of the four major types of multinational operation (UN, NATO, EU and US-led) require nations to negotiate and volunteer contributions. The UN often finds itself in great difficulties in enforcing a Security Council resolution because nations are unwilling to provide the necessary forces. The peacekeeping force for Lebanon in 2006 is one such example, and force requirements were rapidly scaled down as a result. NATO can call on all its twenty-six member nations in the case that one of them is attacked, but for lesser tasks, the Secretary General must tour capitals with a begging bowl to find 2,000 troops and a few helicopters to support an Afghanistan task that all have agreed is necessary. EU defence arrangements are still embryonic, and this is scarcely surprising since little was possible before the UK changed its approach in 1998 at St Malo. The EU suffers from the same volunteerism that dogs NATO and the UN. Finally, the US, which spends as much on defence as the rest of the world put together, is an unequal partner when it leads a coalition. In Iraq, we have seen how it ignores the views of its allies. It often needs partners for political respectability rather than military utility. It looks for bilateral relationships to provide niche capabilities to fill gaps in its own forces.

All of this gives the UK particular difficulty. It has a special position with respect to all four multinational actors. This compounds the problem of over-tasking as we try to show continuing commitment to each. The approach in recent years has been to seek opportunities to take the lead early in an international operation, help to set up the headquarters and structures, and then to try to hand over to others. There have been mixed results with this strategy. There would be much to be gained from greater clarity in our relationship with each of the main actors. We have a different degree of influence in each case.

We have least influence when we undertake military operations as part of a US-led coalition mission. This is unsurprising given that the major military force, and the largest funding, will be provided by the US. It does, however, have unfortunate consequences. If we disagree with the strategy, as it now appears that the British government did during the Coalition Provisional Authority period in Iraq, we must either live with the American policy or withdraw our troops. Given the difficult consequences of being seen to leave the US in the lurch, we find that we lose control of our strategy and commitment. It would not seem to be in the UK national interest to place ourselves in this position.

In the United Nations, we can in theory exert greater influence given our permanent membership of the Security Council and veto rights. Some have argued that the UN should have a standing rapid reaction force to which member nations contribute. This, it is claimed, would make UN response both more assured and faster. Given the diversity of UN operations, this is not necessarily an economical answer to the problem. Certainly, while the current ad hoc system continues, operational success can depend greatly on the troop mix provided, and the UN and national constraints under which they operate. In Sierra Leone in 2000, British forces were deployed independently of UN forces because of such concerns about effectiveness.

NATO is a consensus organisation, and thus in theory every one of its twenty-six members has an equal degree of influence on decision-making. In practice, the US carries great influence because of the scale of its military contribution. The UK is among a second tier of the larger European members. NATO has been in a process of transformation since the end of the Cold War. It has developed peacekeeping skills in the Balkans, and for the past three years has been running the stabilisation and reconstruction mission in Afghanistan. It has also established a new 25,000-strong response force which is to be deployable at five days' notice for thirty days of operations at the high-intensity end of the war-fighting spectrum. It is made up of national forces on standby for six months at a time. NATO has also made limited moves towards procuring equipment at the supranational level to save individual member countries the cost of ownership. The seventeen NATO Airborne Warning and Control System (AWACS) aircraft have been joint owned and joint operated successfully for over twenty years. Unfortunately, the UK is not one of the sixteen participating nations, as it preferred to procure and operate its own fleet of AWACS. NATO has now moved to a similar procurement for strategic airlift with the C17. Again the UK has opted to remain independent and procure its own C17 fleet.

The final multinational security actor is the European Union. Here UK influence can be strong. It is a commonplace that the UK and France dominate all development of European defence capabilities. They have the experience and capabilities necessary for global missions. Yet developments have been slow to start and fitful in recent years. The unblocking of UK opposition to greater EU involvement in defence stems from the

Anglo-French St Malo agreement in 1998. Since then EU members set themselves a challenge to produce a 60,000 troop capability which could be deployed at thirty days' notice and sustained for one year on a challenging crisis management or peacekeeping task short of war. Subsequently more modest battle groups of 1,500 troops have been developed. The EU has also been seeking capabilities beyond the military, such as deployable police forces, for stabilisation and reconstruction. In Bosnia, the EU has taken over the security task from NATO. It now appears that there is emerging a division of tasks where NATO is needed for the more challenging military tasks, and the EU can move in when the stabilisation has proceeded to a stage where its ability to deal with the civil society issues become key. Surprisingly, the EU has as yet made little progress in pooling or sharing national capabilities, although the formation of the European Defence Agency in 2004 has given a focus for such developments.

Vested interests

In looking for ways to structure British defence policy to be affordable while meeting our responsibilities, we must also consider how to deal with the various vested interests. While generals may complain about insufficient funds, the defence budget remains a substantial sum of money that is spent largely at the discretion of the government of the day. Defence equipment is not subject to EU competition law, and therefore procurement can be used to support national industries, and to provide employment in particular areas. This is of course also true for other allies, and is one of the factors which makes efficient transnational consolidation of the industry slower than it should be. MPs with a defence industrial constituency interest will usually give a high priority to the local implications of any national defence restructuring.

The military themselves are also a vested interest. The continuation of multiple headquarters and establishments provides a comfortable career structure. Rationalisation, particularly if it were to have an international dimension, should have the consequence of reducing the number of senior posts. However, the argument in NATO is often about the need for national representation, which leads to an unnecessary number of senior posts.

The public perception of national sovereignty is also a key interest that must be taken into account in any changes to defence arrangements. This is not uniquely a British problem. There is, however, a particular British sensitivity about defence arrangements, which may have their origins in recollections of World War II. There remains a deep sense of unease about the reliability of continental European partners. Opinions may be changing after the Iraq debacle has shown that a special relationship with the US requires a significant loss of sovereignty. This may, however, reinforce the views of those who believe that the UK must be prepared to do everything on its own.

Squaring the circle

Just like the planners in the MoD, we cannot start with a clean sheet of paper and transform the jumble of capabilities, commitments, and future projects into a tidy, rational and coherent defence programme. And even if it were possible, the chances are that events would undermine the plan. When John Nott wanted to reduce surface naval power, he was confounded by the Falklands conflict. The post-Cold-War defence review assumed that the day of the tank battle was past. The first Gulf War disproved that assertion. Yet that does not mean that the only defence planning approach is simply to replace equipment as it wears it out with fewer but more expensive new versions on a like-for-like basis.

The analysis in this chapter suggests that we might begin to lay out a rather different defence template for the future. It would be one that recognised the duty of any government to provide for territorial security and the safety of its citizens. It would also recognise that the UK must play an appropriate part as a serious member of the international community, and that this will often require military contributions as well as other kinds of assistance. However, such international operations will be invariably done in cooperation with allies, and that opens up opportunities to share costs in a more effective way than at present.

We should also attempt to reduce the double-hatting of units against tasks, as this is one of the causes of overstretch. It also gives us a false sense of our real capability, since units cannot be in two places at the same time. The structure of the forces needs to ensure that particular specialisations are not over-tasked when compared to others. The current aim of a twenty-four-month period operating from home base in a non-hostile environment between each six-month operational deployment must be achieved. The Reserves should again become true reserves for emergencies rather than ways of filling gaps in regular forces.

It is sometimes suggested that the high-intensity conflict capabilities should now be left to the United States, and European nations concentrate on the peacekeeping tasks. This does not seem to be an attractive model in a number of respects. In an uncertain future, the national interests of the US may not always align with those of European nations. A military that is trained and equipped only for operations short of war will be constrained, and less able to meet changing circumstances. Nor is it possible to carry influence in international partnerships if it is clear that our options have been limited by capability reductions. Yet it is not possible for the UK to maintain the full spectrum of modern war-fighting capabilities on its own. NATO offers an opportunity to maintain such capabilities as part of a collective security organisation. For the expensive enabling capabilities, costs can be shared on the same basis as AWACS. Instead of keeping the UK outside such shared arrangements, we might explore with other NATO members how we could together start acquiring the already identified capability needs. At the same time, we would build our national high-end military capability around our commitment to the NATO Response Force. This would equate to 10,000 personnel fully equipped and supported for deployable high-intensity operations.

For peacekeeping and humanitarian operations, we would have a similar approach but through the EU. Again pooled and shared high-cost equipment would be needed. In this case it could be in the area of deployment capability through shared strategic air- and sea-lift. EU members spend some €193 billion a year on defence. This is enough to field very significant capabilities if spent more efficiently. For the UK, we should allocate forces to the 60,000 reaction force as well as establish a number of deployable battle groups. The exact scale of such forces would depend on how far we could reduce overhead costs through the shared enablers.

For such schemes as these to work, the current system of voluntary national contributions would no longer be sensible. Both in NATO and the EU, members will need to agree to funding rules both for capabilities and operations. The resources will of course come from national defence budgets, but provided capabilities are not duplicated this should bring cost benefits to the UK. For a period, the cost reductions of such rationalisation at NATO and EU level would reduce the defence inflation effect. However, the need for real budget growth to sustain forces must be recognised. The EU average defence expenditure in 2005 was 1.81 per cent of

GDP. It should be possible to argue for a target of 2 per cent of GDP for all members. Once achieved, the percentage should remain fixed, which would allow for defence costs that rise in line with GDP growth, and would help to sustain force levels.

Conclusion

The UK defence forces are in continuing decline because of the rising costs of maintaining a national range of capabilities. While there is a core national security task, it generates a relatively small part of the overall costs. To meet the international challenges which Liberal Democrats recognise, we need to find a better way to structure and rationalise our capabilities. As we always plan to work with allies, we should look to NATO and the EU to provide economies of scale through shared and pooled capabilities where sensible. NATO should be the focus for our high-intensity war-fighting commitment, and the EU should be the forum for peacekeeping and humanitarian tasks. By shaping our forces in this way, we can reduce overhead costs, share the most expensive enabling capabilities and thus equip and sustain our forces for the long term. The budget costs need to be no greater than now, but will require a mechanism to sustain force levels against the effect of defence inflation.

All of this requires getting used to the idea that the days of Britain standing alone on defence are over. We cannot deal with the challenges of the twenty-first century through the splendid isolation of the late nineteenth century which was flawed even for the twentieth. In defence, perhaps more than any other policy area, we need to reinvent the role of the state by accepting that the sovereignty of the state can be most effectively exercised through international collaboration.

Chapter 22

Communicating Social Liberalism

Steve Webb and Jo Holland

L iberal Democrats are good at coming up with policies. Probably the best policy decision of New Labour – independence for the Bank of England – was actually a policy from the 1992 and 1997 Liberal Democrat manifestos. In many other areas, notably on environmental issues and international affairs, Liberal Democrat policies have set the agenda, only to be picked up in whole or in part by other parties.

But where Liberal Democrats have sometimes failed has been in converting those strong policy ideas into a coherent story about the sort of party that we are and the kind of society that we want to create. In short, we have often got across Liberal Democrat policies, but failed to communicate Liberal Democracy. We have made electoral progress by ruthless targeting of key seats and vigorous grassroots campaigning, but we have failed to promote Liberal Democracy in a way that has won the hearts and minds of large sections of the British public. How, then, do we communicate our philosophy and our principles in a way that will connect with the reality of people's lives, hopes and fears?

At first sight, a collection of essays such as the present one risks falling into the same trap. Eminent Liberal Democrat thinkers have tackled key policy areas such as the environment, health and education, but at the end of the journey do we have a story to tell and a story to sell?

Our contention is that there is a distinctive 'social liberal' narrative, illustrated by the contributions in this book, which is both intellectually coherent and politically saleable.

We would identify three key steps in the social liberal argument:

Step 1 – Relying exclusively on unfettered market mechanisms to deliver a liberal and democratic society is doomed to failure. In some cases markets fail to deliver because there is insufficient competition, leaving individual consumers or service-users at the mercy of monopolistic providers. In other cases markets fail to deliver a socially optimal outcome because the market price fails to include the social cost or benefit of an activity – environmental externalities are one example, but the existence of public goods such as rural post offices would be another. Equally importantly, the outcome of a market process reflects the relative power of the participants, and extreme inequalities of income and wealth mean that unfettered markets will tend to produce highly unequal outcomes. There are many areas in society – such as educational or health outcomes – where such inequalities would be totally unacceptable.

Step 2 – Positive state intervention to tackle market failures is not only perfectly compatible with Liberalism, it may be actively necessary for a full understanding of individual freedom. There is nothing illiberal in tempering the power of a monopolist. There is nothing illiberal in ensuring that market prices are adjusted to reflect the social costs of an activity. And it is surely essential to the concept of an individual's freedom to achieve their full potential that their prospects are not stunted from the start by material disadvantage. To that end, there is nothing illiberal about the state taking an active role in promoting equal life-chances through, for example, high-quality health and education services. In short, in a well-defined set of circumstances, liberals have a duty to intervene where markets fail to deliver.

Step 3 – Liberal interventions in markets are different in kind from socialist interventions. We are constantly wary of the dangers of an over-mighty state. Effective state intervention should be as local as possible and as accountable as possible – it should be the 'state with a human face'. The state, as big bureaucracy, does not know best about the diverse needs of individuals, even if it can be effective at providing the means to meet those diverse needs. The justification for intervention is always in the name of the greater good of enhancing liberty.

In this chapter we set out the basis for these arguments more fully, before considering how best to communicate such a 'social liberal narrative'. In particular, we emphasise the importance of linking this coherent political philosophy to the day-to-day, real-world concerns of the voting public.

Step 1: The failures of unfettered markets

We have identified three main areas where market solutions are likely to lead to outcomes that would be unacceptable to liberals – where effective competition does not exist; where market prices do not reflect society's values; and where inequalities in the initial distribution of income and wealth would give some individuals too much power in the market. In this section we consider examples of each.

a) Lack of competition

In many commercial spheres, market-based competition is undoubtedly good news for consumers. In the market for telecommunications, individuals can now choose between a wide range of providers for domestic telephone and data services. There is innovation, competition and the potential for new entry to the market. Few people would now want us to go back to the world where the GPO was the principal provider of domestic phone lines and customers had to wait months to get a phone put in. Liberals of all stripes are comfortable with a competitive market of this sort, and the role of the state in such a market is now minimal.

It is, however, instructive to note that, even in this example, the state still has a role in promoting competition and preventing monopolistic behaviour. For historic reasons, the dominant incumbent provider, BT, has control over the vast majority of telephone exchanges. It has little incentive to allow rival providers to access its exchanges to set up alternative 'local loop' networks. The state therefore has had to intervene to ensure that competing providers are given rights of access to BT exchanges, thereby undermining BT's monopoly on line rentals and giving consumers enhanced choice.

Among contributors to this collection, Tim Farron (Chapter 14) makes a strong case for intervention in the market for wholesale milk supplies, where a small number of supermarket chains are able to exploit their monopoly position to the detriment of small dairy farmers. Dairy farmers are a 'captive market' – they cannot store their day's output until they get a better price, and the scope for setting up rival supply chains is very limited when most of the eventual consumers buy their fresh milk through one of the large supermarkets. Consumer pressure for a fair deal for producers can have some effect (witness Tesco's new 'local' milk scheme, where a premium price is paid to regional suppliers[1]), but progress is often painfully slow, and the welfare of smaller players in the market cannot be preserved if the power of the big players is not limited in some way.

While there can be some debate about what it means to talk about a 'fair' outcome of a market process, liberals of all kinds must surely be united in the view that a fair outcome requires a fair *process*. Where a small number of players can dominate a market, whether as buyers or sellers, the outcome is unlikely to be conducive to the common good. We should be strong in our condemnation of the abuse of market power, resistant to the lobbying of special interests and forthright in our defence of the individual consumer or supplier.

b) Failures of the price mechanism

Prices convey information about the economic costs of production and reflect the relative level of supply and demand. But where the true costs of an economic activity are not reflected in the price, the market outcome will not be optimal from a social point of view. In some cases, therefore, the appropriate role of the state in a liberal democracy is to adjust market prices to reflect wider social costs and benefits.

Perhaps the clearest example of where unfettered market outcomes do not lead to the best social outcomes is where an activity has a wider environmental impact. If climate change really is the biggest threat that our world faces today, it is clear that government, the business world and individuals all need to change their behaviour. We are living, to use Al Gore's phrase, in an 'age of consequences', in which we can no longer simply take our natural environment and its continual production of resources for granted. As Ed Randall has noted in Chapter 3, a proactive and strong environmental message is an essential component of modern-day Liberalism.

In some cases the most efficient way of achieving the desired change in behaviour is to intervene directly in the market by changing market 'prices' through taxes or subsidies.

One example of how this has been highly successful in the UK context has been the switch from leaded to unleaded petrol. Back in the 1980s, a price differential was introduced by the Chancellor of the day to encourage consumers to switch over to unleaded petrol. This triggered demand for conversion of cars to run on unleaded petrol, to increased supply on station forecourts and ultimately to manufacturers designing and building cars that ran on unleaded petrol from day one. Within a period of just a few years a near total switch-over had been achieved.

However, in an increasingly globalised world there are obviously limits to how far an individual nation-state can take action on environmental externalities without putting itself at a comparative disadvantage. Liberal Democrats, who are internationalists by nature, were the first to recognise that it is only by coordinated international action and market interventions that real progress can be made in this area. For market mechanisms themselves will penalise countries who unilaterally raise the 'price' of pollution. If the UK unilaterally imposes a tax on high-polluting businesses, this will be good for the environment, but not so good for the businesses concerned as they try to compete in the international market. Only by concerted international action can the common good be achieved.

Not only do markets often fail to capture the social costs of an activity, but they also often fail to reflect the wider social benefits of a transaction. The provision of rural post office services is a case in point. The people who run small village post offices often do so on a shoestring, often out of commitment to their community rather than because it is the most profitable thing that they could be doing. Pure market economics – as is increasingly being practised by the present government in the case of post offices – might dictate thousands of post-office closures. But the social impact of such a closure programme could be devastating. Small post offices are often the hub of a local community. They can sometimes provide an invaluable point of social contact, particularly for elderly or disabled people. Yet the value of this 'social service' does not appear on the profit-and-loss account. The market therefore would not deliver the socially optimal number of post office outlets. Only state intervention, perhaps in the form of explicit subsidy for such offices, will produce the desired outcome.

Whether we are dealing with social costs or social benefits, both need to be fully reflected in market prices if the market is to deliver socially optimal outcomes, and only the state can ensure that this happens.

c) Inequalities in income and wealth

A market process can be likened to a horse race. In theory, any number of riders can enter the race and each has an equal chance of winning. The reality, however, is that many markets are like handicap races, where some horses are weighed down and others can run free. Time and again, the same horses win.

In some cases, we would not wish to intervene in this outcome. If someone works hard, makes the most of their skills and attains a higher post-tax income, they are going to be able to buy a larger house, a better car, etc. Even in the presence of redistributive taxation (of which more below), we would not seek to reduce everyone to absolute equality at the start of the race. Liberals can cope with the fact that all races have winners and losers.

However, social liberals believe that there are some races where, at the very least, everyone should be able to finish the race; and others where it matters that the gap between the finishing time of the winner and the loser is reduced. Examples include basic rights to education and health care. Not everyone will receive identical standards of service, but every citizen should have a right to a decent minimum.

The ultimate handicap in a market is having no or a relatively low income. Someone without the money for food, clothing and shelter is not free in any meaningful sense. Therefore, Liberals (and others) accept the case for redistributive taxation to take from those who will suffer least by being taxed in order to provide for those who will benefit most from being supported.

But simply providing a subsistence income is not sufficient in itself to overcome the handicaps in the race of life. Access to key services such as health, housing and education is another key determinant of quality of life.

One option would be to go further with redistributive taxation to provide all individuals not only with enough money for subsistence but also with the something akin to vouchers with which they could buy other services from the market. However, there are many reasons why the state goes further than simply providing the income to buy services, and is actually involved in their direct provision, or at least collective purchase.

One reason why the state provides or purchases services on behalf of the population is that of efficiency. Whilst in principle millions of individuals could strike individual bargains with competing providers of health care or education, it is often far more efficient for the state to act, either as provider or as bulk purchaser of the service. In the case of secondary health care, for example, it is unlikely to be efficient for a community to have competing acute hospitals. It is better for the state to provide or purchase the service and then allow equal access to all.

The second reason for access being regulated by the state rather than being the outcome of a market process is that in a society where all individuals are equally valued we do not want to see undue inequalities in the quality of health care that people receive. For example, even with a highly redistributive tax system providing generous support for those on low incomes, the costs of health care can still be prohibitive to those at the bottom of the pile. We would not want to see someone who, for example, had a chronic condition requiring sustained medication finding themselves unable to obtain treatment because they had run out of money. Access to decent health care is regarded in most liberal societies as something akin to a human right, and this right cannot be guaranteed by a market alone.

A third concern about the market model for the allocation of public services is that too much emphasis on 'choice' over 'entitlement' can again lead to socially undesirable outcomes. The 'choice agenda' so enthusiastically pursued by New Labour has in reality favoured the articulate, well-informed middle classes. Labour has created a market in the NHS, to enable patients to exercise choice over where to go to receive hospital treatment. However, the King's Fund recently found that the middle classes were likely to choose the best hospitals, while those who were less well-educated tended simply to go to the local hospital.[2] King's Fund chief economist John Appleby compared this trend with the education system, where middle-class parents gravitate towards the 'best' schools. He warned: 'If this happens in health care we could see potentially a widening of health and health inequalities between those with formal education qualifications and those without.'[3]

While Liberals are instinctively in favour of 'choice' as part of the exercise of freedom, these examples clearly demonstrate that unfettered markets can simply lead to a beggar-my-neighbour form of choice, akin to the biggest and strongest barging past other people in the queue. If competition and choice genuinely drove up standards for the many and not just the few, we could live with some inequality of outcome. But this is not proving to be the case. Markets make good servants but poor masters.

Step 2: The social-liberal case for state intervention where markets fail

Much of the analysis in the previous section will be familiar to those who have studied the rudiments of micro-economics. Markets can fail where there is insufficient competition or where prices do not reflect the full costs and benefits of an activity. And the outcome in a market is strongly shaped by the starting positions of the participants. Unlike elections, markets do not operate on a one-member-one-vote principle. Those with the most money have the most say and the most influence in the outcome of a market process.

The next question, however, is a political one – does the fact of market failure necessarily imply state intervention, especially for liberals who are instinctively wary of the power of the state?

It is our contention that when market outcomes impinge on the freedom of individuals to maximise their potential, and where effective state interventions are available, then not merely may we intervene, but we must intervene.

Looking at the types of intervention that we have outlined here should also offer some reassurance to the concerned liberal that what we are talking about is strengthening the position of individuals and their communities against vested interests; about adjusting incentives rather than controlling or banning.

Consider, for example, the issue of tackling monopoly power in markets. If a single supermarket chain buys up all the retail outlets in a town – for example in Inverness, where Tesco operates three stores and has sought planning permission for a fourth, giving the town the dubious honour of being the UK's Tesco Capital[4] – it is unlikely to be for the wider social good. Planning restrictions may mean that competitors cannot simply set up shop and compete, and individuals may not readily be able to travel to the next large town, so the monopoly operator has a stranglehold on local consumers. It is hard to believe that acting to prevent such practices offends against liberal sensitivities!

Consider next the issue of interfering in markets to ensure that prices more fully reflect costs and benefits. As Chris Huhne has argued in Chapter 12, on climate change, Liberal Democrats do not argue that people should be prevented from flying or driving their cars, but rather that the true environmental costs of their actions should be reflected in the price that they pay when they fly or drive. Using market mechanisms as a servant in this way will ensure that those who have alternatives are more likely to use them, while the remaining flights are used by those who most value them. Interventions of this sort actually help markets to be more efficient in delivering socially desirable outcomes.

More contentious is the idea of a Liberal case for income redistribution. Most Liberals would accept that redistribution is required to ensure that the poorest do not go destitute. But we would argue that more comprehensive state involvement in the provision or purchasing of public services such as health, education and housing is necessary for all people to be able to achieve their full potential.

One of the authors of this chapter has written elsewhere:

> The sort of freedom that motivates liberals is the freedom to achieve all that you are capable of. Liberals recognise that to do nothing in the battle between the strong and the weak is to side with the strong. Intervention, where it can be shown to be effective, is justified by an enabling state that seeks to empower its citizens and not simply to stand by as a passive spectator and occasional policeman.[5]

Indeed, building on the work of Richard Wilkinson and others, Duncan Brack argues persuasively in this collection (Chapter 2) that inequality of outcome in and of itself can undermine society to the detriment of all. This would seem to imply a greater amount of redistribution than we have sometimes advocated.

Whilst there are obviously pragmatic limits to redistributive taxation (including disincentive effects and the ability of individuals to move to lower tax jurisdictions), and indeed liberal limits to redistribution (the freedom to choose how much to work and to be appropriately rewarded is also one that we value), social liberals would argue that we have been too wary of redistribution as a force for delivering a more liberal society in which all can achieve their full potential.

Step 3: The character of Liberal intervention

Steps 1 and 2 could also be espoused, to a greater or lesser extent, by a socialist. However, unlike socialists, liberals tend to have an inherent distrust of establishments and concentrations of power. Liberals will therefore go further and emphasise that the state must only do what needs to be done, and no more; and that it must perform its tasks in a way that is local and accountable. We consider each characteristic in turn.

a) State intervention must be as local as possible

The arguments that we have advanced in favour of state intervention imply that the form and nature of the intervention will vary from place to place. For example, the extent of competition in a market may be very different in different parts of the country. In some high streets the big supermarkets are all represented and battle it out for customers. In others, one supermarket has a monopoly. The implications for state intervention in each case are quite different.

Similarly, the existence of social costs and benefits that are not included in market prices will vary from place to place. There may well be a case for state subsidy of rural post offices that are the only retail outlet and source of free cash in a community, but much less of a case in a suburban town with many shops and well-served by bank branches. The intervention needs to be tailored to the local situation.

b) State intervention must be as accountable as possible

An inevitable consequence of local variation will be what are pejoratively known as 'postcode lotteries'. But it is quite wrong to think that all variations in services between different areas are necessarily bad. To the extent that such variations reflect genuine differences in needs and preferences, they are not only acceptable but desirable. The problem is that under the present system too many of these variations are apparently arbitrary and are certainly not the result of any expression of preference by local people. This is why intervention needs to be not only local but accountable.

Often state intervention is given a bad name because of the way in which it is carried out. The public does not like the idea that 'Whitehall knows best' – that important decisions affecting local people are taken by quangos and bureaucrats who are un-elected and un-accountable for their actions. This has been clearly seen in the recent NHS reconfigurations where decisions have been taken from afar to reorganise local health services, and to close down wards and even entire hospitals, without meaningful consultation of local people.[6]

'Active citizenship' involves re-engaging people in their communities and in the decisions that affect them. This not only addresses the need for local decisions to reflect local desires, but brings people together where they might not previously have been involved in their local communities; a point that is argued powerfully by Mark Pack in Chapter 8.

But people are not interested simply in elections or consultations for their own sake. Turning again to health, there is always a great deal of local support for the local NHS, but turnout in elections to foundation hospitals is minuscule. Liberal Democrat research found that less than 1 per cent of the population served by a Foundation Trust elect the governors who hold the Trust to account, and in most Trusts, membership is made up of only around 3 per cent of the population it serves.[7] Sham consultations and token elections do not fool people. They want to know what their vote means.

One way in which political decision-making can be made more accountable is by harnessing the power of new technology.

Many of those who are currently disenfranchised or turned off the political process are the young. But these are the very people who are most likely to use the internet, especially for 'social networking' on sites such as MySpace and Facebook. Literally millions of young people spend time on these sites keeping in touch with the latest news on their friends as well as registering support for causes.

The political potential of these sites is massive and is only just beginning to be harnessed. Joe Trippi, one of the key architects of Howard Dean's path-breaking campaign for the Democratic presidential nomination in 2004 writes:

> What we're ... in now is the empowerment age. If information is power, then this new technology – which is the first to evenly distribute information – is really distributing power. This power is shifting from institutions that have always been run top down, hoarding information at the top, telling us how to run our lives, to a new paradigm of power that is democratically distributed and shared by all of us.[8]

While we always need to be wary of opening up new forms of exclusion, the potential of social networking to remould our politics is enormous. Instead of the professional politician being in charge, the citizen can initiate, debate and mobilise. In this model, accountability is not about the politician taking decisions and being answerable for them, but it is about the public being involved from the very beginning in shaping the debate and developing and refining solutions. Technology is not an end in itself

but can facilitate the building of community networks so that local decisions are far more representative than ever before.

For example, politicians are increasingly tuning in to the potential
of the Facebook networking site. At the time of writing, Steve Webb's
online presence has almost 1,500 'friends', of which more than 1,000
are young constituents in their late teens and early twenties – precisely
the age group that has disengaged from the political process.[9] However,
through Facebook, they are able to enter into a dialogue with their local
MP, raising issues of poor local transport or requesting assistance with
claiming benefit entitlements. Most of these young people would not
consider writing a letter or picking up the telephone – or even emailing –
to get in touch with their local MP. But if politicians can go to the places
where their constituents already spend their time, they can connect to
them in a new and genuinely interactive manner.

In sum, where state intervention is driven by local needs and preferences, where the process of decision-making has been transparent,
consultative and accountable, the outcome is likely to command much
greater public acceptance. Indeed this is the only way in which a liberal
and democratic administration should conduct itself.

Communicating social liberalism

Many of the strands of social liberalism that have been identified in this
chapter and throughout this book are ones which strike a chord with the
British public today. For example:

- There is widespread resentment at gross inequalities in income
  and wealth which appear to bear little relation to effort or talent.
  Network Rail bosses were recently forced by public disapproval to
  defer taking the large bonuses to which they were contractually
  entitled, because they were simultaneously withholding payment
  from members of staff, amidst widespread public perception that
  the company had performed poorly.[10]
- There is growing public demand for coordinated international
  action on climate change, recognising that market forces alone are
  not enough to deal with environmental degradation.
- Whilst many people support the basic principle of a market economy, there is growing awareness of the problems that can be caused
  when one player becomes too powerful. The growth of local protests

against various expansion plans by the supermarket giant Tesco is indicative of this.

- The public increasingly wants control over decisions affecting local public services such as hospital reconfigurations. There is a wave of protest against decisions taken behind closed doors by unelected national or regional bureaucracies,
- Concern about the 'nanny state' is increasingly widespread, particularly in reaction to rafts of centralised targets which seek to micromanage the public sphere. The public wants to see common sense and flexibility in the delivery of public services, not a Whitehall-led tick-box mentality.

Against this backdrop there is a golden opportunity for social liberals to set out a message which is both ideologically consistent and in tune with the popular mood.

This social liberal narrative needs to have three main strands:

a) It needs a global dimension

Many of the big issues facing the nation state today – whether climate change, terrorism, economic competitiveness, peacekeeping or managing migration – all have one thing in common: they cannot be solved by individual nation-states acting alone.

On climate change, whilst it is necessary to 'act local' and make individual small changes, it is also necessary to 'think global'. World leaders need to take strategic long-term action if the threat to our environment is to be addressed. For Britain to be seen to be taking action ahead of the rest of the world will not only set an example for other nations to follow, but may offer other first-mover advantages, such as the potential for developing and benefiting from more environmentally friendly technologies.

Similarly, to maintain our economic competitiveness, and having regard to the need to promote well-being and not just wealth, it is necessary to work with other nations. Whilst a fortress-Britain mentality is superficially attractive, it has historically been the most open economies which have prospered the most. Pan-European and global trade deals which ensure fair access to markets and also provide protection for vulnerable developing economies are an essential part of a strategy for sustained prosperity.

Strong states are necessary to harness, control and respond to glo-balisation. They have a role to play in regulating international markets, ensuring that people are well fitted to compete in the new global markets, and helping areas currently dependent on declining and uncompetitive industries to adjust.

Perhaps most potently, in the case of the US-led military action against Iraq, we have seen what can happen when international institutions are not strong enough or are bypassed. Ill-judged unilateral military advances by individual nation-states are guaranteed to destabilise and inflame an already unstable situation. Recent events have show more pressingly than ever the need for international checks and balances on such action.

Despite the siren calls of protectionism and isolationism, there is increasing recognition that effective international institutions and effec-tive international partnerships are the best answer to the nation's and the world's problems.

Social liberals, who are instinctively internationalists, understand this.

b) It needs a local dimension

Paradoxically, at the same time as recognising the interconnectedness of the world and its problems, the social liberal narrative must also be about localism.

At a time when people are anxious about the pace of globalisation and technological change, we need to rediscover the local community. We need a message which is about reconnecting that community with the decisions that are taken in its name.

We have seen a long-term trend of decline in political participation, especially in locally elected bodies which are perceived to have very lim-ited power. But this is not because people are less interested in politics itself. Indeed, the two-thirds of people who declare an interest in politics has remained broadly the same proportion for thirty years.[11] However, many are disengaged from the political process because they do not see how they can make a difference as individuals. The saying that 'if voting changed anything they would abolish it' rings all too true today in Britain's highly centralised system of government, where so many deci-sions are made by those who were not elected and cannot be removed. As Chris Huhne points out in Chapter 15, almost 95 per cent of tax revenue